THE PREPPER'S BLUEPRINT

THE STEP-BY-STEP GUIDE TO HELP YOU PREPARE FOR ANY DISASTER

The Prepper's Blueprint: The Step-By-Step Guide To Help You Prepare For Any Disaster

Published by CreateSpace Independent Publishing Platform

Copyright © 2014 by Tess Pennington

ISBN [1496092589]

First Printing, 2014

www.CreateSpace.com

Table of Contents

LAYER 2 - SHORT TERM PREPAREDNESS

LAYER 3 – LONG TERM PREPAREDNESS

Introduction

Although it is difficult for many to accept, there are and forever will be events that are beyond our control. Emergencies don't announce themselves, they just show up and expect you to make do while they are present. These events could be so severe that they have the capacity to bring us to our knees.

While some choose to prepare for these unforeseen events, there will be others who choose to stay complacent and turn a blind eye. The choice not to prepare could occur for a variety of reasons:

- Some simply do not see the need to prepare.
- Others do see the need, but make excuses why they can't prepare.
- Many are overwhelmed by the enormity of preparedness.
- Lots of people are afraid of the unknown.
- Some people have a fear of other's opinions about preparing for extended emergencies.
- Other people have a fear of admitting to themselves that devastating events can penetrate our lives and affect us.

But in the end, life is all about choices - tough choices. In this prepper's opinion, taking the active steps to prepare for an unforeseen, SHTF disaster (that's "sh*t hit the fan" for those unfamiliar) was the only option that made sense. It took courage and a big leap of faith to get started.

TAKING THE LEAP

Like many of you, when I first began preparing, I started with small-scale situations and then began prepping for longer-term disasters. I made the same mistakes that many of you made in the process, and learned from them. What I didn't understand was the importance of being spiritually and mentally prepared for the magnitude of a long-term disaster. As a result, it sent me into a tailspin of negativity, and the articles I wrote for my website, ReadyNutrition.com, reflected it. I eventually came to the conclusion that even though we sometimes don't see the bigger picture when we're in the middle of chaos, there *is* a larger picture at play, and we have to wait to see what the universe reveals to us in order to take the next steps.

I realized that I didn't want to promote distress, or for that matter, teach others to live in it. Rather than staying in the presence of trepidation, I chose to take another daring step and search for a way to prepare that promotes the freedom and gratification we are all searching for. My goal was to be 100% self-reliant during a short or extended disaster. Luckily, I stumbled across the concept of homesteading and instantly knew that was what I was searching for.

Once I adopted this mind-set, my attitude shifted from living in fear to living with courage to face whatever may come.

I had found my balance.

As Amelia Earhart once said, "The most difficult thing is the decision to act, the rest is merely tenacity. The fears are paper tigers. You can do anything you decide to do. You can act to change and control your life; and the procedure, the process is its own reward."

My new approach to prepping brought a renewed sense of self and a passion that I wanted to share with anyone who would listen. I have mentioned before that showing others how important it is to be prepared and teaching them the necessary survival skills is something very dear to me, and a cause that I feel is greater than myself. This program is a result of this realization. There is nothing more important to me than seeing that communities of people are prepared for what may come. But in order for an entire community to be prepared, it takes consider: "the actions of one person at a time" instead of: one person at a time to keep the preparedness fire lit.

TRUST YOUR GUT

As James T. Stevens says in his preparedness guide, _Making the Best of Basics: Family Preparedness Handbook[1],_ a paradigm shift occurs once the mindset changes from being prepared to living a preparedness lifestyle, "suddenly it's neither so daunting or burdensome – it becomes your routine – the way you live on a daily basis!"

That being said, once I adopted this new lifestyle, I realized that my current living situation did not support what I wanted or needed to achieve. Changes were made. Some of those changes have been met with resistance from friends and family members. (Something I am sure that many of you have first-hand experience dealing with.)

As the saying goes, "Do not go where the path may lead, instead go where there is no path, and leave a trail."

Despite the contradicting viewpoints from others, I still felt strongly enough to take my preparations to the next level. In time, I hope that many will understand why I felt so passionate about this.

ARE YOU A PREPPER, A SURVIVALIST OR A PART OF A COMMUNITY?

---

[1] http://www.amazon.com/Doctor-Preppers-Making-Best-Basics/dp/0983046530/ref=sr_1_3?ie=UTF8&qid=1394753499&sr=8-3&keywords=Making+the+Best+of+Basics%3A+Family+Preparedness+Handbook

As a whole, humans like to compartmentalize things. We naturally gravitate toward this mind-set and feel more at ease when we are part of a group that shares similar traits. I have read in other blogs and forums where people discuss the differences between being self-reliant, being a survivalist, and being a prepper.

Though the titles are different, we are all one in the same. There are however, varying degrees of preparedness and this is where the difference lies. Preppers range from people who have a first-aid kit in the car to those who have an underground bunker. That said, it's about time that we start embracing one another as a preparedness community and be more positive and uplifting towards each other's endeavors.

We are all different, come from a variety of backgrounds, have diverse goals, conflicting points of view, and have various forces that drive us to be who we are. My preparedness goals may not be the same ones that you have. However, my hope is that you take the experiences that I have written about, the lists that I created, and the mistakes that I have made and learn from them so that your transition into preparedness is simpler and easier. Our overall goal is the same: to be self-reliant and have preparations in place to withstand the aftereffects of a disaster so that we do not have to compromise our morals and values.

THE BLUEPRINT'S PURPOSE

For someone to think they are *untouchable* is naive. Roughly, 1% of Americans are adequately prepared for a disaster. The other 99% - well, it's not a great outlook for them. Since disasters tend to have a mind of their own and the capacity to cripple our normal way of life, we want to create a well-rounded approach to your preparedness efforts. Taking the necessary steps to becoming more prepared begins with you.

If you see a need to prepare for something, start taking the steps to get ready for it now. No time is better than today!

I understand the overwhelming nature of preparedness and created the Prepper's Blueprint to help get you and your family ready for life's unexpected events. I simplified and broke down each level and layer of preparedness into comprehensive and easy to follow lists so that small and achievable steps can be made. The entire Blueprint can be read in order, but each chapter also serves as a standalone resource—pertinent information is reinforced and referenced throughout.

My purpose in all of this is not to promote fear and doom, or to teach others to hide from life, but to help others be aware that disasters do in fact exist and can affect us. Moreover, my goal is to teach others that they can find freedom through self-reliance. ReadyNutrition.com is a testament to my personal preparedness journey, and a way for me to help others become more self-reliant in the process.

Introduction

In the Prepper's Blueprint, I have broken up the chapters in order to help you make sense of all the preparedness concepts and supply lists provided. Furthermore, the chapters have been divided into layers of preparedness.

Layer 1 - chapters 1-14
Layer 2 - chapters 15-31
Layer 3 - chapters 32-56

LAYER 1 (CHAPTER 1 - 14)

The first 14 chapters will be the first layer of preparedness you should place your efforts in. This will help you get ready for short-term emergencies that can range anywhere from a few short hours to a several weeks, but the effects could be long lasting. Disasters of any kind can bring on confusion and chaos – especially if you weren't prepared to deal with them in the first place.

In Layer 1, you will read historical accounts of disasters and begin creating an emergency foundation that your family can rely upon when emergencies present themselves. Not only will you learn how to better prepare your family for natural disaster scenarios, but you will plan for emergency evacuations, home security, personal disasters such as job loss, the most likely medical disasters, and a host of other topics.

If you walk away with anything from the Prepper's Blueprint, walk away with this – disasters do not discriminate. In the aftermath of the event, you will be on your own, left to provide for your family with the supplies and knowledge you have accrued. If you are prepared with the mental and spiritual foundation to overcome a disaster, then you will transition into survival mode more quickly.

LAYER 2 (CHAPTER 15 - 31)

In the second layer of preparedness, we will begin extending those first basic preps and turning them into longer-term survival needs. Throughout this layer, you will understand how living through a disaster can have a traumatic effect on one's surroundings. Continued fuel shortages, crime waves, downed local infrastructures, contaminated water supplies, and sanitation-related diseases are a few of the issues we may be up against when a short-term disaster turns into an extended one.

When you plan for extended disasters, you must take into account that you could be on your own for up to a month or longer. To carry you through this unpredictable time, you must add additional layers to your preparedness foundation so that it incorporates essential knowledge and additional supplies.

In this layer, you will learn about how to make your supplies last longer. Some of the concepts you will learn about are food preservation techniques, ways to create a money-saving preparedness pantry, how to effectively organize your supplies, emergency sanitation methods, bush craft lighting, how to prepare yourself for pandemics, and how to maintain anonymity when you want to provide charity.

With the knowledge you can take from the following chapters, you can confidently face a longer-term scenario, knowing that you will have all you need to survive within it.

LAYER 3 (CHAPTER 32 - 56)

Some scenarios go from being a long-term disaster to becoming a different way of life. This brings a new set of challenges to the table – long-term survival. At this point, you are no longer living a preparedness lifestyle, but one of a survivor.

An event that lasts more than 6 months could throw us back to a time before electricity. America would quickly discover itself at the level of a third world country where sanitation-related diseases could be rampant. In order to survive this long-term ordeal, you must be fully insulated with respect to supplies and skills. In a time of uncertainty, your main goal at this point is to be self-reliant in all aspects of your life.

In this final layer, you will learn which types of long term food should be stored, emergency forms of communication, retreat characteristics, homesteading skills, nuclear preparedness, home defense strategies, and much more.

Our goal is to get you and your family to a point where you can not only survive, but thrive, in a world that may be permanently altered. With that, let's begin.

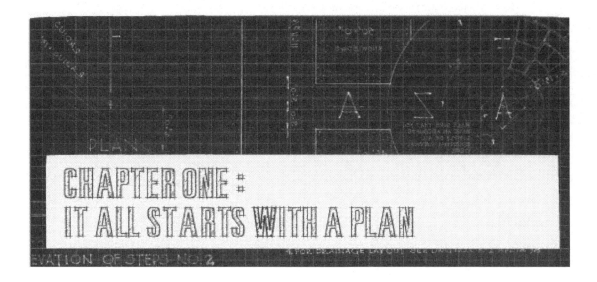

CHAPTER ONE ::
IT ALL STARTS WITH A PLAN

Hurricane Katrina laid siege to the city of New Orleans in 2005, leaving over 81 billion dollars' worth of damage in her wake. Hundreds of thousands of people were evacuated, left to the mercies of the federal government and the Red Cross. Many others were stranded in homes surrounded by high floodwaters, with no power and no means of communication. The graceful old city became a home for vandals and looters as all vestiges of civilization vanished for weeks.

The government hurriedly set up temporary shelters in the Superdome and the New Orleans Convention Center for displaced residents. Thousands crowded into places without adequate sanitation facilities, food supplies, and water.

No one was ready for a disaster on such a grand scale - not the residents, not the responders and not the federal government. As a result, the government and the Red Cross came under fire for not responding quickly enough.

Because of flooded, impassable highways and disorganization on the part of the relief efforts, refugees who were crowded into the Superdome and the New Orleans Convention Center went for four days without supplies. People who had remained in their homes were without electricity, plumbing or running water; they waited even longer for help.

We've seen many disasters over the years from the safety of our living rooms. The aftermath of Hurricane Katrina struck closer to home, and we saw how quickly we could go from civilized to the status of a third world country. Many of us made donations, did volunteer work and assisted the victims. For some, Katrina was a wake-up call. Our eyes became opened to the need to be more prepared. We became aware that help was not always a simple "911" call away and that government relief efforts might not arrive as quickly as we'd previously expected.

In a society filled with people waiting to be rescued, planning ahead can mean the difference between being together or separated, frightened or confident - even alive or dead. To begin to prepare for this short-term disruption, you must begin with a plan. Consider this emergency plan as a map that will help you and your family navigate efficiently through a disaster. You will know what to expect from one another, know how to perform, and know how to get by.

PLAN FOR DISASTERS MOST LIKELY TO OCCUR IN YOUR LOCATION

Chaos and confusion can be as much of an enemy as any act of devastation. Together with your family, decide what to do before a disaster is imminent. Discuss the different threats that are more likely for your area. They could include:

- Winter storms
- Hurricanes
- Tornadoes
- Earthquakes
- Extended power outages
- Floods
- Mandatory evacuation
- Fires
- Epidemics
- Economic downturns

Once the emergency has happened, it's too late to plan. You are *reacting* instead of *acting.* As a family, sit down and discuss likely disaster scenarios that could occur. For instance, when I lived in Houston, TX, my family had to prepare for the likelihood of hurricanes occurring. Not only that, we had to prepare for tornados, chemical leaks from refineries, and flash flooding.

CREATING AN EMERGENCY PLAN

Prepare your children by allowing them to help create the plan. They will feel much more comfortable in a scary situation if they know what to do and what to expect.

Creating practice drills is another way to get family members to think and be focused and calm during an emergency.

As a family, discuss your emergency meeting places, contacts, and plans. Give your children the opportunity to express their feelings and to ask questions so they fully understand the disaster plan.

Ask these questions:

1.) How you will get in contact with one another?

Everyone in the family should know the "emergency job" of the other family members. Will Dad pick up the child at the elementary school while Mom picks up the teen at the high school? Are the kids to attempt to walk home or should they stay put and wait to be picked up?

Plan at least two routes to accomplish these things in case streets are closed due to the disaster.

2.) Who is an out-of-area person that could coordinate communication if you are separated?

Choose a close friend or family member outside the immediate vicinity. This person is less likely to be affected by the same disaster and can be a calm port of communication. In an emergency it is possible that a family member might not be able to get home safely.

Local communications may be inoperable due to a storm or natural disaster. An out-of-area contact can coordinate the locations of the family members and serve as Communications Central until the family can reunite. Every family member should carry the phone number and contact information for the out-of-area person.

3.) What will happen if the kids are in school?

Schools have their own disaster plans in response to evacuations, storms, or other emergencies. The school's disaster plan must be taken into account when making your family preparedness plan. Mom and Dad should visit the school to get the specific details of the schools plan. Knowing what to expect can go a long way towards assuaging fear and panic.

GETTING ORGANIZED

Once you've created your basic plan, it's time to get organized! Having an emergency binder with checklists and instructions allows you to have all of the pertinent information - plans, checklists, phone numbers, etc., in one location. This can help you stay organized during a disaster and minimize chaos and panic during emergencies.

Consider collecting the following information in your binder.

- Family ID information: Current photos, fingerprints from each family member, birth certificates, etc.
- Favorite emergency recipes
- Emergency protocols and evacuation plans and evacuation routes
- Survival instructions for the family members to turn to if an emergency occurs: first aid, constructing a shelter, filtering water, etc.
- Contact information for relatives and close friends
- Veterinary records for pets (you might have to prove they have been vaccinated during an evacuation scenario)
- Medical information for all family members: medications they are taking, medical conditions, allergies, blood types, etc.
- Important documents such as wills, social security cards, custody orders, car registration, marriage license, mortgage
- Maps of the area
- Insurance information: Home inventory (written and video inventory) insurance papers, policy and account numbers, property titles (homes, autos, boats)

SPECIAL DOCUMENTS

Disasters cause things to go awry very quickly, and in some cases, families can become separated. When a family member is separated from the others, providing pertinent information to medical personnel or first responders can be more challenging due to heightened emotions from the stressful situation.

To deal with these unintended separations, disaster organizations have suggested that every family have personal information for the other members of the family before a disaster occurs. Having this information will help responders and medical personnel render aid more quickly, as well as assist you in getting your loved one back safe and sound.

Make Personal I.D. Cards

The Center for Missing and Exploited Children has created a free print out for families to fill out for family members to have on hand. The cards provide a quick reference for phone numbers, personal information and even has a place for fingerprints to be documented. This document will easily fit inside of your emergency binder.

Personal I.D. Cards should include:

- Work and cell numbers for both parents
- The phone numbers for your out-of-area contact
- Doctor's phone number
- The location of your family's designated meeting place
-Any emergency medical needs

You can find printable identification cards for the family at this link:

http://www.take25.org/~/media/Take25/ResourceDocuments/Child_ID_2013-EN.pdf

Creating contact information cards can give your children or vulnerable loved ones an extra layer of protection during any time you are unable to be with them. These cards can help loved ones to reconnect in the aftermath of a crisis.

Emergency documents provide vital information to first responders in case a loved one goes missing. They also provide an extra layer of preparedness for the family. These are especially important for children, the elderly, those with serious medical conditions, and those who are mentally disabled.

Likewise, when you are in an evacuation situation, carrying around a bunch of paperwork (along with all of your other gear) is the last thing on your mind. Thanks to the power of technology, you have options for storing and backing up pertinent data.

What Documents to Back Up

There are a few documents that you obviously should keep in a secured location (a fire safe or safe deposit box). That said, backups can be made by scanning them into computers and saved on other backup storage systems. Some of the information you should consider backing up are:

- Identifying information: Social Security card, driver's license, birth certificate, passport, Marriage certificate
- Financial accounts: Bank, investment, and credit card/loan accounts information, including institution names, phone numbers, and account numbers
- Health records: Immunization records, allergies, dietary restrictions, medications, medical/surgical treatments
- Pet information: Description of each pet, vet contact information, and any important medical notes
- Property: Car information, home purchase papers/deeds, and other home inventory items
- Insurance documents (depending on the disaster you may need to make a claim before you can return to your home)
- Wills and medical directives
- Special sentimental items like photographs, certificates, jewelry or small heirlooms

Protect Your Identity

Emergency contacts, as well as information in your emergency binders, can also be stored online in case you forget your binders or they are lost.

Be aware that if you plan on storing these important documents online, they can be stolen, and your identity along with them. It's a good idea to encrypt the files after they have been scanned in and share them with only trusted sources. If you encrypt the digital files, use an encryption tool such as TrueCrypt.

Flash drives – USB Flash drives are miniature hard drives that you connect to your computer using a USB port. Typically, the capacity for a Flash drive is between 128MB to 1GB. Flash drives are portable, convenient, low cost and easily accessible. A 256-megabyte drive, which runs for $20 or even less, gives you enough space for this type of storage. One of the best ways to prevent data theft and improve information security is to encrypt your data.

Mozy – This is a backup storage system you can use online. It works by syncing your files to the cloud and securely saving it. This eliminates that need to hold onto bulky hard drives or concerns about losing flash drives. This method can store up to 125 GB of data for $120 per year. You could store all of your pertinent documents, family photos, and more with ample storage to spare.

Google Docs – After you have scanned your documents into your computer, simply upload them to Google Docs and share the files with your loved ones. Remember that you can encrypt documents to keep them safe.

Dropbox – This is a free service that lets you store your photos and documents and share them with others. An added incentive to this storage choice is that it gives you a few gigabytes of storage for free.

NAS Drives – If you'd rather store your data with someone you trust, buy two 2 TB network-attached storage (NAS) drives for about $200 each and split them both into two equal partitions. Give one drive to a relative or trusted friend and then have the drives back up to each other over the Internet using rsync software. Both you and your relative/friend will get a local backup and a mirrored remote backup.

PREPS TO BUY:

- 3 ring binder
- Flash drives
- Document protector sleeves
- Pens
- Labels
- Printer paper
- Photographs of family members

ACTION ITEMS:

1. Involve your children in your family preparedness efforts. Educate them on the different types of disasters and on your family's disaster plans. Ready Kids[2] is a great website for fun methods and games to teach your children about what to do in the event of an emergency.

2. Ask your child's school and/or day care about their disaster plans. Here are a few questions that I asked our school: How will you communicate with a child's family during a crisis? Are you prepared for a shelter-in-place situation? If you have to evacuate, where will you go?

3. Find up-to-date pictures of each family member in case one of them gets separated from you during a disaster event, put the pictures in a waterproof or Ziploc bag, or sleeve for a three-ring binder and place it in your emergency kit[3].

4. Get organized, and create an emergency binder using the information provided above. Remember to include a personal information card[4] and a contact information card for each family member.

5. For family members who have special needs, ensure that those needs are accounted for in your emergency plan.

---

[2] http://www.ready.gov/kids/
[3] http://readynutrition.com/resources/are-you-ready-series-72-hour-kits_29082013/
[4] http://readynutrition.com/resources/keep-kids-safe-with-emergency-id-cards_29042011/

SUPPLEMENTAL INFORMATION AND RESOURCES

Play it Safe

Protecting your personal information and your child's personal information is a must these days. Therefore, when creating emergency ID cards, provide the essential information only.

1. Never include any sensitive information or financial information, such as social security number.
2. Put the card in a place that is not easily seen by strangers, such as a wallet or inside of a backpack to keep the card holder safe.
3. If a child is the card holder, only print the initial of their first name. For example: J. Smith.
4. There is no need to print the birth date of the child. Just state the year they were born to give first responders an idea of how old he/she is.
5. During an actual emergency, if a child is too young to carry a card, the National Center for Missing and Exploited Children suggest writing only the necessary information (name, contact number and parents' names) *directly on the back* of the child with permanent marker.

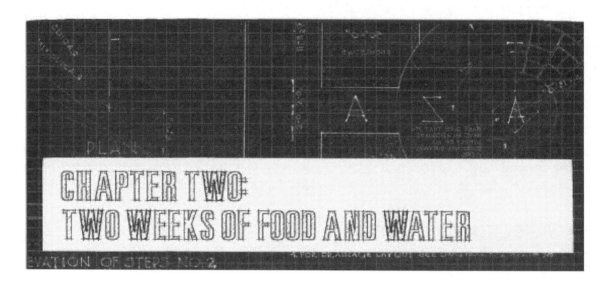

CHAPTER TWO:
TWO WEEKS OF FOOD AND WATER

For tens of thousands of east coast residents, that worst-case scenario is now playing out in real-time with Superstorm Sandy. No longer are images of starving people waiting for government handouts restricted to just the third-world. In the midst of crisis, once civilized societies will very rapidly descend into chaos when essential infrastructure systems collapse. Though the National Guard was deployed before the storm even hit, there is simply no way for the government to coordinate a response requiring millions of servings of food, water and medical supplies...

Limited electricity has made it possible for some to share their experiences:

Via Twitter:

- I was in chaos tonite tryin to get groceries...lines for shuttle buses, only to get to the no food left & closing early.
- I'm not sure what has shocked me more, all the communities around me destroyed, or the 5 hour lines for gas and food.
- Haven't slept or ate well in a few days. Hope things start getting better around here soon.
- These days a lot of people are impatient because they're used to fast things. Fast food, fast internet, fast lines and fast shipping etc.

Source: http://www.SHTFplan.com

FEMA (Federal Emergency Management Agency) has begun to promote personal preparedness. In a press release the agency recommended that all homes be ready for emergencies with a supply of no less than two weeks of food and water.

> *If an earthquake, winter storm or other disaster strikes your community, you might not have access to food, water and electricity for days or even weeks. By taking some time now to store emergency food and water supplies, you can provide for your entire family.*

Can you imagine having to buy an entire emergency supply of food as a disaster is occurring? Not only are you fighting a crowd of stressed-out people who want the same items as you, but your financial budget more than likely did not allot for this!

DISASTERS SHOULDN'T CRIPPLE YOU, BUT BE A MINOR INCONVENIENCE

Rather than having a disaster become a major setback that cripples you financially, we want to ensure it is only a minor inconvenience. Our focus in this chapter is getting your family ready for a short-term disaster. We can prepare for this by creating a family-based preparedness plan and setting up a basic two-week supply of food and water. We must anticipate that help could be a full two weeks away and we must prepare accordingly. What do you and your family need to get by until then?

Plan for water shortages. Following a disaster, water is one of the first items that fly off the store shelves. You need water for consumption, food preparation and for sanitation. Plan accordingly and store an ample water supply. Emergency preparedness sites suggest 1 gallon of water per person per day. Take in mind this is for consumption only, you will need more.

Plan for no electricity. To further prepare your family, you must assume that you will be without power for a week or more. Therefore, create a foundation of preparedness supplies that do not require elaborate cooking methods. Food sources that only require the addition of water to prepare are the easiest meals to rely on during this stressful time.

Create an emergency menu. The best approach to beginning a food supply for your family is to sit down and create an emergency menu. This will help you stay organized for the disaster and to know what food items you need to stock up on.

Base your menus on foods that your family is familiar with – no one wants to experiment with food during a crisis situation.

These are all low cost items that can be stored without refrigeration, and preparation will use minimal fuel. Remember to keep preparation requirements of meals as simple as possible, while also keeping dietary needs in mind. Convenience can be a great gift during the aftermath of a disaster. An added bonus to this method is you don't have to do kitchen clean up and dishes when there is no electricity.

Consider adding these convenient supplies to your stockpile:

- Styrofoam plates
- Paper towels and napkins
- Plastic cutlery
- Baby wipes
- Disinfecting wipes
- Plastic cups

FOOD SAFETY

In the event of a grid-down disaster, begin by using your perishable items located in the refrigerator and freezer to ensure they do not go bad. If the electricity is out, remember to limit opening the door to your refrigerator and freezer. The more often the doors are opened, the less control you have over the temperature of your perishable foods.

If you have some hamburger meat or eggs that need to be cooked to prevent spoilage, prepare those first and save your non-perishable items until later.

CREATE A FOOD SUPPLY WITHOUT BREAKING THE BUDGET

Starting a food supply does not have to be a budget breaker. By slowly accumulating emergency supplies, you will not feel the financial "burn" like you would if you had to pay for everything all at once. To make the best choices for your family, keep these questions in mind:

- What type of emergencies are you planning for?
- Do any of your family members have dietary needs that must be addressed?
- How long do you need for your food supply to last?
- How many people will you be providing for?
- What off-grid method could you use to heat food or boil water if the power goes out?

Before you head to the store with your wallet in hand, assess what you already have. Most of us have at least *some* canned foods and dry goods stashed away. Use the following checklist

Food Safety Tip

If the appliance thermometer stored in the freezer reads 40 °F or below, the food is safe and may be refrozen. If a thermometer has not been kept in the freezer, check each package of food to determine the safety. Remember you can't rely on appearance or odor. If the food still contains ice crystals or the temperature is 40 °F or below, it is safe to refreeze. Refrigerated food should be safe as long as power is out no more than 4 hours. Keep the door closed as much as possible. Discard any perishable foods (such as meat, poultry, fish, eggs, and leftovers) that have been above 40°F for 2 hours or longer.

Source: USDA

and see what items are already lingering in your cupboards. You may be pleasantly surprised to discover that you are more prepared than you expected!

Included in this list is water. Water is the most important item to have on hand during a disaster. Not only do you need water for consumption, but you will need water for food preparation as well.

Therefore, keep this in mind when you are making your two-week food supply list and consider purchasing a water filter for added measure.

2-Week Supply List

For each person in your family or group:

- 1 gallon of water per day for each family member for each day you are expecting the emergency to last.
- 1 jar of peanut butter
- 2 cans of juice
- 2 cans of meat
- 2 cans of soup or stew
- 3 non-perishable items such as saltine crackers, graham crackers, etc.
- 1 box of cold cereal
- One box of quick oats
- 1 jar of applesauce
- 2 cans of fruits or vegetables
- Protein powder
- "Just-add-water meals" such as Ramen noodles, hamburger helper or other boxed foods
- Drink mixes such as tea, Tang or Kool-Aid
- Can opener

Once you've assessed what you already have, make a list of the items you need to acquire. When shopping for those remaining items, take the time to read the nutritional information on the back of the food source to make the best choices. If your family needs to use the stashed food supply, having foods that are high in vitamins, nutrients, and protein will provide their bodies with these necessities. In addition to grocery items, you also want to think about any special needs items that your family may require. Choose high value foods that are shelf-stable. Remember that you may not have electricity for cooking the foods or keeping cold items at a safe temperature.

Off-Grid Cooking Sources

One of the main prepper sayings you need to remember is that it is essential to have backups for your backups. You don't want to rely on one single item to survive. Having backups for off-grid cooking sources are no different. Because survival scenarios have varying time frames, you want to prepare for these differences. For instance, you may be in a bug out situation where you are outdoors and need a lightweight stove, or you may find yourself in a situation where a sturdier cooking tool is needed, as in the case of those who had to go through the long aftermath of Hurricane Sandy.

The Solution:

The key to thriving in these types of events is proper planning and versatility with your preps. The theme of this preparedness guide is to show you that by layering your preparedness supplies with short and long-term preparations, you will better adapt to the situations you are faced with.

When you are planning to cook off the grid, remember that you must have the proper equipment to prepare your food. Some of these stoves and cooking sources may require specific cookware, so look into that on your own.

Have ample lighting sources on hand as well - waterproof matches, several Bic lighters, magnesium fire starters, and fuel stored away.

The following are 10 of the most popular alternative cooking sources to use in an off-grid environment. Some are for outdoor cooking and some for indoor cooking.

Keep what disasters you are planning for in mind when making the decision of which cooking source is right for you, and remember to store additional fuel sources. Further, do research and read reviews on these products before they are purchased.

10 Most Popular Alternative Cooking Sources

1. Fire pit
2. Charcoal and propane BBQ pits
3. Stovetec/Rocket Stoves
4. Collapsible Stoves
5. Solar Ovens
6. Cob Oven
7. Hibachi cast iron stoves
8. Fireplace
9. Wood Stove
10. Wonderbox or insulated cooker

Since most preppers are concerned about OPSEC (operational security) in the midst of a disaster, you may want to consider a level of discretion with your cooking source. Grilling up your food may attract hungry neighbors and if your mission is to feed only your family, then you may want to cook indoors to mask the smell. Here are some other ways to be discreet when preparing food following a disaster.

1. **Cook on the down low.** Plan to prepare and cook food in the early morning or late at night when a majority of people are sleeping.
2. **Stock up on MRE's.** These are self-contained meals that will not require long preparation times.
3. **Have meals with quick prep times.** Prepare meals ahead and can them for quick preparation such as beans, soups and stews. This will cut down on fuel and keep the smell of food down to a minimum.
4. **Go easy on the spices.** As much as we love to add spices to our meals, they will bring added aromas to your food.
5. **Eat foods that are already prepared and are shelf-stable.** Shelf-stable foods are another solution to cut down on strong aromas.
6. **Use a thermal cooker.** This is an insulated crock-pot that will allow you use minimal fuel to heat the food and also help insulate the aromas that the food gives off.

PREPS TO BUY:

- 1 gallon of water per person per day for a two-week period.
- Peanut butter
- Cans of juice
- Cans of meat
- Cans of soup or stew
- Cans of fruits or vegetables
- 3 non-perishable items such as saltine crackers, graham crackers, etc.
- Cold cereal (1 box per family member)
- Pantry staples (flour, quick oats, baking powder, salt, sugar)
- Applesauce
- Protein powder
- Just-add-water meals (macaroni and cheese, Ramen noodles or other boxed foods)
- Powdered drink mixes (Tang or Kool-Aid)
- Baby supplies (diapers, wipes, formula, baby food)
- Protein/calorie drinks
- Prescription medications
- Additional toiletry items (toilet paper, feminine needs, etc.)
- 1 large container of dry pet food

ACTION ITEMS:

1. Inventory the supplies that you already have and shop to supply or resupply needed items.

2. Date perishable goods with a marker.

3. Make an emergency menu with the foods you intend to use and buy for a short-term emergency food supply.

4. Organize your emergency supplies in one place so they are easy to access – consider Rubbermaid bins, 5 gallon buckets, etc.

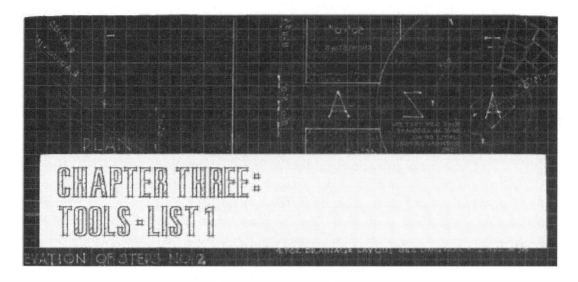

CHAPTER THREE:
TOOLS - LIST 1

Average citizens such as victims' friends, family, and neighbors perform the majority of search and rescue in the first minutes and hours of a disaster. These people locate victims by listening for calls for help, watching for other signs of life, or using information to estimate where the person may be (such as knowing someone would have been home at a certain time of day). It has been estimated that over half of those who are rescued are rescued within the first 6 hours after a disaster, with only 50% of those remaining trapped beyond 6 hours surviving, so the contribution of these average citizens is significant. *These untrained responders, operating without adequate equipment* or expertise, often put themselves at great risk.

Introduction to International Disaster Management, By Damon Coppola

In a search and rescue situation, emergency tools may be vital to reaching and freeing a victim. Tools that can be used to pry open doors, pry off fallen materials, and clear or break through debris will be needed. In many instances survivors resort to desperately using their bare hands to reach a trapped neighbor.

It's essential to have basic tools in order to:

- Evacuate safely
- Protect ourselves and our property
- Aid in search and rescue efforts
- Live in an off-grid/ survival situation
- Repair damaged shelters and other structures

YOU'RE ONLY AS GOOD AS YOUR TOOLS

A good rule of thumb when planning for emergencies is that a person is only as good as his or her tools. Because of my quest for efficiency and frugality, a dear friend reminded me how important it was to have good, quality tools. "With the right tools," he said, "a person can finish the job in half the time it would take with average tools."

> **Quality Tools Are Hard To Come By**
>
> Amish-crafted tools are designed for use in an off-grid world. They are expensive, but are of the finest quality and made to last a lifetime and beyond.
>
> You can find a great selection at these websites:
>
> www.lehmans.com
>
> www.cottagecraftworks.com

That statement really brings to light the importance of quality tools in an emergency situation. We want to be as efficient as possible in the midst of a disaster and having the right tools at our disposal can make a big difference when we are under a time crunch.

THE RIGHT STUFF

Ultimately, if a major disaster threatens, you want to have some tools set aside and ready to go. Of course, power tools come to mind, but for right now, let's focus on those basic tools that are off-grid compatible, compact, lightweight, versatile, and durable to help you get the job done. Power tools can come later.

Like any type of preparedness planning, when it comes to which tools to buy, it all begins with some forethought. Consider the types of emergencies that are common in your area and prepare accordingly. For instance, because gas and water lines can be broken during natural disasters, having a wrench to turn off these lines could be life-saving. Furthermore, if you are anticipating a hurricane or high winds, you may want to board up your windows and will need screwdrivers and screws to do so.

Quality tools are a sound investment that can last a lifetime if properly cared for. However, they do come at a price. Yes, you can save a few bucks here and there on cheaper supplies, but the price could come at a cost. It could be an indicator of the lack of craftsmanship or sub-par quality of the materials. In a dire situation, our tools are just as much a part of our lifeline as our food and water.

In fact, our tools can be the very items that help us to evacuate safely, protect ourselves and our property, aid us in search and rescue efforts, and may even help us to remain alive in an outdoor survival situation.

Many good tools can be found at your local hardware stores or home improvement centers. Look for the best quality tool you can afford.

If you know what you're looking for, check out yard sales, thrift stores, and estate sales. Often older tools are higher quality and you can't beat the secondhand price.

A Note about Quality

Not everything must be top of the line. Some items can be purchased inexpensively without risking your family's financial security. In particular, disposable items such as these can be purchased at the dollar store:

Lighters	Matches
Candles	Baby wipes
Rubbing alcohol	Bungee cords
Small nails	Toiletries

PREPS TO BUY:

- 32-gallon garbage can, large Rubbermaid container or a sturdy water-resistant storage box to hold disaster supplies
- Crowbar
- Hammer
- Multi-tool
- Wood saw
- Axe
- Paracord
- Shovel
- Cordless drill set
- Flashlight with alkaline-batteries or a hand-crank flashlight for each member of household that is over the age of 6.
- Batteries in multiple-sizes.
- Heavy rope
- Duct tape and electrical tape
- Cigarette lighters and matches (store these in a waterproof container)
- Assorted bungee cords
- Baby wipes
- Work gloves (sturdy pair with leather palms)
- Protective eye wear
- Adjustable wrench
- Heavy-duty jumbo sized garbage bags
- Candles
- WD-40
- Vaseline
- Extra parts and maintenance items for vital tools: blades, sharpeners, etc.

ACTION ITEMS:

1. Check to see what you already have. Most people already possess some or all of the basics, like hammers, shovels and lighters.
2. Gather the items you have and begin to organize your SHTF tool kit.
3. Make a shopping list of the other needed items.
4. Check out online resources, home improvement stores, discount stores such as Wal-Mart or Target, estate sales, Craigslist and dollar stores to collect your tools. Remember not to sacrifice quality for price on important items that should last!

SUPPLEMENTAL INFORMATION AND RESOURCES

EMERGENCY GAS SHUT-OFF

If you need to have your gas service turned off following a disaster, call a technician so they can do this for you. However, should a situation arise in which you need to turn off your gas supply immediately, follow these simple steps:

1. Locate the shutoff valve on the riser pipe from the ground to your meter or, on newer meters, the service line going from your meter into the house.
2. Use an adjustable pipe or crescent-type wrench to turn the valve a quarter turn in either direction. When the valve head is parallel to the pipe, it is in the OPEN position.
3. Turn the valve head crosswise (perpendicular) to the pipe and it will be in the OFF position.
4. There are also natural gas shutoff valves on the lines fueling individual pieces of equipment.

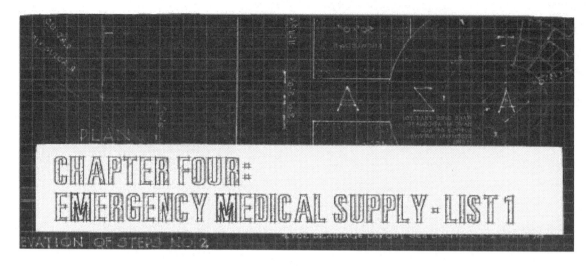

Quiz: Do *you* know how to respond in the event of an emergency?

1.) An adult is choking and cannot cough or speak. What should you do?
- a.) Give them a drink of water
- b.) Hit them on the back between the shoulder blades
- c.) Perform abdominal thrusts

2.) Your spouse has a heavy nosebleed. What is the best treatment?
- a.) pinch the nose and lean forward
- b.) pinch the nose and lean backward
- c.) stuff tissue up the nostrils

3.) Your child is stung by a bee. What should you do?
- a.) remove the stinger using a scraping motion with a straight edge
- b.) apply a paste of baking soda and water
- c.) both of the above

4.) A member of your group has cut her hand and it is bleeding heavily. What should you do to stop the bleeding?
- a.) instruct her to keep her hand below the level of her heart
- b.) apply a sterile gauze pad and apply direct pressure
- c.) apply a tourniquet just below the elbow

5.) Scalding water has splashed onto your mother's arm. Blisters are appearing. How should you treat the burn?
- a.) apply ice
- b.) spread butter on the burn
- c.) submerge the arm in cool water

6.) Which of the following are possible symptoms of a heart attack?
- a.) pale or bluish skin
- b.) persistent chest pain that may feel like indigestion
- c.) back pain along with nausea and vomiting
- d.) all of the above

7.) Someone in your party is having a seizure. What should you do?
- a.) roll him onto his side and move anything in the immediate area
- b.) place a wooden spoon between his teeth
- c.) hold him down by his arms and legs

8.) Your child's hands are frostbitten. What should you do for her?
- a.) massage her hands briskly
- b.) get her into a warm environment and submerge her hands in warm water
- c.) get her into a warm environment and submerge her hands in hot water

Answers: 1 –c; 2-a; 3-c; 4–b; 5-c; 6-d; 7-a; 8-b

Experts suggest that each home have a basic medical kit that is unique to your family's needs. Most of us have our fair share of Band-Aids and antibiotic ointment, but do you have medical supplies that can stop dehydration or bleeding? Do you have medication that can control diarrhea or vomiting? Would you be able to treat a victim of accidental poisoning?

During a disaster, roadways can become blocked or emergency responders can be so overwhelmed, they cannot get to injured victims to provide aid in a timely manner. Keep in mind that the average response time is 20 minutes. In an emergency, it could be much longer. Knowing what type of medical emergencies arise during short-term disasters could help you prepare more efficiently.

WATER-RELATED ILLNESSES

The relationship between communicable diseases and disasters exists and merits special attention. When there is a short-term emergency, there is an increased number of hospital visits and admissions from common diarrheal diseases, acute respiratory infections, dermatitis, and other causes. (Howard, Brillman, and Burkle 1996; Malilay and others 1996[5]). These types of medical issues are due to those coming in direct contact with floodwaters contaminated by oil, gasoline, or raw sewage. These contamination factors will cause irritation to skin and a host of other medical issues.

During a disaster, floodwater typically infests city water sources and should always be viewed as contaminated and never be used for consumption. If ingested, this tainted water can cause medical related issues including but not limited to:

Protozoan cysts *(Cryptosporidium parvum, Giardia lamblia)*
Parasites *(Guinea worm, schistosomiasis, amebiasis, cryptosporidiosis (Crypto), and giardiasis)*
Bacterial infections *(Escherichia coli, or E. coli, Salmonella, Campylobacter jejuni, Yersinia entercolitica, Leptospira interrogans and many others)*
Viral infections *(hepatitis A, rotavirus, enterovirus, norovirus, Norwalk virus)*

Aside from water-related illnesses and skin issues, there are other medical emergencies that can arise. When these do occur, it is important to know which protocols should be followed to care for the victim and perhaps even save their life.

---

[5] http://www.ncbi.nlm.nih.gov/books/NBK11792/#A9202

A significant number of these illnesses can be prevented through healthy sanitation practices, drinking clean water, and avoiding contaminated water all together.

MEDICAL EMERGENCY PROTOCOLS

The following suggestions can help you respond when you are with an individual that is experiencing a medical emergency. This list describes your priorities in an emergency situation.

Follow these steps to care for victims during a medical emergency:

1. Evaluate the situation to protect yourself and others from injury.
2. Be calm and reassuring. Talking to yourself may help keep you calm. It may reassure the individual needing help to hear that you are calm.
3. Do not move the individual unless the individual is in immediate danger or unless you cannot provide assistance without moving the individual.
4. Get help. Call out for someone to call 9-1-1 or, if the individual does not need immediate assistance, make the call yourself.
5. Calmly explain the exact nature of the illness or injury.
6. State the exact location of the emergency.
7. STAY ON THE LINE! The dispatcher will need to ask additional questions.
8. Look, listen, and feel for breathing.
9. Feel for a pulse to determine if the heart is beating.
10. Control bleeding with direct pressure by putting a bandage, cloth, or gloved hand over the spot that is bleeding.
11. Treat for shock. Lay the individual flat.
12. If the individual is unconscious, move him or her into the recovery position.
13. If the situation is a choking emergency, perform the abdominal thrust (Heimlich) maneuver.

Emergency Medical Information

If you have a family member with special medical needs, it is important that first responders have that information immediately available. You will need to provide information about pre-existing conditions such as heart conditions, epilepsy, diabetes or allergies. Also, to prevent potentially fatal drug interactions, a list of all medication the person takes should be available.

This information should be posted in predominant locations around the house and should also be on a card in the person's wallet or backpack. Consider a piece of medic-alert jewelry to warn of a chronic disease or a life-threatening allergy.

MAKE A LIST

Similar to making a list for beginning an emergency food pantry, start building your medical supplies by making a list of most likely medical disasters and what supplies would be needed if these events occurred. Keep in mind any family members that have pre-existing conditions, allergies or long-term health issues. Further, if you plan on caring for infants or elderly members when an emergency arises, ensure you have supplies to properly care for their medical needs.

STORAGE

Remember that medicines can break down and spoil if they are exposed to natural elements such as moisture, temperature fluctuations and light. Did you know that aspirin has a tendency to begin breaking down when it is exposed to a slight amount of moisture? Find an easily accessible area in the home that is cool and dark to store your medical supplies. Make sure that the location is out of the reach of children.

Periodically check the expiration dates to ensure the medicines are still good to use. Rotate things like pain relievers and antacids into your regular medicine cabinet for use the same way you rotate and use your stored food.

PREPS TO BUY:

- First Aid Manual
- Antacid
- Aspirin
- Non-Aspirin pain reliever
- Stool softeners
- Kleenex
- Disposable alcohol pads
- Syrup of ipecac
- Activated charcoal
- Band-Aids
- Triple antibiotic ointment
- Additional childcare needs (diapers, wipes, pacifiers, bottles, medicine, etc.)
- Antibacterial soap
- Instant hot and cold packs
- 1 week of prescription medications
- Extra pair of reading glasses (optional)
- Bandages
- Medical tape
- Tourniquet
- Celox (Emergency Blood Clotting Granules)
- Insect repellent
- Zinc oxide cream
- Calamine lotion
- Vaseline
- Pain and fever relief medication
- Anti-Diarrheal Medicine
- Cold/Flu medicine
- Antihistamine medication
- Contact lens saline solution (for eyewash or sterile rinse)
- Epi-pen
- Scissors

Sunscreen

ACTION ITEMS:

1. Make a list of most likely medical issues you may face during a disaster and list what medical supplies you will need. Remember to keep pre-existing conditions and/or long-term medical needs in mind when making the list.
2. Stock up your medical supplies using the list above. Get a Rubbermaid container or small toolbox in which to store all of your supplies in the same place.
3. Acquire additional supplies for the elderly or young children.
4. Sign up for a CPR/first aid class with your local area Red Cross or through your local Emergency Management Service department. For those of you who are short on time, you can find online disaster skills training courses that can be done in the convenience of your own home.
5. Either purchase a good first aid manual or download and print one to keep in a binder with your kit.

SUPPLEMENTAL INFORMATION AND RESOURCES

CALL

CALL 911

PUMP

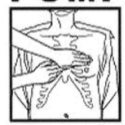

POSITION HANDS IN THE CENTER OF THE CHEST

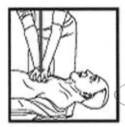

PUSH DOWN IN THE CENTER OF THE CHEST HARD AND FAST TWO INCHES 30 TIMES. PUMP AT 100/MIN

BLOW

TILT HEAD, LIFT CHIN, CHECK BREATHING

GIVE TWO BREATHS

CONTINUE WITH 30 PUMPS AND TWO BREATHS UNTIL HELP ARRIVES

Image Source: http://depts.washington.edu/

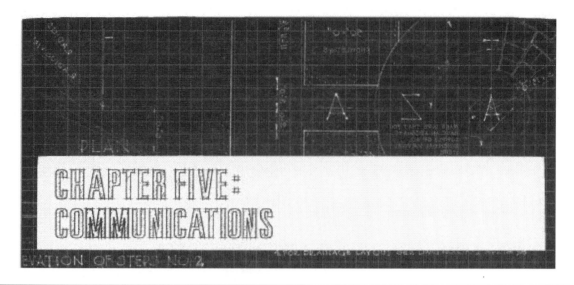

CHAPTER FIVE: COMMUNICATIONS

What's the one thing all of these disasters have in common?

A lack of communication between firefighters at the World Trade Center after the 9/11 attacks contributed directly to the deaths of 300 of those firefighters.

A lack of communication after the earthquakes that caused the Indian Ocean tsunami in 2004 cost thousands of lives because people were not warned to evacuate low-lying areas.

A lack of communication during the aftermath of Hurricane Katrina caused more than 5000 children to be separated from their families.

A lack of communication after the 1995 earthquake in Kobe, Japan left tens of thousands of people without shelter in freezing temperatures, and delayed relief efforts for over a week.

The answer: All of these disasters were immediately followed by an almost total loss of communication with the outside world.

Although our communications systems are still considered among the world's most extensive and dependable, the infrastructure is extremely outdated and unusual conditions can and do put a strain on our grid. Loss of established communications systems occurs for three reasons:

1. The physical destruction of network components
2. The disruption of the supporting infrastructure
3. Network congestion

ALTERNATIVE COMMUNICATION DEVICES

During a natural or manmade disaster, you may not be able to rely on your normal methods of communication such as landlines or cell phones. In fact, during and following disasters, many have issues even using their phones due to the increase in calls to loved ones, so plan on these communication modes not being available. Having alternate communication devices on hand during a disaster can provide a link to the outside world for updates in news, as well as allow you to summon emergency assistance from first responders, assist in coordinating meet up locations with family members, and can help maintain a sense of self-reliance during difficult times. Using a radio to communicate and receive information during an emergency has proven reliable in many disasters in the past.

Communication in a grid-down scenario is going to be *vital* in any serious emergency. Therefore, the best way to prepare for this situation is to layer up your preparedness supplies. Begin your preparedness efforts by purchasing the basic communication supplies for your home and bug-out bag. A whistle or flare may seem too basic, but imagine using that if you happen to be lost in the woods. It would become a lifesaving tool, wouldn't it?

Once you've covered the basics, start equipping your home with a standard radio and then move on to other forms of emergency communication such as a two-way radio or police scanner. Every family should have at least two of the following alternative communication systems:

- Cellular phone
- Whistles
- Flares and beacons
- Police scanner
- Ham radio
- Wind-up radio
- Pre-paid cell phone card

- Amateur radio
- Family radio services offered by the FCC
- Two-way radio (walkie-talkie)
- Police scanner
- CB radio

SETTING UP AN EMERGENCY COMMUNICATION SYSTEM

When making your choices, you should examine your own needs and match them with the appropriate communication system. When you first begin to invest in communication gear, start with low-cost equipment that has a simplistic set-up and operation. Further, you will want to consider emergency communication devices that have an effective range and modest protection against interference. Lastly, seriously consider that these emergency communication tools will likely used in an "off-grid" environment, so find equipment that reflects this.

Like all preparedness matters, you want to "layer up" in terms of having a communication system for short-term emergencies (i.e., two way radios, wind-up radios, etc.).

1. **Table Radio**

    Table radios are contained radio receivers and can mostly be found on eBay. Many can run on battery power, thus making them useful as emergency radios. Because some table radios still use vacuum-tube technology, they are virtually EMP proof. Find a radio with shortwave bands and ensure you purchase additional communication gear (headsets, antennas, etc.).

    Top suggested brands include: Zenith TransOceanic H500, Drake R8B

2. **Cell phones**

    Another communication device to consider is your cell phone – if cell towers are working, you need a way to power your phone. There are many solar chargers on the market that can provide a reliable source of power for your phone.

3. **Shortwave Receiver**

    Shortwave radio is a type of long-range radio transmission that bounces signals off a layer of the atmosphere (the ionosphere) to be received in another part of the world. Unlike AM and FM radio, shortwave radio frequencies can travel thousands of miles away. Your receiver can be a compact, portable general coverage AM/FM/weather band/CB/shortwave receiver.

    Popular brands include: Grundig, Sangean, Eton, Kaito, Sony

4. Police Scanners

Police scanners are convenient to have when you need to monitor local emergencies. Scanners are easy to use and will automatically stop on the frequency when a signal is found. This helps you become more time efficient in an emergency. It is important to note that scanners should be programmed to scan the correct frequencies.

One downfall of standard scanners is that they cannot scan digital frequencies. Because law enforcement is beginning to make the "digital switch" (changing to digital and encrypted communications) this could make the typical scanner obsolete in your area for monitoring these services. Digital scanners are available but are much more expensive at the moment. Some law enforcement and emergency agencies also operate on frequencies above the range supported by most scanner models.

PREPS TO BUY:

- Cell phone
- Extra charger for your phone
- Whistle
- Signal flares, flashing beacon or flashing emergency light. (I bought mine at a camping store.)
- Battery operated or wind-up hand radio, preferably an NOAA weather radio.
- Solar charger for batteries or devices
- Signals such as whistles, flares and mirrors
- Extra batteries for all devices
- Short wave radio
- Two-way radio
- Police scanner

ACTION ITEMS:

1. Spend some time practicing to familiarize yourself with your emergency communication equipment.
2. Certain emergency communications involve a level of knowledge. Download or otherwise acquire instructions and learn the science and mechanics behind the equipment.
3. Get to know people in your community who can offer tips on emergency communication.
4. The National Association for Amateur Radio (http://www.arrl.org/) is a great online resource to assist those seeking more information.

SUPPLEMENTAL INFORMATION AND RESOURCES

Tips for Communication in an Emergency:

1. Limit non-emergency phone calls. This will minimize network congestion, free up "space" on the network for emergency communications and conserve battery power if you are using a wireless phone.
2. Keep all phone calls brief. If you need to use a phone, try to use it only to convey vital information to emergency personnel and/or family.
3. For non-emergency calls, try text messaging, also known as short messaging service (SMS) when using your wireless phone. In many cases text messages will go through when your call may not. It will also help free up more "space" for emergency communications on the telephone network.
4. If possible, try a variety of communications services if you are unsuccessful in getting through with one. For example, if you are unsuccessful in getting through on your wireless phone, try a messaging capability like text messaging or email. Alternatively, try a landline phone if one is available. This will help spread the communications demand over multiple networks and should reduce overall congestion.
5. Wait 10 seconds before redialing a call. On many wireless handsets, to re-dial a number, you simply push "send" after you've ended a call to redial the previous number. If you do this too quickly, the data from the handset to the cell sites do not have enough time to clear before you've resent the same data. This contributes to a clogged network.
6. Have charged batteries and car-charger adapters available for backup power for your wireless phone.
7. Maintain a list of emergency phone numbers in your phone.
8. If in your vehicle, try to place calls while your vehicle is stationary.
9. Have a family communications plan in place. Designate someone out of the area as a central contact, and make certain all family members know who to contact if they become separated.
10. If you have Call Forwarding on your home number, forward your home number to your wireless number in the event of an evacuation. That way you will get incoming calls from your landline phone.
11. After the storm has passed, if you lose power in your home, try using your car to charge cell phones or listen to news alerts on the car radio. But be careful – don't try to reach your car if it is not safe to do so, and remain vigilant about carbon monoxide emissions from your car if it is a closed space, such as a garage.
12. Tune-in to broadcast and radio news for important news alerts.

Recommended Practices for Those with Disabilities

1. Register with your local Police Department. Remind them to keep a record of the help you may need during an evacuation, power outage or other emergency.

2. If you have a Personal Care Attendant, work with that person to decide how you will communicate with each other, such as by cell phone, if you are separated during an emergency.

3. Consider getting a medical alert system that will allow you to call for help if you are immobilized in an emergency. Most alert systems require a working phone line, so have a backup such as a cell phone or pager if the landlines are disrupted.

4. Learn about devices such as personal digital assistants (PDAs), text radio, pagers, etc. that can help you receive emergency instructions and warnings from local officials. Tip: Learn about NOAA Weather Radio for the hearing impaired.

Source[6]

---

[6] http://transition.fcc.gov/pshs/emergency-information/tips.html

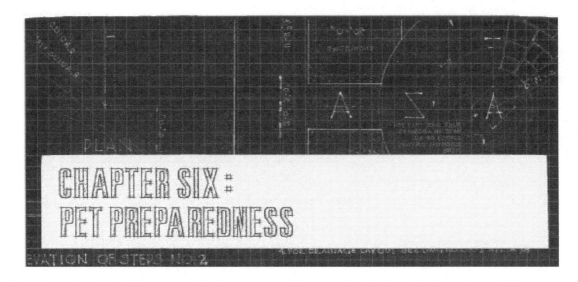

CHAPTER SIX:
PET PREPAREDNESS

More than 300 dogs and cats rescued from around the Fukushima No. 1 nuclear power plant were still being kept at animal shelters and other facilities in Fukushima Prefecture as of Friday, according to a prefectural government-led group taking care of such animals.

After the crisis began, the prefecture rescued 902 animals from around the power plant, including from within the 20-kilometer no-entry zone, that were apparently left at home by owners forced to evacuate after the March 11 disaster.

About 600 dogs and cats have since been collected by their previous owners or placed with new ones, but 305 remain at the facilities. Many are still there because their owners are living in temporary housing units and other evacuation facilities.

"Some of the dogs are sick because they've been here so long. Some have stomach pains from stress," said Tadashi Toyoda, a veterinarian in charge of checking the pets' health.

Source - The Yomiuri Shimbun, March 1, 2012

Our furry, scaled and feathered friends are more to us than just pets: for many of us they are precious members of the family. Caring for them during a disaster is extremely important, not only for the pet, but for our own peace of mind.

In the event of a disaster, terrified pets can easily become lost or injured. Like other vulnerable family members, they are dependent on us to take steps to protect them and keep them safe and secure.

BEFORE

Many times, we are given the gift of time to prepare for an impending storm or natural disaster. However, there are other times when the event is completely unexpected. It's important to make preparations for your pet before the disaster occurs. Because of public health regulations, many emergency shelters cannot accept pets, so effort should be made to locate other accommodations.

When a storm or disaster occurs, many of our animals face anxiety just as we do. Knowing how your pet will react before, during and after an event is the first step in ensuring his/her safety. One of your animal's natural reactions is to run for safety. If the pet is not in a secured yard, then they may run and the last thing you want to do before a disaster occurs is to run around the neighborhood looking for them.

A concerning issue occurs after an animal runs from their home. Or, in an evacuation scenario, if owners are unable to take their pets with them and decide it would be best to release their pets into the wild, they risk dogs packing up and causing harm to others. If you think this would never happen, think again. We saw this occur first hand after Hurricane Ike decimated parts of east Texas. After the storm hit, many locals found themselves dealing with a completely different crisis – feral dog packs[7]. As nature would have it, there is power in numbers and in this case, it was a dangerous group to reckon with. For weeks, many pedestrians and those waiting at bus stops feared that they would become the next victim of an attack.

To prevent this issue, anticipate your pet's needs during an emergency to help them cope with this disruption into their daily routines.

Do some planning in order to ensure that your pet is prepared for a disaster. After all, they are depending on you.

These steps can help your pets be disaster ready.

- Find out which motels and hotels in your area allow pets. There are travel guides that list hotels/motels that permit pets, which could serve as a starting point. An internet search using your city as one of the search words can identify local accommodations as well.

---

[7] http://readynutrition.com/resources/feral-dog-packs-a-rising-epidemic-for-this-nation_23072012/

- Call your local emergency management office, animal shelter, or animal control office to get advice and information.
- Locate pet boarding facilities near your home. Also research some kennels outside your local area in case local facilities close.
- Make reservations at the kennel or pet hotel as soon as possible – they will fill up quickly with the pets of other evacuees.
- Include your local animal shelter's number in your list of emergency numbers. Some shelters will provide temporary foster care for owned pets in times of disaster, but this should be considered only as a last resort.
- Acquire extra copies of licenses and veterinary records to place in your pet's 72-hour bag.
- When a disaster occurs, pets can become separated from their owners. Having emergency information or emergency identification cards on each pet can help you and your pet be reunited faster.
- Be sure that your pet is wearing an ID tag with your contact information in the event that you become separated.
- Never release your pet into the wild.

DURING

If you're riding out the storm or other event at home, these steps can help keep your pet safe and lessen his or her anxiety.

- Bring your pets inside immediately.
- Have newspapers on hand for sanitary purposes. Feeding your pets moist or canned food will help them stay hydrated and they will need less water to drink.
- Animals have instincts about severe weather changes and will often isolate themselves if they are afraid. Bringing them inside early can stop them from running away.
- Never leave a pet outside or tied up during a storm.
- Separate dogs and cats. Even if your dogs and cats normally get along, the anxiety of an emergency situation can cause pets to act irrationally.
- Keep small pets, like ferrets or hamsters, away from cats and dogs.
- If the emergency situation requires evacuation, you must care for your pets differently. **Leaving your pet at home alone places the animal in great danger.** Take the following precautions to give them the best chance of survival.
- Confine your pet to a safe area inside — NEVER leave your pet chained outside!
- Don't crate your animals in an evacuation situation. Leave them loose inside your home with food and plenty of water.
- Remove the toilet tank lid, raise the seat and brace the bathroom door open to provide an additional source of water.
- Place a notice outside in a visible area to alert responders that pets are present in the house. Provide a phone number where you or a contact can be reached as well as the name and number of your vet.

- If your pets include the feathered variety, talk with your veterinarian or local pet store about special food dispensers that regulate the amount of food a bird is given. Make sure that the bird is caged and the cage is covered by a thin cloth or sheet to provide security and filtered light.

AFTER

After the trauma of a disaster, even a beloved, gentle pet can behave differently. Observe them carefully, particularly when they are with children and other pets, until you know that they will interact safely. Environmental hazards may exist that were not there previously, so to keep your pets safe, be sure to watch animals carefully when they are outdoors.

- In the first few days after the disaster, leash your pets when they go outside. Familiar scents and landmarks may be altered and your pet may become confused and lost.
- When outdoors, remember that disasters like floods can bring snakes and other dangerous animals into the area.
- Be alert to the danger of downed power lines.
- The behavior of your pets may change after an emergency. Normally quiet and friendly pets may become aggressive or defensive due to fear and anxiety.

PREPS TO BUY:

- Extra harness, leash, and/or carrier
- ID tags with your contact information
- 1-2 week supply of food for all pets (if not already bought in week 1)
- 2-5 gallons of water for each pet
- Items for your Pet First Aid Kit
- 2 weeks' worth of medication for each animal (if applicable). Note: Pay attention to the expiration date and routinely rotate medicines to ensure they are not wasted.

ACTION ITEMS:

1. Decide if your pet(s) will be going to an animal hotel/kennel, sheltering-in-place with the family, or staying at another home. Make arrangements before the disaster is imminent.

2. If you haven't created a pet survival kit, accumulate your supplies and organize a bag for them. See instructions for creating a pet survival kit.

3. Ensure that your pet's vaccinations are up to date. *Note: If pets do not have their shots up to date, kennels are legally not allowed to accept them.*

4. Get rescue alert stickers for your doors. These will alert rescue workers that a pet is inside the home. Make sure to display these stickers very visibly.

5. Verify that ID tags are up to date and securely fastened to your pet's collar. Attach the address and/or phone number of your evacuation site if possible. **If your pet gets lost, his tag is his ticket home.**

6. In your emergency binder, include a current photo of your pet with your family emergency photos.

7. Always have a pet carrier, leash, and collar or harness. These are essential to your pet's safety, especially if he or she is prone to panicking.

SUPPLEMENTAL INFORMATION AND RESOURCES

Pet Survival Kit

Leash
Harness/collar
Pet carrier
Cat litter/pan
Doggie pads
Can opener
Food dishes
2 weeks' supply of dry food (minimum)

Items for special needs pets:

Pet identification
Veterinary records
Prescription medications
Proof of vaccinations
2-5 gallons of water
Toys, blankets and comfort items

Pet First Aid Kit

Emergency contact numbers
Latex gloves
Gauze rolls
Gauze sponges
Non-stick bandages
Towels
Adhesive tape, hypoallergenic
Elastic cling bandages
Water-based sterile lubricant
Eye-wash or sterile saline wash
Topical antibiotic ointment
Petroleum jelly
Antiseptic towelettes
Diphenhydramine (antihistamine)*
Q-tips

Milk of Magnesia or activated charcoal*Hydrogen Peroxide to clean wounds and induce vomiting*
Thermometer
Eye dropper
Syringe (for oral medication)
Splint
Cold pack
Small scissors
Safety pins
Tweezers
Magnifying glass
Emergency blanket
Muzzle
Leash
Penlight with batteries

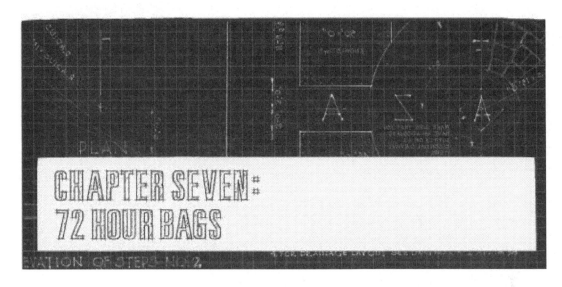

CHAPTER SEVEN:
72 HOUR BAGS

As preppers, we know that despite all of the planning and preparing we can do, things don't always go according to plan – that's why we have backup plans and our bug-out bags packed. It's just the nature of being a prepper to try and be ready for anything life throws at us. Bugging out is <u>dependent on many factors</u>[8] and the more you familiarize yourself with what could go wrong, the post-disaster environment you would be living in, and the dangers that exist, the sooner you can make an informed choice on what is best for the circumstance your family is in.

With certain disasters, you may only have minutes to gather your belongings and evacuate. Therefore, having your <u>evacuation plan</u>[9], your <u>bug-out bags</u>[10] (or BOBs) for each family member, your <u>vehicle prepped</u>[11], and necessary supplies ready to go will save you precious minutes and help you get your family to safety faster. Once you hit the road toward your evacuation route, do not be surprised to find the roads are congested due to the mass exodus of people fleeing. To add insult to injury, plan for gas shortages; this will be a real threat in a mass evacuation. Gasoline is a high commodity during an emergency and one of my largest concerns is bugging out by vehicle and running out of gas. In this case, you're a sitting duck for looters.

---

[8] <u>http://readynutrition.com/resources/the-prepper-conundrum-to-bug-in-or-bug-out-pt-1_26092013/</u>

[9] <u>http://readynutrition.com/resources/emergency-evacuation-checklist_27102013/</u>

[10] <u>http://readynutrition.com/resources/are-you-ready-series-72-hour-kits_29082013/</u>

[11] <u>http://readynutrition.com/resources/5-ways-to-keep-your-vehicle-evacuation-ready_09062011/</u>

As mentioned, bugging out is a time sensitive situation and, if you don't have your gear ready or wait too long to leave, then you could be stuck in gridlock with gas and supply shortages. Therefore, early planning for these events is key and will make all the difference in evacuating smoothly.

Making the decision to bug out will undoubtedly be different depending on the scenario you are facing. In fact, have you considered that due to extraneous circumstances, you may be left with no other option but to bug out by foot?

WHAT GOES INTO THE BAG?

What items could you gather from your home that would save your life for 3 days? Keep the basic needs in mind: water, food, shelter, clothing, safety and communication.

Here are some tips for putting together your 72-hour bags:

- Each family member should have a waterproof duffel bag, large plastic container, backpack or suitcase to store your gear and supplies.
- Be aware that there could be a situation in which the only way to evacuate is on foot. Ideally, the best BOB to have is one that has lots of pockets and/or sections for ease of organization, and has shoulder straps to keep the hands free.
- Have each family member regularly practice walking with his or her bag to be certain that the weight is not prohibitive, that the bag can be carried comfortably and to ensure nothing has been forgotten.
- Try to find items that are lightweight, functional and versatile so that carrying them will not be a strain.

1. Water

In most cases, a person can only survive for 3 days without water. However, after only *one day* without fluids, serious symptoms of dehydration will begin to occur:

The Clock Is Ticking

Each bug-out scenario is different but they all have one similarity – you are working against the clock.

Therefore, consider the different bug-out situations you could be faced with.

1. Mass evacuations due to natural or man-made disasters.
2. Disasters with little or no warning.
3. Massive infrastructure damage that will cause long term implications and roadblocks.
4. Widespread crime waves and lawlessness.

- Headaches
- Visual disturbances
- Decreased blood pressure
- Dizziness
- Fainting

This makes water your most vital priority.

Adults require one gallon of water per day. However, 3 gallons of water adds up to 25 pounds, which, when combined with your other gear, may add too much weight to your 72-hour bag. Because of this, many people carry about a half-gallon (2 liters) of water and pack either water purification tablets or a water filter. Some possibilities are:

- Individual water bottles or gallon jugs in the pack
- Canteen
- Collapsible water container
- Water filter
- Water purification tablets

You can also consider adding drink mixes or vitamin powders to water to increase your calories and add some nutritional content. Also keep in mind that many of the meals packed will require some sort of water for preparation.

2. Food

The foods you carry will make all the difference in the world in terms of maintaining energy levels and nutrition. You will be in a high-stress environment where you may be on foot, walking for long periods, perhaps up and down hills. Many preppers underestimate how much food they will need for their 72-hour bags. A common misconception is that living off of survival bars as a main source of food for 3 days will give you the optimum nutrition. This just isn't so.

When you are preparing your bug-out bag menu, you want your diet to give you ample calories, carbohydrates, protein, vitamins, and fats. Keep in mind that ages and genders will play a role in calorie consumption. As mentioned, you will be operating in a high-stress and high-energy environment, therefore your body needs to be running as efficiently as possible. With this in mind, you should plan to eat small meals every 2-3 hours.

Create a Menu

The best approach to ensuring you have enough food for 72-hours is to sit down and create an emergency menu based on your family's preferences. Map out the nutritional benefits that the chosen foods provide. This will help you stay organized for the disaster and will also help you create a shopping list for bug-out supplies. Your menu should be realistic in providing your body with the necessary energy needs.

The Nutrition Breakdown

Finding foods that are high in complex carbs and dietary fiber is more efficient from a dietary standpoint and will keep you feeling "fuller" longer.

Some energy efficient food sources to consider are:

- **Fruits/Vegetables** – Having these dehydrated will lighten the load and give you something nutritious to snack on. Keep in mind that dehydrated foods can last for 12 months or longer, provided they have been stored properly. Pack fruits and vegetables that are the most calorie dense[12]. Look for small boxes of dried fruits for easy meal assembly.
- **Whole vs. White** – We all know that whole grains are better for you. But did you know that they also keep you fuller longer? Whole grain breads with seeds and nuts can provide added nutrition. Look for whole grain pancake mixes, crackers, pasta, and bread to get good sources of whole grains.
- **Nuts** – This is one of the most nutrient-dense foods and is also full of fiber to help you stay full longer. Due to the high protein count of these lightweight nutrition powerhouses, they can be an efficient meat replacement. Look for non-salted nut varieties to keep you hydrated longer.
- **Meat Source** – Protein is imperative during an emergency and can also cut down on stress. The amino acid in meat, specifically tryptophan, binds to protein and becomes a precursor for the neurotransmitter serotonin. Increased levels of serotonin may help you cope with stress. Freeze-dried meats or TVP (textured vegetable protein), dehydrated meats, or cans of beef, chicken or tuna would be good choices to add to your pack.

According to the FDA, for a normal adult's 2,000 calorie meal plan, 45 to 65 percent of your daily calories should come from carbohydrates, 20 to 35 percent of your calories should come from fats, and 10 to 35 percent of your daily calories should come from proteins. Charts at www.choosemyplate.gov can help in researching caloric needs based on gender and ages.

---

[12] http://en.classora.com/reports/b114961/ranking-of-fruits-with-the-most-calories

Keep this in mind and adjust your dietary intake accordingly to maintain proper energy requirements. Also remember that in a bug-out situation you may be demanding much more from your body, and these demands will increase your caloric needs.

Although your main priority is to keep the weight of your 72-hour bag down, you want to have a way to prepare meals. This can be as simple as having a folding stove, a camping stove or, if you plan on cooking over a fire, a way to light the fire.

Pack enough food for a 3-day period and be sure to consider a few comfort items like gum and hard candy.

Some other examples of food to store in your bug-out bag are:

Crackers
Instant Pudding
Pasta
Powdered Drink Mix
Energy Bars
Dried Fruits and Nuts
Granola Bars
Instant Oatmeal
Instant Rice/Mashed Potatoes
Jerky
Dried Soups
Peanut Butter and Crackers
Gum
MREs[13]
Hard Candy
Powdered Milk
Paper Plates
Plastic Cutlery
Paper Cups
Off-grid Cooking Device

---

[13] http://readynutrition.com/resources/homemade-mres_02102012/

3. Clothing

Essential clothing for a bug-out situation is a commonly overlooked area of prepping. If a person does not have the proper clothing that is suitable for the terrain they are in, then harsh elements such as rain, cold, and snow can cause catastrophic effects. Preparation for an emergency means having the right tools and clothing to meet any emergency situation.

Take into account temperature changes, climate, and season when deciding what clothing to pack in your bug-out bag. Be sure to repack when the seasons change – you don't want long underwear and sweaters in the heat of summer or shorts and tank tops in the winter. Concentrate on items that can be layered for maximum efficiency.

The following are lightweight and multipurpose items that you can justify carrying in your bag.

- At least one change of clothing in your bag and two extra pairs of socks
- A good pair of <u>boots</u> (hiking or combat boots) with a deep trench in the sole
- (For cold climates or weather) Clothing for layering, warm hat, waterproof pants, mittens, etc.
- Work gloves
- Rain Suit or poncho
- Hat or bandana to keep the sun off your face

Create the Best Type of Insulation

To survive in natural environments, it is important to use the layering principle to provide the absolute best protection and flexibility for all types of climates. When you layer your clothing, it creates the best type of insulation in the form of still air between layers of clothing. The more layers that are worn, the greater the insulating effect. Taking off layers of clothing serves as temperature control.

When a person is exposed to harsh, cold terrains, it is important to cover and protect all of the body extremities and to provide maximum warmth with multiple layers. Overheating can be as much of a problem as being cold. If you sweat when it is cold, the body chills when you stop sweating and your sweat-soaked clothing will act as a conductor to draw away body heat into the air.

The best way to prevent this from happening is to layer your clothing. This provides you with a greater ability to control your body temperature in response to environmental factors and exercise.

Proper Layering Techniques

- Thermal underwear should be worn close against the skin.
- A woolen or wool mixture shirt should be worn over the thermal underwear.
- On top of this layer should be a woolen or good woven fiber sweater or jacket (woven fiber tends to be better because it is warmer and more windproof).
- A jacket filled with synthetic fiber should be worn over the last layer. It is advised not to wear a down jacket as it tends to lose its insulating properties when it gets wet.
- The final layer must be windproof and waterproof. This jacket is the outer shell of the thermal protection gear. It should also be made of a "breathable" fabric such as Gore-Tex, which allows sweat to evaporate through the fabric into the atmosphere while at the same time stops rain and water from getting in. These last two layers can be combined into a single jacket.
- Make sure that a durable hat is worn to insulate the heat given off by your head. It is estimated that between 40 and 50% of heat loss from the body in some conditions can occur through the head. Therefore, having proper headgear is essential to maintaining proper body heat. Preferably the hat should be a nylon shell with earflaps that can snap down. A brim on the hat would help keep snow out of the eyes.

When preparing clothing for an emergency situation, bug-out bag, or SHTF scenario, comfortable, non-restricting clothing should be chosen. Keep in mind that you are preparing for an extreme situation. Just because you have a warm home or shelter does not mean that the shelter will always be there. If there is a situation where you are left to walk in the harsh elements of nature, you want to be ready.

4. Footwear

Good footwear has everything to do with survival. A good pair of waterproof boots will protect your feet from the natural elements (water, heat, cold, snow, etc.). Boots that have flexible soles and deep tread are the best type of shoes to have when walking/hiking in rugged terrain.

There is much debate on whether to purchase all leather boots that are fairly heavy or lightweight hiking boots. Several studies have shown that wearing one extra pound on your feet takes as much energy as carrying five or six pounds in a backpack.

Keep in mind the local terrain to make the right decision of the type of footwear that should be purchased. There are many reviews of hiking boots online to determine what the best choice for you is.

5. Socks

Socks are vital in keeping your feet warm and dry. Without a good pair of socks, the feet are susceptible to not only natural factors, but also to blistering and other injuries. Socks should be matched to the intended type of weather condition and the type of walking will be done. Whether you wear multiple pairs of thin-layered socks or wear two thick pairs is your personal preference.

Carrying multiple pairs in your backpack or BOB is a good idea. If one pair gets worn out or wet, then there are extras on hand. Try to keep socks as clean and moisture-free as possible to prevent fungal infections and other unwanted podiatry ailments. A good way to prepare for the worst-case scenario is to have a fresh pair of socks vacuum-sealed and stashed away in your bag.

6. Shelter

If you find yourself in an emergency where you have to evacuate on foot with only the items you are carrying in your bug-out bag, then you must have some type of emergency shelter. You will need some sort of shelter to protect you from the natural elements and maintain your body temperature.

- Tent (lightweight)
- Sleeping bag
- Durable long lasting emergency blankets
- Bivvy sac
- Tube tent (emergency shelter)
- Tarp
- Mylar emergency blankets

In a pinch, garbage bags can even be used for a shelter, but if your bag is well stocked you won't need to improvise.

7. Communication

In a survival situation, communication is key. Ideally, you want a way to be able to contact friends and family members in order to coordinate your locations. It's also important that you be able to access the news. The news reports can tell you if you are in a safe location or a risky one, and can also let you know when the danger has passed and you can safely return to your home.

Our favorite communication device in this day and age is, of course, the cell phone – most of us don't leave home without it. In a massive emergency, though, you can't rely on this stand-by for communication. Everyone else has the same idea and the lines become jammed and overloaded, rendering your phone useless. Because of this, it is beneficial to have a back-up communication device.

Don't overlook simple communication tools like whistles. These can be lifesavers if a member of the group gets separated or is under threat. They are also ideal for children.

Since you can never predict the length of time you may be out of your home, consider a radio or device that is powered by renewable energy. Look for units that are hand-cranked or powered by solar energy.

Some communication options are:

- Cell phone
- Extra charger for your phone
- 2-way radio
- Battery operated radio to get news and information.
- Battery powered TV
- Hand crank or solar radio
- Scanner to hear about police situations and fires that may be in the area
- Extra batteries
- Signals such as whistles, flares, and mirrors

8. Tools

Tools will be used for a variety of reasons. Tools for hunting, shoveling, cutting, and navigational purposes are all essential items for a 72-hour bag.

- Knives (a large machete type and a smaller Gerber hunter)
- Multi-tool
- Camping shovels
- Candles
- Hammer
- Hatchet
- Collapsible fishing pole with hooks, line, bobbers, etc.
- Flares
- Maps, compass or GPS devices (Having extra compasses ensures that navigation is accurate)
- Rope (paracord)
- Knife sharpening stone
- Flashlight with extra batteries, or a hand crank flashlight
- Bungee cords
- Small assortment of hardware

9. Weapons

To maintain safety, you must have the ability to defend yourself. Threats could include wild animals or even other people. Weapons are a vital component of your 72-hour bag.

- Hand gun, rifle or shot gun
- Extra clips and ammo
- Knives
- Taser, stun gun
- Pepper spray, mace, dog spray or bear spray

10. Hygiene

Keeping yourself clean is not only aromatically beneficial to those around you, but vital to maintaining your health. Some hygiene items to pack are:

- Toilet Paper
- Toothbrush/Toothpaste
- Baby wipes
- Soap
- Shampoo/Conditioner
- Laundry Detergent
- Sanitary napkins/tampons

11. Written Resources

In a high stress situation it's easy to forget things that you have studied in the past. Carrying some written information for quick reference can save the life of a loved one or at the very least, make your evacuation less stressful.

- Survival guides
- First aid manual
- Local field guide to identify edible plants
- A Bible, spiritual text or other motivational book
- Favorite children's book for a comforting read-aloud ritual

Fire

Being able to start a fire will help to maintain proper body temperature, and will allow you to cook food and boil water. If an emergency arises and you have to leave, you want to be able to have items on hand to make a fire to stay warm.

- Waterproof matches
- Magnesium fire starters
- Cigarette lighters
- Small camp stove
- Fuel for the camp stove
- Homemade fire starters (see supplement at the end of this chapter)

Personal Documents and Identification

When evacuating to another location, you must have identification and emergency information. These may be needed to present to a police officer, Red Cross disaster worker, state trooper, park ranger, etc. To save space in your bug-out bag, you can download your important papers and documents onto a flash drive.

Examples of the types of identification Information are as follows:

- Driver's license and passports
- Wills
- Marriage licenses
- Birth certificates
- Social security cards
- Proof of address
- Licenses for guns or for fishing, etc.
- Health Insurance information
- Medical information, especially for those with pre-existing conditions
- Local road and topographical maps
- Pet licenses and vaccination records

To ensure that your documents stay safe, place the information in a Ziploc bag or waterproof carrier. You can also upload this information to a computer or flash drive.

Money

Often in a disaster, debit/credit card machines are inoperable due to a down-grid situation. Therefore, it's always important to have cash with you. Your money should be in small denominations in case change cannot be made. You should have enough money to pay for a hotel room, food, and/or other traveling expenses. Many people also take a small amount of precious metals, such as gold or silver coins, in order to have another form of currency.

First Aid

There is no guarantee that everything will go as planned. **Taking a basic first aid course now is instrumental in providing the right type of care.** Packing a well-stocked first aid kit[14] is essential in the event that someone gets injured. First aid kits should be filled with every type of first aid gear that could be needed.

---

[14] http://readynutrition.com/resources/medical-emergency1_09112009/

Band-Aids	Anti-diarrheal medicine	Antiseptic
Gauze pads	Medical tape	Calamine lotion
Tourniquet	Triple antibiotic cream	Anti-nausea medication
Betadine pads	Antiseptic spray	Insect repellent
Vaseline	Prescription medicine	Antihistamine
Sun block	Cold/flu medicine	Pain/fever medication
Epi-pen	Scissors	Moleskins for blisters
First aid manual	Celox (Emergency Blood Clotting Granules)	

Infant/Baby Needs

Any parent can tell you that getting out the door with an infant or toddler just to go to the store for a couple of hours requires almost military precision as well as enough gear to rival a week-long holiday from your pre-baby days. A baby's 72-hour bag contains many of the same requirements, plus their baby paraphernalia.

- Multiple changes of clothing (remember the layering principle)
- Blankets
- Formula (pre-measured in a closed bottle)
- Water (pre-boiled if the child is very young)
- Diapers
- Wipes
- Diaper rash cream
- Pacifiers
- Medications (prescription, Tylenol, etc.)
- Ear ache medications
- Teething gel
- Extra Ziploc bags
- Baby food
- Toys
- Comfort items

Pets

Plan ahead for your furry friends. Leaving home in a bug-out situation is a traumatic event that you don't want to compound by leaving your pets behind to their fate. Invest in a "dog pack" – these look like saddlebags and have pockets to put your dog's gear in. A dog can safely carry his own weight.

- Dog food/cat food
- Dish for food and water
- Water
- Litter pan/small bag of cat litter
- Leashes and extra collars
- Extra id tags
- Vaccination records
- Pet carrier

BAGS FOR THOSE WITH SPECIAL NEEDS

Every 72-hour bag will be unique to the person carrying it. If a member of your family has a disability, it becomes even more important to prepare. Through careful planning and forethought, you can provide the things to keep your family member safe and healthy throughout an emergency evacuation. Consider the type of bag you are using – some bags can easily be attached to a wheelchair, if needed. Another family member may need to carry most of the items for the person, as they may tire more easily. These are some additional items that may need to be added to the 72-hour bag of a person with special needs and should be carried by the person themselves in a smaller bag or fanny pack.

- Prescriptions
- Medical devices: i.e., glucose monitors, C-pap machines
- Items for specific dietary requirements
- Medical records
- Extra Medic-Alert bracelet
- Comfort items

PREPS TO BUY:

Use the lists of suggested items provided above to create a 72-hour kit for you and all members your family. Remember to keep the basic survival needs in mind and ensure you store lightweight items in the case that you must evacuate on foot.

- Food
- Water
- Clothing
- Shelter

ACTION ITEMS:

1. Assemble bags and practice using them to ensure all necessary items are packed.
2. Ensure that all family members have a bag packed. Help distribute items in children's packs to keep weight of pack down.

SUPPLEMENTAL INFORMATION AND RESOURCES

How to Avoid Hypothermia with the Right Clothing

Hypothermia can kill in as little as 20 minutes. Hypothermia is defined as "a body temperature of 95*F or less." Children and the elderly are most vulnerable but hypothermia can strike anyone. Symptoms to look for:

- Mental confusion
- Pale skin
- Blue lips, ears and fingertips
- Violent shivering

The biggest threat to your warmth is becoming wet or damp. Wet clothing can lose up to **90%** of its insulating effect. Select the clothing for your cold-weather 72-hour bag with the risk of hypothermia in mind.

- "Cotton kills" is a common saying among hikers – the fabric does not wick moisture and it loses its insulating effect when damp – avoid cotton!
- Select wool – it insulates even when damp
- Look into synthetic fibers such as polypropylene, found at sporting goods stores – this fabric is designed to wick away moisture from the body
- Water-resistant pants and jacket should be the outer layer
- Hats should cover the ears
- Include a scarf to cover the neck and to insulate the opening of your coat
- Gloves or mittens should be water-resistant
- Bring several extra pairs of socks – change them as soon as they feel damp

How to Make a Homemade Fire-Starter

These thrifty homemade fire-starters are made strictly from items that would otherwise be thrown away.

- cardboard toilet paper roll or paper towel roll
- dryer lint or cotton balls
- worn down candle stubs or crayons
- natural twine

Instructions

1.) Melt the crayons or candle wax down until liquefied. (The addition of wax makes the fire-starter windproof.)

2.) Stuff the dryer lint into the cardboard roll and tie with a piece of natural twine. The twine will be used as a place to light the finished fire starter.

3.) Dip the stuffed cardboard roll into the wax and roll it around until it is completely covered in wax.

4.) Stand the dipped cardboard onto a paper towel or piece of paper to dry.

5.) Once the fire-starters are dry, cut the cardboard rolls in half and vacuum seal them along with a few matches.

Once the fire-starters are lit, they will burn effortlessly. You can then add moss, small twigs, leaves and dry kindling to help the fire grow larger. Depending on how tightly the fire-starters are stuffed, they will typically burn for 5 minutes on their own. This should give you plenty of time to get a fire started.

Examples for a 72-hour Meal Plan:

Day 1

Breakfast – 2 cups oatmeal with raisins and 1 cup reconstituted dry milk powder
*(calories: **568**, fat: **8 g**, carbs: **108 g**, protein: **28 g**)*

Snack: 2 bars Datrex 3600 survival bar
*(calories: **400**, fat: **17.4 g**, carbs: **49.4 g**, protein: **5.6 g**)*

Lunch – Chicken flavored Ramen noodles with dehydrated vegetables
*(calories: **246.7**, fat: **4.7 g**, carbs: **27.3 g**, protein: **9.3 g**)*

Snack – 1 package of whole grain crackers and peanut butter with dried apples
*(calories: **310**, fat: **9 g**, carbs: **23 g**, protein: **5 g**)*

Dinner – 2.5 cups chicken and Rice-a-roni casserole, rehydrated
*(calories: **545.8**, fat: **9.2 g**, carbs: **75 g**, protein: **40.8 g**)*

Total Daily Nutrition of Day 1:

Calories: 2,070.5, fat: 48.3 g, carbs: 282.7 g, protein: 88.7 g

Day 2

Breakfast – 1 cup dry raisin bran cereal with reconstituted dry milk powder and 1 ounce of walnuts
*(calories: **390**, fat: **11 g**, carbs: **66 g**, protein: **14 g**)*

Snack – 8 graham crackers with 4 tbsp. peanut butter and 1 box of raisins
*(calories: **646**, fat: **35.2 g**, carbs: **69.6 g**, protein: **19 g**)*

Lunch – 1 pouch of StarKist Chunk Light Sandwich Ready Tuna Salad, 15 Kashi wheat crackers
*(calories: **230**, fat: **6 g**, carbs: **26 g**, protein: **16 g**)*

Snack – Luna fiber bar and Carnation Instant Breakfast drink
*(calories: **440**, fat: **10 g**, carbs: **67 g**, protein: **23 g**)*

Dinner – Dehydrated bean chili and cornbread, reconstituted and 2 soft oatmeal cookies
*(calories: **605**, fat: **64 g**, carbs: **106.8 g**, protein: **15 g**)*

Total nutrition of Day 2:

Calories: 2311, fat: 126.2 g,

carbs: 335.4 g, protein: 87 g

Day 3

Breakfast – "Just add water" whole wheat pancakes, 1/4 cup of dried blueberries, 2 maple syrup packets, hot chocolate with reconstituted dry milk powder
*(calories: **506.7**, fat: **3.7 g**, carbs: **113.2 g**, protein: **11.7g**)*

Snack – 1 ounce walnuts, dried apples and 8 graham crackers
*(calories: **400**, fat: **13 g**, carbs: **36 g**, protein: **4 g**)*

Lunch – 1 pouch of Star-Kist Chunk Light Sandwich Ready Tuna Salad, 15 Kashi wheat crackers
*(calories: **230**, fat: **6 g**, carbs: **26 g**, protein: **16 g**)*

Snack: 2 soft oatmeal cookies and Carnation Instant Breakfast drink
(calories: **560**, fat: **10 g**, carbs: **66 g**, protein: **16 g**

Dinner – Canned Stew and 14 Kashi crackers
(calories: **370**, fat: **14.5 g**, carbs: **44 g**, protein: **18 g**)

Total nutrition of Day 3:

Calories: 2,470, fat: 47.2 g, carbs: 285.2 g, protein: 65 g

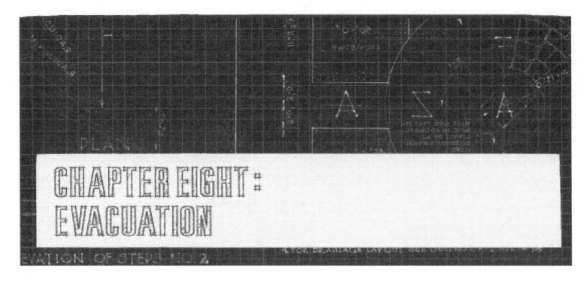

CHAPTER EIGHT: EVACUATION

What would you do if the doorbell rang and a fireman in full turnout gear informed you that you had 10 minutes to evacuate your home? Most evacuations are emergencies where time is of the utmost importance.

This exact scenario can either go smoothly or can be a nightmare. Let's compare the difference in the process between two families: one who was prepared and one who was not.

Family 1, the prepared family, responds with calm urgency to the news from the fireman.

Family 2 immediately begins to show signs of panic.

Family 1 has already divided up the duties for evacuating the house quickly. They have split the house into zones with each family member prepared to perform specific tasks.

Family 2 follow one another around the house, with two people attempting to perform the same tasks and no clear idea on what they need to pack. With only 10 minutes, they are trying to make final decisions on which of their items are the most important.

Family 1 has the vehicle packed and the children buckled into their seats in less than the 10 allotted minutes. The children are calm and cooperative.

Family 2 exceeds the 10 minutes and has a car full of large stuffed animals, mismatched clothing and photo albums. The children are frightened and crying. The parents are arguing about an important item that has been forgotten, each having expected the other to have gotten it.

If you only had ten minutes to evacuate your home, how would you fare? What would you take? How would your children handle it?

Chance favors the prepared mind. ~ Dr. Louis Pasteur

Preparation: it can mean the difference between panic and clarity. If a disaster hits, you may only have minutes to prepare to leave. Mandatory evacuations can happen anywhere, at any time. Some locales are more prone to evacuation-worthy disasters than others. Those that live near chemical refineries, areas prone to wildfires or near flood plains should be ready to go at a moment's notice.

An evacuation is fraught with anxiety, tension and fear. Every decision takes on potentially life-threatening magnitude. You must decide in a matter of moments:

1. What will you take with you?
2. Which family member is responsible for gathering which items?
3. What method of transportation will you use?
4. What route will you take?
5. What is your destination?
6. If something goes awry with the above decisions, what is Plan B?

Remember, from the previous chapter, having a 72-hour bag pre-assembled for each family member can mean the difference between a calm evacuation and a scattered, mad dash out the door.

If time allows, take steps to protect your home

1. Turn off the main gas valves
2. Turn off the water
3. Unplug electrical items
4. Open windows on opposite sides of the house slightly to vent pressure
5. Secure outdoor items by putting them in the garage or shed, or bungee them to ensure they are immobile.

GET ORGANIZED

During an evacuation, tensions run high and you want to be ready to go. The last thing you want to do is run around your home collecting prescriptions, children's special items, and personal documents. You will also be gathering sentimental items that cannot be replaced. As in the scenario at the beginning of this chapter, you may have only 10 minutes to gather the most important possessions in your home.

To ensure that important items are not forgotten, make a checklist of must-have items and keep it in the front of your emergency binder or with your 72-hour bag. This will reduce the fear of forgetting vital items and eliminate the frustration of trying to figure out what to bring when you are in a time crunch.

Include the following items on your list:

- Cash, check books, banking information and credit/debit cards
- Back-up of your hard drive or computer files
- Proof of residence (utility bill, home deed, etc.)
- Insurance documents (depending on the disaster you may need to make a claim before you can return to your home)
- Phone and device chargers
- Special sentimental items like photographs, certificates, jewelry or small heirlooms
- Coloring books and small activities for children
- Comfort items for children – special stuffed animals or blankets
- Prescription medications
- Eyeglasses
- Dental items like dentures and supplies, retainers, mouth guards

DIVIDE AND CONQUER

Simplify the evacuation by dividing up duties amongst the family members. Ensure that each person has his or her own list. This will maximize efficiency, reduce the duplication of efforts, and minimize forgotten items.

One way to divide the packing responsibilities among the family members is to separate them by category.

- Medical needs
- Sanitation needs
- Sentimental items
- Children's needs
- Pet needs

- Documents and money
- Appliances – phones, device chargers, hard drives
- Household responsibilities: turn off gas and water

Make a list for each individual from your master list. Consider performing practice runs or drills to decrease the amount of time it takes your family to get out the door.

WHAT METHOD OF TRANSPORTATION WILL YOU USE?

Another way to prepare for an evacuation is to pre-plan your method of transportation. If you have more than one vehicle which one will you take? Consider cargo space, fuel economy, and the terrain over which you will travel.

The vehicle you've decided upon should always have at least a half tank of gasoline and be prepared with the following:

- Keep your vehicle properly maintained – don't put off repairs
- Maps of the area
- GPS device
- Charger for mobile devices
- Flashlights (if not hand cranked or solar, remember extra batteries)
- Fix-a-flat, engine oil and coolant specific to the vehicle
- Jack and spare tire (make sure the spare is inflated to spec)
- Tool kit
- First aid kit
- Extra blankets
- Battery operated radio

The main goal when you decide to prepare for any type of emergency is to predict and relieve any extraneous stress or frustration. Look at your vehicle as your lifeline - having a vehicle that is well stocked and evacuation-ready is your ticket to a less chaotic and stressful encounter.

Throughout your preparations, keep in mind that while "getting out of Dodge" in a vehicle is your primary goal, sometimes the only option is to evacuate on foot. Evacuating on foot could be because of impassable roads, martial law, or vehicle failure, and may be your only option. In this case, have maps (topographical and maps of highways) of the area stored in your evacuation supplies and keep in mind that railroad tracks typically lead out of a city and are usually away from major roadways.

Emergency destinations may include:

- Hotels/motels
- Extended family member's home
- Friends home
- Emergency shelter
- Camp ground
- Summer home or hunting cabin

WHAT ROUTE WILL YOU TAKE?

When we think of evacuations, we typically think of the mass exoduses we witnessed on television with storms like Hurricane Katrina and Hurricane Rita. Roadways were clogged to the point being impassable.

After Katrina, a report from the National Association of Engineers stated, "One complicating factor is that transportation infrastructure is neither planned nor designed to accommodate evacuation-level demand; building enough capacity to move the population of an entire city in a matter of hours is simply not economically, environmentally, or socially feasible. Roadways are not even designed to be delay-free under routine peak-period conditions."

The last thing you want is to be trapped in your vehicle for hours with an impending storm bearing down on you. As soon as the decision is made to evacuate, be organized and ready to go as soon as possible. This will help you to be ahead of the masses of people leaving an hour later than you.

- Have maps on hand with the planned route already laid out
- Stay off of main highways feeding into the city whenever possible
- During the evacuation keep the radio tuned to a local news channel to keep abreast of the situation—this can alert you to potential delays such as road blocks or accidents
- Develop a plan for picking up children in case the disaster occurs during school hours; find out what the school's evacuation plan is and map these destinations on your route

WHAT IS YOUR DESTINATION?

By choosing your destination in advance, you reduce the likelihood of separation from a family member. If everyone knows where to go, in the event that you are unable to travel together, you will be far more likely to be reunited quickly. A local destination should be chosen, as well as one that is more distant in case of a large regional disaster. Map a minimum of 3 different routes to these locations.

Be sure you have money available in small denominations of cash. Figure out how much you need to make it to your destination. Consider fuel expenses and lodging costs.

WHAT IS PLAN B?

Despite the most careful planning, the very nature of a disaster makes it likely that something will go awry. Anticipate the possible failure of your initial plan by formulating a "Plan B" for all eventualities.

Remember to designate a person outside of the area as a primary contact for the family. This person will be able to coordinate messages and locations for family members in the event that you are separated.

The ultimate Plan B, should you be forced to abandon your vehicle, is to continue on foot. Sometimes circumstances may dictate that you must leave home on foot. You will have to reduce the items that you take to include only what you can carry out. Remember to keep your basic survival needs in mind when adjusting your pack.

The following actions and items take priority in a walking evacuation.

- 72-hour bags that leave your hands free and are not prohibitive in weight
- Pre-planned walking route avoiding populated areas if possible
- Camping gear
- Important documents stored or saved on a flash drive
- Personal defense and security
- Extra food to compensate for the additional energy expended by walking with a fully loaded pack
- Comfortable, sturdy footwear

PREPARE MENTALLY AND SPIRITUALLY

By far, the most important preparation in an evacuation is mental. If all of your best-laid plans deteriorate, a positive mental outlook and a problem-solving attitude can mean the difference between survival and failure.

A little seed of hope can go a long way. Finding faith in hard times can be compared to walking through a desert and finding water. It can save your life and give you the endurance to carry on. In the midst of disappointment and frustration, faith and hope can keep your positive momentum going. Concentrate on all that is good and positive.

"Don't count your problems; count your blessings."

PREPS TO BUY:

- Large Rubbermaid-type containers for gathering items
- Prepared list for medical needs, sanitation needs, sentimental items, children's needs, pet needs, documents and money, appliances, household responsibilities
- Comfortable, sturdy footwear for each family member
- Local maps

ACTION ITEMS:

1. Create an evacuation plan, including an emergency meeting area for family members, multiple evacuation routes, and a list of emergency phone numbers.

2. Assemble evacuation packs.

3. As family, discuss the evacuation plan, and include a discussion on the protocol and emergency exits. Make certain that all family members thoroughly understand the plan.

4. Get a tune-up of the vehicle you plan to evacuate with.

SUPPLEMENTAL INFORMATION AND RESOURCES

72-hour Kit for Vehicles

Having a 72-hour kit for your vehicle is a way to be more prepared for disasters. If packed properly, a 72-hour kit will give you everything you need to keep you alive for 3 days. Having one of these for your car can be used in the case of an emergency evacuation, or if your car stalls in a remote location when help is far away. Adding a few items to the trunk for one of these unforeseen disasters or events will not only help you prepare, but also keep you safe and focused on finding a solution in case you find yourself in one of these situations.

To prepare a 72-hour kit for your vehicle, use a plastic container and fill it with:

- 3 day supply of food
- Water – 3 day supply
- Water purification tablets
- First aid kit
- Blankets
- Emergency shelter
- Flashlight or a light source
- Extra batteries
- Rain poncho
- Work gloves
- Knife or multi-purpose tool
- Chains for tires (if applicable)
- Small shovel or collapsible shovel
- Rope
- Air compressor (to air tires)
- Fix-a-flat
- Extra tire
- Waterproof matches
- Signaling device such as a beacon, flare, mirror, whistle or light stick
- Toiletries (toilet Paper, hand wipes, etc.)
- First aid kit
- Survival book to look to for survival information
- Maps and navigation devices (compass, GPS device, etc.)
- 5-10 gallons of extra gasoline

5 Ways to Prepare Your Evacuation Vehicle

1. **Have vehicle bug-out supplies.** Keep your basic survival needs in mind and plan to have enough supplies for 3 days. The items chosen should be lightweight and functional so that, if need be, carrying the kit will not be a strain. Initially, the most important part of preparing is to have a well thought out *plan*. This plan should be in place before you evacuate. In addition, if you have children, have some child-friendly activities or books packed away to keep their attention diverted. Let's be honest, there is nothing more excruciating than the question, "Are we there yet?"
2. **Keep your vehicle properly maintained.** That means checking and changing the oil on a regular basis, ensuring the tires are inflated, brakes are working, the headlights work, and that the vehicle has been inspected. This is pretty self-explanatory. Whatever vehicle is chosen for evacuation reasons needs to be at optimum performance.

3. **Keep your gas tank full.** When my vehicle gets to half full, I typically fill it up. Not only does this ensure that I could get a far distance from my home, but it also saves on gas money. In addition, during an evacuation scenario, the lines to the gas stations are going to be filled with frustrated individuals, which could lead to run-ins, thus delaying your evacuation further.

4. **Make sure you have extra navigational items.** Items such as GPS, maps and compasses included in your supplies can ensure that you know where to go and how to get there. To take this a step further, having non-electric navigational items can be necessary if your electric circuits are disrupted.

5. **Have multiple pre-planned evacuation locations.** Roadblocks, heavy congestion, and even car accidents can delay your evacuation. Therefore, plan to deviate off course and create multiple escape routes that do not require you to travel through any densely populated cities – this will cut down on traffic jams. Before you leave, listen to the radio and the news to see which highways are open and plan accordingly.

CHAPTER NINE:
HOME SECURITY

According to the United States Department of Justice, there are **more than 8,000 home invasions per day** in North America.

- One in five homes is the target of a home invasion or break-in
- 38% of all assaults occur during home invasions
- 60% of all rapes take place during home invasions
- 50 percent of home invasions involve the use of a weapon
- The most common weapons used are knives or other cutting instruments
- In 48 percent of home invasions, victims sustain physical injuries
- Victims age 60 or older make up 17 percent of home invasion victims
- In 68 percent of home invasions, victims and the accused are strangers
- In 11 percent of these cases, victims and the accused are friends, business associates, or family

We all want to believe that we are safe and sound when we latch the windows and lock the doors. We experience an added feeling of security when we live in an expensive neighborhood, when our home has a security system, or when we are part of an active neighborhood watch program. In reality, security gadgets can protect the outside of your home, but all of the high tech gear in the world is meaningless if you can't protect what's inside. People can be robbed, assaulted, or killed, simply by opening the door to a stranger. Criminals use many ruses to persuade a potential victim to let them in:

- They may pretend to be delivering a package or flowers
- Some wear uniforms from utility companies and act as though there is an emergency
- They may tell you they've accidentally damaged your car or other belonging
- Many ask for help; i.e., to use the phone, asking for food, etc.
- They might act as though they are door-to-door salespeople
- If you are hesitant about opening the door, they may mumble so you can't understand them clearly

Keep this saying in mind!

A popular prepper adage is, "If you can't protect it, you don't own it."

Following an emergency, elements of crime increase due to desperate and unprepared individuals trying to meet their basic needs.

Learn ways of protecting yourself and your home beforehand.

Once the door is opened, invaders can use explosive force to push their way into the home. Many victims are stunned and paralyzed with fear by the violent entrance, giving the intruder vital moments to gain control of the situation.

THE THREE-LAYER DEFENSE SYSTEM

Designing a home defense system that includes multiple layers is a proactive way to protect your family, home and belongings. Security layers are preventative measures that will advertise to intruders that they should avoid your home altogether. The more layers you have in and around your home, the less likely a criminal is going to be to target your home for his/her next "job."

Layer 1: The Outside Layer

This layer comprises the outer perimeter of your home. Due to the poor architectural designs of homes these days (doors with decorative windows and transoms, sliding glass doors, picture windows, and easy entry from streets and highways) homes are now more vulnerable than ever to break-ins.

Installing visible, preventative measures around your home will advertise to anyone staking out your neighborhood that you mean business. Walk around your home and figure out where the vulnerable areas are. Minor adjustments to the outside of the home can help secure it from the outside in. One of the most vulnerable areas of your outside perimeter is the windows. A heavy lawn chair can easily be tossed into a window, shattering it and creating an easy entry. Investing in shatterproof window film is one solution to this potential problem. Make the exterior of your home look inhospitable to criminals with these adjustments:

- Thorny bushes beneath windows (see box for more about security landscaping)
- "Beware of Dog" signs near all doors (even if you don't have a dog)
- Barred windows or European-style security/storm shutters.
- Security company stickers in all windows
- Infra-red motion lights
- A video camera pointed at the front door (even a fake one with a blinking light)
- Locks on the back fences
- A gated entry at the front of the driveway that has spikes at the top to prevent someone from jumping over the fence

Many of us unknowingly put our families in danger by being predictable. For example, have you ever placed a key under the mat? Surprise: burglars know that trick! You want to make breaking into your home difficult. Avoid leaving keys under flowerpots, under the mat, or inside fake "rocks". If you need to leave an extra key, your best option is to leave it with a trusted neighbor.

Layer 2: The Inside Layer

Small preventative measures can help secure the inner sanctity of your home. This layer focuses on "hardening" your home by making it more difficult to access.

- Ensure your doors are strong (a hollow-core metal or solid wood door is best)
- Reinforce the door frame – a door is only as strong as the frame that holds it in place
- If your doors are comprised of glass, apply a shatterproof film
- Install a double cylinder lock to reinforce strength
- Install 1-inch deadbolt locks on all exterior doors
- Close all curtains and blinds at nighttime and set the alarm
- Keep purses, car keys, money and jewelry away from windows where the items are visible from outside
- Put a peephole in the door
- Burglarproof your glass patio doors by setting a pipe or metal bar in the middle bottom track of the door slide. The pipe should be the same length as the track
- Put anti-lift devices in your windows
- Add an intrusion detection system

- Install a noisy home alarm with panic buttons in different locations around the house – intruders do not want the attention that a loud siren will attract
- Position hidden web cams strategically throughout your home. Be sure to place the computer that is monitoring the locations in a hidden spot so the criminals cannot walk off with it
- Add a 2-way voice feature to an existing alarm system. This feature enables your security system to communicate directly through the control panel. This feature also allows you to call into your system and be able to listen to any activity or speak to your child or other family members who are home
- Consider adding a safe room to the home

Layer 3: The Personal Layer

This layer is the most critical because it is based on all of the protocols, defense training, and emergency plans you have established.

The personal layer is the only layer that you can take into the outside world. If you are walking and someone tries to mug you, you will be able to use your defense training and emergency protocols to deal with the attacker(s).

The personal layer is the final defense. If all of your deterrents and preventative measures are not enough to keep a determined intruder out of your home, you must take action to defend yourself and your family.

It is prudent to have multiple strategies to defend yourself. If the first strategy fails, always be prepared to move on to the next strategy.

- Learn self-defense: Find a class that specializes in rapid response techniques like Krav Maga or Wing Chun.
- Get a gun and learn to use it safely and accurately. Go to the gun range and practice on a regular basis.
- Learn to improvise. Your home is full of weapons of opportunity such as:
    - Hot coffee
    - Fire extinguisher
    - Aerosol hairspray
    - Lamps
    - Baseball bat
    - Salt thrown in the eyes
    - Butcher knife
- Have emergency plans and protocols set up and put in writing where children or teens can see them. Included in these protocols should be important contact phone numbers next to the plan.

- Teach the household how to call 9-1-1, and have a script ready for them to read to the dispatcher. This will help keep them calmly explain the emergency situation to the dispatcher.
- Teach family members different escape routes to use in case they need to leave the home, as well as a code word to use for the family to immediately leave the home to go to a safe location.

PREPS TO BUY:

- Thorn-bearing plants for landscape
- "Beware of Dog" signs
- Barred windows or European-style security/storm shutters
- Security company stickers for windows
- Infra-red motion lights
- A video camera (even a fake one with a blinking light)
- Locks for fences
- Double cylinder lock
- 1-inch deadbolt locks
- Peephole kits
- Metal pipes or other blockers for sliding doors and windows
- Intrusion detection systems
- Alarm system
- Web cams
- Weapons

ACTION ITEMS:

1. Create an emergency protocol and discuss it with your family members. Be sure to include a list of emergency phone numbers and escape routes.

2. Take the time to walk around your home and yard and look at it through the eyes of a criminal. Check for vulnerabilities. If you were to break into this home, how would you do it? Do this to identify your weak points, and then address them.

SUPPLEMENTAL INFORMATION AND RESOURCES

Design Your Landscape to Minimize the Risk of Invasions

Thorn-bearing plants, trees and shrubs can help to keep the perimeter of your home inhospitable to criminals. Check your garden zone to see which varieties are best for the area where you live. Some of these plants are very prolific and can cover an area in a rapid amount of time.

Thorn-Bearing Trees

Trees with thorns on their trunk can help protect upstairs windows from being broken into. Who wants to scale a tree of thorns?

- Argentine Mesquite - This variety of tree bears 2-inch thorns in its bark making it a very intimidating tree to climb up.
- Honey Locust – This plant is a multi-purpose plant that not only provides a security defense with its sharp red thorns, but has edible parts as well. The seedpods are edible and sweet and can be fed to livestock. In addition, the flowers of this tree attract bees.
- Black Locust – This tree has smaller, 2-inch thorns on its main trunk. Despite their smaller thorns, they cause swelling and pain on contact.

Thorn-bearing Vines

These vining plants are good multi-taskers. They are aesthetically beautiful and provide preventative security at the same time!

- Bougainvillea
- Climbing roses
- Blackberry vines
- Catclaw creeper

Thorn-bearing Bushes

Locate these bushes beneath windows to deter peeping toms or intruders.

- Pyracantha or fire thorn bush is not a bush to get caught up in. The sting will radiate a burning feeling for hours. It spreads prolifically and will definitely make a statement of "back off."
- Catclaw acacia conceals its thorns under beautiful leaves and yellow flowers.
- Cacti are a great way to keep intruders away. Look for varieties such as the thorny chollas with 2-inch thorns.

- Rugosa roses are a thorn bearing variety, but are also functional: they attract bees with their pollen and nectar.
- Oregon grape holly is both attractive and a deterrent with its 2-inch thorns.
- The Washington hawthorn tree has attractive red berries and thorns. It can be allowed to grow or be pruned into a bush.

Creating a Safe Room

A safe room is a great starting point for preparing a personal layer. This gives you and other family members a safe place to retreat if someone enters your home with evil intent.

Most of us aren't wealthy enough to build a separate room with a hidden entrance, camouflaged by a fake bookcase. That doesn't mean you can't create a safe place for you and your family members to retreat if someone enters your home. A safe room can be created on a budget.

Choose a location in your home, most likely a bedroom or walk-in closet, and add security reinforcements to make it extremely difficult, if not impossible, for someone to enter the room. This room is an investment in the safety of your family, so purchase the best quality products you can afford.

1. **Replace the door with an exterior door.** This is the most expensive component in the conversion of your safe room, but it is a vital one. Most interior doors are simply two thin sheets of plywood with air in the middle. Replace the door to your safe room with one designed for the exterior of the house. The best choices are solid core wood or steel. Ideally, go with the heaviest steel door you can afford. Once the door is installed, simply paint it the same color as the other doors and it will hardly be noticeable that one room entrance is different than the others. Hang the door so it opens outward.

2. **Reinforce the doorframe.** Most exterior doors come with a heavier frame than the one that will exist to house your current door, and you'll want to install that too. Reinforce the doorframe with steel angle iron. A door is no better than its frame – you want a frame that will help protect the door from being kicked in by intruders, so if the frame that accompanies your new door is not substantial enough, look for a sturdy steel door-jam. Always use at least 3-inch screws to anchor the components of your door and its frame.

3. **Install locks.** Once you've installed your new door in its sturdy frame, install a heavy duty locking knob and a one-sided deadbolt that you can lock from the inside. When choosing a deadbolt, look for a keyless Grade-1 deadbolt (the American National Standards Institute tests locks with an arsenal of tools, and then grades them: Grade 1 is the most impenetrable).

4. **Install hardware for a door bar.** If you are extremely serious about deterring intruders, you can also install hardware and have a bar that goes across the door from side to side. The bar can be a very heavy piece of wood, or it can be iron or another metal. Picture the bars reinforcing doors in medieval castles or on barns. Once you've engaged the deadbolt, you can quickly slide your bar into place. Without a police battering ram and a full SWAT team, no one will get through that door.

5. **Fortify the windows.** If money is not an object, you can replace your bedroom windows with security windows. Security windows are shatterproof and bulletproof, but very expensive. For most of us, the application of shatterproof film on the windows will suffice. Be certain that you have heavy curtains over the windows so that no one can see in. Being visible makes you more vulnerable.

6. **Keep your gun/weapons in the safe room.** If you store your firearms in a gun safe, this is the room where you want it located. Storing weapons differs from state to state – be certain to follow local laws. Keep your firearms and extra ammunition in the safe room to defend yourself on the very slim chance that the room is breached before help can arrive.

7. **Have a phone in the safe room.** It's best to have more than one type of communication available in the room. A landline, a cell phone and/or a two-way radio will allow you to call for help. Keep in mind that cell phones that are not activated can still be used to call 911 in most areas. If your landline is cut, then a deactivated cell phone could still be used. Make certain that the cell phone is constantly plugged in and charged.

8. **Install security devices.** If you have a home alarm system, a panic button should be located in the safe room. Cameras and monitors can now be purchased for less than $200 and can feed into the television in your room. These devices can allow you to see where the criminals are in your home and what they are doing. With a camera to show you what is going on elsewhere in your home, you can also verify that help has arrived.

9. **Stock your safe room.** Keep food and water in the safe room, as well as a first aid kit and any supplies for medical conditions. A fire extinguisher should also be included – a very determined intruder may use fire to attempt to force you out of the room. If there is not a bathroom connected to the safe room, consider some sanitation supplies.

If a situation arises during which you must retreat to the safe room, **do not exit the room until help has arrived.**

Remember that your safe room is the *absolute last defense* against intruders. If the safe room is breached you **must** be prepared to use force to defend yourself. The most reliable weapons in your personal arsenal must be stored in this room, along with sufficient ammunition. Make sure you keep the weapon clean and well maintained. Your life and the lives of your family may depend on it.

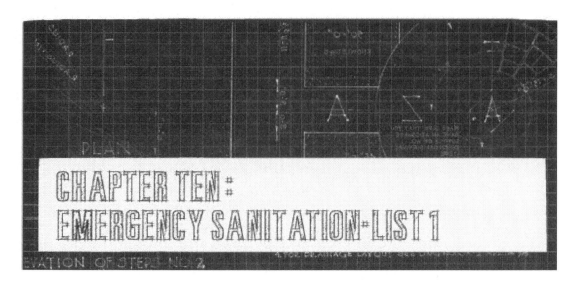

CHAPTER TEN:
EMERGENCY SANITATION - LIST 1

Outbreaks of infectious diseases following hurricanes, cyclones, floods, tsunamis, and earthquakes are not uncommon. Most post-disaster disease is spawned by poor sanitation, a lack of safe drinking water and contaminated food.

Cholera, typhoid fever, dysentery, hepatitis A and E, balantidiasis, and leptospirosis are some of the diseases that can afflict survivors of disasters. They are typically spread under unsanitary conditions, mainly through contamination of food and water with human feces. All of these diseases can potentially be fatal if not treated properly and immediately.

For those who survived the disaster but lost their homes and had to seek shelter in an emergency center, there are additional risks. Diseases such as infectious hepatitis, gastroenteritis, measles and tuberculosis could catch up with victims of a catastrophe stuck in a crowded shelter with insufficient sanitary facilities and garbage management.

Source: The Humanitarian Coalition

Sometimes surviving the actual disaster is only the beginning. The aftermath of a disaster can be just as hazardous. In a grid-down situation, access to normal methods of sanitation may be limited. Trash may not be collected, water may not be running, toilets may not be flushing and you may be without power to properly cook your food.

GARBAGE DISPOSAL

Have you ever wondered what it would be like if your trash wasn't picked up each week? Have you thought about how you would dispose of it? What would happen to your town if garbage was left to sit out in the sun to bake for weeks on end without anyone arriving to take it away?

The odor alone would be enough of a nightmare to face, but what about the contents of the garbage itself (i.e., dirty diapers, contaminated medical supplies, rotting meat and food)? This type of situation would cause E. coli and bacteria to invade almost everything that you touch. If a situation like this was allowed to fester, the potential for diseases and epidemics would create an entirely new disaster to be dealt with.

The city of Toronto, Ontario accumulated over 48,900 **tons** of garbage during a 36-day strike in 2009. Mountains of garbage overflowed city trashcans and dumpsters. The strike took place in July, so the heat exacerbated the dilemma.

No one really wants to discuss sanitation because it's an unpleasant and dirty subject; however, it is one of the most important areas to focus on when preparing for a disaster. In a disaster where water resources are compromised, people within a 50-mile radius could be adversely impacted by illness and disease if even *one person* handles the trash improperly. You need to plan to dispose of garbage and human waste, as well as methods to maintain personal hygiene.

How can you safely dispose of garbage after a disaster?

1. **Reduce:** Try to reduce the amount of garbage that you produce after a disaster. Obviously, you can't eat the package the food came in, but you can attempt to choose items with less packaging in the first place. If you go elsewhere to purchase items, dispose of the packaging at the store. Limit your use of disposable items like paper plates and cups.
2. **Reuse:** Many items can be rinsed and used for another purpose. For example, soda bottles or water bottles can be refilled with newly filtered water.
3. **Recycle:** If your locality has recycling services, you can separate your waste and put aside your glass, metal and paper for this purpose. Bear in mind, though, in a large scale disaster these services may not be available for some time.
4. **Compost:** Non-meat food scraps and newspaper can be added to the compost bin.
5. **Dump:** In some situations, when transportation is available, you can take your garbage to the dump.

6. **Bury:** If you must bury your garbage, add some powdered lime to the bag to help it decompose more quickly and reduce foul odors.
7. **Burn:** Many items are suitable for burning: paper, cardboard, waste food, plant clippings, used feminine hygiene products and wood. **NEVER BURN:** plastic, rubber or other man-made materials – this can release toxic fumes.

HUMAN WASTE

According to the Center for Disease Control, contamination by human feces is the number one cause of communicable disease after a disaster.

Prevention is the key to spreading communicable diseases, so prepare appropriately. If water services are interrupted during a short-term emergency, you will be unable to flush your toilet. Consider this alternative:

1. Clean and empty the water of the toilet bowl out.
2. Line the bowl with a heavy-duty plastic bag.
3. Once the bag has waste, add a small amount of disinfectant and deodorant (e.g. cat litter) and securely tie the bag and dispose of it.
4. A large plastic trashcan (lined with a heavy duty bag) can be used to store the bags of waste. Once waste services begin, the city will come and collect these.

If waste services do not begin, then you may need to consider burning or burying your waste. There are some considerations when choosing a site to bury waste.

- Select a cat hole site far from water sources, 200 feet (approximately 70 adult paces) is the recommended range.
- Select an inconspicuous site untraveled by people. Examples of cat hole sites include thick undergrowth, near downed timber, or on gentle hillsides.
- If camping with a group or if camping in the same place for more than one night, disperse the cat holes over a wide area; don't go to the same place twice.
- Try to find a site with deep organic soil. This organic material contains organisms that will help decompose the feces. (Organic soil is usually dark and rich in color.) The desert does not have as much organic soil as a forested area.
- If possible, locate a cat hole where it will receive maximum sunlight. The heat from the sun will aid the decomposition.

Disposing Feminine Products When the SHTF

It is important to properly dispose of items with menstrual blood. Menstrual blood can carry blood-borne pathogens and bacterial infections. Tampons and feminine napkins do not decompose quickly, and items with blood attract rodents and other animals, even when buried.

The best way to dispose of used feminine napkins and tampons is to burn them. The fire must be very hot in order to thoroughly destroy the used items.

- Choose an elevated site where water would not normally run off during rainstorms. The idea here is to keep the feces out of water. Over time, the decomposing feces will percolate into the soil before reaching water sources.

PERSONAL HYGIENE

Keeping clean after a disaster is one of the most important things that we can do to remain healthy. Many diseases and illnesses can be spread by the inability to wash our hands with soap and clean running water. In some situations, you will have to improvise. If running water is unavailable there are other options to keep your hands clean.

1. Use soap with some of the bottled or stored water that you have available
2. Use antibacterial hand sanitizer containing at least 60% alcohol
3. Use baby wipes
4. Use rubbing alcohol

Take care to always clean your hands in the following situations:

- Before, during, and after preparing food
- Before eating food
- Before and after caring for someone who is sick
- Before and after treating a cut or wound
- After using the toilet
- After changing diapers or cleaning up a child who has used the toilet
- After blowing your nose, coughing, or sneezing
- After touching an animal or animal waste
- After touching garbage

Source: Center for Disease Control

There are other personal hygiene issues in the aftermath of a disaster. Follow these tips to keep your family safe from disease.

---

1. Only wash dishes in water that is uncontaminated – you can use boiled water or bottled water for this.
2. Only use water that is safe for consumption for brushing your teeth. Even if tap water is running it may not be safe for use in dental hygiene.
3. Clean and treat all wounds immediately. If the skin is broken at all you must immediately take steps to care for the wound. A potentially fatal infection can set in much more easily in times of disaster. If the wound develops redness, swelling, a foul odor or discharge, seek immediate medical attention.

PREPS TO BUY:

These suggested preps will specifically target creating a sanitation kit.

Disposable bucket or luggable-loo

- Toilet paper (1 roll per family member for each week)
- 1-2 rolls of paper towels
- Diapers for infants
- Additional infant supplies (baby wipes, diaper rash cream, etc.)
- Rubber gloves
- Sanitary items for women (at least one- month supply)
- Garbage bags with twist ties (i.e., to line toilets or luggable-loo)
- Bleach
- Cat litter or absorbent material (i.e., saw dust or dirt)
- Baking soda (to eliminate odors)
- Vinegar
- Shovel
- Soap
- Antibacterial sanitizer (one per family member)
- Baby wipes
- Rubbing alcohol
- Lime (calcium hypochlorite)
- Disposable latex gloves
- Masks (N95 or surgical)

ACTION ITEMS:

1. Create a sanitation kit for your family.

2. If you are preparing a sanitation kit with infants in mind, ensure that you have accounted for their short- and long-term needs.

3. Familiarize yourself with different methods of handling the sanitation problems that arise during short- and long-term emergencies.

SUPPLEMENTAL INFORMATION AND RESOURCES

How to Build an Outhouse

1) Choose your location. Make certain you are at least 200 feet away from all water supplies: wells, lakes, streams, springs, etc. A shady area will reduce odors in the summer.

2) Dig a hole at least 3-6 feet deep.

3) Build a box without a top or bottom to insert into the hole to keep the sides from caving in.

4) Build a floor over it – make sure there will be enough space for a person to sit over the hole and still have room for his or her knees – approximately 4'x4'.

5) Making it as simple or as elaborate as your skills allow, build 4 walls and a roof. One of the walls should have an opening for the door.

6) Cut a hole in your newly constructed floor to go over the pit you've dug.

7) Build a bench over the hole. The bench should go all the way across the outhouse and have a closed front. Cut two holes into the bench. The first one will be centered where you will install the toilet seat, and should be just smaller than the toilet seat's diameter. The second hole should be against the back wall, and big enough to accommodate ventilation pipe from the pit.

8) Cut a hole in the roof directly over the smaller hole in the bench. Then install a PVC pipe that runs the full height of the outhouse, with an open bottom terminating a couple of inches below the bench surface in the pit area, and a lidded top about 1 foot above the shallow end of the roof. Use a silicon caulking to seal these holes.

9) Add a door with a latch.

10) Use the dirt from the hole you dug to mound around the outside of the outhouse – this helps to keep the gases from escaping and causing odor.

11) Stock the outhouse with toilet paper, baby wipes and hand sanitizer.

12) Add one or more small windows for ventilation and light. Feel free to cut a crescent moon in the door for classic outhouse charm!

HOMEMADE HAND SANITIZER

Essential oils have been used for thousands of years to combat disease. You may already have all of the oils in your home that are necessary to make your own hand sanitizer. Using essential oils with disinfectant, antiseptic and antiviral properties will allow you to create a homemade hand sanitizer with no alcohol at all.

Cedarwood, lavender, lemon, lemon grass, myrrh, neroli, patchouli, peppermint, rose, sandalwood, tea tree, thyme and ylang-ylang essential oils all have **antiseptic properties**.

Clove, neroli and pine oils have both **disinfectant and antiseptic properties.**

Tea tree oil is the most powerful of these essential oils and has antiviral, antifungal and antibacterial properties, making it the recommended essential oil to use in the following recipes. The effectiveness of your hand sanitizer will be reduced if you do not use tea tree oil

Always be careful with essential oils and consult an herbalist before using if you have any current health conditions. Some oils (like tea tree, cedar wood and hyssop) are not suitable for children, infants or pregnant and nursing women.

One essential oil blend option that is safe for families is a combination of lavender and pine. This will create a disinfectant, antiseptic hand sanitizer with calming effects. Add a little citrus or rosemary to enhance and round out the aroma.

Aloe vera gel is in ingredient in all of these recipes. This means pure aloe vera gel, not juice, without the coloring. It should say "100% aloe vera gel" somewhere on the bottle. If it doesn't, it's the wrong stuff.

Use a glass bowl for mixing your hand sanitizer - plastic may take on the aroma of the essential oils and metal may react with the ingredients. Add the ingredients together in your mixing vessel, then shake or stir to combine. Funnel the mixture into small plastic bottles or glass jars. Some recipes may need to be shaken before use to distribute the oils.

Alcohol Free Hand Sanitizer Gel

- 1 cup pure aloe vera gel
- 1-2 teaspoons of witch hazel (add until the desired consistency is reached)
- 8 drops of essential oils (as listed above)

Mostly Alcohol Free Hand Sanitizer Gel

- 2 cups pure aloe vera gel
- 2 tablespoons 90% SD40 alcohol (perfumer's alcohol if you can get it)
- 2-3 teaspoons essential oils (as listed above)

Alcohol-based Hand Sanitizer

- 1/4 cup pure aloe vera gel
- 1/4 cup grain alcohol or vodka
- 10 drops essential oils (as listed above)

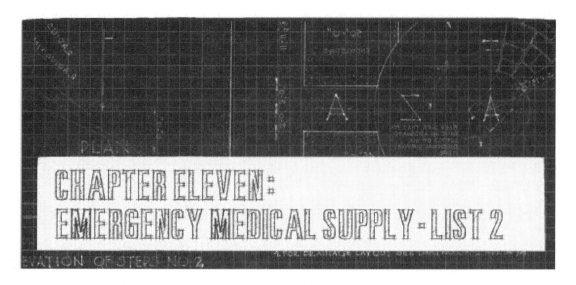

CHAPTER ELEVEN:
EMERGENCY MEDICAL SUPPLY - LIST 2

At approximately 5:30 pm we received a warning that a tornado had been spotted. At 5:42 pm a security guard yelled to everyone, "Take cover! We are about to get hit by a tornado!" ... We heard a loud horrifying sound like a large locomotive ripping through the hospital. The whole hospital shook and vibrated as we heard glass shattering, light bulbs popping, walls collapsing, people screaming, the ceiling caving in above us, and water pipes breaking, showering water down on everything ...The whole process took about 45 seconds, but seemed like eternity. The hospital had just taken a direct hit from a category EF5 tornado.

We had to use flashlights to direct ourselves to the crying and wounded... There was no power, but our mental generators were up and running, and on high test adrenaline. I remember a patient in his early 20's gasping for breath, telling me that he was going to die. After a quick exam, I removed the large shard of glass from his back, made the clinical diagnosis of a pneumothorax (collapsed lung) and gathered supplies from wherever I could locate them to insert a thoracotomy tube in him. He allowed me to do this without any local anesthetic since none could be found. With his life threatening injuries I knew he was running out of time, and it had to be done. Imagine my relief when I heard a big rush of air, and breath sounds again; fortunately, I was able to get him transported out.

A small child of approximately 3-4 years of age was crying; he had a large avulsion of skin to his neck and spine. The gaping wound revealed his cervical spine and upper thoracic spine bones. This was a child, his whole life ahead of him, suffering life-threatening wounds in front of me, his eyes pleading me to help him... Fortunately, we were able to get him immobilized with towels, and start an IV with fluids and pain meds before shipping him out.

~ Dr. Kevin Kitka, Mercy/St John's Regional Medical Center, Joplin, MO

In the event of a disaster, calling 911 or going to the doctor may not always be an option. If you are following this book chapter by chapter, then you have taken a basic first aid course and purchased a first aid manual. But what will you do if an illness or injury occurs that is beyond the scope of that training and information? If there is no way to get the victim to the hospital, you could be on your own to treat them. When a disaster occurs, every second counts and every person is needed to help others survive.

In Chapter 4, you began the process of accumulating your first aid kit. A lot goes into being medically prepared, so this will be a recurring theme in this book. After gathering the basic first aid supplies, you will continue accumulating more advanced medical preps, as well as learning alternative medical therapies towards the end.

Medical reference books are a necessity of every SHTF library for this very reason. Buying multiple reference materials gives you a broader spectrum of information in how to provide different types of medical treatment. Different books will also recommend different treatment techniques, which will allow you to be versatile with potentially limited supplies and tools.

Don't forget to consider eBook references as well. Scribd.com carries a variety of electronic books and references that can easily be downloaded. EBooks or kindle edition electronic books can often be downloaded for a far lower price than you would pay to purchase the book itself.

Be certain to print a copy of what you have downloaded for your emergency resource library or to put in your emergency binder. In a down-grid situation, you may not be able to access your references if they are only stored on the computer.

Great Medical Resources

When There is No Doctor
By David Werner with Jane Maxwell and Carol Thurman, Hesperian Health Guides

The Doom and Bloom Survival Medicine Handbook
By Joseph Alton and Amy Alton, CreateSpace

A Barefoot Doctor's Manual: A Translation of the Official Chinese Paramedical Manual
By John E. Fogarty, Running Press

Field Guide to Wilderness Medicine
By Paul Auerbach, Mosby Publishing

Wilderness Medicine: Beyond First Aid
By William Forgey, Globe Pequot

PREPARE FOR YOUR FAMILY'S UNIQUE MEDICAL NEEDS

During short-term disasters, it is imperative that you prepare for medical situations if you want to keep your loved ones and yourself healthy. When buying your medical supplies, remember the things that are unique to your household. Some family members may have preexisting conditions or allergies, or may simply be accident-prone.

Another item for your emergency medicine kit is prescription medications. If one of your family members suffers from a chronic condition that requires daily medication, begin to stockpile that medication until you have a minimum of one month stored. If your medication is covered by insurance, this can be tricky. However, if you purchase your refills one week early each time, you can have your extra month of medication stockpiled in short order, while still being covered by insurance.

Avoid pre-assembled medical kits - they tend to be overloaded with unneeded items (i.e., 500 band aids) for a grossly exaggerated price. Selecting your own medical supplies allows you to customize your kit on a budget.

Remember to store your kit properly. Medicines can break down and spoil if they are subject to moisture, temperature fluctuations, or are exposed to a light source. Unless a particular medication requires unique storage, store the supplies in a cool, dark place out of the reach of children.

PREPS TO BUY:

- Medical reference books or eBooks on handling medical crises
- Sunscreen
- Aloe vera gel
- Gauze pads in assorted sizes (3×3 and 4×4)
- Sterile roller bandages
- Antibiotic ointment
- Expectorant
- Decongestant
- 2-3 bottles of disinfectant (Betadine, isopropyl alcohol or hydrogen peroxide)
- Sterile adhesive bandages in assorted sizes
- Adhesive tape or duct tape
- Latex gloves
- Scissors
- Tongue depressors
- Medicine dropper
- Tweezers
- Thermometer
- Liquid antibacterial hand soap
- Disposable hand wipes
- Eye care (e.g., contact lens case, cleansing solution, eye moisture drops)

ACTION ITEMS:

1. Expand your existing first aid kit and ensure the kit is situated in an accessible location.

2. Take a basic first aid class, if you have not done so already. Further, look into a local outdoors/wilderness first aid course. Since this will be geared towards your local terrain, it will prepare you by using local items to assist in rendering aid.

3. Research medical reference books and select one or more for your library.

4. Prepare a medical kit for your vehicles from your supplies. Be cautious of adding items that might be negatively affected by extreme changes in temperature.

SUPPLEMENTAL INFORMATION AND RESOURCES

Signs of Medical Distress

Those who are preparing for medical emergencies need to familiarize themselves with signs of medical distress. Recognizing these signs when they first appear can help take the appropriate next steps in a timely fashion.

You can help by learning these warning signs and symptoms of some common medical emergencies.

- Difficulty breathing, shortness of breath
- Chest or upper abdominal pain or pressure lasting two minutes or more
- Fainting, sudden dizziness, weakness, seizure
- Possible serious bone fractures
- Major burns
- Changes in vision
- Difficulty speaking
- Confusion or changes in mental status, unusual behavior, difficulty waking
- Any sudden or severe pain
- Head pain that lasts longer than five minutes
- Uncontrolled bleeding
- Shock symptoms, e.g., confusion, disorientation, cool/clammy, pale skin
- Severe or persistent vomiting or diarrhea
- Coughing or vomiting blood
- Unusual abdominal pain
- Suicidal or homicidal feelings

Knowing these signs and acting quickly could save the individual's life. Get treatment promptly. For many medical emergencies, time is very important. Some people experience the symptoms of an emergency, such as a stroke or a heart attack, but do not get help right away. A delay in treatment could lead to a more serious illness.

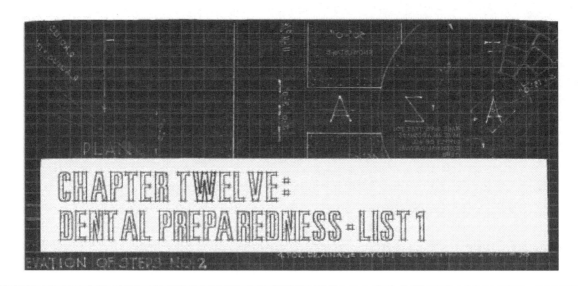

CHAPTER TWELVE:
DENTAL PREPAREDNESS - LIST 1

Death from Dental Abscess

If a dental abscess is left untreated, it can lead to life-threatening disease. In the lower jaw, the infection can spread into the neck. Extreme neck swelling can close off the windpipe, resulting in asphyxiation and death. An upper jaw abscess can spread into the sinus and even migrate into the brain, causing a stroke or uncontrollable swelling.

In March 2007, Mary Keel died from a dental abscess in Petaluma at age 76. A stroke victim, Mary Keel's dental health was neglected at Pleasant Care Convalescent of Petaluma. The nursing home neglected Keel's dental hygiene to the point that she developed an oral abscess from tooth decay. The abscess spread to her neck, causing extreme swelling. She died of cardiac arrest brought on by blood poisoning and reduced ability to breath. Mary Keel's death is a sad story and a reminder of the importance of good oral health.

Before the advent of modern medicine and the use of antibiotics, dental abscesses were frequent causes of death. Ancient human skulls often show large bone loss at the tip of teeth, indicating an abscess and the probable cause of death.

Source: Dr. George Malkemus, DDS

Dental emergencies can hit out the blue. Without warning, pain and soreness can occur in the gums or teeth and cause an extreme amount of discomfort. Frighteningly, that pain is sometimes just the tip of the iceberg. A dental emergency, if not properly cared for, can quickly become life threatening.

How many people actually have emergency dental supplies on hand? Most of us probably have little beyond some toothpaste, mouthwash and floss.

THE MOST LIKELY DENTAL EMERGENCIES TO PREPARE FOR

Anticipating a dental emergency is difficult to say the least, but, according to Douglas W. Stephens, DDS[15], the most common types of dental emergencies are:

1. Toothache: This is the most common dental emergency. The pain generally indicates a badly decayed tooth. As the pain affects the tooth's nerve, treatment involves gently removing any debris lodged in the cavity (being careful not to poke deeply - this will cause severe pain if the nerve is touched). Rinse vigorously with warm water. Then soak a small piece of cotton in oil of cloves and insert it in the cavity. This will give temporary relief until a dentist can be reached.

At times the pain may have a more obscure location such as decay under an old filling. As this can be only corrected by a dentist, there are two things you can do to help the pain. Administer a pain pill (aspirin or some other analgesic) internally or dissolve a tablet in a half glass (4 oz.) of warm water holding it in the mouth for several minutes before spitting it out.

Note: Do not place a whole tablet or any part of it in the tooth or against the soft gum tissue, as it will result in a nasty burn.

2. Swollen Jaw: This could be caused by several conditions, with an abscessed tooth being the most probable. In any case, the treatment should be directed towards the reduction of pain and swelling. An ice pack held on the outside of the jaw, (ten minutes on and ten minutes off) will take care of both. If this does not control the pain, an analgesic tablet can be given every four hours.

3. Oral Injuries: Broken teeth, cut lips, bitten tongue or lips, if severe, should be seen by a dentist as soon as possible. In the meantime, rinse the mouth with warm water and place cold compression on the side of the face opposite the injury. If there is a lot of bleeding, apply direct pressure to the bleeding area. If bleeding does not stop, get the patient to the emergency room of a hospital, as stitches may be necessary.

---

[15]

https://www.google.com/url?sa=t&rct=j&q=&esrc=s&source=web&cd=1&cad=rja&uact=8&ved=0CCYQFjAA&url=http%3A%2F%2Fwww.textfiles.com%2Fsurvival%2Fdental.txt&ei=9GUiU5iGPJXZoASrpYHQCQ&usg=AFQjCNFnSFsERWEgyk2eQjhOX_gpCcUlGw&sig2=dT02eqt1XqyJfgLCliBigg&bvm=bv.62922401,d.cGU

4. Prolonged Bleeding Following Extraction: Place a moistened tea bag over the socket and have the patient bite down gently on it for 30 to 45 minutes. The tannic acid in the tea seeps into the tissues and often helps stop the bleeding. If a tea bag is not available, use a clean gauze pad. If bleeding continues after two hours, call the dentist or take patient to the emergency room of the nearest hospital.

5. Broken Jaw: If you suspect the patient's jaw is broken, bring the upper and lower teeth together. Put a necktie, handkerchief or towel under the chin, tying it over the head to immobilize the jaw until you can get the patient to a dentist or the emergency room of a hospital.

6. Painful Erupting Tooth: In young children, teething pain can come from a loose baby tooth or from an erupting permanent tooth. Some relief can be given by crushing a little ice or frozen fruit (if they are old enough) and wrapping it in gauze or a clean piece of cloth and putting it directly on the painful tooth or gum tissue. The numbing effect of the cold, along with an appropriate dose of a children's analgesic, usually provides temporary relief.

In young adults, an erupting 3rd molar ("wisdom tooth"), especially if it is impacted, can cause the jaw to swell and can be quite painful. Often the gum around the tooth will show signs of infection. Temporary relief can be had by giving aspirin or some other painkiller and by dissolving an aspirin in half a glass of warm water and holding this solution in the mouth over the sore gum.

Note: Again, do not place the tablet directly over the gum or cheek or make the aspirin solution any stronger than recommended: This will burn the delicate tissue.

Using an ice pack on the outside of the face at intervals of ten minutes on and ten minutes off can reduce swelling of the jaw.

7. Cold Sores, Canker Sores, and Fever Blisters: Sores in the mouth, on the lips or on the tongue can be caused by many things: irritation, injuries which bruise or cut the lip or a general run-down condition. The germs that cause most of these sores are always lurking just below the surface, waiting for a chance to flare up.

Usually these lesions last five days no matter what treatment you use on them. Such preparations as Blistex, Carmex, Butyn Dental Ointment or Spirits of Camphor will relieve pain but it is debatable whether they aid in healing any sooner. New studies suggest that high levels of the amino acid "arginine" can give the body increased resistance to these painful mouth and lip sores.

In the event of a dental emergency, your goal will be to relieve the pain and to provide temporary treatment until the patient can be seen by a dentist. Prompt emergency treatment can spell the difference between permanently losing a tooth and saving it.

Keep in mind that dental emergencies can be far more serious than the loss of a tooth. I cannot stress how important it is to take your oral health seriously. Failure to treat a dental emergency could result in one of the following:

- Mediastinitis (an infection causing inflammation of the tissues in the mid-chest)
- Sepsis (blood poisoning)
- Spread of infection to soft tissue (e.g., facial cellulitis, Ludwig's angina)
- Spread of infection to the jaw bone (osteomyelitis of the jaw)
- Spread of infection to other areas of the body resulting in brain abscess, endocarditis, pneumonia, or other complications

A good reference book can help you correctly identify and treat a dental issue, in either a long-term or short-term emergency. I recommend:

> **When There is No Dentist**
> By Murray Dickson
> Hesperian Health Guides

PREVENTION IS BETTER THAN TREATMENT

Be proactive and take the time to schedule regular dental visits and develop good dental hygiene habits. By doing this, it will ensure that your teeth and gums stay healthy. When your family dentist suggests elective procedures, take the opportunity to go the extra mile for your teeth. The last thing you would want to face during a disaster scenario is a dental emergency.

We have a tendency to forget about the importance of having a stock of dental supplies on hand. Having supplies and natural alternatives to remedy flare-ups will help keep a bad situation from getting worse. Take care of any existing problems now before they become more aggravated. Note: If you plan to have older adults staying with you during a short or long-term disaster, do not forget to anticipate their dental needs.

PREPS TO BUY:

- Dental emergency reference book
- Dental exam gloves
- Toothpaste (for 3 months)
- Toothbrushes (for 3 months)
- Floss (3)
- Baking soda
- Toothpicks
- Fluoride rinse (3 bottles)
- Hydrogen peroxide
- Oral-gel
- Cotton balls
- Cotton gauze pads
- Pain reliever such as Tylenol or aspirin
- Temporary cap filler
- Instant ice packs
- Dental mirror
- Salt (for rinsing)
- Clove oil (for toothaches)
- Penlight or headlamp
- Orajel or other OTC topical pain reliever

ACTION ITEMS:

1. Get an annual check-up and cleaning.

2. Start a vitamin regimen to assist in oral health.

3. Begin brushing your teeth for at least 1-2 minutes, and floss daily. Teach your children to do the same.

4. Read your dental emergency resource to be familiar with treatment plans.

5. Invest in a Waterpik or other water flossing device and use it daily for maximum dental cleanliness.

SUPPLEMENTAL INFORMATION AND RESOURCES

Natural Dental Remedies

- Valerian Root – pain reliever
- Kava Kava – muscle relaxant and mild sedative
- Passionflower – pain reliever
- Clove oil – relieves teeth pain
- Charcoal – can make a compress that relieves swelling and pain.

Storing Vitamins

Vitamins tend to expire after a year; however, there has been contradicting information regarding taking medicines and vitamins after the expiration dates have passed. Since the expiration date is probably conservative to ensure full potency (and to benefit the prosperity of manufacturer and retailer) taking vitamins passed their expiration date will not put a person in danger. Keep in mind that the potency of the vitamin may be reduced if the vitamin is taken after the expiration date.

Keeping vitamins in a cool, dark area of the home will ensure they maintain their potency for as long as possible. Over time, vitamins will gradually oxidize and become less effective. It happens faster if the environment you keep them in is humid (e.g. your kitchen or your bathroom).

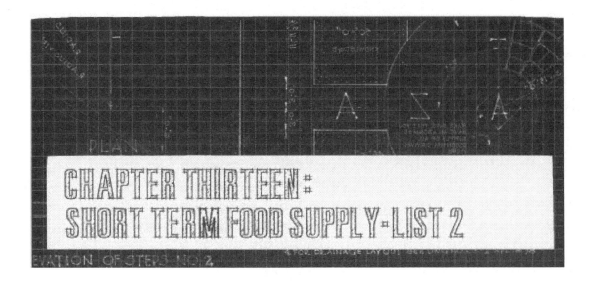

CHAPTER THIRTEEN: SHORT TERM FOOD SUPPLY - LIST 2

When a disaster is imminent, our first instinct is to run to the store and stock up on emergency food and supplies. Of course, everyone else has the same brilliant idea, which means emergency food and supplies will be in high demand and will be depleted if you didn't time your trip to the store well. There is nothing worse than leaving a crowded store with no storm supplies when a disaster is bearing down upon you.

In 2012, after a severe summer thunderstorm in the metro Washington, DC area, store shelves were utterly bare, and that was in the few stores that were open. Without power, many stores locked their doors because they would be unable to ring through purchases. It was a sad message that our nation's capital was shut down and unable to keep its citizens in food and water, all due to a thunderstorm. In the week that followed, as crews worked around the clock to restore power, temperatures crept up to the triple digits. Half a dozen people died from heat-related dehydration. Many more were without food as everything in their refrigerators spoiled in the intense heat.

Unlike a hurricane, the storm that caused this massive outage gave no hints as to the severity to come. "Unlike a polite hurricane that gives you three days of warning, this storm gave us all the impact of a hurricane without any of the warning," Maryland Gov. Martin O'Malley said.

A SOUND INVESTMENT

Storing food for storms is not the only reason you should have an emergency food supply. Due to the current state of the economy and the widespread droughts that continue to cripple our growing seasons, you are more likely to run into an emergency caused by a disappearing food budget. Food prices have been soaring during the past few years, and there doesn't seem to be any relief in sight.

Consider looking at your emergency supply as an investment. Many of the food items you will be purchasing over the next year are considered commodities (e.g., sugar, wheat, corn, rice, etc.). Treat your food purchases as a financial decision or investment: this means that you will purchase food at today's prices and consume at tomorrow's higher prices. If we see the same 20% increase in price that is being predicted, where else will you find an investment with that type of return?

Water

First, you need to get your water supply in order. Remember the rule of three: 3 minutes without air, 3 days without water and 3 weeks without food. Prioritize your purchases accordingly.

The standard recommendation is to expect to use one gallon of safe consumable water per person per day. The amount needed would go up during extremely hot weather. And those with special medical needs, the elderly, children, and pregnant women will need more water. Take into account your pets as well when considering how much water to store.

> A family of four, by this formula, would require approximately 120 gallons of water for a one-month supply.

Methods to Store Water

Water Bricks - Those of you who have begun storing water know that it takes up a lot of space. When storing a short-term water supply, purchase the 5- or 10-gallon water containers or water bricks. Note: These choices easily store and organize water if you place them on their sides and stack them.

Re-Use Soda Bottles - You can also reuse your juice and soda bottles. As long as the container is comprised of food-grade plastic, it is safe to reuse. Make sure that the plastic container is washed well before reusing it. These two-liter bottles can be laid on their sides to slide under a bed for future use. Milk jugs, unfortunately, are not recommended because of bacteria that cannot be removed and could multiply during storage time, tainting the water within.

Water Bob - Another short-term water storage need is a "water bob". This device is made of food-grade plastic and is designed to turn your bathtub into an emergency water storage container you can use during short-term emergencies.

Water Filtration Systems - I also highly recommend investing in a water filtration system. While water filters, such as Katadyn or even Berkey, are a little pricey, they can be used multiple times and would be a good preparedness item to have on hand in case of a longer-term emergency. Take it a step further and purchase extra filters and spare parts for your filtration system.

WHAT DO YOU HAVE?

If you don't know what you have[16], then you don't know what you need. The only way to know what you need is to perform frequent and accurate inventories[17] of your supplies. Especially if you are new to prepping, don't start out trying to load up and get a year's supply of food. Put thought into what you need. This is a great time to make a weekly menu for your family and then list the ingredients needed to make these dishes. Once you have enough ingredients to last a month, start small and work on stocking *one month*[18] at a time, working from your list so that you don't replenish grains in an already grain-heavy cupboard. Keep the end result in mind, which is a nutritionally balanced one-year *long-term food supply*[19] with a reasonable amount of variety.

When you do an inventory of your current food supplies, this is a great time to organize them as well. Take a look at your storage and make sure that you are organizing the items in a way that they are easy to find, as well as in optimum conditions to make them last longer.

Short and long-term food supplies should be placed in a safe and dry spot preferably out of sunlight. Many people make use of unused wall space and create shelving units to use as their storage area.

Another method is to commandeer unused closets or spare bedrooms. As long as the space is dry, is climate controlled and large enough to store foods, it can be used. To make the best use of a small space, additional shelving units can be purchased. This is also a great way to accommodate larger food supplies.

---

[16] http://readynutrition.com/resources/if-you-dont-know-what-you-have-you-dont-know-what-you-need_02102012/

[17] http://readynutrition.com/resources/inventory-management-for-survival-supplies_15022010/

[18] http://readynutrition.com/resources/week-20-of-52-1-month-supply-of-food_16092011/

[19] http://readynutrition.com/resources/week-45-of-52-long-term-food-and-water-needs_18052012/

Follow these steps to organize your food pantry:

- **Take all items off the shelf and sort items into categories.** Sort items into categories such as baking supplies, breakfast cereals, canned goods, medical supplies, bartering/charity, etc.
- **Store items next to one another that are used together**. For example, keep baking needs such as flour, sugar, baking soda, salt, etc. next to one another for easy access.
- **Place goods with the longest expiration date in the back and work forward to the closest expiration date.**
- **Have an inventory management spreadsheet or listing system.** Keeping an inventory list of foods that have been purchased and adding to the list when more items have been purchased will provide a well-rounded supply. Categorize the inventory into sections such as items for baby, baking, water/beverages, cleaning, condiments, 72-hour bag, emergency supplies. The Prepared LDS Family[20] has a thorough suggested inventory organizational method that would be helpful for those starting out.
- **The food storage inventory should be checked every 6 months to make sure that food items are properly rotated and are used within their expiration date.**

WHAT SHOULD YOU BUY?

Ideally, you want to store shelf-stable foods that are items your family normally consumes. An emergency or stressful situation is not the time to experiment with unfamiliar foods.

A few other points to consider when starting an emergency food pantry are:

- Store emergency foods that will not require refrigeration, and should require little electricity or fuel to prepare
- Look for foods that serve multiple purposes[21]
- The food should have a long shelf life
- It should provide ample nutrition
- It should contain minimal salt

In the book, The Prepper's Cookbook: 300 Recipes to Turn Your Emergency Food Into Nutrition, Delicious, Life-Saving Meals[22], the following essential food staples were used as the basis for the recipes. These are all popular food staples that should be considered as "must haves" for your emergency pantries.

---

[20] http://preparedldsfamily.blogspot.com/2009/04/food-storage-step-4-taking-inventory.html

[21] http://readynutrition.com/resources/7-kitchen-essentials-that-deserve-to-be-on-your-preparedness-shelves_15032012/

[22] http://www.amazon.com/The-Preppers-Cookbook-Nutritious-Life-Saving/dp/1612431291

An advantage to storing these items is that they encompass all of the key points listed above. Best of all, these items are very affordable and versatile, thus making them worthy of being on your storage shelves for extended emergencies.

Focus on these foods:

1. Canned fruits, vegetables, meats, and soups
2. Dried legumes (beans, lentils, peas)
3. Crackers
4. Nuts
5. Pasta sauce
6. Peanut butter
7. Pasta
8. Flour (white, whole wheat)
9. Seasonings (vanilla, salt, pepper, paprika, cinnamon, pepper, taco seasoning, etc.)
10. Sugar
11. Bouillon cubes or granules (chicken, vegetable, beef)
12. Kitchen staples (baking soda, baking powder, yeast, vinegar)
13. Honey
14. Unsweetened cocoa powder
15. Jell-O or pudding mixes
16. Whole grains (barley, bulgur, cornmeal, couscous, oats, quinoa, rice, wheat berries)
17. Non-fat dried milk
18. Plant-based oil (corn oil, vegetable oil, coconut oil, olive oil)
19. Cereals
20. Seeds for eating and sprouting
21. Popcorn (not the microwavable kind)
22. Instant potato flakes
23. Packaged meals (macaroni and cheese, hamburger helper, Ramen noodles, etc.)
24. Purified drinking water
25. Fruit juices, teas, coffee, drink mixes

These items will create a broad selection of foods that can be consumed in an emergency situation. You can create meals such as biscuits and jelly, cereal and milk, oatmeal, sandwiches, soups, pastas, casseroles, etc. Be sure to have items that do not require lengthy cooking times, in case power and fuel are a concern.

Construct an emergency menu now before a disaster happens – this will enable you to see what foods you have and what foods you may need. Further, keep in mind that some family members may have allergies, restrictions, or intolerances to certain foods. Remember this when you are purchasing food for your pantry.

PREPS TO BUY:

[Per person]

- 1-gallon of water per day for each member of the family (i.e., 1-2 weeks' worth)
- 2 bottles of juice per family member
- 2 canned goods (e.g., meat, veggies, soup, and fruit) per family member.
- 1 each of the following food condiments: peanut butter, jelly, honey, mustard, ketchup, BBQ sauce
- 2 large size drink mixes/tea/coffee per family member
- Spices (e.g., salt, pepper, taco seasoning, apple pie seasoning, etc.)
- 1-gallon of cooking oil
- 2 each of the following pre-packaged foods: beans, dried peas, rice, noodles, oats, grains, cereals and pasta
- 2 bags of flour (Note: For those with wheat allergies, see below for alternatives.)
- Ramen noodles
- Powdered milk
- Potato flakes
- Canned meats such as ham, tuna or flaked chicken
- Powered nutritional shakes

ACTION ITEMS:

1. Date perishable goods with a permanent marker.

2. Find a storage area in the home where emergency food supplies can be placed. Some people who are living in small spaces have rented air-conditioned storage facilities in which to store their supplies.

3. Organize the food[23] and begin creating a list of the items you have according to categories (e.g., condiments, baking supplies, canned goods, medical supplies, etc.).

---

[23] http://readynutrition.com/resources/inventory-management-for-survival-supplies_15022010/

SUPPLEMENTAL INFORMATION AND RESOURCES

Gluten Free Prepping

An allergy or intolerance to wheat products does not need to stop a person from prepping. There are alternatives available. These alternatives may not have the same consistency as wheat products, but most do the job nicely. Note: bread made from flours that do not have gluten will not rise. Unleavened breads can still be made.

Here are some suggestions for gluten-free pantry staples:

- Arrowroot Flour- This type of flour is ground from the root of the arrowroot plant - it is tasteless and ideal to use as a thickener.
- Brown Rice Flour – Brown rice flour has a higher nutritional base compared to white rice flour. It is much heavier in comparison to white rice flour and is suggested not to be purchased in bulk as it is better used when it is fresh.
- Corn Flour – Corn is ground into a very fine powder. It has a bland taste and is therefore good to use for multiple recipes.
- Corn Meal – Cornmeal is much heavier and coarser than corn flour.
- Nut Meals – Such as almonds, hazelnuts or walnuts can provide rich flavor as well as a good flour substitute for cookies and cakes. Their shelf life is brief and proper storage is necessary. Most nut meals require a bonding agent such as eggs. Note: chestnut flour has a longer shelf life.
- Potato Flour – potato flour is not potato starch flour. It does have a stronger flavor compared to other wheat alternatives. Due to the heaviness, a little can go a long way. The shelf life for this type of flour is not very long; so long term storage could be a problem.
- Potato Starch Powder – This has a lighter potato flavor which is hardly detectable in recipes. This type of flour keeps very well.
- Quinoa Flour – "The Mother Seed" as the Incas call this has a large variety of vitamins and is high in protein. Quinoa flour is not readily available in many stores, so locating this could pose a problem.
- Soy Flour – This flour is a fine powder ground from soybeans. It adds a pleasant texture to different recipes and is also high in protein and a good vitamin source.
- Tapioca Flour - Tapioca flour adds chewiness to baking and is a good thickening agent. It also stores well.
- White Rice Flour - This type flour does not have a high nutritional value. The taste is bland and ideal for recipes that require light texture. The shelf life is adequate as long as it is stored properly.

Try substituting 1-cup wheat flour with one of the following alternatives:

Oat flour 1-1/3 cups
Rice flour 3/4 cup
Soy flour 1-1/3 cups
Corn flour 1 cup
Potato flour 3/4 cup
Rye flour 1-1/3 cups
Tapioca flour 1 cup

Potato and soy flours are best used in combination with other flours. They have a strong flavor and soy flour has a darker coloring. Rice flour gives a distinctively grainy texture to baked products. Rye flour is frequently used although it has a dark color and distinctive flavor. Barley, oat, and rye flours all contain slight amounts of gluten. Other grains are available that do not. Here are some suggestions:

Gluten-Free Flour Mix: 1 part white rice flour, 1 part corn starch, 1 part tapioca flour, 1/2 part white bean flour.

Rice Flour Mix: 3 cups brown rice flour, 1-1/4 cups potato starch or cornstarch, 3/4 cup tapioca flour.

Bean Flour Mix: 1-2/3 cups garbanzo/fava bean flour, 2 cups potato starch or cornstarch, 2/3 cup tapioca flour, 2/3 cup sorghum flour. Mix all ingredients together, use in place of wheat flour.

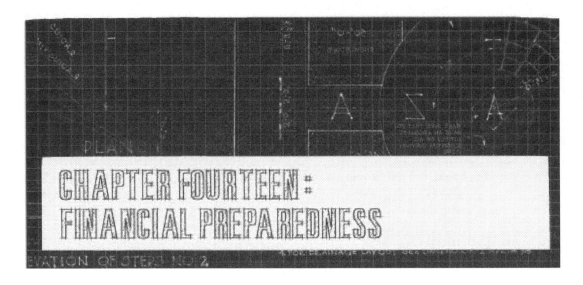

CHAPTER FOURTEEN:
FINANCIAL PREPAREDNESS

There was a time in the not-too-distant past when I was enslaved to debt. I supplemented my income with credit cards in order to maintain an overindulgent lifestyle, and when my daughter needed emergency medical care, my financial situation worsened because I didn't have medical insurance. The medical bills were a nightmare, and paying them off seemed like a never-ending uphill battle.

For years we had to live below our means in order to sort out our financial mess. During this time frame, I repeatedly asked myself, "Why didn't I set some money aside for harder times? Why didn't I prepare for this?" It was these questions that led me on a journey toward financial freedom. Instead of wallowing in self-pity, I educated myself in finding practical ways to fight back and to simplify my lifestyle. This became a huge lesson in self-control.

Tess Pennington, Ready Nutrition

Sometimes, the life you are living no longer makes you happy. A vital component is missing from your day-to-day existence, but you are unsure what it is. There is so much chaos and clutter spinning around you that nothing seems to make sense the way it used to. What you need is total financial security and the peace of mind that comes with it.

You realize that the lifestyle you've become so accustomed to is a necessary evil, a constant struggle between the life you want to achieve and the life you have to give up right now to achieve it. But you don't have to live your life dreaming of what it could be – you can stop spinning and start simplifying right now!

It starts with the courage to change and the willingness to realize that you need to get back to basics and focus on the things that matter most, not at some time in the future, but right now.

SHIFTING YOUR DIRECTION

Those who live a stress-filled life tend to be very familiar with the three C's: Chaos, Clutter, and Confusion. These elements do not make for a happy existence. In fact, they drag you and your spirit down. In plain words, this lifestyle is toxic.

The key to achieving your goals, is to break them down into their smallest, most manageable parts. Where you may feel tired or overworked attempting to achieve a single, massive goal in one fell swoop, simplifying that goal into micro-movements will seem like you're hardly working.

Realizing that you want to take this journey towards simplicity requires some pre-emptive planning on your part. To begin this, you must find some time to reflect and think about what is important and how to enhance those priorities. For example, if family is a main priority, start scheduling designated family time. The football game can wait. Or, if you have been putting off planning your off-grid home, sit down with the family and start planning what you want your homestead to incorporate. Nothing should interfere with those designated priorities.

Here are some additional tips to get closer to achieving financial freedom and simplicity.

- Sit down and **contemplate the priorities in your life**. What matters most in your life? What can you live without?
- **Set short- and long -term financial goals** to get to your simplified destination.
- Break down each goal and **create micro-movements**, or mini-goals, that will help you to achieve success
- **Take action** and start integrating your micro-movements into your daily life.

---

6 PRACTICAL TIPS TO SIMPLIFY YOUR LIFE

After shifting your direction toward simplifying your life, you will find that you only need a few things to really make you happy. Somehow in the middle of everything, you realize that whatever void you had in yourself before, filling it with superfluous products, services, and habits often leaves you feeling just the opposite – unfulfilled.

Many are adopting this voluntary simplicity. In fact, trend researcher Gerald Celente has been quoted in saying that "between 5%-7% of adults are pursuing some type of voluntary simplicity." It should be no surprise, then, that the percentage of those who are simplifying their lives are also the same percentage of individuals who are prepping. Preppers are already making it a point to practice and live a more simplified lifestyle.

Here are a few tips to help you begin your road to a simpler life:

1. **Simplify your finances** - Having debt creates a lot of unwanted stress and uneasiness in your life. Take responsibility and begin taking steps to live within your means and start paying off any unnecessary debt. Research on your own what credit solutions seem right for you. There are websites available that can give tips on how to reduce debt. Creating a manageable budget can also be an invaluable tool for minimizing credit-induced stress.
2. **Simplify your life** - Get back to the basics and downsize your life. Start weeding out the areas in your life that cause you pain, suffering and confusion. Sometimes you have to weed out those toxic friends, stop hanging out late at night, and learn to say "no" to people. Over-committing yourself can also cause a build-up of chaos.
3. **Start prepping** - <u>Preparing for emergencies</u> beforehand creates a safety cushion to fall back on when a problem arises. It eliminates the headache of gathering supplies in a high stress environment. There are plenty of resources to help you start your preparedness journey.
4. **De-clutter your home and office** – It's easy to have those organized "catch all piles" lying around the house. But the more clutter that piles up, the more disorganized things are in your life. Clutter brings uneasiness to your life. Make a short-term goal to clear these piles out. If you are not using these items, then throw them away, give them away or sell them.
5. **Simplify your health** – Research has shown that stress takes its toll on a body. Those who live a stress-free life are more inclined to live longer, be healthier and are overall pleased with their lives. So, start getting some fresh air every day. Additionally, cutting back on those greasy junk food items or taking steps to quit those unhealthy habits are a few ways to cleanse and detoxify your body.
6. **Rely on yourself** – What a great concept! <u>By relying on yourself, you will find freedom</u>. This is the threshold to prepping. Once you realize that you can be self-reliant, everything changes. Your goals change, your attitude changes, you change.

THE TIME/ENERGY YIELD

In the spin cycle we call life, we spend our time and energy on work and other distractions that keep us from doing what we need to thrive. Rather than spending our time on what's important in life and sitting back in quiet thought, we have to entertain ourselves with thoughtless television programming, gossip websites, Facebook, glossy fashion magazines, etc. It's important to relax, but these activities will not relax you. They will only stimulate you into not moving or thinking. Your time/energy yield is not a positive reflection of what you are trying to accomplish.

An example of good time/energy yield would be: rather than exchanging your time for excessive work at the office to generate more money to buy more food at the store; take that time and spend it building and developing a home vegetable garden. You will use your time and energy to not only fulfill your consumptive needs, but you will be feeding your spiritual, emotional and physical wellness needs at the same time.

STARTING FRESH

It's a new day where anything is possible. Simplifying your life will create more room for you to do what you need to be at peace. I've read stories of people who dreamed of living near the water. So, in order to save money, they sold their McMansion, their gas-guzzler truck and put that money into a boat. They found a creative solution to their problem that ended up being the right decision not only for their stress load, but also for their spirit.

Making the decision to simplify does not mean that you are giving up your life in order to live a life of poverty. Quite the contrary, it means to get rid of the non-essentials that cloud your life. By doing so, you begin to clear the distortion and haze, and then you start to focus on the important things in life. This sensible lifestyle creates a well-balanced and harmonious living environment.

Think of it, you are deliberately taking the reins and slowing down your life to actually give yourself the opportunity to look at the beauty and treasures surrounding you.

PRACTICE BLACKBELT FRUGALITY

Emergency agencies suggest that you save a minimum of 3 months of living expenses to fall back on. Although this can be a difficult amount to save in our economy, it is possible if you make some adjustments to your lifestyle. Use some or all of these tips to reduce your expenses

Counteract financial emergencies by preparing for them in advance. Even when times are financially prosperous, it is a good idea to have a financial contingency plan in place and some emergency funds set aside to fall back on; this money can act as a buffer when things do go financially awry.

Cut out frivolous spending and focus on meeting your practical needs: food, water, shelter. As long as you can provide these things for your family, you are ok. The rest of the financial mess will eventually sort itself out.

Take advantage of grocery store advertisements and coupons. You can save a substantial amount of money when you search for discounted goods; throw away brand loyalty.

Buy products in bulk. Learn from businesses: they save more money buying in bulk than they would by buying individual products. Use what you can and store the rest for another day. Due to the increasing food prices, it's a positive way to buy your food staples at the most economical price. This is a great time to start an emergency food supply[24]. Foods such as flour, sugar, oatmeal, and popcorn can be bought in bulk quantities at discounted prices. Instead of paying $2.50 for a pound of sugar, you can buy 25 pounds at $13.00.

Trim the budget and shift your focus to the bare necessities. If you have children and one of the parents isn't working, don't spend money on daycare. If you are concerned about a lay-off, start conserving your money by cutting back on energy bills, cable bills, etc. Speak with family members and let them know that you may be losing your job. Sometimes friends and family have good advice and possibly some contacts.

Have a garage sale to get rid of items that are no longer used. "One man's trash is another man's treasure." You may be surprised at how much money you could get for the gently used items that are collecting dust in your garage.

Remove the phantom charges. Did you know that when you leave your appliances (computer included) plugged in to the electrical socket, they still consume electricity? You can reduce your electricity charges by 10% simply by unplugging the kitchen appliances, TV and computer. Consider plugging items into a power bar so that you can easily unplug everything at once.

Create a rotating refrigerator. Just like rotating your stored preps[25], rotate perishable food items in the refrigerator. Once a week, check for foods such as produce, eggs and meat. If no one has eaten the fresh fruit or vegetables you bought last week, dehydrate them and store them for another time. *Each household wastes close to $600 a year on spoiled food.* Start making an effort to cut down on this.

Go vegetarian a few nights a week. Who said that you have to have meat with every meal? Buying meat for every meal is expensive. Make a few vegetarian dinners or pastas to save money. For instance, vegetarian pizzas are filling and healthy. Or make use of all those beans and make a vegetarian chili!

---

[24] http://readynutrition.com/resources/store-your-food-and-be-ready_14122009/

[25] http://readynutrition.com/resources/simple-techniques-to-organize-your-preps_22032010/

When you do buy meat, make sure it's on sale: When you see deals for meat, buy as much as you can and try one of these tricks to save it for a rainy day:

- Frozen meals can be enjoyed at a later date and can be a lifesaver on those days that get away from you.
- On weekends, my family enjoys eating buttermilk pancakes. I always make an extra batch and freeze them for weekday breakfasts when we are running late.
- Another way of saving time is to freeze a crock-pot-ready meal[26]. Adding some vegetables, meat, rice or potatoes and spices and freezing it will save 20 minutes in preparation time. Just take it out of the freezer, put it into the crock-pot and voila!
- Another easy solution to free up time is to take frozen vegetables and add a cheese sauce or an herbed butter sauce and freeze it for another time.
- Use your pressure canner to make beef stew, soup or chili when you have an abundance of meat. You can also use the raw pack method to can meat purchased on sale, and then you have a quick heat and eat ingredient for a rushed dinner.

Homemade is better tasting and cheaper. Let's be honest, a lot of the products we buy are to make our lives easier, but this can be costly, both in finances and health. Find ways to make it yourself. For instance, make your own granola or trail mix for healthy snacks. This can later be made into granola bars, cereal or yogurt toppers. Another easy snack to make is homemade fruit leathers. Kids love them and they are healthy. It's a win-win situation!

Do-it-yourself. Start simplifying[27] your finances by doing things yourself. Mow the lawn yourself, fix the plumbing and wash the car by yourself. There are great how-to articles, as well as helpful neighbors who would be more than willing to help you out if you need some pointers. This has more than one benefit: not only are you saving money, you are learning skills to be more self-reliant. Some of the ways I cut back and became more self-sufficient were learning to bake my own bread, learning to can and learning to make my own condiments. If I hadn't made the choice to be more frugal, then I never would have learned how much more healthy and delicious these homemade items are!

Go solar! Some of us can't afford all the solar gadgets, but that shouldn't stop you from harnessing the power of the sun in simple ways. Dry your laundry outside on lines to save money on the electricity bill. Make a simple solar cooker for summer meals that won't heat up the kitchen.

---

[26] http://readynutrition.com/resources/8-slow-cooker-freezer-meals-made-from-leftovers_06012014/

[27] http://readynutrition.com/resources/simply-simplifying_06102010/

PREPS TO BUY:

Rather than purchasing emergency supplies, concentrate your attention on your family's short-term and long-term financial goals and discover ways to trim your budget.

ACTION ITEMS:

1. Create a financial contingency plan.
2. Get a notebook and track every penny you spend this month. You may be surprised to find out how much money you could have saved by eliminating all the little items that add up!
3. Look at your budget and begin eliminating unnecessary debt.
4. Make a goal to save 5-10% of your paycheck to use as an emergency fund.

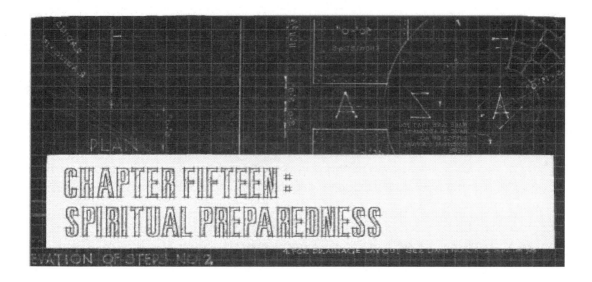

CHAPTER FIFTEEN ::
SPIRITUAL PREPAREDNESS

We tend to play stories in our head. Whether they are truth or fiction, we live through these stories and feel them as if they are really happening. As a beginning prepper, I plunged myself head first into every preparedness book and article and studied every possible disaster or grim scenario I might run into. Needless to say, I was playing a 24-hour TEOTWAWKI (The End of the World as We Know It) station in my head and became very weary as a result. In my mind, I wasn't just studying it, I was *living* it. Even though I prayed regularly, I found it hard to cope because there was something missing. I realized I had not put any thought into my spiritual preparedness before I began this arduous journey of physical preparations.

I am sharing this experience with you because I want each of you to know that the end result of not preparing your spirit for hard decisions and troubling times will affect your overall well-being and make it all the more difficult for you to shake the effects of the disaster away. I have often heard that the first three days after a disaster are the most difficult. Psychologically, people are dealing with the trauma of the moment and it can be difficult to think about something as simple as preparing a meal or ensuring that your children's needs are met. The longer you stay in the shock and awe of the disaster moment, the longer it takes for you move into survival mode.

Tess Pennington

Choosing to prepare now is a choice you made with your spirit – a choice to survive. You are putting plans in place, purchasing basic living items, and stashing away supplies. Now is the time to put your spiritual house in order. When you are spiritually prepared, the groundwork is then laid for <u>mental preparedness</u>[28].

As James Allen once said, "Every man thinks, lives and acts in exact accordance with the belief which is rooted in his inner most being." Essentially, spiritual preparedness is your moral compass that guides you through the good and bad times. It is a sum of the core beliefs that makes up who you are and serves you throughout your walk through life. These beliefs can guide you, motivate you, and sustain you, or they can do the complete opposite. The inner beliefs will either become a negative or positive influence depending on what each of us hold as truths about the nature of ourselves and our reality.

Exercising these core beliefs will help you to further develop and be more aware of where your spiritual growth is and what you need to improve on.

DEVELOP YOUR MENTAL PREPAREDNESS

You can develop this further by being aware of it and by utilizing these mental exercises:

1. Sit and reflect. Ask yourself moral questions such as:

> - Am I who I want to be?
> - Do I have the courage to make the hard changes to be a better person?
> - Do I have the courage to turn away from bad habits?
> - Do I have faith that I can bring my family through a bad situation, against the odds?

And going even further, asking the tough preparedness questions and really investigating why you chose to answer the way you did can help you in developing your spiritual preparedness. In a true TEOTWAWKI situation there will be life and death decisions that must be made and the only way to make your decisions will be to tap into your personal moral compass for the answers. Here are some examples of these types of questions:

- What would I do if a neighbor needed my help? How far would I go to help my neighbor?
- If a relative needed food, would I help them? What are my guidelines on helping others?
- Would using a gun on a home intruder be something I could do? How would I feel about it?
- Would I feel responsible if I could not help someone medically and they died? Why am I taking that burden on?

---

[28] http://readynutrition.com/resources/are-you-ready-series-using-mental-preparedness-to-survive_27122009/

2. Knowledge is power. Reading inspirational books and printing out inspirational passages that call to you is a tool that many use to stay spiritually awakened. In addition, reading survival books and survival fiction can help the reader look at preparedness from different perspectives and learn more about their spiritual foundation through the characters of the books.

3. Acknowledgement and gratitude. These are other ways that you can begin laying a spiritual foundation. Recognize your good fortune that you have been called upon to prepare and that you have had the wherewithal to do so. Acknowledge those little blessings in your life that help you move along your life's journey. I often start my prayers with how thankful I am for the family, friends and events that shaped who I am. Even the bad events played a part in who I am. I then follow the gratitude with further prayers. After I am done, I feel at peace.

4. Find passages and quotes. Inspirational materials found in a book or religious reference that have been printed out or written down to turn to later also helps. In my emergency binder[29], I have an entire section of my book that has inspirational quotes and bible passages that I have printed out or found that have touched me in some way. In addition, I have all of the church handouts that I have received over the years to turn to. Collect stories that give you a sense of peace and dedicate a portion of your library to these things that nourish your soul.

5. Listen to that little voice within. Some people call it instinct and others believe that it is Divine in nature. Think of all the times your "early warning system" alerted you before an event – maybe you had a funny feeling that you just couldn't put your finger on, or maybe it was something blatant like a flat tire that caused you not to be on a highway that had a huge accident. Spend time in prayer or meditation and learn to tap into this voice. Allow it to guide you and protect you.

6. Spend time in contemplation. This might be prayer, meditation, devotional, inspirational reading or time communing with nature. Whatever your personal path is, spend time each day seeking comfort and peace. Like any skill, you improve with practice, and if you are well versed in this, you will be able to find comfort and peace in the most desperate of times. In a disaster situation, fear and panic can be deadly – if you are able to find your peace, your decisions will be clear and logical while those around you reel from the event, weeping and trying to process what has occurred.

> ## Develop Your Moral Compass
>
> Working on your spirit and further developing your moral compass will help you in finding the answers to tough situations during disasters. And, most importantly you will find peace in the midst of adversity. Possessing this spiritual preparedness will lay the groundwork for being mentally prepared for disasters.

---

[29] http://readynutrition.com/resources/good-manuals-every-family-should-have-one_22102009/

PREPS TO BUY:

The best way to begin training your mind for mental preparedness is through knowledge, faith and practice. Go online and purchase some books to add to your survival library. Some books that I have read and have found helpful in this area are:

- The Holy Bible, if you are Christian, or the sacred book of your personal faith
- Devotional books
- *A New Earth: Awakening to Your Life's Purpose* by Eckhart Tolle
- *The Unthinkable* by Amanda Ripley
- *Are You Ready for Change? Preparing for Tribulation in America* by Philip Lewis
- *Survive!: Essential Skills and Tactics to Get You Out of Anywhere* – Alive by Les Stroud
- *One Second After* by William R. Forstchen
- *Last of the Breed* by Louis L'Amour

ACTION ITEMS:

1. Find some time and think about your core beliefs. What do you believe in? What drives you to be a better person?

2. If you feel open in discussing your belief system, talk with family members and find out what they believe.

3. Set up a time daily where you can sit and meditate on your spirit.

4. Begin exploring ways to advance your core beliefs to spiritually prepare yourself.

5. Practice your spiritual beliefs daily.

6. Talk with a spiritual advisor, pastor, or priest if you reach a place where you need guidance. If you don't already, consider practicing your faith by attending the church, synagogue or service of your choice on a regular basis.

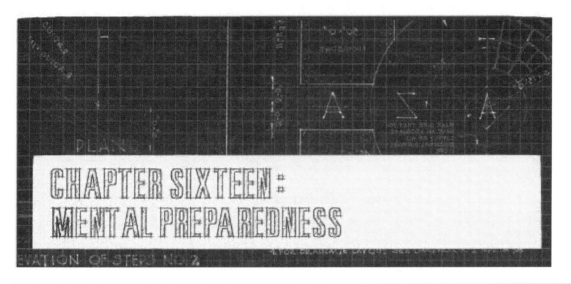

CHAPTER SIXTEEN: MENTAL PREPAREDNESS

I am from Bosnia, and as some of you may know it was hell here from 1992-1995. Anyway, for 1 whole year I lived and survived in a city of 50,000- 60,000 residents WITHOUT: electricity, fuel, running water, real food distribution, or distribution of any goods, or any kind of organized law or government. The city was surrounded for 1 year and in that city actually it was SHTF situation. We did not have organized army or police force, there was groups of defenders, actually anybody who had a gun, fight for his own house and his own family. Some of us was better prepared, but most of families had food for couple of days, some of us had pistol, few owned AK-47 when all started. Anyway, after one month or two, gangs started with their nasty job, hospital looked like butchery, police force vanished, 80 percent of hospital staff gone home.

I was lucky, my family was big in that time (15 members in one big house, 5-6 pistols, and 3 Kalashnikov s) so we lived and survived, most of us. I remember US Air force dropped MREs every 10 days (god bless USA for that) as help for surrounded city, it just was not enough. Some of houses had little gardens with some vegetables, most did not.

After three months rumors started about first deaths from starvation, deaths from low temperatures, we stripped every door, window frame from abandoned houses for heating, I burned all my own furniture for heating, lot of people died from diseases, mostly from bad water (two of my family members), we used rain water for drink, several times I ate pigeons, once I ate rat. It was almost 20 years ago, but believe me, for me it was just like yesterday, I remember everything, and I think I learned a lot.

~ Selco
SHTFSchool.com

So many get caught up in compiling survival tangibles we forget about the most important asset – our mental preparedness. Mental preparedness[30] implies possessing the right frame of mind to handle stress before, during and after a disaster. This aspect of preparedness is directly connected to spiritual preparedness, a subject we covered in the last chapter. Spiritual preparedness is based on the established core belief system that guides and serves you throughout your walk of life. Once your spirit is prepared, you will become more mentally prepared for dealing with a disaster situation.

UNDERSTANDING THE BIOLOGICAL REACTION TO STRESS

Mental preparedness sounds great, but there are natural responses you must take into account when disasters occur. In a critical emergency, how quickly we respond to a disaster directly impacts how successful we are at coming out of the situation. Many of us typically go through a processing phase, or what many call the normalcy bias[31].

This bias is actually a coping mechanism that occurs when we are trying to register and sort out a traumatic event or impending disaster. It is very natural to slip into this phase – but getting out of it is takes a little longer. The reason being is we are creatures of habit and resist change at every turn. When we begin to come out of the normalcy bias, only then do we open our eyes to the changes that have occurred in our lives; and we must react to them. Sometimes these changes are short-lived and sometimes, depending on the disaster, will be long lasting. Our military forces train for reacting quickly in a situation, and we must train for this as well.

As much as I do not like to spew doom, mark my words – after a disaster, times will quickly change, and the sooner we can adapt, the better our chances at survival will be.

Stress is another factor that takes a physical toll on the body. How can we prepare for that? Understanding chemical and biological reactions to stress will shed some light on how stress affects us all. Biologically speaking, stress or anxiety (especially after an unexpected event) leads to a short-term imbalance of neurotransmitters such as serotonin and norepinephrine.

Whether you are packing up to get out of Dodge, or if you get in a car accident on your way to pick the kids up from school, there are elements of frustration, confusion, anger, helplessness, nervousness and even physical responses related to the neurotransmitters, such as shaking, heart palpitations and headaches.

Knowing how to curb these natural reactions can reduce the emotional and physical elements, allowing you to adapt to the issue at hand and focus on the problem. Using these daily bursts of

---

[30] http://readynutrition.com/resources/are-you-ready-series-using-mental-preparedness-to-survive_26082013/

[31] http://readynutrition.com/resources/the-dangers-of-the-normalcy-bias_17022014/

stress in a constructive manner, rather than viewing them as a nuisance, can help propel you to the next level of preparedness.

HELPFUL TIPS TO COMBAT DAILY STRESS

- Control your breathing when in a stressful situation. Keeping your breath as steady as possible will keep you focused and alert.
- If you find yourself losing control, STOP! Give yourself a few seconds and visualize an immediate plan of action.
- Read your emergency binder and read over contingency plans, supply lists, etc. to stay organized.
- Have your preferred or enjoyable music nearby.
- Sip on some herbal tea such as chamomile, Valerian root[32], or kava kava[33].
- Try herbal therapy such as Clarocet[34], which is a natural supplement that combines herbs for relieving stress and anxiety.
- Make sure you are getting your daily dose of vitamins and nutrients.
- Try to get enough sleep at night.

PLAN AHEAD FOR SMALL EMERGENCIES

Pre-planning for small-scale emergencies can assist in decreasing stress.

- **Have a plan.** Have emergency plans and protocols set up[35] where children or teens can see them. Additionally, have important contact phone numbers next to the plan.
- **Practice.** Test out the emergency plans with test drills.
- **Get some back up.** Have an emergency phone list in the home, in the car and programmed in cell phones so that you can call for assistance if needed.
- **Prepare for the unexpected when you're on the go.** Have a small amount of money hidden in the car in case you run out gas, keep your vehicle well maintained, and keep a well-prepared emergency kit for each vehicle[36].

---

[32] http://www.clarocet.com/ingredient-reference-library/

[33] http://www.clarocet.com/ingredient-reference-library/

[34] http://www.clarocet.com/

[35] http://readynutrition.com/resources/home-invasion-preventitive-security-layers-to-protect-the-home_30062010/

[36] http://readynutrition.com/resources/what-do-a-hurricaneteotwawki-and-a-flat-tire-have-in-common_16082010/bug%20out%20vehicle%20and%20ready%20nutrition

> - **Keep a kit ready.** You should have some <u>survival gear on you</u>[37] at all times.
> - **Prepare for the expected, too.** If children are acting up in the car, have some sticker books, activity books or car-appropriate games, toys, music and snacks available for them.

Preppers have prepared for long and short-term emergencies where there is a high stress event involved. As much as we pride ourselves on preparedness, there are those unexpected events that occur in our daily lives that can create unwanted stress and frustration. By using these stress bursts as a way to further mentally prepare yourself for unforeseen events, you can increase your tolerance for stress and frustration.

CHANGE IS INEVITABLE

One principle you must keep in mind when dealing with emergencies is that change is inevitable. Change is the one true constant in this universe, yet it is something we tend to stress about and avoid all together.

Many do not handle stress well because they are unprepared to deal with what has been thrown at them. They are resistant to change. This rigidity will only hinder them from finding solutions. Disasters bring change and a lot of it

An aspect of mental preparedness, therefore, is learning to be more fluid and respectful of change in your day-to-day life. This ease in movement and acceptance of change will help you adapt more quickly to all situations. The more flexible you learn to be, the more adaptable you will be in an emergency.

Rehearse To Be Ready

We have all heard that practice makes perfect. One way to be mentally prepared for situations of extreme stress is to practice rehearsal drills. Consistent practice will turn your life-saving plans into muscle memory.

This rehearse-to-be-ready concept is how many emergency personnel and even athletes train to condition their mind and body.

Schools practice fire drills so that the children know what to expect and aren't panicked. Soldiers drill in various manners so that their reactions are rehearsed and second nature. This readiness could make all the difference when stress is sending your neurotransmitters out of whack.

Even implementing stress relief techniques when responding to daily stress helps. The daily "minor disasters" give valuable insight into your mental and physical reaction to stressors, allowing you learn how you perform under pressure and the things to look out for.

---

[37] http://readynutrition.com/resources/lighten-up-your-load-with-a-mini-survival-kit_12052010/

KNOW WHAT TO EXPECT

If you know what to expect in a bad situation, things won't be quite as terrifying in the midst of the event itself. If we can all agree on something, it's that disasters happen time and again and it seems that only a small percentage are prepared for them. The rest still have not learned from past mistakes.

That said, personal responsibility goes a long way in terms of preparing your family and loved ones for an emergency. Learn about what disasters are the most likely in your area. Are you near a fault line? Are you in an area prone to frequent hurricanes or other powerful storms? Are you living close to a nuclear power plant? Once you have identified the threats that are local to you, take the time to learn about the worst-case scenarios if disaster strikes.

Also learn about the aftermath of disasters. Depending on whether your location is rural, suburban or urban, you will face different threats. For example, in an urban area: expect serious sanitation issues in a down-grid event, clean water may be impossible to acquire, and crime and looting are frequent in the aftermath of a disaster in any large populated area. Knowing all of this, how can you prevent becoming a victim and what is your plan of action if, despite your best-laid plans, you are faced with an aggressor intent on stealing your supplies or harming your family? Thinking through all of the possible scenarios will help you to mentally prepare yourself for handling these events if they occur.

PREPS TO BUY:

- In this chapter, the focus is on actions and learning, as opposed to a shopping list. The best way to begin increasing mental preparedness is through knowledge and practice.
- Read, watch, and walk through any information on disaster preparedness you can get your hands on.
- Enhance your mental and literal survival library. Increasing your knowledge of disasters will increase your perspective of your preparedness options.
- Start learning about disasters, how people are affected by them and the dangers they may encounter.

ACTION ITEMS:

1. Decide which emergencies and disasters you need to be mentally prepared for.

2. Take some time and brainstorm potential disaster scenarios from this list. What stands in your way of preparedness? Think about how your family could be affected, what types of dangers you may face as a result of being in these disasters, and find ways to be prepared respecting your mental reaction to stressors.

3. Research first-hand accounts of survivor stories and recent disasters to learn what the victims came up against and how they survived.

4. Invest in some survivor literature such as: *Patriots* by James Wesley Rawles, *One Second After* by William R. Forstchen, *Lights Out* by David Crawford, the *Left Behind* series by William Tim LaHaye and Jerry B. Jenkins, *The Stand* by Stephen King.

5. Watch some survival/apocalyptic movies.

6. Watch disaster documentaries.

7. Discuss disaster scenarios and plans with other like-minded individuals. This is a great way for you to become aware of your community, your plans, and your current state of being.

SUPPLEMENTAL INFORMATION AND RESOURCES

Prepper's Night at the Movies

Grab some popcorn and do some "research" with the following prepper classics!

The Road	Red Dawn
The Walking Dead series	Waterworld
The Book of Eli	Independence Day
Jericho series	2012
Outbreak	Contagion
Survivors	Terminator movies
The Book of Eli	Children of Men
The Postman	The Colony
Tremors	The Day After Tomorrow

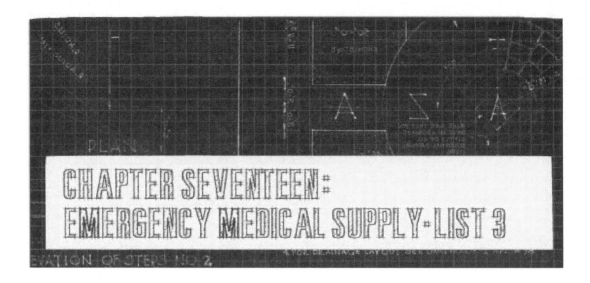

CHAPTER SEVENTEEN: EMERGENCY MEDICAL SUPPLY LIST 3

It was a scorching hot day in August and my family and I, along with a friend and her daughter, decided to go for a day of fun at the river. We walked down the trail and deviated off the main path at one point and scrambled down a steep ravine 30 feet or so to get to the river below. Due to the dry conditions the summer had caused, the ground was very dry and one could easily lose their footing.

I was preoccupied with making sure the kids were safely making it down the ravine. Before I knew it, my friend began to tumble down the ravine, hitting large rocks and thorny bushes along the way. While watching her fall, something snapped in me - everything went in slow motion. After she tumbled 5 or 6 times, a large boulder had finally stopped her fall. The children were hysterically screaming, not knowing what to do. I got their attention and told them to hike back to the car and the get the first aid kit, then have my husband (who was 1 mile back) call 911.

As I started to make the descent down into the ravine, I was immediately aware of my breathing – it was very rapid and I made a point to control my breaths. I also noticed that I was acutely aware of everything going on around me. I was weighing every possible path back up, looking for dangers and thinking about all of the injuries I would have to assess. All the while, I noticed how strangely calm I was. Anticipating the worst, I could already see how getting my injured friend back up the ravine was going to be a challenge. By the grace of God, she had no broken bones, but was badly cut and had a likely concussion. She was dizzy and she wasn't steady on her feet. Two hikers happened to come by and help me get her up back up so that we could take her to the hospital.

Tess Pennington

As I previously mentioned, to be fully prepared for a medical disaster, you need to have a well-rounded medical supply. Since there are so many different types of medical supplies to store, I have broken them up to make the list more affordable and less overwhelming. Refer back to Chapters 4 and 11 to see the other lists.

Because medical emergencies can occur suddenly, stored medical supplies should be diverse and unique to your family's needs. After an accident, getting to the store or the emergency room may not be a viable option. Therefore, having a wide array of medical supplies and medical resources to turn to can help you find the best solution to dealing with medical emergencies.

When creating a medical supply, think about which medical issues will most likely occur and prepare accordingly for them. For instance, if you have small children at home, prepare for bumps and bruises, small-scale skin abrasions, fevers, etc. Also, have some supplies on hand for any family members who have pre-existing conditions. This will make a prolonged disaster more comfortable and less stressful.

> ### The 4 Most Likely Ways to Die When the SHTF
>
> 1. Illness due to poor water conditions and sanitation
> 2. Malnutrition
> 3. Acute respiratory infections
> 4. Infection from wounds

THE MOST COMMON ISSUES REQUIRING TREATMENT

In 2006, The National Hospital Ambulatory Medical Care Survey (NHAMCS) released a 2006 Emergency Department Summary that gathered statistics of emergency department use, including the most common reasons adults and children sought medical care and treatment. Having medical supplies that could assist in these common emergencies would be a proactive approach.

- Childhood fevers
- Childhood earaches
- Various injuries such as sprains, strains, broken bones
- Chest pain
- Abdominal pain
- Back pain
- Shortness of breath
- Ensure that your medical supplies are stored appropriately and organized[38] in a way that they are easy to access. When there is a medical emergency, time can be of the essence.

---

[38] http://readynutrition.com/resources/storing-medical-supplies-to-be-ready_18122009/

Typically, medical rescue workers who respond to accidents work swiftly by having their supplies organized and at times, pre-assembled (wound care, trauma packs) to treat patients more efficiently. Having these items pre-packaged cuts down on response time, and gives the responders an advantage in properly caring for the wounded. That efficiency can easily be replicated for your medical supplies or added to your SHTF sick room.

Medical first response packs can be made ahead of time using most of the medical products that you have on hand. In fact, these first response packs are not limited to medical emergencies; they can also be used for dental emergencies[39] as well.

To prepare for a SHTF scenario, it would be beneficial to take into account the most likely medical situations you may come in contact with and plan accordingly.

---

[39] http://readynutrition.com/resources/are-you-ready-series-dental-emergencies_07072011/?preview=true

Response packs for superficial wounds

- Latex-free or Nitrile gloves
- Alcohol wipes
- Antiseptic
- Antibiotic ointment
- Gauze
- Tape
- Scissors
- Steri-strips
- Bandage
- Instant cold packs
- Response packs for hikers
- Adhesive bandages (assorted sizes)
- Tourniquet to open or bleeding wounds
- Knuckle adhesive bandages
- Butterfly closures
- Israeli battle dressing compression bandage
- Gauze pads (assorted sizes)
- Non-adherent pads
- Sterile top sponges
- Moleskins
- Abdominal/pressure pad
- Stretch gauze roll
- Medical tape
- Antibacterial wipes
- Triple-antibiotic ointment packets
- Sting relief wipes
- Iodine wipes or swabs
- Antimicrobial hand wipes
- Safety pins
- Latex-free or Nitrile gloves
- Bandage scissors
- Splinter forceps

Response kits for wounds that require sutures or staples

- Suture scissors
- Latex-free or Nitrile gloves
- Hemostat, probes, forceps, surgical scissors, suture lip scissors
- Alcohol pads
- Antiseptic
- Non-adherent sterile pads
- Israeli battle dressing compression bandage
- Gauze bandage rolls
- Absorbing and non-absorbing sutures or nylon fishing line
- Non-suture wound closure strips
- Suture needles
- Suture removal kit
- Suture scissors
- Forceps
- Skin stapler
- Staple remover
- Tweezers
- Gauze sponge
- Iodine swabs
- Gauze wrap

Response packs for advanced wound treatment: open or bleeding wounds fractures, falls

- Latex-free or Nitrile gloves
- Tourniquet to open or bleeding wounds
- Roll bandage
- Israeli battle dressing compression bandage
- Gauze
- Iodine swabs
- Sterile medical sponge

- Abdominal pad
- Triangular bandage
- Tape
- Steri-strips or butterfly closures
- Antiseptic wipes
- CPR microshield
- Respirator mask
- QuikClot® sponge

Response packs for 72-Hour Kits: Intended for the treatment of open or bleeding wounds caused by gunshots, knife cuts or punctures

Note: Items in the response pack for hikers can also be included in your 72-hour response pack

- Latex-free or Nitrile gloves
- Roll bandage
- Israeli battle dressing compression bandage
- Tourniquet to open or bleeding wounds
- Gauze
- Abdominal pad
- Triangular bandage

- Tape
- Antiseptic wipes
- Iodine swabs
- CPR microshield
- Emergency signal whistle
- Thermal Mylar blanket
- QuikClot® sponge

Don't forget vitamins and nutritional supplements. They can help prevent problems before they start by fueling a healthy immune system. Furthermore, vitamins are essential in regulating body functions and also help in the healing process. Storing the right types of food[40] - ones that have the highest amounts of nutrients - would be one way of ensuring that your diet is vitamin packed. Prepare by having firsthand knowledge of what vitamins the body needs on a daily basis. Storing multivitamins like Centrum multivitamins or Centrum Silver multivitamins is a great way to keep your body running at optimum levels.

Special thanks to Dr. Bones and Nurse Amy for reviewing the contents of this chapter. Their survival medicine handbook[41] would be a valuable resource to turn to for medical emergencies.

---

[40] http://readynutrition.com/resources/be-nutrition-ready-and-store-super-foods_23022011/

[41] http://www.amazon.com/Doom-Bloom-Survival-Medicine-Handbook/dp/0615563236/ref=sr_1_1?ie=UTF8&qid=1353040649&sr=8-1&keywords=dr.+bones+and+nurse+amy

PREPS TO BUY:

[In quantity]

- Sunscreen
- Anti-fungal cream or powder
- Hydrocortisone cream
- Tourniquet
- Nasal spray (saline)
- Saline solution
- Lip balm
- Flashlight (Small)
- Allergy relief medication
- Vitamin supplements
- UTI (urinary tract infection) meds
- Medical reference books or e-books on handling medical crises
- Sterile adhesive bandages in assorted sizes
- Adhesive tape or duct tape
- Gauze pads (assorted sizes)
- 2-4 instant ice packs
- Sterile roller bandages
- Sterile surgical gloves
- Latex-free or Nitrile gloves
- Gallon size plastic zip-lock bags, Mylar or Vacuum sealer bags to store contents

ACTION ITEMS:

1. Create some first response medical packs[42] to make emergency situations easier to care for.

2. Take another first aid course, or purchase a first-aid book.

3. Practice basic first-aid techniques regularly

---

[42] http://readynutrition.com/resources/shtf-survival-first-response-packs-for-medical-emergencies-2_13082011/

CHAPTER EIGHTEEN:
SURVIVAL TOOLS-LIST 2

In this chapter, we will be expanding on the topic discussed in Chapter 3, tools for home emergencies, with a focus on acquiring the most useful items to include in your 72-hour bag to help you survive.

Preparedness requires the ability to fall back on a foundation of equipment and supplies to aid in your survival. Our ancient ancestors depended on tools to meet their needs, and we are no different. Having the right gear on hand for when unexpected emergencies occur can help assist you in meeting your basic needs, catching food, communicating with emergency officials, and even finding your way in the dark.

Good quality survival implements are a sound investment that can last a lifetime if properly cared for. The ten tools listed below are the most important items that should be in your 72-hour bags[43] or bug-out bags. Practice using them regularly so that you know their capability and their strength.

---

[43] http://readynutrition.com/resources/are-you-ready-series-72-hour-kits_04122009/

TOP 10 SURVIVAL TOOLS FOR YOUR 72-HOUR BAG

1. Water treatment: We simply cannot live without water. The more energy you consume, the more water your body will need. Having a means to purify water during a disaster will help keep you hydrated, your brain functioning properly and your focus on thriving. In addition, if you sustain an injury, clean water can be poured over the wound for cleaning.

Water filters use microfiltration to rid water of harmful bacteria and protozoa. This level of protection is considered quite sufficient for emergency water filtration methods. Water purifiers typically use microfiltration plus a chemical treatment (UV light is an alternative approach) to meet an Environmental Protection Agency standard for eliminating viruses as well as bacteria and protozoa. Purifiers are often recommended for international travel where the risk of viral contamination is greater. See Chapter 17 for more details on water filtration systems.

2. Compass and map: Knowing which direction you are headed and where you need to be is essential – especially in an emergency situation. In this electrically driven era, many heavily rely on GPS-assisted navigation. But it is important to understand that a GPS receiver does not replace the humble compass and map. Most importantly, these tools can be used in an off-grid scenario and do not need batteries or satellite signals to function. A detailed topographic map and a compass are still the primary tools for navigation in the wilderness. Keep maps of your surrounding area at home (in case you have to evacuate by foot), in your car and in your 72-hour bags and practice orienteering regularly to increase your skill level.

Compass Features:

- Magnetized needle
- Liquid-filled capsule
- Rotating bezel (or azimuth ring)
- Base plate and ruler
- Orienting arrow and parallel meridian
- Index line or direction-of-travel line

Floating-needle compasses, as opposed to digital compasses, are those that use a magnetized needle that aligns with the earth's magnetic field. Needle housings are often filled with a liquid that steadies the needle, making precise readings possible.

3. Fire-starters[44], flint bars, matches or a lighter: Having a way to produce fire can help you cook food, keep warm, and prevent hypothermia. Be sure these items are stored in waterproof containers. Get creative and make your trash work for you. Fire-starters can be made at home using materials such as cotton balls dipped in Vaseline or cardboard toilet paper rolls stuffed with dryer lint.

---

[44] http://readynutrition.com/resources/how-to-make-homemade-fire-starters_18052011/

4. First aid kit: You do not want to be caught in an emergency situation without a first aid kit. This kit will assist in injury treatment and helps prevent infections from perpetuating. Ensure you have supplies for abrasions, a wound cleaner, antibiotic ointment, assorted gauze pads, anti-diarrheal medicines, etc. Essentially, you want to be able to care for minor medical emergencies and be able to stabilize the wounded in a major medical issue.

5. Mirror: Used for signaling, checking face for wounds, looking at your back for wounds/ticks, and can be used to start fire. This basic survival tool is often overlooked and could be one of the most important to have in your bag.

6. Rope: This can be used for making snares or assisting in making other traps, lashing branches together to build a shelter, assisting in first aid (splints, tourniquets, slings), or to make essential tools such as spears. Paracord is ideal to have on hand because it is lightweight in nature and is very durable. There are at least 50 ways to use a paracord[45] in a SHTF scenario.

7. Survival blanket or bivvy: These are lightweight and multipurpose items that can be used as an emergency shelter, sleeping bag or can be an extra layer added to your existing sleeping bag if you are expecting a cold night. Additionally, if your survival blanket is made of Mylar, you can also use this to collect rainwater, can be used as an emergency poncho and even a signaling device.

8. Multi-tool: A multi-tool is the ultimate compromise between the flexibility of a generalist and the expertise of a specialist. A multi-tool is one of the items that should really be of the highest quality the buyer can afford, because a poor-quality tool could break or potentially harm its user.

Selecting a multi-tool begins with deciding which components the tool should have, based on the needs of the user. Design considerations should reflect SHTF scenarios you plan to find yourself in. For example, a hunter will likely need a tool with at least two blades, one straight, the other serrated, as well as a flat head screwdriver, a can-opener, and a pair of needle-nosed pliers with a wire-cutting blade. A fish scaler, an LED flashlight, and a ruler may also be appreciated, depending on the needs and habits of the user. Ensure that the multi-tool you choose has a clip or a ring to tie a lanyard to. This can be a critical feature, since a multi-tool dropped in two feet of snow, marsh mud, or anywhere in the dark, does nobody any good at all.

Uses for a multi-tool include: notching or more complex wood working skills, opening cans, altering equipment, medical uses, and cutting snare wire…the list is nearly infinite. Once you get a multi-tool, carry it on you regularly to see how often you use it.

---

[45] http://readynutrition.com/resources/paracord-the-most-versatile-item-in-your-bug-out-bag_07062012/

9. Lighting: Lanterns, light sticks, flashlights, and headlamps can help you find your way in the dark. LEDs, solar and hand crank will get you the most for your money. There are a variety of flashlights. The Streamlight LED pen flashlight is one of my favorites. It's lightweight and gives off 65 lumens of light. This is a great tool to put in your car, as well as in your bug out bag.

10. Survival Knife: Knives should be made of good quality steel. Invest in one you can rely on. Make sure it is well made, is strong enough for rough field use, and is the best you can afford. It is always a good idea to have a variety of different knives. For instance a machete can clear brush, slice through wood and would be ideal to have if you are in a densely wooded area. That said, a boning knife would be essential in dressing small game. My all-time favorite is the multi-tool. I have used my multi-tool is a variety of different scenarios and never leave home without.

Your preparedness tools are your lifeline. The equipment you choose should be ones that you can depend on to assist in meeting your basic needs. Without them, you could be ill equipped in a survival situation.

PREPS TO BUY:

- Candles or hurricane lamps
- Matches (regular and water-proof)
- Batteries (an assortment of sizes)
- Collapsible shovel or trowel
- Water treatment supplies
- Compass
- Map
- Fire-starter
- First aid kit
- Mirror
- Duct tape
- Rope
- Signal flare or flashing beacon
- Survival blanket or bivvy
- Multi-tool
- Lighting (lantern, light sticks, flashlights, head lamps)
- Survival knife (If you have not already purchased one)

ACTION ITEMS:

1. Prepare a survival kit or 72-hour bag[46] with your essential preparedness tools included. Have this ready in case you have to make a quick evacuation.

2. Consider a camping drill – go 24 hours using just the items in your 72-hour bag. This will help to identify the shortcomings of your bag.

3. Look for an in-depth pocket-sized field guide to include in your bag as a reference.

4. Take a wilderness-training course to increase your chances of survival if exposed to natural elements. Practice these skills[47] regularly.

---

[46] http://readynutrition.com/resources/are-you-ready-series-72-hour-kits_29082013/

[47] http://readynutrition.com/resources/teaching-kids-how-to-survive-in-the-forest_17082011/

SUPPLEMENTAL INFORMATION AND RESOURCES

How to Make a Water Compass

A water compass is a very simple device that indicates north, as any other compass, but is based on the direction a needle points while floating in water. Take a needle and slightly magnetize it by rubbing it against a magnet. Then poke it through a small piece of Styrofoam or cork. This ensures that it floats in water. Place the compass in the water and it will point north. To test the compass, blow it so it points another direction and see if it reorients to point north again.

You will need:

- Sewing needle about one to two inches long
- A small piece of Styrofoam or a cork (corks from wine bottles work well, but not the plastic stoppers)
- A small glass or cup of water to float the cork and needle
- Small bar magnet or refrigerator magnet
- Pair of pliers

Instructions:

1. Rub a magnet over the needle or paperclip a few times, always in the same direction. This action magnetizes the needle.
2. Use a piece of Styrofoam or cut off a small circle from one end of the cork, about 1/4-inch thick. Lay on a flat surface.
3. Carefully poke the needle into the Styrofoam. Or, if using a cork, poke one edge of the cork and force the needle through the cork so that the end comes out the other side. Push the needle far enough through the cork so that about the same amount of needle is sticking out each side of the cork.
4. Fill the glass or cup about half full of water, and put the cork and needle assembly on the surface of the water.
5. Place your "compass" on a flat surface and watch what happens. The needle should point towards the nearest magnetic pole —north or south, depending upon where you live. Try placing a magnet near your compass and watch what happens. How close does the magnet have to be to cause any effects?

Making a Stove from a Coffee Can

1.) Select a large empty metal coffee can or other #10 can.
2.) The bottom of the can will become your cooking surface – the top of your stove. The open end of the can is now the bottom of your stove.
3.) Wearing safety gloves and using tin snips, cut a small rectangular access door at the bottom side of the can – the open end - this door will be used to tend your fire.
4.) On the opposite side of the access door, use a bottle opener to puncture 3 small holes near the top of the stove. This will release smoke. You can also use a hammer and nail or an awl for this.
5.) To use the stove, build a fire small enough in diameter to fit inside the can. Place the can over your fire.
6.) Food can be cooked directly on the surface of the can or in a camp skillet placed on top of the can.

CHAPTER NINETEEN:
WATER PREPAREDNESS

227 of the 2,600 buildings operated by the New York City Housing Authority remained without power going into the second week after Hurricane Sandy wrought devastation across the waterfront.

Perhaps more so than in any other place in the city, the loss of power for people living in public housing projects forced a return to a primal existence. Opened fire hydrants became community wells.

Any bathtubs filled with water are now empty. Unflushed toilets stink.

Open hydrants in Coney Island and at East Sixth Street and Avenue D became lifelines, drawing residents on foot and skateboards to fill buckets and bottles, which were then hauled up darkened stairways for use as drinking water, for baths, and for flushing festering toilets.

       Source – The NY Times[48]

[48] http://www.nytimes.com/2012/11/03/nyregion/in-public-housing-after-hurricane-sandy-fear-misery-and-heroism.html?pagewanted=all&_r=0

Water is the foundation of life, and as such, water preparedness is one of the most important aspects of being prepared. Disaster officials suggest the importance of having a 3-day water supply, equating to one gallon of water per person, per day. However, in the event of a natural emergency such as a hurricane or tornado, water can be interrupted for many days, or even weeks. Within a three-day period of not drinking water, dehydration will have set in, the body starts shutting down, and death occurs. Infants, pregnant women, and the elderly are especially prone to dehydration and their needs should be taken into account.

Water is essential to life, so why not be prepared? Keep some alternative water treatment sources on hand in case of a water shortage. Along with learning about various treatment options, store enough bottled drinking water for short-term emergencies and consider having multiple alternatives on hand to treat and filter water if a short-term emergency becomes an extended one.

In a disaster where water sources are compromised, people within a 50-mile radius could be adversely impacted by illness and disease if just one person incorrectly handles water or incorrectly disposes of waste. Learning how to safely handle and treat water before an emergency occurs will ensure that your family does not become ill from poor water conditions.

Some of the symptoms of ingesting contaminated drinking water include:

- Severe gas
- Diarrhea
- Vomiting
- Severe abdominal cramps
- Headache
- Weakness due to the above symptoms

As discussed in chapter 4, properly treating water will eliminate microorganisms and the possibility of contaminants in the water. Microorganisms such as protozoan parasites, bacteria and viruses can make a person very ill. Drinking contaminated water can even cause death[49] in extreme cases.

There are multiple water treatment options on the market. On your own, research to find which one is suitable for your family. On a personal note, my family has all of the following options and has found them to be viable for both bugging in and bugging out.

Water Treatment Options:

---

[49] http://readynutrition.com/resources/the-4-most-likely-ways-you-can-die-if-the-shtf_29062011/

- Pump-style filters and purifiers
- Gravity-fed filters and purifiers
- Ultraviolet light pen purifiers
- Sip/squeeze bottles with in-line filtering straws
- Chemical tablets
- Boiling

THE PREPPER RULE OF THREE

The need to duplicate certain preps ensures that you have extras in case the first choice breaks or doesn't work. Many preppers believe in the Rule of Three and use it throughout their prepping endeavors.

The Rule of Three goes on to say that if you have three, then you know that you can count on two; if you have two, you know you can count on one; but if you have one, you really have nothing in a worst case scenario. Basically, have alternatives to fall back on.

WHEN IN DOUBT, TREAT IT

Anytime water for the home has been interrupted, it is a good idea to use a water pump to prevent the ingestion of harmful parasites. If you are out in nature and need to purify water, try and find a running water source as opposed to a standing water source. Water purification tablets are also suitable in treating water for consumption. Bear in mind that water pumps do not always remove viruses or giardia cysts, therefore if at all possible, treat the water chemically as well as filtering it.

A way to integrate the Rule of Three into your water preparations is to have separate filtration systems for the home, the 72-hour bag, and in emergency vehicle kits. In addition, keeping extra filtration parts on supply would be very proactive in the event that a short-term emergency extends into a longer-term emergency.

Water is only as safe as its source. When there is any doubt about the quality of water you are drinking, treat it chemically, through distillation, through the boiling method, or through a combination of methods.

WATER STORAGE TIPS:

- Keep emergency water in a cool, dark place in your home, each vehicle, and your workplace.
- Keep water in food-grade containers intended for water storage.
- Containers must be thoroughly washed, sanitized, and rinsed.
- Only store clean, ready-to-drink water. After a disaster, tap water will likely need to be purified. Ask public health authorities or your water provider whether tap water should be used and how to treat it.
- Plastic soft drink containers can be used in a pinch. Clean and sanitize containers thoroughly before they are used.
- Do not use milk or juice bottles to store water. It is extremely difficult to clean off the leftover sugars and proteins. Over time, these can become a breeding ground for bacteria to grow.

Some suitable emergency water storage containers are:

- Bottled water
- Water bricks
- Water bob
- 2-liter soda bottles
- Collapsible water containers
- Plastic gallon sized bags
- Sealed water pouches (similar to Capri Suns, but with water)

Many of these water containers are portable and can be used in a bug-out situation as well. Further, with the exception of the plastic gallon-sized bags, these containers are made of food grade plastic and are suitable for long-term storage.

To prevent drinking contaminated water, ensure that the containers you decide to use are properly cleaned and sanitized.

Take the following steps to clean reusable containers or plastic soft drink bottles:

1. Wash the inside and outside of the container with water and dishwashing soap.
2. Rinse thoroughly until all the soap is gone from the inside -- clear water goes in and clear water comes out, no suds or bubbles.
3. Sanitize the inside of the bottle with a bleach solution. Use 1 teaspoon of non-scented chlorine bleach to a quart of clean water for the solution. Fill the container about a quarter of the way and swish the solution all around the inside of the bottle, touching every surface including the cap or lid. Rinse the solution out of the bottle with clean water.

To fill emergency water storage containers:

1. Fill containers to the top with clean, drinkable water from the tap or other source. Any questionable water needs to be treated before storage.
2. If your water source is chlorinated like many municipal water systems, then just seal the container (step 3). If not, then add two drops of non-scented chlorine bleach per gallon of water (unless you already chlorinated it as described below).
3. Seal container tightly with the original cap. Don't touch the inside of the cap to avoid contaminating it.
4. Replace water every six months if you're not using commercially bottled water.

Source - cdc.gov

TREATING WATER FOR CONSUMPTION

When water is unavailable, we must trust in the skills and knowledge we have amassed. One essential skill is knowing how to properly treat water.

Boiling

Boiling is the easiest and safest way to treat water. Bring the water to a rolling boil for 1 full minute, keeping in mind that some of it will evaporate. (If you're more than a mile above sea level, boil for 3 minutes.) Let the water cool. The taste of boiled water can be improved by adding oxygen back in, which you can do by pouring the water back and forth between 2 clean containers.

Chemical Treatment

If boiling water isn't possible, chemical disinfection is advised. As an extra measure, once the water has been treated, to ensure that all microorganisms are removed, many will also boil their water for up to 1 minute

Bleach — Sodium hypochlorite of 5.25% to 6% concentration should be the only active ingredient in the bleach you use to treat water. There should be no added soap or fragrance. Make sure the bleach is fragrance free before using it to treat water.

1. Filter the water through a piece of cloth or a coffee filter to remove any solid particles.

2. Add 8 drops or 1/8 teaspoon of liquid chlorine bleach per gallon of cooled water. Ensure that your bleach bottles are within their expiration date. Bleach expires after one year and loses its effectiveness. Stir to mix, then let stand for 30 minutes.

Iodine tablets — Follow the manufacturer's instructions. Iodine must be stored in a dark container, since sunlight will inactivate the tablets.

Be aware that some people are allergic to iodine and cannot use this form of water purification. Persons who have thyroid problems or are on lithium, women over age 50, and pregnant women should consult their physician prior to using iodine for purification. Also, some people who are allergic to shellfish are also allergic to iodine.

Chlorine (Calcium Hypochlorite) granules—Chlorine granules can be used by those who have iodine allergies or restrictions. An advantage of storing chlorine granules is the shelf life is much longer compared to bleach. To make a bleach solution using chlorine, add one teaspoon of chlorine granules per 2 gallons of water. To disinfect water, add 2 ½ teaspoon of the solution to 1 gallon of water. Ensure that when storing granular chlorine, it should be kept it in its original container and stored in a cool, dry place away that is not located near any flammable objects.

Try this camping trick: if you add a vitamin C tablet to chlorine-treated water, the chlorine taste vanishes. Make sure the purification process is complete before you add the vitamin C.

Micropur tablets—According to Katadyn, the maker of these tablets, this is the only disinfection system effective against viruses, bacteria, cryptosporidium, and giardia. One tablet is used per 1 quart of water - follow the manufacturer's instructions. The tablets leave no residual chemical taste.

Ensure that you are able to drink clean water during times the water supply may be cut off by having multiple ways to treat water and a good supply of potable water. This will ensure that your family has what they need to survive and thrive.

HIDDEN WATER SOURCES IN THE HOME

Those of you who do not have access to natural water sources will need to be cleverer at finding water in an emergency situation. Knowing the hidden water sources inside your home can help you find immediate water (for short term use) when you need it the most.

Hidden Water inside your Home

Safe Sources

- Melted ice cubes
- Water drained from the water heater (if the water heater has not been damaged). Treat water accordingly.
- Liquids from canned goods such as fruit or vegetable juices.
- Water drained from pipes. Treat water accordingly.

- To use the water in your pipes, let air into the plumbing by turning on the faucet in your home at the highest level. A small amount of water will trickle out. Then obtain water from the lowest faucet in the home.
- To use the water in your hot-water tank, be sure the electricity or gas is off, and open the drain at the bottom of the tank. Start the water flowing by turning off the water intake valve at the tank and turning on the hot water faucet. Refill the tank before turning the gas or electricity back on. If the gas is turned off, a professional will be needed to turn it back on.
- Toilet tank. The water in the tank (not the bowl) is safe to drink unless chemical treatments have been added.

Unsafe Sources

- Radiators
- Hot water boilers (home heating system)
- Water beds (fungicides added to the water or chemicals in the vinyl may make water unsafe to use)
- Water from the toilet bowl
- Swimming pools and spas (chemicals used to kill germs are too concentrated for safe drinking but can be used for personal hygiene, cleaning, and related uses)

PROTECTING WELL WATER

Those who have wells with electric pumps may want to consider investing in an alternative hand or solar pump to have in the event of a disaster that causes a power outage. Hand pumps such as Flojak pumps[50] are very popular among preppers and would be a solid investment for those of you who require a non-electric pump for your well.

If there are reports of broken water or sewage lines, steps should be taken to protect your water sources. To close the water source, locate the incoming valve and turn it to the closed position. Be sure several family members know how to perform this important procedure.

If there is time before the impending emergency, attempt to plug or cap your well to reduce the potential for damage and contamination. After the disaster, go to the well or aquifer and check for the possibility of contamination and investigate the area to assess the situation.

---

[50] http://www.flojak.com/

Check the following:

- Surface water running into or collecting near the well.
- A defective or improperly installed well casing, cover or pipe connection which would allow surface water, animals, insects or plant material to enter the well. (Well casing not sealed).
- Nearby septic systems or manure piles: within 30M (100 ft.) of the well.
- Openings in the well seal.
- Well casing not being deep enough.
- A source of contamination not related to the well construction.

If any of these have occurred, treat any water that comes from the well.

Source – www.cdc.gov

Water is a finite resource, and in the case of emergency preparedness, it is paramount that it is in your supplies. We use water for everything: hydrating our bodies, cleaning our bodies, brushing our teeth, for cooking, cleaning the dishes, and cleaning wounds. Ensure that you have enough for these purposes.

PREPS TO BUY:

- 1-2 week supply of bottled water for each family member (at 1 gallon each per day)
- Secondary water filtration system
- Water purification tablets and extra filters
- Collapsible 2-gallon water containers (as many as you think your family needs).
- Water bricks are also a great investment for holding larger quantities of water in your home. They also are stackable!
- Bathtub storage unit – This is a large food grade plastic container that holds up to 65 gallons of water and fits conveniently into your tub.
- Water purification tablets – My family has stocked up on Micropur tablets, but there are a host of other purification tablets out there. These tablets are great to carry in your bug-out bags, evacuation vehicles and even to use on camping trips.
- Unscented bleach *(Bleach only stores for 12 months, so do not buy large quantities of this item unless you plan to use it for other reasons.)*
- Chlorine granules (available at most super stores or pool stores)
- Iodine
- Tarp or plastic sheeting (for solar stills and collecting rain)
- Electrolyte[51] or rehydration powders
- Anti-diarrhea medicines
- Vitamins (to help the body absorb needed nutrients after being ill from untreated water)

ACTION ITEMS:

1. Research different types of water filtration systems to see which type is best suited for your family. Some great choices that have excellent reviews are Berkey water filtration systems, Katadyn water filters, LifeStraw, Micropur tablets and Steripen. These are all products that I have in my own preparedness supplies and use regularly.

2. Learn about natural ways to filter water. YouTube is an abundant source of information on how to filter water for survival situations. Devote some time to learning methods such as: how to build a solar still, how to live on seawater, how to make your own water filter, making a sand filter, making a gravity filter.

3. Practice filtering and treating your water. This is a crucial skill to learn!

---

[51] http://readynutrition.com/resources/diy-electrolyte-powders_21062011/

SUPPLEMENTAL INFORMATION AND RESOURCES

Homemade Water Distiller Instructions

Materials You Will Need:

- Dish-washing soap
- Stove
- Drill and drill bit
- Stainless steel feed-through fitting that has a barbed end and an inner diameter of 3/8-inches
- A 3-ft. long plastic hose that has an inner diameter that matches the stainless steel feed-through fitting
- Large glass jug
- A one-gallon metal pot with a tight lid

1. **Drill Holes.** Begin making your homemade water distiller by using the drill to make a hole in the metal pot's lid. Once the hole has been successfully drilled, insert the stainless steel feed-through fitting through it, taking care to keep the fitting's barbed end outside of the metal pot.
2. **Wash the Metal Pot.** Give the metal pot a vigorous washing with warm water and dish-washing soap. Be sure to thoroughly wash the pot's lid, the glass jug and the plastic hose as well. Once your materials have been sufficiently cleaned, give them all ample time to air dry before proceeding any further.
3. **Place Metal Pot on the Stove.** Fill the metal pot exactly three-fourths of the way up with the water you wish to distill, then place the partially filled pot on the stove and heat it up to about 200 degrees Fahrenheit. After steam has escaped from the stainless steel feed-through fitting for about five minutes, you will be ready to continue with the next step.
4. **Attach the Plastic Hose.** You're almost finished with your homemade water distiller. You'll now need to slowly attach one end of the plastic hose to the stainless steel feed-through fitting, thus venting away any remaining contaminants and preventing them from being condensed into the freshly distilled water. Place the other end of the plastic hose into your jug. Steam that is being condensed will slowly drip into the glass jug in the form of pure water. After the dripping slows down considerably or stops completely, take the metal pot off the stove, after which it will require at least half an hour of cooling-down time before it and the plastic hose can be cleaned.

Solar Powered Water Distiller

Materials You Will Need:

- 2 liter soda bottle
- utility knife
- lighter
- Black rag

1. Cut an empty bottle in half using the utility knife.
2. Using the top half of the bottle (the part with the lid), fold the bottom edges of cut bottle inward making a 1" or 2" lip back into the inside of the bottle (this is the trough). If needed, use the lighter to heat to help the bottle in order to easily bend back in.
3. Thoroughly soak a black rag with the dirty water and set it inside the plastic bottle in full sun for 4 hours or more. The water will evaporate and condense on the inside sides of the bottle and find its way down into the trough.
4. When you notice enough water has collected in the trough, carefully remove the bottle from the nasty black rag and flip it over quickly. The water now flows the other way and ends up in the cap. Carefully remove the cap and drink the water.

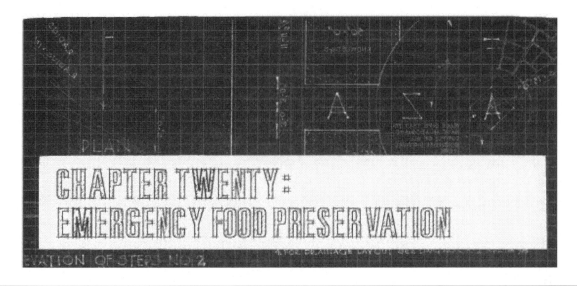

CHAPTER TWENTY:
EMERGENCY FOOD PRESERVATION

In 1795, Napoleon Bonaparte offered a cash prize of 12,000 francs to whoever could develop a safe, reliable food preservation method for his constantly traveling army.

French confectioner Nicolas Appert took on the challenge, and after much trial and error with the food sterilization processes, 14 years later he finally had a breakthrough. He introduced a method that involved heat-processing food in glass jars reinforced with wire and sealing them with wax. He took a cue from the way that wine was preserved in glass bottles. To ensure his vegetables were packed at their peak of freshness, he grew his own tiny peas. He tested his discovery for a year before telling Bonaparte.

As promised, in 1810, Napoleon Bonaparte awarded him 12,000 francs. Nicolas Appert is now known as the Father of Canning.

If a short-term disaster is turning into a longer-term predicament, you need to have the skills and supplies to preserve the food you have available before it spoils. Later chapters will go into more detail about these skills.

It is important to emphasize that preparedness isn't about how many items you have stored away - it's really about learning the skills necessary for survival. Food preservation is economical, you know exactly what your food contains, and you know where it came from. Most of all, it takes you one step closer to being self-reliant[52] during a disaster.

Acquiring items to preserve food is a good investment for your short and long-term disaster supplies. The best way to start is by collecting various types of food preservation resources.

One great advantage of learning how to preserve food is that you can use just about any type of food that you have on hand. You can even preserve your own fruit juice! All you need are the right tools and your imagination. Having knowledge on how long foods last will help you preserve foods when they are at their best. This convenient food storage chart[53] is a great tool to have in your kitchen to ensure your foods are within expiration.

Here are some canning and preserving tips:

- Nutritionally speaking, canned food is comparable to its cooked fresh and frozen counterparts.
- Canned fruits and vegetables are packed at their peak of harvest, which means they are packed at their peak nutrient value.
- Crops that go directly from the field to the processor often retain vitamins better than those that travel hundreds of miles across the country and sit for days in produce bins.
- Canners use only top-quality ingredients, which are picked, packed, and canned within hours.
- No preservatives are added or necessary in the canning process and many canned foods are available in low- and no-sodium varieties.

The Canning Process

Did you know that most fruit and vegetable canning facilities are located within a few miles from the point of harvest and meats, soups and stews are canned within the facilities in which they are prepared? The canning process was developed to preserve food safely and for an extended period of time. Virtually any food that is harvested or processed can be found in a can. Every food can is hermetically sealed, which prevents contamination.

---

[52] http://readynutrition.com/resources/freedom-through-self-reliance_02022010/

[53] http://www.uga.edu/nchfp/how/store/ksu_cupboard.pdf

Providing the can remains sealed and not damaged, the food maintains its nutrition and flavor for more than two years.

Benefits of the Canning Process

- Canned food allows seasonal favorites to be enjoyed year round.
- According to a 1997 University of Illinois study, the canning process actually may help to enhance the nutrient profile of certain foods.
- Canned pumpkin contains 540 percent of the Recommended Daily Intake of vitamin A, while the same amount of fresh pumpkin has only 26 percent.
- Foods like canned beans have higher fiber content and are excellent sources of protein and iron.
- Canned tomatoes contain significantly higher quantities of the essential phytochemical lycopene than fresh.

It's also important to realize that nearly all of the contents of your refrigerator and freezer can be preserved during a grid-down emergency. For example, canning those foods before they spoil can make them last another 12 months without refrigeration! Use your imagination and combine meats, sauces, and vegetables into tasty combinations like soups and stews.

FOOD PRESERVATION METHODS

- **Canning** - This process destroys microorganisms and inactivates enzymes that exist naturally in food. The heating and later cooling forms a vacuum seal to prevent other microorganisms from contaminating the food within the jar or can. Acidic foods such as fruits and tomatoes can be processed or "canned" in boiling water (also called the "water bath method") while low acid vegetables and meats must be processed in a pressure canner at 240°F (10 pounds pressure at sea level). Because the foods are canned at the time of their peak nutritional content, they will retain most of their value through the canning process. Canned food[54] will keep 12 months or longer in some cases.
- **Freezing** – This is by far the easiest way to preserve your food. Many simply blanch their fruits or vegetables for a minute or two and then throw them in the freezer. I have a vacuum sealer and seal up ready-to-cook dinners so that they are sitting in my freezer to use on nights when I'm really busy. It's best to eat frozen food within 6-12 months. This is a very time efficient way of preserving food; however, if the electricity goes out for an extended time, the food will spoil. So my advice is to not put all your "eggs in one basket" (or store your food by one method!). Know the pros and cons[55] of freezing your food storage.

---

[54] http://readynutrition.com/resources/canning-makes-a-comeback_15102009/

[55] http://readynutrition.com/resources/using-your-freezer-as-a-long-term-food-storage-solution_25012013/

- **Drying or Dehydrating** - This method is a very low-cost approach to use for long-term storage. It is a great way of including needed nutrition into diets with minimal investment. You can purchase a food dehydrator for a reasonable price, or you can dehydrate foods in the oven at a very low setting. Some people have even used their cars as a dehydrator during the hot summer months. This method preserves foods for 6-12 months and the items can easily be rotated into your food pantry[56]. Dried fruits and vegetables will add much needed flavor, nutrients, and variety to your off-grid pantry. Keep in mind that large amounts of potable water will needed in order to rehydrate dried foods[57].

- **Cure & Smoke** - This time honored preservation method is very popular due to the intense flavor it adds to meats. Many foods are cured before smoking, especially cold-smoking, to draw out the moisture, which would otherwise promote spoilage. Ensure that you use cure mixtures that contain nitrate. *Caution: Nitrites are considered carcinogens and are toxic if used in quantities higher than recommended; therefore caution should be used in their storage and use.* Curing is when a mixture of salt, sodium nitrate, nitrites, and sometimes sugar, spices, and other seasonings are combined to kill off any bacterial growth and to flavor the meat at the same time.

- **Fermenting and pickling** - This method of food preservation is one of the oldest ways to prolong food sources. The acidity level makes it difficult for bacteria to grow. Ensure that you select fresh, firm fruits or vegetables free of spoilage. Distilled vinegar or cider vinegars[58] of 5 percent acidity (50 grain) are recommended. Aside from the correct type of vinegar, no special equipment is required for fermentation.

As with all foods in your storage pantry, ensure that your supplies are stored properly in a cool, dark place away from natural elements (sunlight, moisture, and insects). Natural elements and insects are your food's worst enemies and should be avoided at all costs.

Food preservation is one of the oldest technologies known to man. Humans have depended on preserved foods for centuries. Take a look at the lost art of food preservation and revive it for use in your future survival situations.

---

[56] http://readynutrition.com/resources/complementing-your-food-storage-pantry-with-dehydrated-foods_01092013/

[57] http://readynutrition.com/resources/rehydration-chart-for-dehydrated-foods_22012013/

[58] http://readynutrition.com/resources/make-vinegar-from-apples_23092010/

PREPS TO BUY:

- Kosher Salt (10 lbs.)
- Sugar (20 lbs.)
- Morton's Sure Curing Salt (10 lbs.)
- Pickling Salt (5-10 lbs.)
- White Vinegar
- Apple Cider Vinegar (5-10 gallons)
- Molasses (5-10 lbs.)
- Powdered Fruit Pectin
- Canning Jars (in an assortment of sizes), Lids and Rings
- Food Drying Racks
- Pressure Canner
- Food Strainer
- Large Water Bath Canner

ACTION ITEMS:

1. Begin researching and finding resources to have on hand for the different food preservation methods discussed. There are some great resources for preserving food on different homesteading websites and even homesteading magazines.

2. Practice makes perfect! So, begin now to perfect the necessary skills!

3. Start a garden[59] and preserve your harvest for later use.

---

[59] http://readynutrition.com/resources/survival-gardens-25-seeds-you-need_05112009/

SUPPLEMENTAL INFORMATION AND RESOURCES

Meet Your Emergency Food's Worst Enemies

Moisture

Problem: Foods can become contaminated by moisture through humidity, rain, and standing water. As a result, molds, mildew, and microbial infestation can form and rot stored food, thus making it inedible. Since some foods draw in moisture, such as wheat, rice and grains, the best way to avoid moisture from coming in contact with stored food is to store it properly.

Solution: Remedy this by using a multi-barrier approach and making sure the food items are away from any possible areas that can flood (laundry rooms, bathrooms, near water pipes, etc.), and have been properly sealed to avoid moisture. Additionally, storing your food grade buckets or round cans on shelves or stacked on wooden platforms 6 inches off the floor is another method of preventing decontamination of food. Providing ventilation between the stored containers can also assist in preventing increased moisture levels.

Sunlight

Problem: When sunlight shines directly onto your food pantry or food storage area, photo-degradation (spoilage) occurs and results in losses of pigments, fats, proteins, and vitamins, as well as surface discoloration.

Solution: Storing food in Mylar bags is an easy solution to remedy this concern. Mylar bags are metallized foil liners that prevent sunlight, moisture, and bugs from ruining food. Investing in the thickest grade of Mylar would be a good investment for your food storage endeavors. Additionally, store your food items in a dark area not prone to sunlight or temperature fluctuation. If you have to store your food supply in a room with a window, put up curtains or black out material over the window.

Oxygen

Problem: Oxygen is another force to reckon with where food storage is concerned. Over time, oxygen will break down food, cause discoloration, and create staleness in foods.

Solution: Using oxygen absorbers greatly prolongs the shelf life of stored food. Because it absorbs the oxygen from the container, it inhibits the growth of aerobic pathogens and molds. Oxygen absorbers come in vacuum-sealed packs and begin working the moment they are exposed to oxygen. Oxygen absorbers come in different sizes, so pay attention to the size needed for the container. Manufacturers of this product suggest that, 2,000-4,000 cc's of oxygen absorbers should be added in one #10 can, and roughly 15,000 – 20,000 ccs for 5 gallon pails. If working with smaller containers such as Bell jars, 50 ccs of oxygen absorbers should be used.

Temperature Fluctuations

Problem: Fluctuations in temperature create an imbalance in the food storage environment. Ideal temperatures for stored food are between 65-80 degrees F.

Solutions: Typically, people store their stockpiles in unused closets or areas in the home that do not have large exposure to sunlight. Ideally, the area where the food is stored should have access to air conditioning. Those that do not have extra space within their homes have used basements, root cellars, and even temperature controlled storage warehouses. To ensure the area where the food is stored maintains adequate temperatures and moisture levels, install an indoor thermometer and humidity gauge.

Bugs

Problem: Bug infestations can be present on food sources when purchased and can also occur from improper storage methods. Typically the stored food product becomes infested at the warehouse in which it was processed. Nearly all dried food products are susceptible to insect infestation, including dry goods, seeds and dried fruit. Insects will chew their way through cardboard, plastic or foil liners, or folds in the packaging system. This is why a multi-barrier approach to food storage is suggested.

Solutions: There are few different ways to prevent bug infestations:

> **Freezing Method** – Freeze food that will be stored for 72 hours. Freezing will kill any bug eggs.

> **Heating Method** – Heating the food to be stored at 150 degrees F for 15-20 minutes will kill any bugs or eggs as well.

> **Organic Option** – Diatomaceous earth are the fossilized remains of diatoms. They are organic and are safe to use on food. Use 1 cup to each 25 pounds of food.

Dry Ice Method – This method can be done two different ways. According to the <u>Family Preparedness Handbook</u> by James Talmage Stevens, the proper method for this technique is:

Basic on-top method:

- On top of almost-full 5-gallon container, place 1/4 lb. dry ice on non-conductive (insulating) material such as Kraft paper.
- Press lid down gently so some air can escape.
- After 20-30 minutes, check to see if dry ice has completely evaporated.
- If not, wait another 5 minutes, then check again.
- When dry ice has completely evaporated, remove material and seal container.

Basic on-bottom method:

- On bottom of 5-gallon storage container, place 1/4 lb. of dry ice under non-conductive (insulating) material, such as Kraft paper.
- Press lid down gently so some air can escape.
- After 20-30 minutes, check to see if dry ice has completely evaporated.
- If not, wait another 5 minutes, then check again.
- When dry ice has completely evaporated, remove material and seal container.

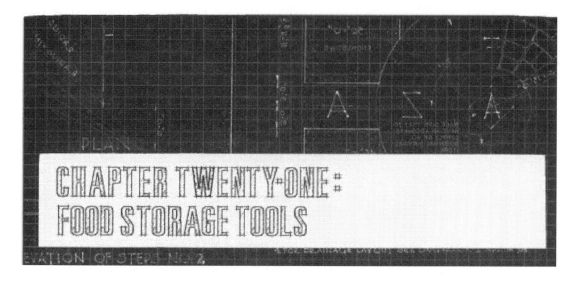

CHAPTER TWENTY-ONE:
FOOD STORAGE TOOLS

When emergencies last longer than originally expected, your basic needs such as food and water become the highest priorities. Finding ways to prolong your food source should be at the forefront of your mind. A secure supply of food and water is one of the greatest advantages you can have in being prepared for longer-term emergencies. In order to understand the importance of having a long-term food supply, you need to begin seeing food as a necessary investment[60] for your family's well being.

Due to the likelihood of a food shortage, as well as an increase in prices from inflationary periods[61] from a major recession, the cost of food is expected to increase at least 20% or more. Buying foods[62] before this crisis hits will help sustain your family longer than foods bought later on during the inflationary period. Depending on what is purchased, lasting foods such as seeds, dry goods, dehydrated foods, dry beans, and rice can be stored for up 20 years.

Additionally, begin looking at longer-term solutions to storing water[63]. Water may be hard to come by in future.

---

[60] http://readynutrition.com/resources/safe-investment-commodities-for-a-volatile-market_07052010/

[61] http://www.shtfplan.com/headline-news/hyperinflationary-depression-no-way-of-avoiding-financial-armageddon_12152009

[62] http://readynutrition.com/resources/25-must-have-survival-foods-put-them-in-your-pantry-now_03042013/

[63] http://readynutrition.com/resources/having-a-water-supply-during-a-long-term-disaster_25032010/

SHELF-STABLE FOODS

It is best to store dry goods that have long shelf lives and ones that you regularly use in your menus. Dry goods such as grains, rice, beans, oats, wheat, corn kernels, powdered milk, sugar, salt, baking powder, etc. are the best types of foods to store for long-term use and an added benefit is that many of these are multipurpose items. Having an understanding of how long certain foods last can help you in your food supply endeavours.

Usually, foods that are purchased at a grocery store are packaged for short-term use. The thin, flimsy packaging is not designed for long-term storage and does a sub-par job at keeping out your food's worst enemies: sunlight, oxygen, temperature fluctuations and pests. If these foods are destined to become part of your long-term food supply, they will need to be re-packaged.

LONG TERM FOOD STORAGE METHODS

Listed below are some of the most post popular long-term food storage methods for bulk quantities of food.

1. **Multi-barrier system** – Many preppers opt for a multi-barrier approach to store their food. This barrier system will keep natural elements such as sunlight, moisture, and air out of the container when sealed. The multi-barrier method uses Mylar bags (also called food liners) to initially seal the dry food. The Mylar bags are then placed in a food grade plastic container. There are different sizes of Mylar bags that can be used. I have small Mylar bags to use for my short-term food sources and larger sized Mylar bags that fit into 5-gallon plastic containers to use for my longer-term food sources.
2. **Vacuum sealing method** – I use this method for short-term food storage. I vacuum seal dry food in food sealer plastic packaging and then I add the sealed packages to Mylar bags. Then, I seal the Mylar bag. This is a little more work, but when I go to grab the food, I know that I have taken every precaution to ensure its quality. In the many years I have been doing this, never once have I found a tainted bag.
3. **Dry Ice Method** – Dry ice is frozen carbon dioxide and works through the sublimation process. When the dry ice sublimates (changes from a solid state to a gas state), it replaces the oxygen in the container with carbon dioxide. As dry ice slowly evaporates, the cool carbon dioxide fills the bottom of the bucket, displacing the warmer and lighter atmosphere. In an average 5-6 gallon container, it takes roughly two to four hours for the light air to exit from the top. This process makes it impossible for bacteria or insects to live in this environment.

   An advantage of this method is that dry ice is extremely economical (5 pounds of dry ice for $5) and can be easily purchased at many grocery stores, ice cream stores, and even welding stores. Preppers who do use this method emphasize that you should only buy enough dry ice that you plan on using. You will not be using very much of the dry ice when putting food away – the typical 5-gallon bucket will need 3-4 ounces. Dry ice is very cold, so if you use this method, use gloves when handling, and ensure that you work in a ventilated area. Also, if you are using oxygen absorbers, there is no need to use the dry ice method.

4. **Mylar bags technique** – Some prefer only using Mylar bags to store their foodstuffs. This is a popular approach for storing one's short-term food supply because the food is usually in smaller quantities and will be used more frequently. However, there is some risk to using this method because it can leave the food supply vulnerable to natural elements and also to insects.

FOOD STORAGE TOOLS

In order to have your foods stored properly, you need to use the right tools. The tools suggested below are used for short and long-term food storage preparation. These products are a necessary investment will ensure that your food sources are protected from pests and the elements. These products as well as many others can be found at www.PrepperPackaging.com.

Food Storage Containers – Any large quantities of food that you plan to store indefinitely should be stored in food grade containers. These non-toxic containers will not transfer any hazardous chemicals into the food.

> ### Food Grade Containers
>
> Food grade containers have a #2 by the recycle symbol or the acronym "HDPE" stamp on the bottom (HPDE stands for "high density polyethylene").

Before any food is stored, clean the containers with soapy water, then rinse and dry thoroughly. 5-gallon plastic containers are the most popular amongst those who store bulk quantities of food. Ensure that you have an airtight lid.

Mylar Food Liners – Thick Mylar bags have a middle layer of aluminum and two different plastic layers on the inside and outside, making them ideal for long-term food storage. Research has shown that over time, slow amounts of oxygen seep through the walls of plastic linters typically used for commercial food storage. Eventually, natural elements and even insects can find a way inside the container. To add additional protection to your food source, use Mylar food liners that are at least 5-mililiters thick to ensure there are multiple barriers protecting the food. Food liners come in an assortment of sizes and should fit the size of container you are using. For example, if you are using a 5-gallon plastic bucket, you will want to use an 18-inch x 28-inch or a 20-inch x 30-inch Mylar bag.

Further, Mylar bags make for a good investment because they can last up to 20 years if properly cared for, are reusable, and because the contents is well protected, they help preserve the taste of stored food.

Food Sealers – Food vacuum sealers remove and lock out air and moisture using specially designed bags and canisters. This preserves the longevity of the food. Using a food sealer is a great way to ensure that all oxygen is removed from food sources before it is placed in a long-term environment. Ensure that you have ample food sealer bags and the food is properly sealed. Learn more about the pros and cons of food sealers[64].

Oxygen Absorbers – Using oxygen absorbers greatly prolongs the shelf life of stored food. Because it absorbs the oxygen from the container, it inhibits the growth of aerobic pathogens and molds. Oxygen absorbers begin working the moment they are exposed to oxygen. Therefore, it is best to work as efficiently as possible. Oxygen absorbers come in different sizes, so pay attention to the size needed for the container. Oxygen absorbers are not edible, not toxic and do not affect the smell and taste of the product. For an oxygen absorber chart, check the supplemental information at the end of this chapter.

Desiccant Packets – Desiccant packets moderate the moisture level when placed in a food container. *They do not absorb the moisture.* Please note that desiccant is not edible. If the packet somehow breaks open and spills onto the stored food, the entire contents of the container must be thrown away. There are certain foods that desiccants should not be added to, specifically: flour, sugar and salt. These items need a certain amount of moisture to stay activated, and if a desiccant is added to it, they will turn into a hard brick.

Heat Clamp – A person can use a heat clamp to seal the Mylar bags, or they can seal their Mylar bags with an iron used on the highest setting. The heat clamp is usually around $85 and is specially made for sealing Mylar bags. If the clothing iron method is chosen, use a hard surface such as a cutting board or book to iron on and slowly go over the Mylar bag. Note: if using an iron to seal Mylar, this method must be done gently and slowly or the Mylar will be damaged.

WHERE CAN YOU PURCHASE THESE ITEMS?

- www.PrepperPackaging.com
- Latter Day Saint Food Distribution Warehouses[65]
- Ask local restaurants and bakeries in your area to see if they have any food grade containers with lids that you can have. Typically, restaurants are happy to give these away as they have no need for these containers after they are used. This could save you a lot of money investing in food grade containers.

---

[64] http://readynutrition.com/resources/vacuum-sealing-for-long-term-food-storage_13022013/

[65]

http://lds.about.com/gi/o.htm?zi=1/XJ&zTi=1&sdn=lds&cdn=religion&tm=40&f=20&tt=2&bt=1&bts=1&zu=http%3A//store.lds.org/webapp/wcs/stores/servlet/StoreLocationsView%3FcatalogId%3D10557%26langId%3D-1%26storeId%3D715839595

- Storing food is a continual process of using, rotating and resupplying. If you invest in a food supply, the food should be used and more food purchased to resupply the storage shelf. Think of your food supply as a small store where the foods in the front have the shortest expiration date and the ones in the back have the longest.

A little preventative maintenance can go a long way in terms of food storage. Understanding the different methods for storing your food supply for short or long-term storage will help you avoid waste and get the most out of your investment.

PREPS TO BUY:

- Mylar bags (in different sizes)
- Oxygen absorbers
- Desiccants
- Plastic food storage containers
- Food vacuum sealer with plastic liners
- Heat clamp or iron

ACTION ITEMS:

1. Find a safe, dry area in the home to store your longer-term food supplies. Those who are tight on space can use creative methods such as shelving units high in their closets, extra bedrooms or closets. As long as the space is dry, free from temperature fluctuations, and large enough to store the foods, it can be used. *It is best not to use a garage or attic as a food storage area due to the drastic temperature fluctuations that occur in these areas of the home.*

2. Make a list of what types of long-term foods you plan on storing for your supply. Those who have family members with special dietary needs should do further research on which types of foods they will need, as well as storing substitutes for the foods the person needs to avoid.

3. Practice using your food storage tools on short-term foods to perfect your method before using them on bulk amounts of long-term foods.

SUPPLEMENTAL INFORMATION AND RESOURCES

Guidelines for Food Storage:

Use within 6 months:
- Powdered milk (in box)
- Dried fruit (in metal container)
- Dry, crisp crackers (in metal container)
- Cereal
- Dried potatoes
- Flour

Use within 1 year:
- Canned condensed meat and vegetable soups
- Canned fruit, fruit juices and vegetables
- Ready-to-eat cereals and uncooked instant cereals (in metal containers)
- Vitamins
- Peanut butter
- Jelly
- Hard candy and canned nuts
- Vegetable oil

May Be Stored Indefinitely (in proper containers and conditions):
- Wheat
- Dried Corn
- Sugar
- Honey
- Soybeans
- Instant coffee, tea and cocoa
- Salt
- Non-carbonated soft drinks
- White rice
- Bouillon products
- Dry pasta

Freezer Storage Chart (0 °F)

Note: Freezer storage is for quality only. Frozen foods remain safe indefinitely.

Item	Months
Bacon and Sausage	1 to 2
Casseroles	2 to 3
Egg whites or egg substitutes	12
Frozen Dinners and Entrees	3 to 4
Gravy, meat or poultry	2 to 3
Ham, Hot Dogs and Lunch Meats	1 to 2
Meat, uncooked roasts	4 to 12
Meat, uncooked steaks or chops	4 to 12
Meat, uncooked ground	3 to 4
Meat, cooked	2 to 3
Poultry, uncooked whole	12
Poultry, uncooked parts	9
Poultry, uncooked giblets	3 to 4
Poultry, cooked	4
Soups and Stews	2 to 3
Wild game, uncooked	8 to 12

Learn about which <u>foods are best and worst to freeze</u>[66]. By freezing your food source, the frigid temperature kills any insects or eggs that may be present on the food.

---

[66] http://readynutrition.com/resources/the-best-and-the-worst-foods-to-freeze-for-long-term-storage_24012013/

	1-quart pouch (8" x 8") — 947 CCs)	#10 can(0.82 gallon) — 3,910 CCs)	5-gallon bucket —18,942 CCs	6-gallon bucket—22,730 CCs
Flour, pancake mix, fine powders	50–100 cc	200–300 cc	750 cc	1000 cc
Sugar, salt, dry milk	50–100 cc	200–300 cc	750 cc	1000 cc
Rice, grains (wheat berries, oats, etc.)	50–100 cc	200–300 cc	750–1,000 cc	1000–1,500 cc
Dried beans	100–150 cc	300–500 cc	1,000 cc	1,500 cc
Pasta	100–200 cc	300–600 cc	1,000–1,500 cc	1,500–2,000 cc

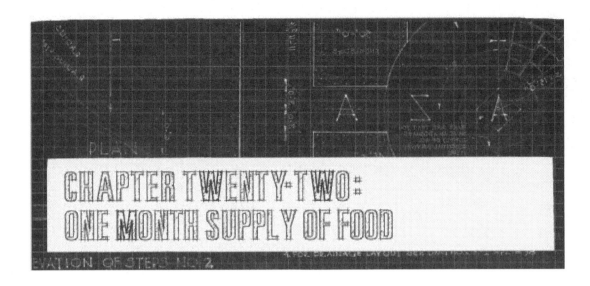

CHAPTER TWENTY-TWO: ONE MONTH SUPPLY OF FOOD

A reader writes….

I've been a prepper for a long time, stockpiling food, medical supplies, and health and beauty aids. If it was on sale and looked useful and storable, I added it to my pantry, neatly organized so that I'd be able to find it when needed. I felt very prepared for any natural disaster that might come my way.

The disaster I wasn't expecting was a job loss. I'd worked for the same company for many years and the layoff was completely out of the blue – I had been downsized. In my small town, jobs were few and far between. I was a single mom of two children with a mortgage and bills to pay. I applied for unemployment and was greatly dismayed to discover there was a 6-8 week waiting period before my first check was to arrive.

Although the disaster I had been planning for was something along the lines of an earthquake or a devastating storm, my well-stocked pantry stood us in good stead. I was able to make it the NINE weeks until my first check arrived by only supplementing our stockpiled goods with about $10 per week at the grocery store for some fresh items. In fact, the entire time I received unemployment (6 months) I was able to rely on my pantry for nearly everything. I replenished some of what I was using with sale items and when I eventually found another job, I rebuilt my stores as quickly as possible.

All disasters are not related to Mother Nature – a personal economic disaster can be just as devastating. There is no better feeling than the security that comes from knowing that your family will be fed, clean and cared for despite a financial downturn.

We are all preparing for different reasons and to different degrees; however, most of us agree that we are all preparing for a scenario where we will need to have emergency supplies to fall back on when the time comes. We have discussed in previous chapters how storing food is economical and promotes self-reliance and personal responsibility. Knowing that you can sustain your family in a disaster also provides peace of mind, which is priceless.

IT'S BETTER TO BE OVER PREPARED

When storing food for long-term emergencies, it is hard to calculate how much food a person or family will need. One of the golden rules of prepping is "it's better to be over prepared rather than under prepared." Ensure that your family has enough food for long-term emergencies by figuring out how many calories per day are needed. Use the formulas below to calculate the Active Metabolic Rates of family members to come up with these numbers. Use a simple food storage calculator to figure out how much food to store.

Basal Metabolic Rate

Women: BMR = 655 + (4.35 x weight in pounds) + (4.7 x height in inches) - (4.7 x age in years)
Men: BMR = 66 + (6.23 x weight in pounds) + (12.7 x height in inches) - (6.8 x age in years)

Active Metabolic Rate

Calculate your AMR by using your BMR and estimating your current level of activity. If you are:

- Sedentary (little or no exercise) - your AMR = BMR x 1.2

- Lightly active (light exercise/work 1-3 days per week) - your AMR = BMR x 1.375

- Moderately active (moderate exercise/work 3-5 days per week) - your AMR = BMR x 1.55

- Very active (hard exercise/work 6-7 days a week) - your AMR = BMR x 1.725

- Extra active (very hard exercise/work 6-7 days a week) - your AMR = BMR x 1.9

This number represents the number of calories you need to maintain your current bodyweight.

Certain foods can stand the test of time and are lifelines to families. The following is a detailed list of the suggested prep items for you to purchase this week. Most of these items are lifetime survival foods[67], meaning their shelf life is 20 years+ and would be a good investment to make towards your food security. Purchase these products and more at www.ReadyNutrition.com.

- **White Rice** – White rice is a major staple item for preppers because it's a great source for calories, is rich in starches and carbohydrates, is cheap, and it has a long shelf life. Although some prefer brown rice, white rice is the better storage choice. Even though brown rice has more nutrition, it is considered a "living" food and tends to not last as long as white rice does. If properly stored, white rice can last 30 years or more. Rice can be used for breakfast meals, added to soups, made into a variety of side dishes and is also an alternative to wheat flour.
- **Dry Beans** – These low cost prep superstars are not only packed with nutrition, but are also extremely versatile. Beans[68] are packed with protein, iron, fiber, folate, antioxidants and vitamins. When beans are accompanied with rice, it makes a complete protein that provides all the amino acids needed to survive. One serving of beans and rice provides 19.9 g, or 40 percent of your recommended daily allowance.
- **Wheat** – Wheat is one of your long-term emergency must-haves! Besides being a high carbohydrate food, wheat contains valuable protein, minerals, and vitamins. Wheat protein, when balanced by other foods that supply certain amino acids, is an efficient source of protein. Wheat berries are best to store as they will last longer than flour. The berries can also be used as a breakfast cereal, added to soups for additional nutrition, popped like popcorn, ground into flour for baking, used to make alcohol, fed to livestock, used as a leavening agent, and used for sprouting.
- **Oats** – Steel cut, rolled or quick cooking oats are the most common types of that can be purchased in bulk. Oats are considered a whole grain and can be a valuable protein source during a long-term situation. In addition, oats can be used in a variety of recipes, ground into flour, sprouted[69] for "fresh veggie" nutrition, and used as livestock feed. Oats also have proven to be very effective in soothing the skin, and can be used medicinally. The alternative medicine community boasts that infusions of oat straw have also been used to assist in nicotine withdraws, and can be used to treat flu symptoms and coughs.
- **Salt** – Salt is a multipurpose, low cost prep that will be highly desirable if a long-term disaster were to occur. Prepping calculators suggest having 25 pounds of salt stored for one year. Salt can be used for curing, as a preservative, in cooking, as a cleaning aid, medicinally, and for tanning hides. Salt that is stored in its paper packaging can be subject to caking due to exposure to moisture. Re-housing salt into long-term packaging is suggested.

---

[67] http://readynutrition.com/resources/11-emergency-food-items-that-can-last-a-lifetime_20082013/

[68] http://readynutrition.com/resources/rice-and-beans-arent-so-boring-after-all_15062011/

[69] http://readynutrition.com/resources/simply-sprouting_16042010/

- **Sugar** – Sugar will be highly desirable in a long-term emergency mainly because it will add a bit of normalcy to the situation. If you have a little sugar stored away you can use it as a sweetener for beverages, in breads and cakes, as a preservative, to make alcohol, for curing, in gardening, and as an insecticide (equal parts of sugar and baking powder will kill cockroaches). Much like salt, sugar is also prone to absorbing moisture, but this problem can be eradicated by adding some rice granules into the storage container. It is suggested not to add any oxygen absorbers or desiccant packets to sugar, as it will cause the sugar to brick.

- **Bouillon Granules** – Bouillon granules are a great way to add flavor to dishes during a long-term situation. This could be a great way to beat food fatigue (eating the same types of food repeatedly that causes one to lose their appetite). Because bouillon products contain large amounts of salt, the product is preserved. However, over time, the taste of the bouillon could be altered. If storing bouillon cubes, it would be best to repackage them using a food sealer or sealed in Mylar bags. Bulk quantities of bouillon granules can be found at most super stores.

- **Powdered Milk** – Because dry milk will probably be the most sensitive food item you are storing, the drier powdered milk can be kept the better. In fact, adding a desiccant packet when repackaging for long-term would be helpful in preserving this necessary food item. Powdered milk is not just for drinking. It can be used in a variety of recipes, added to soups, used to make breads, and has many beauty uses as well.

- **Cooking Oil** – Many overlook this critical prep item. Having oil is not only essential to use for cooking purposes, but it can play a large role in our diet as well. The fats contained in oil have nine calories per gram compared to the four calories contained by either carbohydrates or protein. This makes fat a valuable source of concentrated calories that could be of real importance if faced with a diet consisting largely of unrefined grains and legumes. Keep in mind that storing cooking oil could pose a problem. If you are planning to store food for longer-term emergencies, look for a hand crank oil expeller. Keep in mind that due to the instability of most cooking oils, unopened bottles of oil have a shelf life of 1 year. This is one example of why it is so important to use the foods that we store. Plant-based oils are better for you and have a longer shelf life. Ironically, coconut oil has a longer shelf life of 5 years when properly stored in cool, dark place. Although darker colored oils have more flavor than paler colored, the agents that contribute to that flavor and color also contribute to faster rancidity. For maximum shelf life buy paler colored oils.

PREPS TO BUY:

- White rice in bulk quantities
- Beans in bulk quantities
- Wheat in bulk quantities
- Oats in bulk quantities
- Sugar in bulk quantities
- Salt in bulk quantities
- Bouillon granules in bulk quantities
- Powdered milk in bulk quantities
- 2-gallons of cooking oil

ACTION ITEMS:

1. Calculate the amount of food your family will need for a month long disaster with the <u>food calculator</u> at Ready Nutrition.

2. With the food storage items purchased from the last chapter, begin assembling Mylar bags and storage containers. Repackage and seal for long-term storage. Have a print out on hand with the <u>directions for packing food</u>[70] to ensure that you are storing items correctly.

3. Ensure that all lids are sealed correctly.

4. Store sealed food containers in a cool, dark, and dry area of the home.

5. As a reminder, don't forget your pets in your long-term food storage plans and ensure that you have packed enough food away for your pets. Dog and cat food can also be stored in food grade plastic containers for long-term use.

---

[70] http://readynutrition.com/resources/are-you-ready-series-best-practices-for-long-term-food-storage_03042011/

SUPPLEMENTAL INFORMATION AND RESOURCES

Lifetime Survival Foods

These food items have a shelf life of 20 years + if stored properly.

1. Honey
2. Salt
3. Sugar
4. Wheat
5. Dried corn
6. Baking soda
7. Instant coffee, tea and cocoa
8. Non-carbonated beverages
9. White rice
10. Bouillon products
11. Powdered milk (in nitrogen-packed cans)

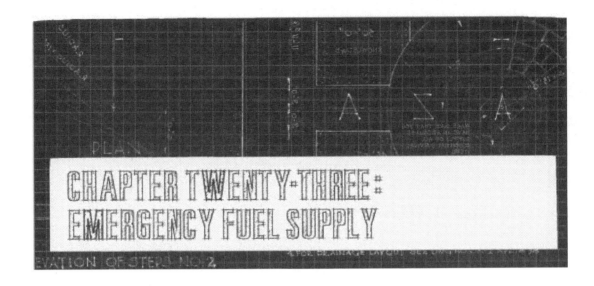

CHAPTER TWENTY-THREE: EMERGENCY FUEL SUPPLY

In the wake of Superstorm Sandy, gasoline might as well be gold. With lines snaking for blocks -- miles, even -- outside gas stations in New York and New Jersey, tensions flare as people wait for the chance to pump gas into cars or gas cans.

The demand is high, and the fuel isn't just for empty car tanks. Many people still have no electricity and are using gasoline-powered generators, adding to the demand. To make matters worse, a winter storm hit after the hurricane causing temperatures to fall below freezing and are endangering Hurricane Sandy victims who huddle in cold homes that lack heat or insulation.

At a station in Queens, New York, police arrested a man early Thursday after he cut in line and then pulled out a gun when he was challenged by other residents. Most major gas station chains, from ExxonMobil to Hess, were experiencing disruptions. In fact, some 60% of gas stations tracked by AAA in New Jersey were not operational, according to the motorist group. In New York's Long Island, that figure was 65%.

A lot of the closed gas stations simply don't have electricity to operate their pumps, while others cannot get gasoline delivered to the station from the refinery because of blocked roads or other logistical problems created by the storm.

Source: CNN[71]

When a disaster threatens a given area, fuel is one of the first emergency prep items people begin stocking up on. Fuel helps power you through an emergency by providing means to keep warm, cook, power emergency generators, and run appliances.

---

[71] http://www.cnn.com/2012/11/02/us/sandy-gas-woes/index.html

When choosing which types of emergency fuel to store, consider the following issues:

- Any dangers the fuel may pose by being stored
- How much fuel needs to be stored for the most likely emergencies
- The appliances or tools for which the fuel is needed
- The length of time the fuel will remain viable
- Storage methods and safety requirements

Because storing fuel for short- or long-term use presents its own set of unique challenges, ensure that you safely store your fuel supply according to safety regulations. Also check your local by-laws regarding fuel storage.

To ensure maximum safety, follow these guidelines when storing fuel:

- Use a proper container for storing fuel.
- Keep fuel dry.
- For safety reasons, store fuel in an isolated area. Do not store fuel near your home or near appliances such as water tanks.
- Do not store fuel near ammunition.
- Store fuel downwind from any homes or buildings.
- Store fuel in a cool, dark area away from sunlight or temperature fluctuations.
- Rotate your fuel supply regularly.
- Have a fire extinguisher on hand in the area where the fuel is stored.
- Check the storage containers or tanks regularly to ensure that the fuel is safely stored and that there are no signs of leaking.

FUEL STABILIZERS

When storing certain fuels, over time the fuel will separate and you will need to use a stabilizer to prevent this.

When water is present in a fuel tank with gasoline that contains ethanol, the water will be drawn into the fuel until the saturation point is reached. Beyond this level of water, phase separation will cause the ethanol and water to separate from the gasoline and drop to the bottom of the tank.

Moreover, writers for the Fuel School[72], state the effects can be catastrophic.

When this Phase Separation occurs you will have an upper layer of gasoline with a milky layer of Ethanol and Water below it, and then in many cases a third layer of just water at the bottom.

If this happens and you try to start the engine you can have one or more of the following problems.

1. If your fuel tank pick-up tube is in the water layer, most likely the engine will fail to start.
2. If the engine is running and suddenly draws water you can have damage from thermal shock or hydro-lock.
3. If the pick-up tube draws the Ethanol-Water mixture or just Ethanol you can have problems where the engine will operate in an extreme lean condition, which can cause significant damage or even catastrophic failure.
4. If the pick-up tube draws the gasoline, it will operate very poorly due to lower octane that is the result of no longer having the Ethanol in the fuel.

Some of the most popular fuel stabilizers are Stabile and Pry-G or Pry-D. Both are relatively inexpensive and can be purchased online or at most super store centers. Most preppers like to have enough fuel on hand for at least a 72-hour period. To be on the safe side, plan on storing enough fuel to provide power through your predicted "worst case scenario".

DIVERSIFY YOUR FUEL SOURCE

If fuels are to be stored for emergencies, use containers that prevent evaporation and prevent the signs of fuel phase separation. If the storage container is made of plastic, ensure that the following requirements are present:

- It should be made of durable HDPE with barrier materials to eliminate hydrocarbon emissions.
- It must have an airtight seal to reduce spills when not in use.
- The container should have a pour spout that controls variable flow.
- Look for automatic venting and automatic locking when lever is released.

Plastic is permeable and the fuel can seep through. Because of this, some preppers have found that metal fuel cans are best. An auto grade silicone like Sil-Poxy or 3M Super Silicone Seal can be used to coat the metal cans in order to preserve them longer.

DIFFERENT TYPES OF FUELS

---

[72] http://fuelschool.blogspot.ca/2009/02/phase-separation-in-ethanol-blended.html

It is in your best interest to store more than one kind of alternative fuel. In the heat of the summer you won't want to burn wood inside the house for cooking and alternatively you won't want to stand outside in a blizzard cooking on your propane barbecue. The six most popular fuel sources[73] to store are listed below.

- **Firewood** – This is the most basic of fuel sources. It is inexpensive and depending on where you live, there could be a plentiful supply nearby. Many preppers believe that firewood is one of the greatest self-sufficiency advantages of off-grid living. On a side note, many have found free firewood being given away on Craigslist. All one needs to do is pick it up and haul it out.

  Ensure that your firewood is seasoned at least six months and is kept dry. In cold climates, invest in a tarp or cover to place wood under. This will ensure that it stays as dry as possible. Firewood is also the only fuel that has reusable byproducts. Firewood can be made into charcoal. Ashes can be used in the garden or compost pile, and can be used in the snow for extra traction in place of salt. Ashes are also the basis for lye soap.

- **Gasoline** – Because of the oxygenate additives that are added to gasoline, its shelf life is greatly affected. The shelf life for gasoline is about 1 year if properly stored. This type of fuel will more than likely need a stabilizer such as Sta-bil added to it to preserve the viability of the gasoline. The life of the fuel can be even more diminished if gasoline is subjected to heat or moisture. Most cities prohibit large quantities of this type of fuel from being stored above ground, so check with a fuel dealer in your area.

  Additionally, there is strong evidence that these fuels pose dire health and environmental consequences, so please follow the safety suggestions provided above.

- **Diesel fuel** – This fuel lasts longer than gasoline and is safer to store because of the difficulty in ignition - it is almost impossible to ignite by accident. According to Back Woods Home[74], a homesteading website, there are two grades of diesel fuel:

  Two grades are available: #1 diesel which is old-fashioned yellow kerosene, and #2 diesel which is the same thing as #2 home heating oil. (You may see literature to the contrary, but #2 diesel is #2 heating oil. Period.) Diesel fuel presents its own unique storage problems: The first is that it is somewhat hygroscopic; that is, it will absorb moisture from the air. The second (and related) problem is sludge formation. Sludge is the result of anaerobic bacteria living in the trapped water and eating the sulfur in the fuel. Left untreated, the sludge will grow until it fills the entire tank, ruining the fuel. Stored diesel fuel should be treated with a biocide like methanol or diesel Sta-Bil as soon as it is delivered. Unique to #2 is the fact that some paraffin wax is dissolved in the

---

[73] http://readynutrition.com/resources/the-6-most-popular-types-of-fuel-to-store-for-emergencies_10092013/

[74] http://www.backwoodshome.com/articles/warner43.html

fuel and will settle out at about 20° F, clogging the fuel filter. This "fuel freezing" may be eliminated by adding 10% gasoline or 20% kerosene to the diesel fuel. Commercial diesel fuel supplements are also available to solve the same problem. Diesel should be filtered before use.

- **Kerosene** – This is one of the more versatile fuels that can be stored for disasters for long-term use. This fuel does not evaporate as readily as gasoline. Although some preppers add stabilizers to kerosene to ensure it remains viable, no special treatment is necessary. Did you know that many pre-1950 farm tractor engines were designed to run on kerosene? In fact, diesels will run on kerosene if necessary. Kerosene stoves and refrigerators are also available and would be very beneficial to have on hand during a disaster situation, especially a longer-term disaster.
- **Propane** – Propane is a very popular choice to store for disasters, mainly because it is so widely available, easy to use, and versatile and will last indefinitely. Propane is widely used in "off-grid" areas as an alternative to natural gas and electricity. There are even some automobiles that run on this fuel source. Steel cylinders can be purchased in different sizes to contain the desired amount of propane.
- **Biodiesel** - Biodiesel is typically made by chemically reacting lipids (e.g., vegetable oil, animal fat, and tallow) with an alcohol producing fatty acid esters. Biodiesel is meant to be used in standard diesel engines and is thus distinct from the vegetable and waste oils used to fuel converted diesel engines. Biodiesel can be used alone, or blended with petro diesel.
- **Solar power** - Harnessing the sun's power is another alternative to powering your home. Consider adding solar preparedness supplies to your power options. There are a host of solar products that can make your life far more convenient during an emergency. Consider doing some research on solar ovens, solar lamps, solar powered lights and lanterns, water heaters, well pumps and even farm equipment. The benefit to solar power is that you have an unlimited source of fuel beaming down on you during the better part of the year.

HOW MUCH FUEL SHOULD YOU STORE FOR A DISASTER?

The answer of how much fuel to store is largely dependent on what the fuel will be used for during an emergency and how long you predict the disaster might last.

If you wanted to only run a generator with gasoline to power your home and appliances during the day, plan on using 1-2 gallons of fuel per hour. In a 72-hour emergency where you are reliant on yourself to provide power, plan on needing a minimum of 48 gallons of fuel. Some generators run on alternate fuels. You can find diesel, biodiesel, propane and natural gas generators as well.

Those who live in apartments or duplexes will probably not be allowed to store fuel in or around the buildings because of the close living proximity to others. That said, if your apartment has a fireplace, you can store large amounts of wood and set it on the balcony. Fuel dealers in your local area can tell you about the EPA and regulatory issues associated with storing fuel in a tank on your property. Contact them for this information as well as a host of other useful information about fuel storage.

PREPS TO BUY:

- Multiple amounts of plastic or metal fuel storage containers
- Seasoned fire wood (ample supply)
- Fuel of choice to run generators, appliances, and to provide electricity for 1-3 month duration (if legally allowed to do so)
- Fuel for cooking (ample supply)
- Alternative cooking sources (a solar oven, Korean cook stove, Volcano Stove, reflector oven, Dutch Oven, Rocket Stove, propane grill or stove)
- Propane (one week supply)
- Long burning jarred candles (unlimited amount)
- Extra wicks for candles (can be purchased at Amazon or EBay)
- Matches

ACTION ITEMS:

1. Read about the different types of fuel and decide which fuel choice(s) will work best for your family.

2. Find an appropriate area outside of the home where the fuel can be stored.

3. Ensure that you rotate your fuel regularly and check to make sure there are no signs of leakage.

SUPPLEMENTAL INFORMATION AND RESOURCES

Making Biodiesel

Materials needed:

- 1 heavy-duty blender that will not be used for food preparation purposes any more. Glass is the best way to go, as the plastic might melt after repeated uses.
- Keep a fire extinguisher and the phone handy.

Ingredients:

- 200 ml (about 6.7 ounces) methanol (caution: methanol can cause blindness. Be careful!)
- 3.5 grams (about .12345 ounces) lye
- 1 liter (about 1.056 US quarts or .264 gallons) oil -- if it's reused, you'll need to filter it and heat it to at least 215 degrees F, to remove any water

Instructions:

Place methanol and lye in blender. Blend. Stop. Blend some more. You have now created sodium methoxide. The sides of the blender should be getting hot. At this point, the mixture can eat through your skin and the fumes are explosive and dangerous to inhale. Don't let that fire extinguisher and telephone get too far out of reach.

Pour vegetable oil in with the sodium methoxide. Blend for 15 minutes. Cheaper blenders can and will fall apart during this process of continuous blending. I like to sing to the mixture right about now. Any good country song will do—something with a good beat. Stop blending and singing after 15 minutes. If done correctly, two layers will form. The bottom layer is glycerin, a by-product of the procedure, and the other layer is biodiesel. The glycerin can be safely composted or made into soap to clean up the mess in the kitchen.

Yield: 1 liter biodiesel

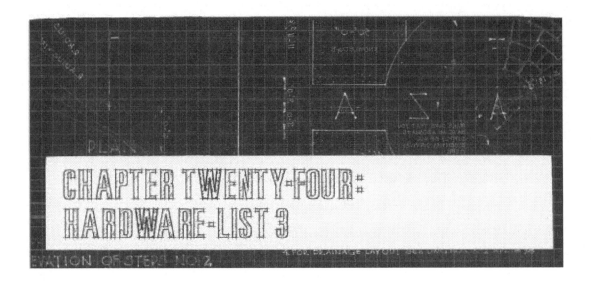

CHAPTER TWENTY-FOUR: HARDWARE-LIST 3

Rebuilding is an inevitable part of putting our lives back together after a disaster. When an emergency occurs, we need tools to build, repair and maintain our homes to make them livable once more. Those who survived the Haitian earthquake know this all too well. We are all familiar with the devastation that occurred there, the lives lost and the reconstruction still taking place.

According to an article in Popular Mechanics[75], relief workers who responded to the disaster were asked to bring their own tools in order to rebuild parts of Haiti. They did so using simple hand tools. The tools used for reconstruction not only created shelters for families and areas for sanitation, but they gave the Haitians hope that one day their island would be restored.

In the backbreaking early stages of rubble removal, simple hand tools played a vital role in transporting and removing debris. Acquiring basic hand tools—shovels, axes and hammers—meet immediate demolition needs and then take on a long-term role once construction resumes.

---

[75] http://www.popularmechanics.com/outdoors/survival/gear/4346954?click=main_sr

Keeping essential tools in your preparedness supplies will help you operate in a non-technological environment. As we move into preparing for longer-term situations, we have to think about what our life will be like during an extended disaster. You must expect to be without power for a longer period of time in such a scenario. Cooking, laundry, sanitation, and a host of other daily activities will have to be done without the convenience of electricity. We will require tools to build, repair, and maintain our homes and gardens in the face of damage or breakdown. Keeping traditional tools on hand can help in this department.

Not only will tools make ideal barter items[76], they are one of your top priorities in creating a survival homestead[77]. During times of grid-down disasters, you will require specific tools to chop firewood, build a shelter, repair damage from the event, and fulfill a host of other important duties. The tools you invest in should be of the "traditional sense" and of good quality. If you buy cheap tools, you will get what you paid for. In the end, you will end up paying more for a replacement tool because the cheap one was not well constructed.

There are a lot of tools that will be required for a survival retreat and we will continue to add to our list in the future. Right now, we are focusing on starting simply. This is a list of the basic tools that are needed for any retreat.

- **Hammers** – There are a lot of specialized hammers but to get started, you need a minimum of two types: a claw hammer for hitting nails, and a ball peen hammer for striking metal.
- **Saws** – Handsaws are cheap and easy to use. For the long term, think about learning to sharpen them by hand.
- **Hacksaw** – Buy plenty of blades, they wear out. For cutting metal objects such as pipes.
- **Screwdrivers** – A complete range of slotted, Phillips and Robertson screwdrivers would be the minimum for me. There are other specialist types such as Torx, but if you've got the big three, you'll be okay in most situations.
- **Allen wrenches** – Also known as hex keys, these are used for the recessed hexagonal headed screws/bolts seen in many applications. A good quality set with a range of sizes.
- **Measuring tape** – At least one of 25' or so. If you can afford a large reel tape of the sort you see surveyors use, that's nice to have as well.
- **Squares** – Two types here, roofing, or framing square, and a smaller combination square.
- **Levels** – Two again, a short one and one that is at least four feet.
- **Bit and brace** – This is what you'll use after your electric drill doesn't run. You might need a little practice using it, and make sure you know how to keep the bits sharp. Try to have a nice variety of lengths and sizes of bits.

---

[76] http://readynutrition.com/resources/the-barter-boom_01122009/

[77] http://readynutrition.com/resources/ten-things-tha-make-a-survival-homestead_20012010/

- **Hand drill** – NOT a bit and brace, but similar in use. Generally a hand cranked, geared drill, you can use it for lighter, tighter, and finer work than the bit and brace.
- **Socket set** – ½" size, with a good variety of sizes and some extras like extensions and a breaker bar.
- **Combination wrenches** – A wrench with an open jaw at one end and a box end on the other, other wrenches in a variety of sizes.
- **Adjustable wrenches** – At least two, and more in a variety of sizes if you can afford it. There's always an off size bolt you'll need these for.
- **Pipe wrenches** – Always in pairs, in larger and smaller sizes.
- **Vise grips** – There probably isn't a more abused tool out there, but it is invaluable for many jobs. Multiple sizes and styles if possible.
- **Pliers** – The traditional style to start, then add needle nose and other types as you see fit. There are dozens of types, but lineman's pliers and fencing pliers are especially useful. Your mileage may vary.
- **Pump pliers** – In two sizes. These are adjustable long handled pliers that come in handy in a variety of situations.
- **Files** – A variety of sizes and types, used for metal work and sharpening.
- **Tin snips** – For cutting sheet metal.
- **Cold chisel** – Used to cut heavier metal.
- **Wire stripper** – Self-explanatory, I would think.
- **Side cutter pliers** – Designed to cut wire, but you'll find other uses the manufacturer never imagined.
- **Wood chisels** – A moderate range of sizes will keep you going in most circumstances.
- **Wood plane** – A general-purpose plane such as a jackplane. Learn how to use it.
- **Bolt cutter** – Also known as a chain cutter, this is a specialized tool, but one I think necessary for certain uses. Buy a large one.
- **Crow bar** – Used in demolition mostly, but pretty handy to have around.
- **Nail puller** – You can use the claw on your hammer, but the specialized tool is easier on wrists and hands if you're salvaging a lot of lumber.
- **Box cutter and blades** – multiple uses.
- **Stapler** – I mean the construction type here. Great for tacking up almost everything. Buy lots of staples.
- **Clamps** - If you have room and money, clamps make building anything easier, especially when you haven't got someone around to 'just hold this here'.
- **Bench vise** – And some bolts to mount it. You'll find many tasks are easier when the components are held securely. It is nearly indispensable when sharpening tools.
- **Pencils** – Having sharpened pencils on hand will assist you in your projects.

Source: Manitoba Prepper's Network[78]

---

[78] http://www.manitobapreppersnetwork.com/

Keep the prepper's rule of multiples in mind when making these tool investments: "Two is one, and one is none." Instead of purchasing two tools, consider investing in spare parts for the tools such as extra blades, sharpening tools and lubricants such as WD-40 or <u>Vaseline</u> to keep these solid investment items up to par.

We will all have to make certain sacrifices during a grid-down scenario. The best way to understand what those sacrifices will be is to practice them periodically. Take a weekend - or even a day - and drill for a grid-down situation to experience what your life would be like during those times. This exercise will help you understand how dependent you may be to certain conveniences. Being without them can help you find solutions now, while extra supplies are as close as your local department store. This can also help you to identify gaps in your preps.

Spend some time getting acquainted with your tool investments and practice using, cleaning, and sharpening these tools.

PREPS TO BUY:

- Work gloves for all members of the family
- Protective eyewear for all members of the family
- Dust masks
- Paracord rope
- Hammers (a claw hammer for hitting nails, and a ball peen hammer used for striking metal)
- Saws (hand saws and hack saws with extra blades)
- Screwdrivers (4-in-1 screwdrivers, Phillips, Robertson)
- Wrench sets (Allen wrenches, pipe wrenches, combination wrenches)
- Adjustable wrench set
- Ax with a sharpening device
- Wedge to help in cutting firewood
- Pliers (an assortment of sizes)
- Socket set
- Vise grips
- Squares (roofing squares and framing squares)
- Levels (short square and a 4-foot level)
- Bit and brace
- Measuring tape
- Pre-sharpened pencils

ACTION ITEMS:

1. If you are not handy with tools, purchase a how-to guide and begin practicing this essential skill. Remember, you only have to be 10% smarter than the tool to get it to work.

2. Simulate a grid-down scenario in your home and practice what life will be like without the modern conveniences we are dependent on today.

SUPPLEMENTAL INFORMATION AND RESOURCES

The 50 Tools and Supplies Used to Rebuild Haiti

1. Round point and square nose shovels, preferably heavy-duty variety with extra-long blade socket
2. Pick axe
3. Pulaski axe
4. Rig builder's hatchet
5. Axe
6. Bow saw
7. 24-oz. framing hammer
8. Sledge hammer
9. Digging bars, preferably both pointed and chisel tip varieties
10. Crow bars
11. Leather or synthetic work gloves
12. Protective eye wear
13. Hard hats
14. Dust masks
15. Contractor-grade wheel barrows
16. Bolt cutters
17. Large-diameter heavy-duty weatherproof rope; small-diameter light-duty line
18. Rope hoist/pulley, minimum 250-lb. capacity
19. Folding knife
20. Rotary hammer and bits
21. Hammer drill and bits
22. Reciprocating saw and bi-metal blades
23. Chainsaw (with necessary tools and spare parts: gas cans, funnel, spare spark plug, bar and chain oil, gasoline, chain with carbide-tipped teeth, chainsaw chaps, chainsaw gloves)
24. Gas-engine driven welder/generator and selection of stick electrodes and accessories (welding mask, gloves, welding hammer, C clamps)
25. Right angle grinders and spare grinding wheels
26. Portable concrete mixer, bags of ready-to-mix concrete
27. Basic set of concrete and brick/block mason's tools, rock-working tools: float, trowel, brick/block trowels, plumb bob, brick set, mason's level, jointer, stone tracer, stone chisel
28. Simple optical level, such as a builder's level or transit

29. Basic electrician's tool kit (Haiti uses 110-volt power, the same as North America): side-cutting pliers, diagonal pliers, needle-nose pliers, electrician's multi-tool wire stripper/screw cutter, solenoid voltage tester, fork meter, and spare AA batteries.
30. Metric/SAE tap and die set
31. Kerosene and kerosene lanterns, waterproof matches
32. Charcoal and charcoal grills
33. Chlorine bleach for water disinfection, Lifestraws or similar filtration tools, and refillable water bottles
34. Anti-bacterial soap, shop towels, and toilet paper.
35. 1/2-inch exterior-grade plywood, which has the structural stability to help frame out a building's wall.
36. 2 x 4 x 8 lumber by the pallet
37. 8-d common nails
38. 12-d and 16-d common nails
39. Blue tarps in various sizes (5 x 7, 10 x 10, 12 x 20)
40. 6-mil plastic sheet, roll
41. 5-gallon plastic buckets
42. Self-stick roll roofing
43. 8-point crosscut saw
44. Carpenter's pencil
45. Carpenter's square
46. Framing hammers and carpenter's hammers—smaller sizes for various family members, in addition to the 24-ounce tool above
47. 25-foot Metric/English tape rule
48. Bit Brace and a set of solid-center auger bits, ¼ inch through 1 inch
49. Utility knife, spare blades
50. High-tension hacksaw and selection of spare blades

Source: Popular Mechanics

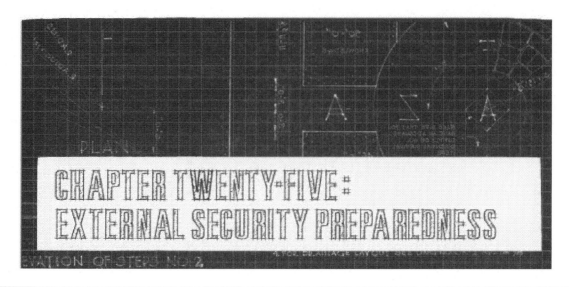

CHAPTER TWENTY-FIVE:: EXTERNAL SECURITY PREPAREDNESS

The narrative of those early, chaotic days — built largely on rumors and half-baked anecdotes — quickly hardened into a kind of ugly consensus: poor blacks and looters were murdering innocents and terrorizing whoever crossed their path in the dark, unprotected city.

Today, a clearer picture is emerging, and it is an equally ugly one, including white vigilante violence, police killings, official cover-ups and a suffering population far more brutalized than many were willing to believe. Several police officers and a white civilian accused of racially motivated violence have recently been indicted in various cases, and more incidents are coming to light...

"I done seen bodies lay in the streets for weeks," said Malik Rahim, who lives around the corner from Mr. Bell and came to his aid. "I'm not talking about the flooded Ninth Ward; I'm talking about dry Algiers. I watched them become bloated and torn apart by dogs. And they all had bullet wounds."

... The highest-profile case involving the police is the Danziger Bridge shooting in eastern New Orleans, where six days after Katrina, a group of police officers wielding assault rifles and automatic weapons fired on a group of unarmed civilians, wounding a family of four and killing two, including a teenager and a mentally disabled man. The man, Ronald Madison, 40, was shot in the back with a shotgun and then stomped and kicked as he lay dying, according to court papers...

Source: **Rumor to Fact in Tales of Post-Katrina Violence,** _NY Times_

Shortly after Hurricane Katrina struck the Louisiana coast, reports out of New Orleans on September 1st stated that victims of the disaster were being raped and beaten and that fights and fires were out of control, leaving corpses laying in the open as the city descended into anarchy. Emergency responders in the New Orleans area were overwhelmed, and as a result their response time was lapsed.

Furthermore, in places where police did respond, many complained that their 2nd Amendment rights were violated and their guns were seized by authorities. Police officers have since been convicted of looting and violence against the victims of the storm.

Sometimes a "bug-in" scenario is our only choice after a disaster strikes and we must prepare not only for our basic needs, but also for our safety. When the grid goes down, it causes anarchy and chaos amongst the unprepared, so each household should prepare for crime. Looting and home invasions will more than likely be at the forefront of these crime waves and a defensible home will help your family stay safe.

Need and Greed in the Wake of Katrina

Evident is the criminal lawlessness. Hospitals being ransacked. Armed pirates on the prowl. Looters trashing stores. The wanton disregard for human life and property stands as a sobering reminder that, when freed from social constraints and driven by greed the human animal can become both feral and (unlike most other creatures in the animal kingdom) cruel.

...we must not forget that people have been without water, electricity, and sometimes food for almost a week now. Many of these despised looters have lost everything: left homeless, their cars literally flooded in three feet of water, their livelihoods suspended, and little in their bank accounts to fall back on.

Before rushing to blanket judgment, we must be examining our own moral pretensions. The first law of nature is self-protection. I myself would steal bottled water if my children were crying out in thirst and food if they were aching with hunger. Any moral judgment that doesn't place our own sin within its purview is incomplete.

Source: Rev. Forrest Church - Beliefnet[79]

IMPROVE YOUR HOME SECURITY

Most of us recognize that our home security needs to be beefed up. In fact, some homes are defensive nightmares due to variables like geographic location, structural design, neighborhood, or city. Because the home will be more vulnerable when the grid goes down (due to electrical alarm systems not working, lapsed emergency response time, etc.), consider

---

[79] http://www.beliefnet.com/News/2005/09/Need-And-Greed-In-Katrinas-Wake.aspx

having some alternative security features for the home. A barking dog is a great deterrent against anyone trying to break in. Properly trained or not, most dogs are territorial and protective.

In an emergency where civil unrest is a problematic issue, criminals look for accessible targets. They will concentrate on vulnerable "easy-pickings" and bypass the more secured areas. This was seen during the Rodney King trial verdict riots in Los Angeles and its suburbs: the only structures that were spared from active looting by large gangs were some stores owned by armed Korean Americans. Bulking up your home security features for the outside can be your first line of defense in preventing any criminals from trying to enter your home.

- **Doors should be sturdy and steel core**. The frame around the door is equally important. (There is only 1" of wood protecting you in normal door locks.) Even the strongest door will not hold up to a determined intruder if it is seated in a flimsy frame. Look for a sturdy steel door-jam. Always use at least 3-inch screws to anchor the components of your door and its frame.
- **Install hardware for a door bar**. Envision the bars reinforcing doors in medieval castles or on barns. By installing brackets into studs on either side of doors to the exterior of the house, you can have a bar that goes across the door from side to side. The bar can be a very heavy piece of wood, or it can be iron or another metal. Unless you are in a high crime neighborhood, this barricade would not be necessary under normal situations. However, during a SHTF scenario, it will make your doors virtually impenetrable without the aid of a battering ram with a team of burly men behind it.
- **Secure your windows**. Particular attention should be paid to windows on the ground floor. Install a sturdy piece of wood, cut to fit so that the window cannot be raised from the outside. Consider coating windows with a shatterproof film. Keep valuables out of sight from the windows. If your door has a window in it, or if it has sidelights, a piece of decorative metal grid work can easily be screwed in over the window, making it impossible for an intruder to break the window and reach through to unlock the door.

MAKE YOUR HOME AN UNINVITING TARGET

Minimize the threat of a home break in or home invasion by adding layers of security (before a disaster is imminent) in order to prevent your home from being a possible hit. Security layers are preventative measures put into place that will advertise to possible intruders to avoid your home altogether. Once these security layers are put into place, follow the suggestions below to zombie-proof your home.

Once you've made the house itself more difficult to penetrate[80], concentrate on making it less appealing to criminals. They do not want to draw attention to themselves and will pass by homes that look more difficult to access.

[80] http://readynutrition.com/resources/home-invasion-preventitive-security-layers-to-protect-the-home_30062010/

Here are some tips to make your home look uninviting to criminals:

1. **Install motion lights around the perimeter of your home**. If they are solar-powered they will also work in a SHTF and grid-down scenario.
2. **Practice defensive landscaping**. Use <u>thorn-bearing plants</u>[81] around your home to make ground floor windows less vulnerable to access.
3. **Install cameras**. Even fake cameras give criminals the feeling they are "being watched" – just make sure they are the kind with a light on them.
4. **Beware of dog**. People who don't have a furry friend can still make use of this tactic by posting signs on their property. Criminals are looking for easy targets – fending off a growling canine can be dangerous for them and also draws attention to them. Often, they will choose a different home to rob based on this factor alone.
5. **Fence your yard**. Enclosing your entire property with a fence is a deterrent. Doorbells and cameras can be installed at the gate, giving you a safer distance from those who come to your home. Moreover, add sturdy locks that cannot be accessed from the other side of the fence. This added layer of distance can make a home invasion-style attack far more difficult to perpetrate. If the top of the fence is "decoratively" spiked, it serves to make it difficult for someone to jump or climb the fence.

If you find yourself in the midst of a disaster and are concerned about displaced persons breaking in, the following suggestions could come in handy, especially if you are planning for Golden Hordes or looters after a widespread disaster.

- Barricade or fortify all points of entry (doors, windows, basement entries, etc.)
- Remove all lawn furniture or objects that can be thrown at windows to gain entry.
- Replace all exterior doors with steel doors (no window glass, only a peep hole to allow viewing of outsiders).
- Use solid hardwood doors with steel frames. Additionally, if time permits, apply screw-in hooks to the door frame/wall and string a crisscross pattern of chain over the door (it won't stop anyone, but the point is to make them stop to deal with the obstacle long enough to get a good, solid sight picture on your target). Lacking the chain, pile obstacles at doorways to make them pause to clear them, again giving you a chance for a good, solid shot.
- Attach thick heavy dead bolt locks to the door. Two or more would be advantageous.
- Locking security bars/grates over all windows (they can be unlocked from the inside to allow escape and allow daylight to come in).
- Motion detectors to turn on outdoor floodlights can frighten away anything from a fox after your chickens to burglars. In a SHTF situation, they can illuminate your enemies outside without giving away your position (like shining a flashlight through the window would).

---

[81] http://readynutrition.com/resources/using-plants-to-secure-the-home_09092010/

- Outdoor security cameras (camouflaged to reduce chances of being detected by raiders) can allow you to see what's going on outside your home, without exposing yourself to any hostile fire.
- Large windows and sliding glass doors should be covered in sheet steel for the best protection. Plywood is more affordable, but less bullet resistant (Nail a tangle of razor wire over the plywood to discourage raiders from trying to work on removing the plywood. A motion detector activating a light/noise maker (alarm), or even a tin can with a handful of pebbles attached to the razor wire, can make enough noise to alert you to someone messing with the razor wire/plywood and allow you to respond accordingly. If sheet steel or plywood isn't available, sandbags can be used to "wall up" the weak points of windows and sliding doors. If sturdy "factory" sandbags aren't available, any burlap or canvas bags full of dirt will do (in a pinch, heavy duty trash bags full of dirt can be used, just make sure the bags aren't too big, or the weight of the dirt may cause them to rip while you are working with them).
- Maintain a low profile and exercise noise discipline. Reduce or eliminate the sounds of generators, chain saws, radios, vehicles, farm animals, etc., as much as possible. Black out your light sources so that they cannot be seen from the outside (Light is a tip off that someone is there). Be aware of smells, such as burning wood smoke from a wood stove can be detected for quite some distance.
- Common sense precautions: make sure you have fire extinguishers and smoke detectors, just in case your dwelling is set on fire.
- Create a safe room for your home.

BUILDING COMMUNITY

Don't forget the importance of community[82] in a SHTF or disaster scenario. To survive a SHTF situation, especially in the city or suburbs, it will take a group effort.

The neighborly way can extend itself far more than just helping a neighbor out in the yard. A group of people banded together with the same goal can defend far more effectively than each family for themselves.

Start now to build a community you can count on:

1. **Get to know your neighbors**. If you don't already know your neighbors well, take the time to be more outgoing. Say hello when you see them outside, compliment their landscaping and do little things to be helpful.

---

[82] http://readynutrition.com/resources/sustainable-in-the-city-community-solidarity-when-the-shtf_20052013/

2. **Have a block party**. Another good way to pull the community together is through social interaction. Organize a block party or host a barbecue as a way to help people become better acquainted. Getting to know your neighbors better is not only a good way to make allies, it's a good way to subtly identify those who might be a problem in an emergency situation.

3. **Organize a neighborhood watch.** If you and your neighbors are already accustomed to looking out for one another, it won't require as much additional organization if disaster strikes.

4. **Make a plan**. If some of your neighbors are like-minded, you might be able to do some advance planning, like choosing the most defensible property as a place to send the children, creating defense strategies for your cul-de-sac or figuring out the best way to patrol your immediate area.

5. **Don't forget the importance of OPSEC**[83]. No matter how much you like your neighbors, never put all your cards on the table. Be sure to keep some things private, like your food stores, back-up weapons, caches and ammo stores. If desperate people have to one day make decisions between their families or their neighbors, you can be certain that their own families will win every time. They cannot take what they do not know about.

---

[83] http://readynutrition.com/resources/mums-the-word-using-opsec-with-preps_21032010/

PREPS TO BUY:

- Reinforced doors and locks.
- Barred windows or European-style security/storm shutters.
- Place <u>thorny bushes or plants</u>[84] around windows or near vulnerable areas of the home.
- Install a peephole and add a bolt and chain to the door.
- Infrared (IR) floodlights to illuminate the property (these can be motion-sensor activated).
- Solar garden lighting can also be an inexpensive way to illuminate areas outside the home.
- Fence the entire property, if it is not done so already. Consider adding a gate at the front of the driveway that has spikes at the top to prevent someone from jumping over the fence.
- Cameras placed strategically around the home and near the entry points of the home can also deflect an intruder.
- Create a safe room or vault to which a family can retreat to evade their attackers.
- Buy a gun and know how to use it.

ACTION ITEMS:

1. Walk around the perimeter of your home and see where the vulnerable areas are. Make necessary changes to the outside of the home by bulking up on <u>security layers</u>[85].

2. Contact a security expert or friend in the police department and see if they can provide you with additional advice.

3. If it is a good fit with your family, look into purchasing a firearm or going to a concealed handgun course.

4. Create a neighborhood watch program.

---

[84] http://readynutrition.com/resources/using-plants-to-secure-the-home_09092010/

[85] http://readynutrition.com/resources/home-invasion-preventitive-security-layers-to-protect-the-home_30062010/

SUPPLEMENTAL INFORMATION AND RESOURCES

Inside the Mind of a Looter

If you're a law-abiding citizen I suggest you don't read this section. In some historical instances extraordinary measures have been taken against looters during times of crisis. It's not uncommon in some countries for looters to be shot, either by police, army, or business owners. Some governments will justify the shooting of looters with the excuse of "preventing further damage to the economy". I suggest you get out of countries that value the economy over your life.

Warnings aside... Let's get down to business!

What is Looting?

Looting is essentially the act of stealing goods during a catastrophe, riot, war, or natural disaster and can also be referred to as sacking, plundering or pillaging. Looting is almost always opportunistic and usually occurs during a collapse in authority.

Looting can be justified in many ways. Some people may feel that if the goods are not stolen, they will be wasted. Another common belief is that if you don't steal the goods, they will be stolen by someone else. In the aftermath of a large disaster, these beliefs both hold credence and are good reasons for you to be looting!

Preparing

As with any endeavor, preparation is the key to success. In order to take optimal advantage of a disaster and loot effectively you'll want to get several things handled ahead of time. The next few pages will cover all the information you need to become a master looter.

Make a Looting Kit

There are a few items that will make looting a lot easier. You'll want to keep these items ready and on hand for when shit hits the fan. They should be kept together in the location for easy access so you just pick them up and go when it's time.

Crow bar

The ultimate urban survival tool! A nice, heavy crowbar can be used to break into stores, clear your way through rubble and it can be used as a weapon! Don't underestimate the crowbar. There are a million things you can do with a crowbar, just use your imagination.

Bump keys

These are keys that have been ground down in such a way that they can be used to open almost any lock. Bump keys are used by locksmiths and they're relatively easy to use. A crowbar will get you through any door or window but a bump key will get you through without making a mess.

Laundry bag

A strong, large drawstring bag is a definite must for looting. Laundry bags are great for the purpose of looting. They have a large carrying capacity and when empty they can be folded to fit in your pocket. You can always go for a large backpack, duffle bag or rucksack but they're cumbersome, expensive and made for looks more than anything else.

A dollar coin or quarter

You may be wondering... a dollar coin or quarter? What the hell for? Well the answer may be a lot simpler then you imagine. The coin is for a shopping cart! Just make sure you get one before the other looters! If you don't want to use a coin, you can always use the crowbar to break the chains holding them together.

Flash light / Lantern

It's very likely that if the situation permits looting, the power is probably out. Good luck getting over fallen shelves and getting food in the dark. Looting with one hand will also be difficult but there are a few methods around that. I suggest placing the lantern or flash light in the shopping cart, get a headlamp, or just bring someone along to shine the light and push the cart.

Make a Looting Team

Find several friends or family members and make a plan! It's all about leverage, you can get a lot more done if you work as team. Get everyone together in a room and discuss a plan of action. Here are the questions you'll want to have answered:

- Under what circumstances will looting take place?
- Where will the goods be kept?
- Who has a vehicle for transportation?
- What are the best locations for looting?
- Should each individual go to a different store?
- Should everyone go as team?
- What goods have priority?

If each person focuses on acquiring a certain type of item, you'll collectively save a lot of time and effort. What I mean by this is that one person will collect water filters, one person will collect rice and beans, and the other person will collect fuel. That's just an example and should be customized to fit your team needs.

Mapping and Creating a List of Target Addresses

Get a detailed map of your city and mark off important looting locations. Make a legend with symbols to represent different types of locations, for instance, use a circle for food stores, triangles for hunting/outdoor stores, squares for hospitals and pharmacies etc. A good resource for finding addresses and locations is Google maps, Just type in a store name and Google will give you all the addresses for that store in your area. Copy and paste the results into a .txt file and print it out for future use. This map is extremely important and should be kept in a safe area. The map should be copied and distributed among friends and family. Here's a list of some locations to keep in mind:

- Hospitals
- Restaurants
- Grocery stores
- Large stores and warehouses
- Police stations
- Fire stations
- Factories

- Shipyards
- Pharmacies
- Liquor stores
- Shopping malls
- Hotels
- Schools
- Sporting goods stores
- Outdoor living stores

- Garden stores
- Hardware stores
- Military / Armory bases
- Gas stations
- Airports
- Shipping container sites

What to Loot

Some items are important to loot and some aren't. A wide screen TV for instance will not contribute to your chances of survival. The highest priority should be on food and water but depending on location, finding water may be a problem. Water is too heavy to move around so instead of looting water bottles the focus should be on buckets and water filters. The value of money may be worthless in a disaster situation and therefore should not be a high priority. The most important items to loot are as follows:

- Personal medicine (if required)
- Water filters and water
- Rice
- Dried lentils, legumes, beans
- Salt
- Oatmeal
- Whole wheat flour
- Sugar
- Cooking oil

- Coffee
- Money (preferably in change)
- Alcohol
- Cigarettes
- Energy bars
- Kool-aid/ electrolytes
- Fuel/oil

Places to Avoid

The family run corner stores should be avoided as the owners actually have an interest in the store. The best historical example to illustrate this point occurred during the LA riots... remember Korea town? Go for the super stores as the employees could care less about you looting (they have no vested interest in the store).

Looting When Shit Hits the Fan

You have a plan and you know what to do but what happens next?

It's my personal belief that violence will not break out in the first stages of a disaster since food and supplies are still in relative abundance and people have what they need to survive. This has been proven during hurricane Katrina and many other disasters. The first few weeks of a disaster should be spent looting and acquiring resources. Everyone in your team should loot the area and acquire as much as a possible. It's only after several weeks of looting that gangs and groups will have formed and violence will erupt. Fighting will most likely occur over food and resources. All looting from that time on should be executed with extreme caution.

Source: No Bullshit Survival

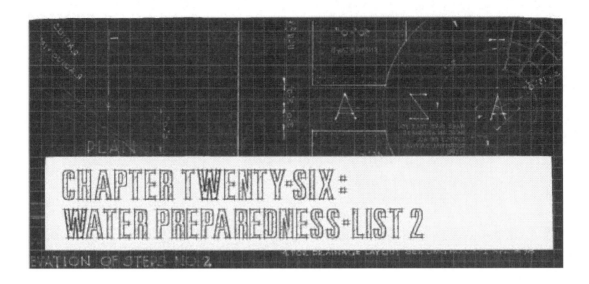

CHAPTER TWENTY-SIX:
WATER PREPAREDNESS-LIST 2

Rosemene Meristil carries a large pot brimming with water atop her head and gingerly navigates the rocky path to her home. She's knocked on the gate of a neighbor's mansion up the road to ask for *dlo* — water — from their cistern.

Most, like Meristil, are water-dispossessed. Their huts have no taps. They beg or buy their water from private tankers or kiosks that aren't regulated by the government, or they take their chances and drink from pipes emerging from the ancient underground water system.

Meristil steps into the muddy yard beside the family's temporary, two-room stone house and lowers the bucket for today's bathing, cooking and cleaning. She follows the local church pastor's instructions and adds three drops of bleach. Then, when her daughter Lovely returns from school, she calls her over to wash her hands in a bucket of sudsy clothes.

Her family has outlived the earthquake, and the hurricane. Meristil hopes they will survive Haiti's newest deadly threat.

"We're still praying to God to keep cholera away from us," she says.

Rosemene is Haitian Earthquake Victim

Never can enough be said about water purification and quality water sources during an emergency. One of the reasons I am placing so much emphasis on potable water is because improper drinking water is one of the leading causes of death in third-world countries. Mentioned in a previous chapter on this subject, it is also one of the four most likely ways to die in a SHTF scenario. Not only must we have water to drink, we must also have clean water on hand for cooking, cleaning ourselves and ensuring that our households are properly sanitized.

The foundation of this preparedness program is to use a layered effect for emergency supplies. Likewise, you should do so with your water needs. Have water methods stored for short-term emergency[86] needs as well as prepared for your longer-term needs.

Those who do not have access to their own water sources run the risk of being completely dependent on the city or town municipal water supply. When that supply is consumed or contaminated, emergency contingency plans must be put into place to find another water source. Learning how to be less dependent on the local water supply will ease this burden and, in the process, make you more self-reliant.

Having knowledge on how to harvest water through means of rainwater catchment systems is a great place to begin this path towards self-reliance. Depending on the amount of rainfall and square footage of the roof, you could collect adequate amounts of water from one rainstorm. This could be used to water gardens, feed livestock or store for long-term emergencies.

Ensure that the container you use to collect water did not contain pesticides, chemicals or oils. Some suggested low-cost options are:

- Collapsible water containers or 5-gallon buckets
- Rain harvesting containers or 50-gallon barrels
- Rainwater downspouts routed to water tanks by PVC pipes
- Having knowledge beforehand on where local streams, ponds and rivers are located.

If you plan on collecting a lot of water, get two or three barrels and connect them so they are all part of the same water collection system. This way, you can have hundreds of gallons of water at your disposal. Make sure that you leave the top over the container or a screen to prevent mosquitos from laying eggs. Here's what you need:

- 1 standard 1-inch hose spigot with ¾-in. pipe threads, so you can access water from your rain barrel.
- 1 ¾-inch x ¾-inch coupling
- 1 ¾-inch x ¾-inch bushing

---

[86] http://readynutrition.com/resources/5-methods-to-have-water-stored-for-emergencies_18092013/

- 1 ¾-inch pipe thread with a 1-inch hose adapter
- 1 ¾-inch lock nut
- 4 metal washers
- 1 roll Teflon thread tape
- 1 tube silicone caulk
- 1 "S"-shaped aluminum downspout elbow, to direct water from your downspout to your rain barrel
- 1 piece of aluminum window screen, to keep leaves, bugs and other materials out of your water
- 4-6 concrete blocks

In addition to knowing how to harvest water, ensure you know how to appropriately treat it to make it safe for consumption.

Store Your Water for a Rainy Day

- Before you start, conserve, conserve, conserve. Cutting your water usage will reduce the size of tank you need and save you money.
- Remember – water is very heavy. (i.e., 500 gallons weighs over 2 tons!)
- Make sure the tank is easy to access and maintain.
- Tank should be opaque or darker, either upon purchase or painted later, to inhibit algae growth.
- For potable systems, storage tanks must never have been used to store toxic materials.
- Tanks must be covered and vents screened to discourage mosquito breeding.
- Tanks used for potable systems must be accessible for cleaning.
- Install first-flush and screening devices prior to water reaching the tanks to keep it as fresh and clean as possible.
- Keep tops of tanks free of debris to make it harder for animals to reach the top of the tank.
- Buried tanks should be located in well-drained soil and location.
- Water weighs about 8 pounds per gallon so plan your pad, if any, before installing your tank.
- Plan where storage tank overflow should be piped or directed to. Keep it away from underneath your holding tank to prevent pad erosion and to keep animals away.
- Be prepared. Keep some alternative water treatment sources on hand in case of a water shortage and begin learning ways to set yourself apart from those who are dependent on local water supply.

Water is a finite resource and essential to life. Learning to be more self-reliant and creating a water supply to depend on if a water shortage occurs is a proactive approach to dealing with this pressing issue. Ensure that your family has the water they need to maintain health and if possible, to perform daily tasks.

PREPS TO BUY:

- Collapsible water containers or 5-gallon buckets
- Rain harvesting containers or 50-gallon barrels
- Rainwater downspouts routed to water tanks by PVC pipes
- Begin investing in long-term water storage containers and the equipment that goes along with it.
- Tarps for rain collection or solar stills
- Resources about long-term water supply and storage.

ACTION ITEMS:

1. Look at your local jurisdiction to determine if you can harvest rainwater.

2. Ensure that you have water purification systems for the home and bug-out bag. This gives you a back-up plan for your back-up.

3. Start practicing water conservation in your home.

4. Learn some alternative and off-grid ways to collect and treat water.

SUPPLEMENTAL INFORMATION AND RESOURCES

Homemade Water Purifier

To avoid water-related illnesses, learn how to filter your water using materials available to you. This is also a great project to do with children to teach them this important skill. When you begin to filter water from lakes, rivers and groundwater, there are 4 steps to keep in mind:

1. Coagulation: removes dirt, metals and other particles suspended in water. Chemicals like Alum are added to the water that form sticky particles called "floc" which attract the dirt particles.

2. Sedimentation: the combined weight of the sediment and chemicals stuck together become heavy and sink to the bottom.

3. Filtration: smaller particles are removed as water passes through a series of filters (sand, gravel, charcoal).

4. Disinfection: to kill bacteria or microorganisms found in the water, a small amount of chlorine is added.

MATERIALS NEEDED:

- 1-liter soda bottles cut in half
- Napkins, cheesecloth or paper towels
- *Gravel
- *Sand
- Activated Filter Carbon (available at pet stores)
- Large water container for dirty water (pitchers or gallon jugs)

- Dirty water (made by adding dirt, twigs, leaves, etc., to water)
- Large waste container (plastic container, thick garbage bag, etc.)
- *Potable Aqua Chlorine Dioxide, water purification drops or tablets
- 2 clean pitchers for filtered water

1. Cut 1-liter soda bottle in half and put top of soda bottle upside-down (similar to a funnel) inside the bottom half. The top half will build the filter, the bottom half will hold the filtered water.
2. Add napkin, cheesecloth or paper towel at the neck of the inverted bottle.
3. Add filtration materials in this sequence:
    a. 1 inch of charcoal
    b. 2 inches sand
    c. 1 inch gravel
    d. 2 inches sand
    e. 1 inch gravel
4. Add unfiltered water and allow water to seep through the filter.
5. For added measure, it is recommended to chemically treat filtered water to kill off any pathogens that were not filtered.

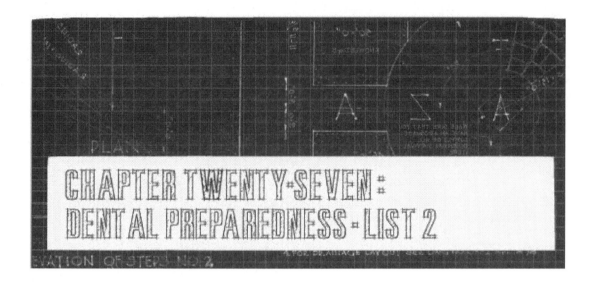

CHAPTER TWENTY-SEVEN: DENTAL PREPAREDNESS - LIST 2

A simple toothache can be fatal.

That is the sobering message a 12-year-old Maryland boy left when, after his dental problems went untreated, he succumbed to a severe brain infection.

Deamonte Driver's life could have been spared if his infected tooth was simply removed...

When a cavity goes untreated for months or years, the decay eats into the center of the tooth, and eventually enters the nerves and blood vessels.

From there, bacteria get into the blood stream and can travel virtually anywhere.

Source: Toothache Leads to Boy's Death, ABC News[87]

---

[87] http://abcnews.go.com/Health/Dental/story?id=2925584&page=1#.UKuP-4edPmQ

In Chapter 12, dental preparedness was introduced and preventative dental health was stressed. In this chapter, we are taking dental issues to another level… a longer-term level. It is important to remember that your teeth and gums are living body parts that respond to vitamins, minerals, and fatty acids just as your skin, hair, muscles and organs do.

We must do all that we can do to keep them healthy. When teeth do not get the proper amounts of vitamins[88] and nutrients[89], their overall health diminishes.

10 FOODS THAT ARE HEALTHY FOR THE TEETH

Did you know there are foods and beverages that are not only nutritious, but also good externally for the teeth and gums? Having access to some of these items during short and long-term emergencies can be beneficial to your overall health as well as to your teeth.

1. Green tea: It contains polyphenols, antioxidant plant compounds that prevent plaque from adhering to your teeth and help reduce your chances of developing cavities and gum disease. Tea also has potential for reducing bad breath because it inhibits the growth of the bacteria that cause the odor.

2. Milk and yogurt
Unsweetened yogurt and milk are good for your teeth. Because yogurt has low acidity, the gradual wearing away of the teeth (also called dental erosion) is lessened. In addition, yogurt is low in sugar, which means less dental decay, too. As we all know, calcium is the main component of teeth and bones, and dairy is a good source of this essential mineral.

3. Cheese
Cheese is low in carbohydrates and has a high calcium and phosphate content that provides important benefits for your healthy teeth. It helps balance your mouth's pH, preserves and rebuilds tooth enamel, produces saliva, kills the bacteria that cause cavities and gum disease. Cheese also is high in calcium.

4. Fruits
Different fruits such as apples, strawberries, and citrus fruits (especially kiwis) contain a lot of vitamin C. It is considered the cement that holds all of your cells together. Just as it is vital for your skin, it is equally as important for the health of your gum tissue. If you don't get enough vitamin C, research shows that the collagen network in your gums can break down, making your gums tender and more susceptible to the bacteria that cause periodontal disease.

---

[88] http://readynutrition.com/resources/shtf-survival-7-vitamins-that-help-prevent-dental-emergencies_05072011/

[89] http://readynutrition.com/resources/top-10-foods-that-naturally-clean-teeth_27102011/

5. Vegetables

Pumpkin, carrots, sweet potato, and broccoli are full of vitamin A. This vitamin is absolutely necessary for the formation of tooth enamel. Apart from that, crunchy vegetables cleanse and stimulate your gums, making them healthy.

6. Onions

This vegetable contains powerful antibacterial sulfur compounds. Tests showed that onions kill various types of bacteria. Researchers indicate that they are most powerful when eaten freshly peeled and raw. It may be not so tasty, but good teeth are guaranteed!

7. Celery

This food protects your teeth through extra chewing. It produces plenty of saliva, which neutralizes different bacteria that causes cavities. Additionally, celery massages gums and cleans between teeth, keeping them healthy and clean.

8. Sesame seeds

Sesame seeds are another way of keeping the teeth healthy by sloughing off plaque and helping build tooth enamel. Sesame seeds are also high in calcium, which helps preserve the bone around your teeth and gums.

9. Animal food

Beef, chicken, turkey, eggs – all of them contain phosphorous. Calcium, with the help of vitamin D and phosphorous, creates our bone system. These elements keep teeth stronger and healthier by protecting them from teeth decay.

10. Water

Healthy water cleanses the mouth, allowing the saliva to work wonders by depositing essential minerals back into the weakened teeth. Drinking water keeps gums hydrated and helps wash away trapped food particles that decompose in the mouth and cause bad breath.

(Source: World Dental.Org)[90]

Most Common Dental Emergencies

Since our goal is to create an all-encompassing preparedness supply, knowing what the most likely scenarios are, and planning for them is better than going into the situation blindly. The most common types of dental emergencies to prepare for are:

- Toothache
- Swollen jaw
- Dental injuries
- Prolonged bleeding after an extraction
- Painful jaw
- Painful erupting tooth
- Cold Sores, Canker Sores, Fever Blisters

Most of these issues can be eradicated through preventative maintenance, so I'll stress again: Keep your teeth healthy.

---

[90] http://worldental.org/nutrition/10-most-healthy-foods-for-teeth/

DEAL WITH EXISTING DENTAL ISSUES BEFORE A DISASTER STRIKES

Preventative dental health is the best type of oral care you can give your teeth and gums. Schedule regular check-ups with your dentist to keep your oral health up to par. You don't want to be dealing with any existing dental problems during a long-term emergency.

DENTAL CARE ALTERNATIVES

In the midst of an emergency, dentist appointments will be hard to come by. Therefore, it's important to learn some alternative approaches to keeping your teeth and gums in top shape.

Eventually, your disaster supply of toothpaste and toothbrushes may run out. Having supplies and knowledge about natural alternatives to turn to during longer-term emergencies will help keep you thriving.

Chew sticks - Traditional people the world over use natural toothbrushes made from healing plants. These primitive twig "brushes" actually work quite well, and provide a natural-bristle, disposable brush with healing herbs already incorporated right into the plant. People would chew on the tip of a twig to make it spread out into several small strands. They would then use it in the same way that a toothbrush is used. If this is the only option to brush your teeth, look for twigs that contain oils to help stimulate blood circulation, tannins that tighten and cleanse gum tissue, and other materials, such as vitamin C, which maintain healthy gums. Twigs from bay, neem, eucalyptus, oak, fir, and juniper trees are good choices for making primitive toothbrushes.

Salts - Salt is a multipurpose item that every prepper should have a good supply of. In the case of dental health, it is a mild cleanser that can be used multiple times daily or as a mouthwash to help with bad breath or used as a disinfectant rinse. Salt has natural healing properties, removes plaque, tartar and fights bad breath.

To clean your teeth with salt:

Pulverize salt with a blender or roll it on a kitchen board, then mix one part salt to two parts baking soda.

This combination whitens teeth, helps remove plaque and is healthy for the gums. (Another recipe for cleaning teeth with salt is one teaspoon each of ground sage, baking soda, and table salt.)

Mouthwash: Mix equal parts of salt and baking soda with water for mouthwash that sweetens the breath.

Baking soda - Baking soda is a classic amongst natural teeth cleaning methods, and is harmless. It is very effective in removing stains and killing plaque-causing bacteria, and it also reduces the acids that harm your tooth enamel. Hippocrates recommended a mixture of salt, alum, and vinegar as a mouthwash for preventative measures.

Baking Soda Toothpaste Recipe

Ingredients:

1/2 cup aluminum free baking soda
5 drops peppermint essential oil
2 drops cinnamon or clove essential oil

Mix all ingredients together and use as you would normally for toothpaste.

Essential oils - Incorporate essential oils into your dental preparedness supplies. The oils can function as natural antibacterial and antimicrobial agents, as well as natural cleansers for well-rounded mouth health. Essential oils such as peppermint and spearmint can be mixed with water to make dental rinses too.

Three popular essential oils amongst preppers are:

- **Clove oil** contains eugenol, a natural painkiller and antibacterial. Mix 2 to 3 drops of pure clove oil with 1/4-teaspoon olive oil. Saturate a cotton ball with the mixture and place the cotton ball beside the tooth.
- **Cinnamon oil** - Cinnamon naturally contains antimicrobial and antibacterial properties and can help fight harmful mouth bacteria. Cinnamon bark oil has been known to effectively destroy 21 different types of bacteria. Rinsing with diluted cinnamon oil after you brush your teeth or using toothpaste made from cinnamon oil may help kill harmful bacteria and prevent cavities. Its warming properties will also stimulate the blood circulation in gums. *Note: Using cinnamon oil can cause some irritation and inflammation, so always dilute it first. If you suffer from any inflammation in your mouth, discontinue using cinnamon oil and the symptoms should disappear within 24 hours.*
- **4 thieves oil** – A combination of clove, lemon, cinnamon, eucalyptus, and rosemary, this oil possesses both antimicrobial and antibacterial properties. A few drops of this oil[91] can be used to prevent and treat gum disease. Drops can be applied orally to maintain healthy teeth and reduce cavities, to clean teeth and be used as an effective mouthwash, or applied to gums and teeth for pain relief from toothaches.

If you are faced with swollen gums, nightly gum packs made from herbs or herbal infused oils rolled in gauze can be tucked into the corners of the mouth. In Ayurvedic medicine, a

---

[91] http://readynutrition.com/resources/antiviral-germacide-could-be-the-new-alternative-for-flu-shots_21022010/

combination of turmeric, aloe, willow bark, vitamin E, and powdered alum can help relieve pain and swelling. If this regimen is regularly used and followed with a healthy diet and vitamin supplements, it can reduce symptoms significantly.

Hydrogen peroxide 3% - This product assists in healing canker sores, helps kill off bacteria living in the mouth, and fights gingivitis. There is conflicting information about the abrasiveness of hydrogen peroxide on teeth, so to be on the safe side, dilute this product with water if you decide to use it in your mouth.

A mouth rinse can be made by mixing equal parts of water and a 3% solution of hydrogen peroxide. This mouth rinse should be swished (not swallowed) around the entire mouth for 15-30 seconds. Using the diluted mouthwash and then following it with your normal brushing regimen will thoroughly clean the mouth and teeth, as well as kill off harmful bacteria. Don't limit using hydrogen peroxide to inside your mouth. Use it to clean your toothbrush after use to kill off any bacteria that may still remain.

Water - This is the most basic you can get for cleaning your teeth. Brushing your teeth with water may not have any healing properties, but it will at least get any residual food off of your teeth. And anything is better than nothing at all.

To conclude, without our normal dental items being readily available to us during a long-term emergency, we may have to fall upon more natural approaches to dental health. Having supplies and possessing knowledge on natural alternatives to maintain healthy teeth and gums will prevent and may control any current issues from exacerbating.

Also, if you plan to have any elderly family members staying with you during a short or long-term disaster, do not forget to anticipate their dental needs.

Having some dental supplies to rely on during short-or long-term emergencies is vital to your preparedness plan. Your emergency dental supplies should be all encompassing with regard to multiple dental emergency resources, first aid supplies, vitamins, pain relief, anti-inflammatory needs, and antibiotics.

PREPS TO BUY:

Many items on this supply list were recommended by Dr. Bones and Nurse Amy. I'd also like to recommend their book, The Survival Medicine Handbook[92], as a must-have medical resource.

- Salt (in quantity)
- Baking soda (in quantity)
- Essential oils (in quantity) such as clove oil, cinnamon oil, or 4 thieves oil
- Hydrogen peroxide (3%)
- Toothpaste (in quantity)
- Soft bristled toothbrush (in quantity)
- Dental floss (in quantity)
- Toothpicks (the rounded end type)
- Fluoride rinse (optional, but could come in handy)
- Tweezers
- Instant hot and cold packs (in quantity)
- Dental wax (to place over sensitive areas)
- Dentemp
- Cotton balls (in quantity)
- Gauze pads (in quantity)
- Black teabags (tannic acid in tea is a natural blood clotting agent)
- Activated charcoal
- Suture kit
- Vitamins
- Monofilament or suture "thread"
- Suture needles
- Celox or QuikClot
- Antibiotics
- Ibuprofen or pain reliever
- Rubbing alcohol to sterilize dental tools
- 2 Dental Extractors #150 and #151 (upper bicuspid #150, lower bicuspid #151)
- 1 #301 Dental Elevator all metal
- 1 dental scraper/pick combo all metal
- 1 clove oil (anesthetic for gum and tooth pain, like Anbesol product)
- 2 packs zinc-oxide powder (mixed with clove oil, will make a temp dental filling)
- 1 dental mirror
- 6 pill cups
- 20 cotton swabs (2 per package)

---

[92] http://www.amazon.com/Doom-Bloom-Survival-Medicine-Handbook/dp/0615563236/ref=sr_1_1?ie=UTF8&qid=1353040199&sr=8-1&keywords=The+Doom+and+Bloom%28tm%29+Survival+Medicine+Handbook

- 10 tongue depressors
- 10 Gum Soft-Picks, disposable
- 1 oral analgesic with 20% benzocaine
- Dental resources

ACTION ITEMS:

1. If you haven't done so, get a check-up with your dentist and have any necessary dental work performed as soon as possible.

2. Begin stocking up on vitamins that can help dental health.

3. Download a PDF version of "When There Is No Dentist[93]" by Murray Dickson. Then begin studying this resource to familiarize you with how to provide care.

4. Start changing some bad eating habits (i.e., eliminating sugars, sodas, honey, molasses and junk food from the diet). If you do eat or drink any sugary items, make a habit of brushing your teeth within 30 minutes to remove any sugars left on your teeth. This can significantly reduce cavities.

5. Get in the habit of flossing regularly.

---

[93] http://hesperian.org/10408695.php

SUPPLEMENTAL INFORMATION AND RESOURCES

Vitamins for Dental Health

It's no surprise that the more vitamins and minerals your body is able to absorb, the healthier you will stay. Maintaining a proper diet rich in high protein meats, grains and a combination of fruits and vegetables benefits your overall health.

If a long-term emergency were to occur where your daily vitamin intake suddenly decreased, or you failed to properly care for your teeth because of lack of dental supplies, then your overall health, as well as your teeth could suffer and degrade. Taking vitamins during a long-term emergency will assist in:

- regulating body functions
- maintaining mental alertness
- maintaining good eyesight
- keeping teeth and gums healthy

1. **General Multivitamin**: This basic multivitamin will provide your body with its basic daily vitamin and minerals. Buying the multivitamin for mature adults will give a person increased levels of certain needed minerals that may further improve health.
2. **Vitamin A**: Vitamin A is responsible for maintaining healthy gums. Without it, gum infections do not heal as fast and calculus tends to form more quickly under the gums. Lack of vitamin A is also associated with abnormal bone and tooth formation.
3. **B-Complex Vitamins**: These are also a big player in fighting gum disease. B vitamin deficiencies can make gingivitis more severe and cause sores in the gums, tongue and other soft tissues in the mouth.
4. **Vitamin C**: Without it, your gums become more vulnerable to infection, bleeding, and gum disease. A vitamin C deficiency makes whatever gum issues you have much worse. If you have periodontal disease, a lack of vitamin C increases bleeding and swelling and accelerates destructive effects. Studies have revealed that people who consume less Vitamin C tend to be 25% more likely to suffer from gum disease.
5. **Vitamin D**: This vitamin not only strengthens your immunity against disease, but it also absorbs calcium that is needed for healthy teeth and also assists in keeping the teeth anchored into their sockets. Vitamin D has been shown to reduce gingivitis because of the anti- inflammatory effects of the vitamin.
6. **Calcium**: 99% of the calcium in your body is in your bones and your teeth. Dietary calcium is needed to make sure they're in good shape. It is important to understand that the calcium that is present in bones and teeth is constantly in a state of movement. The calcium gets reabsorbed into the bloodstream if levels are low, and it is put back into bones and teeth when levels are higher. This is why vitamin D is so important because it regulates this entire mechanism. People with low intake of calcium and vitamin C are more likely to suffer from periodontal disease. Children's teeth need calcium to develop properly.

7. **Phosphorus**: Calcium alone cannot take all the credit for proper tooth formation. In fact, about 85% of phosphorus in the body can be found in bones and teeth. It has been found that vitamin D compliments this mineral by boosting its effectiveness.

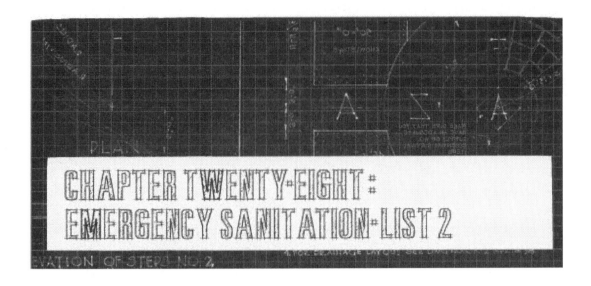

CHAPTER TWENTY-EIGHT: EMERGENCY SANITATION-LIST 2

Billions of gallons of human waste have poured into New York Harbor since Hurricane Sandy hit the region, NBC[94] reports.

The waste is coming from the fifth largest sewage treatment plant in the nation, based in Newark, New Jersey. A 12-ft surge of water flooded the plant that serves some three million people when Sandy struck on October 29.

The Passaic Valley Sewerage Commission plant has pumped more than three billion gallons of untreated or partially treated wastewater into local waterways since then.

Mike DeFrancisci, executive director of the plant, could not say when the mess would stop. Until repairs are made, the plant will continue to dump millions of gallons of partially treated human waste into waters near the Statue of Liberty every day.

The pathogens in partially treated waste are a health hazard and a threat to safety. The New York City Department of Environmental Protection issued a warning to residents to avoid contact with the water.

---

[94] http://www.nbcnewyork.com/news/local/Passaic-Valley-Sewerage-Commission-Newark-Plant-Human-Waste-179571291.html

The contamination described above sets the scene for an epidemic similar to the one that Haiti has faced after a devastating earthquake leveled the island nation in 2010. The reconstruction process was put on hold in order to deal with a massive cholera outbreak, an illness spread from the contamination of food and water. This epidemic, which sickened over half a million people and killed 7,050, was caused by open defecation and could have been avoided if individuals knew where and how to properly dispose of waste.

READY FOR THE SHOCKER?

It is a documented fact that more people die *after* a disaster due to poor sanitation than from the disaster itself. You can do everything right regarding emergency sanitation measures, but that will in no way protect you from all those around you who did not. During times of extended disasters, those who live in close proximity with others will be at the greatest risk for contracting illnesses from unsanitary conditions. Teaming up with those around you to create a community-led sanitation system can assist in avoiding epidemics caused from unsanitary conditions.

Quite simply, wherever humans gather, their waste also accumulates. This creates a perfect storm for E. coli and bacteria to invade nearly everything that you touch, not to mention carrying the risk of infectious disease, particularly to vulnerable groups such as the very young, the elderly, and people suffering from diseases that lower their resistance. Fly infestations can also pose a health risk. If waste is left out in the open, then it will lead to the possibility of epidemics. The following are a few examples of structures that can be built to maintain sanitation during a longer-term disaster:

- Simple pit latrines[95] are the easiest and cheapest way to dispose of waste.
- Ventilated latrine and an odorless earth closet that prevents fly infestations are also good choices. Do research on your own to learn more.
- Decomposing toilets are above ground latrines that are another option and once the waste is decomposed, it can be used in the garden.

Ever hear of humanure[96]? Solid and liquid waste can be decomposed and composted for use in the garden.

---

[95] http://www.who.int/water_sanitation_health/hygiene/emergencies/fs3_4.pdf

[96] http://humanurehandbook.com/instructions.html

Toilet paper is always a concern for emergency preparations. For the lovers of disposable toilet paper, you can purchase larger quantities at super stores or via the internet at www.Amazon.com or at online janitorial supply stores. According to Wikipedia, the average American uses 23.6 rolls of toilet paper per year. In a long-term disaster, toilet paper will be a hard to find luxury item and could be great for bartering[97].

However, that stocking up on thousands of rolls of toilet paper will take up a lot of space. So, while having some on hand for extended emergencies is a good idea, for longer-term scenarios, you may need to get creative.

There are alternatives and you might one day need to begin thinking outside the box. Some off-gridders use rags and thoroughly wash the soiled cloth between uses. However, if you are opposed to this, there are many types of toilet paper alternatives to use in case the toilet paper reserve runs out. Leaves are nature's alternative to toilet paper.

A WORD TO THE WISE

By far, the single most effective way to ensure the health of your family or group members is to wash your hands frequently during disasters. Have ample bars of soap, hand sanitizer and wipes on hand.

HOMEMADE ALTERNATIVES FOR WASHING CLOTHES

Toilet Paper Alternatives

Leaves

Baby wipes (these don't take up a lot of space, so you store a larger amounts)

Phone books and catalogs

Unused coffee filters

Corn cobs (that's right- corn cobs)

Dilapidated kitchen towels or other rags that will not be used for cleaning

Cut strips from a worn sheet

There are many other aspects to sanitation. You must keep your hands and body clean, your home clean, and your clothing clean. Not only is this vital for good health, but it is an important morale booster too.

Learning how to make your own cleaning and washing products is invaluable. Instead of being a slave to store-brands, you can learn to be more self-sustainable as well as save money for the family budget at the same time. As well, learning how to make your own detergents and cleaning products helps you learn how to find multi-functional items that have a long storage life.

---

[97] http://readynutrition.com/resources/the-barter-boom_01122009/

HOMEMADE LAUNDRY RECIPES

- 1 bar of soap – whatever kind your prefer
- 1 box of washing soda – in the laundry detergent aisle of stores. It comes in an Arm and Hammer box and will contain enough for 6 batches.
- 1 box of Borax – optional, but really kicks the cleaning up a notch.
- 5-gallon bucket with lid – or a container that can hold up to 15 liters.
- 3 gallons tap water

Instructions

1. Put about 4 cups of water into a pan on your stove and turn the heat up on high until it's almost boiling. While water is heating up, begin shaving strips off of bar soap into the water until most of the bar of soap is shaved off into the water. Make sure the soap shavings have dissolved into the water.
2. Put three gallons of hot water, or 11 liters or so into the 5-gallon bucket. Then mix in the hot soapy water from step one, stir it for a while, then add 1 cup of the washing soda. Keep stirring it for another minute or two. Add a half-cup of borax if you are still using borax. Stir for another couple of minutes, then allow it to sit overnight.
3. Once the mixture has settled overnight, it will look a pale shade of gelatinous mixture. One measuring cup full of this mixture will be roughly what one would need to do a load of laundry.

3 gallons of this mixture will give you 48 loads of laundry detergent. The cost of this recipe breaks down to 3-cents/per gallon. Not a bad deal, if you ask me.

HOMEMADE FABRIC SOFTENER

- 3 cups of vinegar
- 2 cups hair conditioner
- 6 cups water

Mix it all together and add to washing machine at the proper cycle.

Note - some people only use 1/4-1/2 cup of vinegar as their chosen fabric softener, but the above mentioned is another version.

HOMEMADE STAIN REMOVER

- 1 cup water
- 1/2 cup hydrogen peroxide
- 1/2 cup baking soda
- 1 tablespoon distilled white vinegar

Instructions

1. In a spray bottle, combine all ingredients. Shake well.
2. To use, spray directly on stained clothing and allow solution to set on clothes for 15 minutes. Wash as usual.

SOAP NUTS

Another option that can be used for laundry or body care is soap nuts[98], or soap berries. These are the dried fruit of the Sapindus tree that contains a natural soap ingredient called saponin. This dried fruit has a multitude of other uses, and even has some anti-inflammatory and anti-microbial properties.

Soap nuts can be used whole or made into liquid form to clean the body and hair. They can be used on pets and are also a gentle but effective mosquito repellant for use on children and pets. The best part is they can be reused several times and then composted[99]. A liquid detergent can be made from soap nuts and essential oils can be added to make the formula more powerful or water can be added to dilute the formula for other uses. See the directions below.

They also work as a natural fabric softener (which is great for line drying) and they are gentle enough to use with septic and gray water systems.

In dried fruit form, soap nuts can last for years as long as they are stored properly and kept away from humid conditions. Soap nuts can be stored along with your other preparedness items in a five-gallon bucket with a lid. While the color of the dried fruit tends to deepen with age, the active ingredients are still at your disposal.

---

[98] http://readynutrition.com/resources/soap-nuts-who-knew_10112011/

[99] http://readynutrition.com/resources/composting-feeds-the-earth_03112009/

Making a Liquid Cleaner from Soap Nuts

To preserve the liquid for washing:

You will need re-sealable and sterilized quart jars and soap nut shells.

Place the equivalent of 7-10 soap nuts in each jar. (It's better to use smaller soap nut pieces). Fill with boiling water but leave a 1/2-inch space at the top. Place the lid on securely.

PRESSURE COOKER: Place the jars in the canner, and process according to manufacturer's instructions for 15 minutes at 10 lbs. of pressure.
Use only canning jars if you use this method.

WATER BATH: Place the filled jars in a large pot of boiling water. Make sure to cover the jar completely. Bring to a rolling boil and set the timer for 30 minutes. Remove jar from boiling water and let cool.

OVEN METHOD: Preheat the oven to 250F. Place 7-10 soap nuts in a clean glass quart jar with a resealable lid. Fill with boiling water but leave 1/2 inch at the top. Place lid on securely. Watch until it starts to bubble and then time it for 30 minutes. Turn off oven and let cool a little. Remove from oven.

HAND SANITIZER

Another multipurpose sanitation product to have in your supplies is hand sanitizer. It has a myriad of uses other than keeping your hands clean.

- Add salt to hand sanitizers to scrub dishes
- Use to sanitize food preparation surfaces
- Clean minor wounds (ouch!)
- Clean glass
- Add to cotton balls to start a fire
- Use when cleaning guns to remove gunpowder residue
- Use in place of Sterno gel
- Use to treat acne

Other uses include:

- Hand soap
- Dishwasher soap
- Window cleaner
- All-purpose cleaner
- Shampoo
- Pest and mosquito repellant
- Carpet cleaner
- Pet shampoo
- Lice remover
- Jewelry cleaner

PREPS TO BUY:

- Toilet paper for two weeks or longer
- Cat litter
- Bleach
- 5-gallon bucket
- Janitor's bucket with mop wringer
- Clothespins
- Laundry plunger (optional)
- Wash boards (optional)
- 2 large storage bins to do laundry
- Women's sanitary needs[100] (in bulk)
- Soap or a multipurpose alternative (in bulk)
- Hand sanitizer (in bulk)
- Mesh screening to use for long-term latrine
- Space bags to store toilet paper
- Peroxide (in bulk)
- Baking soda (in bulk)

ACTION ITEMS:

1. Ensure that you have sanitary items for all members of the family, including women, children, and the elderly.

2. If you have not done so, create a sanitation kit[101] for the home.

3. Print the Hesperian health guide on sanitation and add it to your emergency manual[102].

---

[100] http://readynutrition.com/resources/shtf-survival-womens-health_13012011/

[101] http://readynutrition.com/resources/what-to-do-when-the-sanitation-hits-the-fan_22122010/

[102] http://readynutrition.com/resources/good-manuals-every-family-should-have-one_22102009/

SUPPLEMENTAL INFORMATION AND RESOURCES

No Boys Allowed: Female SHTF Preparations

Clearly, the first plan of attack is to stockpile sanitary napkins and tampons by the truckload. During a stressful situation, you'll want to make things easier on yourself and you'll want to keep things as familiar as possible.

However, in the event of a long-term survival situation, you will require items that (1) can be reused indefinitely and (2) don't require disposal.

Sanitary Napkin Solutions

Before the 20th Century, most women used cloth pads or "rags" during their menstruation. Because disposable pads do not biodegrade very quickly, a good measure would be to have cloth pads at your disposal.

Cloth pads can be purchased from a variety of online sites. Many of them are made of organic cotton and they are designed with "wings" much like the disposable pads we buy from the pharmacy. Many of them are decorated with fanciful designs. Two sources for reusable cloth sanitary napkins are Luna Pads or Glad Rags.

A more budget-friendly option is to make your cloth napkins. A pattern for homemade cloth feminine napkins can easily be found online.

To make washing your cloth pads easier, it is recommended that you rinse them in cold water immediately. (It's best if you can soak them in water with some white vinegar and peroxide.) They can later be washed by machine or by hand, using your regular detergent. Avoid the use of fabric softener, as this can make the pads less absorbent. If your pads are purchased, some manufacturers recommend that you do not use chlorine bleach when washing the pads.

Internal Protection

Many women prefer tampons to pads. If the corner drugstore is no longer an option, there are some options that are equivalent to tampons as far as convenience and discretion.

The Diva Cup is a reusable silicone cup that is inserted into the lower vagina. It simply collects the flow. It is removed, emptied and reinserted. It can be worn for up to 12 hours at a time. You can locate sellers of the Diva Cup here.

Another option is the use of natural sea sponges. Many women currently use sea sponges as an alternative to tampons (which are laced with dioxin, synthetic fibers and pesticide-soaked cotton).

When purchasing sea sponges, don't buy the ones advertised as sea sponge tampons. Instead, pay a fraction of the cost and get them at your cosmetics counter. They are identical. Select sponges that are dense in texture and very firm when you squeeze them.

Before using your sponge for the first time, sterilize it by soaking it in hydrogen peroxide. Air-dry thoroughly.

To use your sponge, dampen it and then squeeze out as much water as possible. Insert the sponge as you would a tampon. Remove, rinse thoroughly, and reinsert as necessary. At the end of your cycle, again sterilize the sponge using hydrogen peroxide, then air-dry completely.

A sponge will last up to 6 months and can be composted afterwards, as it is easily biodegradable. You can store many years' worth of sponges in the same amount of space as a two-month supply of disposable tampons.

It's best to prepare with a variety of feminine hygiene options. Also, think ahead if you have daughters that are not yet menstruating. It's only a matter of time until they will also need supplies.

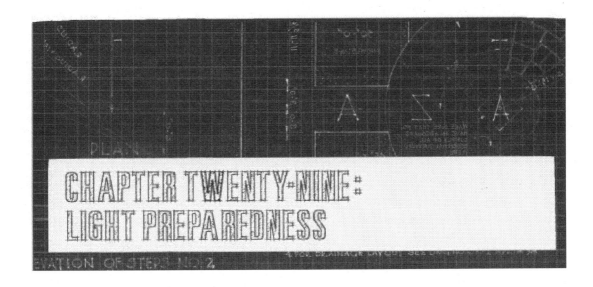

CHAPTER TWENTY-NINE:
LIGHT PREPAREDNESS

It would be dark soon at the Coney Island Houses, the fourth night without power, elevators and water [after Hurricane Sandy struck New York City].

Another night of trips up and down pitch-black staircases, lighted by shaky flashlights and candles.

Another night of retreating from the dark.

On the second floor of Building 4, an administrative assistant named Santiago, 43, who was sharing her apartment with five relatives, ran through a mental checklist. Turn the oven on for heat. Finish errands, like fetching water for the toilet, before the light fades.

"We don't dare throw out garbage at night," she said. "We make sure everything's done."

Elsewhere in the building, Sandra Leon, 35, a mother of two, kept an eye on her door fearing another attempted break-in.

Source: NY Times[103]

---

[103] http://www.nytimes.com/2012/11/03/nyregion/in-public-housing-after-hurricane-sandy-fear-misery-and-heroism.html?_r=0

Facing a disaster is a frightening ordeal. But facing a disaster in the dark can be terrifying.

Many do not anticipate the sheer amount of light sources needed for a standard power-outage, let alone for a long-term emergency. In a previous chapter, while we were still preparing for short-term disasters, it was suggested to stock up on flashlights, candles, and matches for a short-term disaster to get by until the electricity comes back on. However, if you find yourself in an emergency where the lights go out permanently, being able to sustain yourself for a longer-term scenario requires a more permanent means of producing light.

Before we get into producing light, it's important to note that some people worry about attracting unwelcome attention by having light in the home during a longer-term emergency. Further, powering up a loud generator to turn the lights on may also draw unwelcome attention to the homestead. If you are concerned with this issue, take special precautions ahead of time. Invest in blackout curtains to provide a barrier and keep the light from spilling out.

Plan to have a means of emergency light for not only getting around in the dark, but for essential rooms that will need to be illuminated. In particular, rooms used for medical/triage reasons will need ample light to help treat any serious medical issues that occur, especially at night. The kitchen and bathroom will also require illumination.

EMERGENCY LIGHT SOURCES

Developing your survival skills, investing in preparedness supplies, and gaining know-how can help put you ahead in the survival game. Here are a few suggestions of emergency light sources to invest in for a longer-term disaster:

- **Candles** – It is recommended to have candles for an emergency. Many people worry that certain types of candles and waxes are best in this type of situation. But candles are candles, so save yourself some money and look for the cheaper varieties. The Catholic style devotional candles range between three and five dollars and may be even cheaper at dollar stores. A case of these candles can be purchased at discount stores for a modest price. Keep in mind that candles do emit carbon monoxide, so ensure that candles are placed in a well-ventilated room. The light the candles emit may also be considered dim compared to other light sources you can find, so numerous candles may be needed to light a room effectively.
- **Solar lighting** – Solar lights are an efficient alternative for emergency lighting. Solar garden lights can be purchased for as low as $1 at the Dollar Store and can be used as a torch (the solar panel/LED top can be unscrewed to be used as a night light), or could be altered to provide overhead lighting. In the morning, take lights out to a sunny area to recharge. Get creative!
  Purchasing solar panels to use to light and power the home is an expensive investment that could pay itself off, especially in a long-term scenario. These panels would be an ideal purchase for those interested in going off-grid. Keep in mind that solar cells are

very fragile, and because of the fragility of solar equipment, it would be wise to invest in replacement parts for any solar materials purchased. Remember: two is one, one is none.

- **Fuel powered light sources** – Gas powered lamps[104] and overhead lights are also available for those interested in a more off-grid solution. Bear in mind that additional fuel[105] will need to be stored in order to provide light. Hurricane lanterns can be purchased at outdoor stores, but can also be found at garage sales or donation centers such as the Salvation Army for a fraction of the cost. Remember to invest in extra parts and fuel for these types of light sources.

- **Rendered animal fats** – If you find yourself with no means of producing light, tallow can be made from rendered animal fats. Note the smell that tallow emits may not be what you expect, but it will do the job it is intended to do (rendered animal fats can also be a means of producing alternative fuel for certain engines).

- **Alternative fuel** – Although having kerosene fuel on hand is a great preparedness item to have to fuel lamps, in a long-term emergency, it is a precious item to that many would want to conserve. Olive oil, Crisco or other types of cooking oil are great options to use in lieu of fuel to create illumination. A few ounces of oil can burn for several hours, so it is also cost effective. Olive oil is 99% pure renewable fuel and does not produce smoke or odor.

Other cooking oils such as canola or corn oil may have the potential to produce smoke and odor, so use caution. According to Mother Earth News, olive oil is much safer to use compared to using candles or kerosene. Because of the high flash point olive oil has, it is not a very flammable material and will stop burning if spilled or knocked over.

- **Recycled food oils** – These would be a great way to make use of what you have on hand. Used cooking oils and even oil packed canned goods can be used to create lighting.

- **Alternative wicks** - In a long-term emergency, you will never have too many wicks. Stock up on this low cost, essential prep item while you still can. Candle-making supply stores will have a large assortment of wicks to choose from. Self-sufficiency stores such as www.Lehmans.com or even Amazon.com can also help. Eventually your wicks will run

---

Alternative Wicks

Make your own wicks out of cotton materials like old towels or even socks. Some alternatives to candle wicks can be:

- Cotton string or twine
- Paper towel
- Torn pieces of cloth
- Shoe lace (with the plastic coating removed)
- Old cotton sock (that is clean) torn into strips
- Cotton towel torn into strips

---

[104] http://www.cottagecraftworks.com/self-sufficient-living-batterygas-powered-lamps-c-42_125_49.html

[105] http://readynutrition.com/resources/the-6-most-popular-types-of-fuel-to-store-for-emergencies_10092013/

out. Keep in mind to find alternative wick materials that do not produce any harmful fumes that could cause any health problems. I like to stick with cotton materials when making wicks.

- **Light from water** – That's right, you can light your home using a clear soda bottle and clean water. The light it emits is comparable to a 50-watt light bulb. Instructions can be found on the Internet.
- **Night vision goggles** – Investing in a pair of night vision goggles would be good not only for perimeter security, but also helpful in other situations where you do not want to draw attention to yourself. The price of night vision tools vary from $250-$500. Night vision scopes are also available for rifles and could be an advantage for hunting. In online reviews, it was mentioned that some service members who used the night vision binoculars have said they prefer the monocular version. Because of the mass manufacturing of this product, ensure that you buy from a reputable dealer.

Generally speaking, the American lifestyle is largely dependent upon the power grid[106]. When the grid goes down, our population's Achilles' heel will be exposed. Our inability to function in a realm without power, coupled with the extremely stressful nature of disasters and emergencies, will be an antagonist for chaos and unwelcome encounters with the unprepared.

How to Make an Orange into a Candle

Step 1: Cut an orange in half and scoop out the flesh, leaving the long piece of white pith in the middle.

Step 2: Fill with olive oil and light the piece of pith.

---

[106] http://readynutrition.com/resources/when-the-grid-goes-down-you-better-be-ready_28102013/

PREPS TO BUY:

The following list is not meant to be comprehensive. Decide which items would benefit your family the most and invest in those. Personally, I believe the more supplies you have, the better. Don't forget that the following would also make good bartering items.

- Long lasting candles
- Hurricane lamps
- Hanging lanterns battery powered, solar and/or gas powered
- Flashlight – hand cranked, solar, battery powered, or LED
- Solar garden lighting
- Light sticks
- Matches and water proof types
- Cigarette lighters
- Strobe light – as a signaling device
- Flash lights and head lamps
- Extra glass mantels for lamps
- Extra candle wicks
- Extra propane or fuel
- Extra batteries for flashlights, lanterns and head lamps
- Solar panels
- Solar chargers
- Battery chargers
- Black out curtains
- Night vision goggles

ACTION ITEMS:

1. Understand your light dependency. Turn the electricity in your home off for 2 days to simulate a lights-out scenario. Take notes along the way to find out what you really need or miss.

2. Ensure that you have flashlights with extra batteries in your bug-out gear, short-term emergency preps, and in your emergency vehicle supplies.

3. Ensure that you have enough light sources to last you through an extended disaster.

4. Look into some non-traditional light sources on the Internet and practice alternative ways of producing light.

SUPPLEMENTAL INFORMATION AND RESOURCES

Canaanite Lamps

The most simplistic and archaic type of lamp is the Canaanite lamp and dates back to 1500 BC-600 BC. This type of lamp is made of terra cotta. Although it isn't the safest type of lamp to walk around with, it would definitely be a good source of light for stationary use. This type of light source demonstrates the simplistic nature of creating a lamp. All that is needed is a vessel, oil or fuel and a wick. When you do not have the normal items on hand to create a lamp, there are many items that can be substituted to make an alternative source of light.

Alternative Vessels - An expensive lantern is not needed to create an emergency lamp. All you really need is a container that can hold oil and will not catch fire. Some items to consider are:

- Glass bottles
- Glass or porcelain bowls
- Used tuna cans or pet food cans
- Fruit peels with the pulp removed and cut in half (citrus fruits work very well).
- Hollowed out potatoes
- Wide-mouth glass jar or recycled glass jars
- Terra cotta containers

Tricks with Wicks

Salt your wick to make it burn longer. To salt your wick, take your cotton twine, put it in a bowl with a little water, and then cover with table salt. Squeeze it dry and let it dry overnight, or until it is no longer damp.

If you need your lamp to emit more light, try using a braided, flat wick (a half inch or narrower), adjusting the way the wire supports this kind of wick by crimping it to accommodate the extra girth.

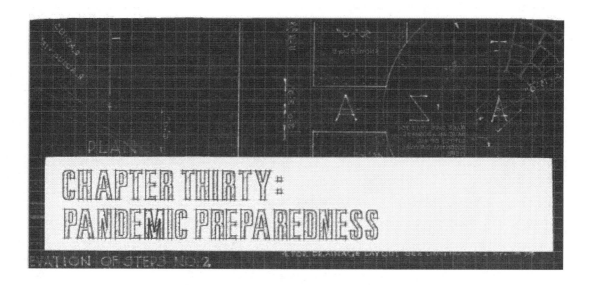

CHAPTER THIRTY: PANDEMIC PREPAREDNESS

There are no exact death tolls for the 1918 Flu Pandemic (which actually came in 3 waves and lasted into well 1919). It was called the "greatest medical holocaust in history." Because of a rare shift of genetic material in the virus, no one had been able to build an immunity to the virus. The death toll was estimated at between 30 million and 50 million people worldwide. It moved so fast that within the first 6 months, 25 million people had caught the "Spanish Flu." More people died in one year of this flu than in the entire 4 years of the medieval "Black Plague." By turning into a vicious form of pneumonia, this strain of influenza killed people, often within hours of the first signs of illness.

The first confirmed outbreak in the United States occurred at an army base in Kansas. Within hours of the first reported illness, dozens of sick soldiers were in the infirmary. Within a week, more than 500 soldiers on that base had fallen ill. Meanwhile, 2 million troops were mobilized to Europe, where they introduced the deadly virus to France, England, Germany and Spain. One ship could not be put out to sea because more than 10,000 soldiers on board were suffering from the virulent strain. More American soldiers died of the Spanish flu than deaths in combat in WWI, but what's more, they carried the flu with them as they shipped out all over the world.

So many people died at once that there was a shortage of morticians, coffins and gravediggers. Morgues were forced to stack bodies like "cordwood' in the hallways and mass graves were dug to try and deal with all of the corpses in an effort to prevent even more health risks. Public health ordinances were created to try to contain the pandemic, to little avail. Gauze masks were distributed, trains required a certificate of health before passengers were allowed to travel, and some towns required such certificates before a person could enter.

There are still no answers as to why this flu mutated and spread so quickly—there are also no answers on how to prevent such a thing from occurring again.

According to the Center for Disease Control[107] (CDC), serious, contagious disease outbreaks can and do happen. The CDC investigates new contagious diseases—averaging one new contagion per year. Given our vast array of transportation systems, modern society causes infectious diseases to spread far more rapidly compared to any other time in recorded history. Further, because pandemics are fast moving, vaccines cannot be created fast enough to be of help.

We need not look any further than the most recent Ebola scare that swept the world into a frenzy. For months, health officials were reporting an increase in cases of Ebola in Africa. The world watched as it quickly spread. Inevitably, the first case of Ebola appeared in America and caused pandemonium for the better part of October 2014. The government was not ready, the hospitals were not prepared, nor were the funeral homes that would have to handle the possibility of massive amounts of Ebola infected bodies. The entire country was guarded, and some families scrambled to acquire pandemic kits, masks and needed supplies before the virus had an opportunity to spread. There were fears of the virus mutating, forced quarantining by government officials, and concerns of closing the border to prevent the spread of this deadly virus. No one was prepared to handle such a deadly virus on a massive scale – not even the CDC. Preparedness experts explained to the public how this event is a perfect example of why one should be prepared—because you never know when an emergency will strike.

PREPARING FOR A PANDEMIC

It is imperative to understand how contagions behave, how quickly they can spread and how important it is to be prepared ahead of time. When an outbreak occurs, those living in close proximity to others (especially in cities with high density populations) will be more at risk. Pregnant women, infants, elderly people, or those with chronic medical conditions are at the highest risk and could be the first of the population to contract the contagious illness. Moreover, schools and daycares, workplaces, and community events are germ-ridden cesspools for attracting unwanted illness and diseases. Studies are finding that sneezes and coughs cause illnesses to travel much farther than originally estimated.

In a novel study by Massachusetts Institute of Technology[108], researchers show that coughs and sneezes have associated gas clouds that keep their potentially infectious droplets aloft over much greater distances.

---

[107] http://www.pandemicflu.gov/news/contagion_outbreakcontrol.html

[108] http://newsoffice.mit.edu/2014/coughs-and-sneezes-float-farther-you-think

This cloud actually enhanced the range and travel length of the smaller droplets, helping them travel farther than was previously thought—particularly the smaller ones, which travel up to 200 times farther than previously estimated. According the study, the fluid droplets expelled in coughs and sneezes are a combination of sizes—ranging from 1 micrometer to 800-900 micrometers that can span the entirety of a room. Therefore, they can penetrate the room and ventilation systems more insidiously. Understanding this phenomenon can help you better prepare your home to prevent airborne viruses from spreading.

PREVENTION PLAYS A ROLE

Preventing the transmission of an illness rests in the hands of not only the individual, but the community as well. Prevention plays a very large role in preparing for a pandemic. There is a lot to be said for preventative measures.

> ### Pandemics are naturally occurring disasters
>
> Pandemic outbreaks are fast moving and vaccines may not be able to stop it. This natural occurring disaster is not one you should take lightly. Not only are our bodies under attack, but our way of life is as well.
>
> Community and individual preparation are critical in regards to prevention.

As a whole, communities should take the necessary steps to be ready for potential challenges before a threat exists. Understand that areas where large numbers of people congregate (i.e., malls, schools, airports, grocery stores) pose the highest risk of spreading the epidemic more quickly. Breakdowns in communications, supply chains, payroll service issues, and healthcare staff shortages should be anticipated when preparing for a pandemic. To assist communities in planning for a pandemic, the federal government has developed a Pandemic Severity Index. This index assists the government in gauging the severity of the epidemic based upon the amount of fatalities. Being familiar with the government's protocols before this type of emergency arises can help put you ahead of the game.

Some of the categories they use for determining their pandemic countermeasures are:

- Covered countermeasures
- Category of disease
- Population
- Time period
- Geographic area
- Means of distribution

Source – flu.gov

If the government sees fit, they can activate pandemic mitigation measures. Some of these measures include the following:

1. Isolation and treatment (as appropriate) with influenza antiviral medications of all persons with confirmed or probable pandemic influenza. Isolation may occur in the home or healthcare setting, depending on the severity of the individual's illness and/or the current capacity of the healthcare infrastructure.
2. Voluntary home quarantine of members of households with confirmed or probable influenza case(s) and consideration of combining this intervention with the prophylactic use of antiviral medications, providing sufficient quantities of effective medications exist and that a feasible means of distributing them is in place.
3. Dismissal of students from schools (including public and private schools, as well as colleges and universities) and school-based activities and closure of childcare programs, coupled with protecting children and teenagers through social distancing in the community to achieve reductions of out-of-school social contacts and community mixing.
4. Use of social distancing measures to reduce contact between adults in the community and workplace, including, for example, cancellation of large public gatherings and alteration of workplace environments and schedules to decrease social density and preserve a healthy workplace to the greatest extent possible without disrupting essential services. Enable institution of workplace leave policies that align incentives and facilitate adherence with the non-pharmaceutical interventions (NPIs) outlined above.

Source: www.flu.gov

Mandatory Quarantines

When there is a concern for dangerous communicable diseases spreading, the CDC activates pandemic mitigation measures. Among these measures are: isolation and quarantines. These are the first steps in protecting the public by preventing exposure to infected persons or to persons who may be infected. Social distancing measures will follow in order to reduce further contact between the community members. Quarantines can last anywhere from days to months depending on the severity of the contagion. Mandatory quarantines are backed up by laws and executive orders. The official CDC website details 'Specific Laws and Regulations Governing the Control of Communicable Diseases,' that even healthy citizens who have no existing symptoms would be forced to adhere to. Additionally, executive orders have been put in place that allows for the "apprehension, detention, or conditional release of individuals to prevent the introduction, transmission, or spread of suspected communicable diseases."

This type of disaster is very unique in that you will not be able to run to the store if your supplies run out. A mandatory quarantine of this nature will require that the roads are clear of anything other than non-essential travel. Further, the shops and stores that you are dependent on will no longer be available; therefore, you need to have everything in place before mitigation measures are activated.

Depending on the severity of the contagion, a quarantine period can last up to 6 weeks. Ensure that your family has enough food and water to sit out an extended event. If you are forced to exit your home, you're going to want to be fully protected, and that includes covering your hands, eyes, nose, and mouth.

Many preparedness experts suggest stocking up on N95 and N100 masks. Understanding the differences in the respirator masks on the market can help keep you and your family safer.

When the National Institute for Occupational Safety and Health (NIOSH) specified there be requirements for different respirator filters, they created three divisions for the filters with differing specifications: N series, R series and P series. Using masks with air-purifying respirators protects by filtering particles out of the air the user is breathing. There are seven classes of filters for NIOSH-approved filtering face piece respirators available at this time.

- N95 – Filters at least 95% of airborne particles. Not resistant to oil.
- Surgical N95 – A NIOSH-approved N95 respirator that has also been cleared by the Food and Drug Administration (FDA) as a surgical mask.
- N99 – Filters at least 99% of airborne particles. Not resistant to oil.
- N100 – Filters at least 99.97% of airborne particles. Not resistant to oil.
- R95 – Filters at least 95% of airborne particles. Somewhat resistant to oil.
- P95 – Filters at least 95% of airborne particles. Strongly resistant to oil.
- P99 – Filters at least 99% of airborne particles. Strongly resistant to oil.
- P100 – Filters at least 99.97% of airborne particles. Strongly resistant to oil.

The difference between the N-series, R-series and P-series of masks has to do with whether or not the mask will be worn in an environment where oils and their vapors can be inhaled. In short, N-series filters are not resistant to oil, R-series filters are resistant to oil, and P-series filters are oil proof.

INDIVIDUAL PREPARATION STARTS AT HOME

Disasters of any kind have the potential to cause grid-down scenarios. In this case, if a pandemic ensues, people will not risk exposing themselves to a deadly contagion just so the public has electricity. If you are serious about protecting yourself from a potential pandemic, prepare to live off grid for up to 6 weeks or longer. Further, plan to bug in and not venture out in the community until the threat has passed.

Being prepared before the masses realize there is a problem will ensure that you can avoid chaos as the hordes run to the store to stock up. The following guidelines can fast track your preparedness and contingency plans.

Bug-In Supplies

Water – Have a stored water supply. Emergency organizations suggest 1 gallon per person for 30 days. If one goes by this suggestion, to have 1 gallon per person per day, a family of 5 will need 35 gallons of water per week. Further, it would be ideal to have some tools to treat water such as a portable filtration system, chemical treatment tablets, etc.

Note: As a backup plan, consider investing in manual water pumps, tarps, rain gutters for the home to collect rainwater and condensation from the ground, trees and bushes. This could save your life!

Food – Have a 30-day supply of shelf-stable foods. You need to assume that electricity could go out, therefore look to foods that do not require refrigeration. Create a menu based around your shelf-stable foods to ensure you have enough food to feed your family. Your menu should be realistic in the sense that it will provide your body with the necessary energy needs. At the very least, plan for 1200 calories per meal. Keep healthy whole grains in mind when adding carbohydrates to your larder.

Sanitation – In a pandemic, everyone will fear going to their jobs and all forms of normal life will be on hold. This includes your trash pick-ups. Have a basic sanitation kit and prepare for the likelihood that toilets won't flush, trash won't be collected and you will be on your own. Keep in mind that when sanitary conditions are not up to par, there is an increase of diseases such as cholera, typhoid and diphtheria. Typically, women and children are the most affected by poor sanitary conditions. Taking proper precautions and stocking up on sanitary items will help eliminate most issues regarding poor sanitation.

Alternative power – It would be advantageous to invest in alternative means of power before the grid goes down. Further, invest in rechargeable batteries, solar battery chargers, generators, ample supplies of fuel and even a siphon for fuel. As well, if cold weather threatens the area where you live, have ample firewood and matches or a way to start a fire.

Communication – You cannot cut yourself off from the world, especially in a disaster. Our normal forms of communication – television, cell phones, and landlines may not be available following a disaster. Therefore, you will need alternative forms of communication to communicate with neighbors, loved ones or to learn what is happening in your community. Having police scanners, radios, Ham radios to communicate to the outside world will give you a huge advantage in survival and security.

Security – Never underestimate the desperation of those who are unprepared or ill equipped to survive. When one's needs are not met, there is nothing they will not do. Bugging in will require more planning and security on your part. Although living in an urban center may be the most difficult in terms of survival, those that live on the city's outskirts and suburban areas will not be without their own set of challenges.

Considering that the majority of the U.S. population is centered in 146 of the country's 3,000 counties, chances are most of us live in urban areas, and special attention must be placed on security. We've read enough survival stories to know that drug addicts, released prisoners, those with mental illnesses and the unprepared will be the ones looting and pillaging. Those that live in densely populated areas will be the most vulnerable to this. To curtail this, amp up your security endeavors and preps.

1. Prepare a sick room for the home to limit family member's exposure to the virus. If someone in the house is infected, then the person needs to be segregated to a room of the house. That room needs to be sealed off from the rest of the home, either using plastic sheeting or duct taped closed with limited interaction from other family members.
2. Consider all items coming in from the outside to be contaminated. They should be washed with antibacterial soap or a chlorine mix before being handled with bare hands.
3. Seal air leaks in your home. All it takes is one particle of infectious material to doom your whole family.
4. Any time you come into near-contact with anybody who is infected, you will need a shower. This is not an option.
5. All common items in the house should be disinfected after use regardless if anyone is sick. The kitchen and bathrooms should be meticulously cleaned after use.
6. If a family member dies in quarantine, seal off the room until professionals can deal with it. Don't risk it. If you decide to take matters into your own hands, wear long pants and long sleeves. Tuck your sleeves into your gloves. Dig the grave prior to moving the body. Spray the areas of the deceased you intend to touch with your bleach solution and wait 10 minutes before touching the body. Avoid touching the torso and head of the deceased person and only touch the disinfected extremities. Disinfect your clothing and shower after the operation is complete.
7. Looters and crime waves can occur during this time, so ensure you have a means to protect yourself and your preps.

In the event of a pandemic, because of anticipated shortages of health care professionals and widespread implementation of social distancing techniques, it is expected that family members, friends, and other members of the community who are not trained health care professionals will care for the large majority of infected individuals. Persons who are more prone to contracting illnesses include those who are 65 years and older, children younger than five years old, pregnant women, and people of any age with certain chronic medical conditions or compromised immune systems.

PREPS TO BUY:

- A one-month supply of shelf-stable emergency foods.
- 1 gallon of water per person per day, in clean plastic containers.
- Tychem protective suit and shoe covers
- Protective eye wear
- Plastic sheeting
- Supply of nonprescription drugs
- Pain relievers
- Cold medicines
- Decongestants
- Stomach remedies
- Duct tape
- Anti-diarrheal medication
- Essential oils
- Vitamins that have immune boosting enhancers
- Fluids with electrolytes
- Bleach or disinfectant
- Tissues
- Garbage bags to collect soiled clothing and bedding
- A thermometer
- Latex gloves
- Disposable cleaning gloves (in quantity)
- Soap
- Hand wipes
- Hand sanitizers
- An extra supply of your regular prescription drugs and medical supplies.
- N95 and N100 respirator masks (in quantity)

ACTION ITEMS:

1. Understand your community's role in pandemic preparedness. Find out ahead of time what your community's protocols are in the case of a sudden onset pandemic.

2. For those with special needs, ensure that you have supplies ready for them (infants, elderly, handicapped, etc.).

3. Plan accordingly for pets as well.

4. Talk with family members and loved ones about how they would wish to be cared for if they became ill.

5. Find out your employer's plans and ask your child's school or day care what their protocol is during epidemic or pandemic outbreaks.

6. Have some supplies prepared in your workplace.

7. Identify how you can get information, whether through local radio, TV, Internet or other sources.

SUPPLEMENTAL INFORMATION AND RESOURCES

Taking a Natural Approach to Pandemics

Herbal lore has it that, while the Plague was raging in France, a rash of burglaries of plague victims' homes was discovered. No effort was made, however, to apprehend the thieves, as it was assumed that they would soon succumb to the contagion in the homes they had robbed.

The thieves carried on their crime spree for some time, and people began to wonder why they had not become ill and died. It was then that the authorities began to pursue them... to discover the secret of their immunity to the Plague.

Once the burglars had been apprehended, they struck a bargain with the authorities that they should be set free in exchange for revealing the secret to their immunity to the Plague. It was then that the four thieves revealed the herbal disinfectant formula that rendered them immune to the Plague.

ALTERNATIVE FOUR THIEVES OIL
1 part eucalyptus
1 part rosemary
1 part cinnamon
1 part clove
1 part lemon
50 drops of a carrier oil (olive, jojoba, or your choice)

Put 50 drops of each oil in a 2 oz. bottle and then top it off with jojoba oil (I like jojoba oil because it never seems to go rancid).

APPLICATIONS:

- For personal protection, add a teaspoonful to bath water.
- Use as a topical spray for disinfecting surfaces and/or skin.
- Apply 1-2 drops of Four Thieves on the bottoms of the feet and on the nape of the neck.
- Apply under the arms and on the chest.

FOUR THIEVES VINEGAR

Current theorists suggest that this formula, now called "Four Thieves Vinegar," may offer protection against fearsome possible threats, such as the flu, smallpox, and biological weapons, as all of its ingredients are either strong anti-bacterial agents, or have potent anti-viral properties.

This vinegar can be taken daily to ward off any potential pathogens, used in salads as a nutritious salad dressing or added to the bath water.

- 1 part lavender, dried
- 1 part sage, dried
- 1 part thyme, dried
- 1 part lemon balm (Melissa), dried
- 1 part hyssop, dried
- 1 part peppermint, dried
- 1 handful garlic cloves
- Raw (unpasteurized), organic apple cider vinegar

1. In a glass jar, place all dry ingredients.
2. Add raw (unpasteurized) organic apple cider vinegar and cover.
3. Set jar at room temperature for 6 weeks.
4. Strain off herbs and garlic, and add to a glass bottle or jar with a tight fitting lid.

Homemade Electrolyte Replacement Powders

Staying hydrated and keeping your electrolytes balanced is critical for optimum use of your body and brain functions. The following recipes for electrolyte replacement powders can be made with ingredients typically found in the home.

Sugar Option

2 quarts water
5-10 teaspoon of sugar
1 teaspoon of salt
1 teaspoon of baking soda
½ teaspoon of salt substitute (potassium salt)
1 pack of sugar-free drink flavoring

Sugar-Free Versions

Sugar free: Although adding sugar to your drink will help you keep your energy levels up, it's not a good option for everyone. People on a low-carb diet or people with diabetes, can choose a recipe that doesn't add sugar to the electrolyte drink:

Version 1

1 quart of water
2 tablespoons fresh lemon juice
3-4 tablespoons raw honey
¼ teaspoon of sea salt

Version 2

2 quarts of water
1 teaspoon of sea salt
1 teaspoon of baking soda
½ teaspoon of salt substitute (potassium salt)
1 pack of sugar free drink flavoring
Artificial sweetener to taste, optional

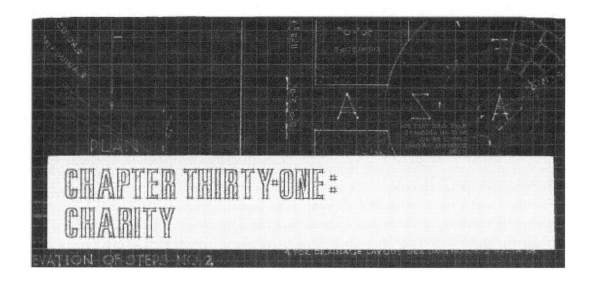

CHAPTER THIRTY-ONE: CHARITY

Carl Evett was inside his small, uninsured home when the tornado struck and while he survived, dazed, but unharmed, the home was destroyed. "The tornado took it all away, except me and the couch and the living room," he said.

Herman McDade's home wasn't badly damaged, but his yard was littered with 40 fallen trees. When he heard that Evett was struggling to rebuild, he and another neighbor, Jack Brassfield, wanted to help. "The rest of us got hit by it, and we were busy taking care of our business, but every day we drove by, we'd see Carl out there picking up debris," Brassfield said. "Every day. All by himself." The two leveraged connections from their long careers in construction to help Evett rebuild with donated materials, volunteers and the money he received from the Federal Emergency Management Agency. This holiday season, the volunteers along with Bayside Baptist Church helped build a new home for Evett about 50 feet away from the ruins of his former basement.

"You have no idea how many good people there are," Evett said. "We go through life kind of pessimistic about people, until you have something like this happen and so many good people come out of the woodwork to help you." Last week, Evett, who previously worked as a janitor at the Chattanooga Times Free Press, was painting the frame around his new front door. There are still final touches left to complete and furniture to bring in, but he hopes to be in the home by New Year's. "It was really bad in the beginning, but I'm better off now," he said, standing on his new front porch. "I mean, people suffered because it was really horrible — when you lose everything you have and you don't know which way to turn. But when you do turn that corner and things start looking up, you're better off."

The Claims Journal[109] (January 4, 2013)

---

[109] http://www.claimsjournal.com/news/southeast/2013/01/04/220188.htm

Preppers tend to find themselves in conflict over the subject of charity during an extended disaster. Although many want to help, there is a large concern with drawing unnecessary attention to oneself when lending a hand, and in the process, endangering those around you.

With regard to the unprepared, many believe that desperation knows no boundaries. If a person were desperate enough, they may not only want the hand out you are giving them, but the "whole enchilada." Many fear that the unprepared would make attempts to overtake your home to get to all of the supplies, or get a group together to attack your home. In the case of a disaster, especially a widespread disaster, a person can never be too cautious.

WHAT WOULD YOU DO?

Many believe that helping others is not only the right thing to do, but may help improve your own survival situation. Of course, if you help the wrong person they may come back and take the rest of what you have by any means necessary. But if you help the right person out, they may be there to help you when that wrong person comes knocking for more supplies. Many of us are "cut from the same cloth" as far as our belief systems go, and will feel compelled to help our fellow man when the right situation presents itself. In previous chapters, we discussed how being spiritually and mentally prepared for these moral ordeals will help you make the right choice for you and help you feel less conflicted. Dealing with those asking for charity is no exception.

PROVIDING SECURITY FOR YOUR FAMILY WHILE GIVING CHARITY

Those who are at odds with how they could provide charity, maintain good OPSEC and keep a secure home at the same time can take alternative measures to ensure their safety. If you want to help those in need, ensure that you provide charity inconspicuously and/or *anonymously*.

This can be achieved by going through a third party to give out the charity. This eliminates the danger involved in face-to-face donations and blowing your operational security. A third party could be a member of a church, a charitable organization, a friend or family member. For example, you could drop the donation off at the church door with a note asking that the donation be given to someone who could benefit the most from it. Further, if someone comes by your property asking for help, you can direct them to the church or organization that you donated to.

ALWAYS KEEP THE WELL-BEING OF YOUR FAMILY IN MIND

Ensuring the well being and safety of your family is the reason you are getting prepped in the first place. In my humble opinion, before any charity occurs, you must ensure that your family has enough to survive before giving away precious supplies. We never know how long a disaster can last, so keep this in mind before you decide to provide charity.

To gauge how much food your family needs for extended emergencies, use the <u>food calculator</u>[110] at Ready Nutrition.

PRE-PLANNING FOR CHARITY

We wouldn't be preppers if we didn't consider planning for future charitable issues. If you are fortunate enough to have any extra supplies, consider setting the charitable items aside in a separate location from your family's supplies. This will keep your supplies more organized. For the most part, keep basic survival needs in mind when setting aside items for charity, such as food, water, baby supplies (diapers, formula), medical supplies, blankets, etc. Some of the most popular pantry goods to store can be seen in the supplemental information at the end of this chapter.

Kits filled with beans, rice and some water keep the basics in mind and are frugal too. My family purchased starter food kits from the Latter Day Saints Food Warehouse to give away to those in need. For $20, the kits have #10 cans of rice, beans, red wheat, white wheat, flour, and quick oats. This is enough food for a month and more than enough to keep a family fed during an emergency.

During times of strife, we do not want to lose sight of our humanity. Our ability to help our fellow man is what sets up apart from the animals, and in all honesty, if you are not in an isolated area, it will be very difficult to ignore those in need. Survival during a long-term disaster depends not only on making the right choice, but the smart choice that is right for your family. And we all know that sometimes the smart choice is the hardest one to make.

---

[110] <u>http://readynutrition.com/resources/category/preparedness/calculators/</u>

PREPS TO BUY:

- Canned goods of soups, stews, vegetables or fruit
- Boxes or cereal
- Dry goods (rice, beans, oats, etc.)
- Water
- Jars of peanut butter
- Protein bars
- Diapers and wipes
- Infant formula
- Infant cereal
- Baby food
- Powdered milk
- Protein/calorie drinks
- Soap
- Feminine hygiene supplies
- Medical supplies
- Pocket bibles

ACTION ITEMS:

1. Use the food calculator at www.ReadyNutrition.com to determine how much food you need to have for an extended disaster.

2. If you are planning on storing charitable items, store them away from your family's supplies to ensure they do not get mixed in.

3. When purchasing charitable items, keep the basic survival needs in mind.

4. Focus reading on your spiritual preparedness again and reflect on moral dilemmas you may be faced with in a long-term emergency.

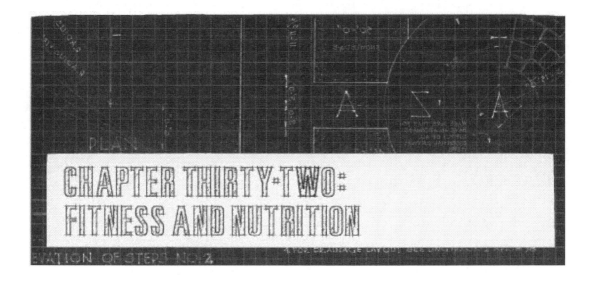

CHAPTER THIRTY-TWO:
FITNESS AND NUTRITION

In 1959, popular Tibetan resistance was crushed by the Chinese army; the Dalai Lama and 80,000 Tibetans fled to India, Bhutan and other countries in a mass exodus.

When Kunsang's monastery was destroyed, she left with her husband and two small daughters, trekking across the mountains with few possessions. They took enough food to last them a few months, some clothes and blankets, and a heavy bronze mold for making tsa tsa, sacred Buddhist images, out of clay. They knew that wherever they went they would have to preserve their culture, which was in danger of disappearing.

Their journey was arduous: they walked along the Pang Chu River, through narrow, icy mountain paths, avoiding Chinese soldiers. The girls cried with cold and fatigue; their shoes, which were homemade of thin leather and filled with snow that turned to ice, soon wore out, and their parents took turns carrying them. The paths were slippery; the cold was numbing. They walked sometimes not knowing where they were going, only aware that they were leaving their country behind. The fear of the unknown, the cold, the hunger and the exhaustion were overwhelming...It took a month to reach India.

Source: telegraph.co.uk[111]

---

[111] http://www.telegraph.co.uk/culture/8362276/Across-Many-Mountains-escape-from-Tibet.html

Each emergency provides us with its own set of unique challenges. One often-overlooked aspect of emergencies is the fact that we must adapt to various physical challenges. Whether you find yourself chopping more firewood, scaling rooftops, bending over more while gardening, or hiking through the bush with a fully-loaded bug-out pack, if your body is not prepared to handle this sudden influx of physical activity, you will be more susceptible to injuries and strain.

It doesn't take much for your body to become strained and injured if it isn't conditioned to handle rugged activities.

SURVIVAL OF THE FITTEST

The term "survival of the fittest" is not just applicable to describing the evolution of organisms who best adapt to the environments. In a survival sense, those who are the fittest will have the greatest chance of surviving.

Our bodies were not designed to sit lethargically at a desk for 8 hours a day. We have large muscular systems that were created to help us maintain a physical activity level. Yet, we have been conditioned to be sedentary due to our jobs and the ease of modern transportation. How will you survive a different lifestyle if your body is not conditioned for it?

Here's another scenario: say you and your family have made the decision to bug out of the city[112]. If you end up evacuating on foot and have not conditioned your body to hike with multiple pounds of gear strapped to your back, then you will have a very difficult time bugging out. Lugging around extra pounds on your body on top of all the gear you have in a bug-out scenario will quickly wear you out, could potentially cause an injury, and even put you in harm's way.

We must begin preparing the body now for those physical activities we may find ourselves in. Recognizing your physical weaknesses[113] and figuring out how to make things work despite those weakness will also be vital to your survival. An effective prepper fitness routine[114] contains three components: cardio, strength, and flexibility. Neglecting any of those three categories of fitness opens you up to the risk of injury.

---

[112] http://readynutrition.com/resources/the-prepper-conundrum-bugging-out-pt-3_10102013/

[113] http://readynutrition.com/http:/readynutrition.com/resources/prepping-with-physical-limitations_20092013/prepping-with-physical-limitations_21082012/

[114] http://readynutrition.com/resources/bug-out-boot-camp_30072012/

CARDIO

Cardiovascular fitness might also be called "endurance." It is the ability of your heart to supply oxygen to your body while you are under physical strain. Cardio is important in many scenarios:

- In a bug-out situation, you may have to evacuate on foot over rough terrain.
- When chopping wood you are swinging an axe over and over for an extended period of time.
- When hunting, you may have to hike through the woods, dragging your kill behind you.
- In a battle situation, you may need to run for cover (or even run away!)
- In a flood you may need to haul sandbags to build a wall.

You can't leap from your desk and run 5 miles to evade a threat without a huge health risk if you don't prepare for this in advance.

To build your cardiovascular fitness, start out simple. You don't need an expensive membership to a gym. Just lace up your shoes and start walking. Make it a point to incorporate walking into your daily activities. For example, instead of taking the car to run errands, go on foot. I also specifically walk for fitness, plugging into my iPod and bringing along my dog.

As your fitness increases, look for more challenging routes with hills. Walking or hiking off road is more of a challenge because of uneven terrain. Finally, you can add a loaded pack for some resistance training. Build your fitness level so that you can meet the challenges that you may face without stressing and overworking your heart and lungs.

Beginner Prepper Fitness Program

Here is an example of how you might put the three components together for an all-around fitness building routine.

Monday: Stretching 10 minutes, Moderate walk, Strength

Tuesday: Stretching 10 minutes, Moderate walk

Wednesday: Stretching 10 minutes, Training walk with weight

Thursday: Stretching 10 minutes, Moderate walk

Friday: Stretching 10 minutes, Moderate walk, Strength

Saturday: Stretching 10 minutes, Training walk with weight

STREGNTH

Strength is also known as muscular fitness. It refers to the ability to lift, pull, drag or push. Muscular fitness can come into play in many ways in a SHTF scenario:

- When bugging out you'll likely be carrying a heavy pack while traversing difficult terrain.

- If you are farming, you will be plowing and tilling, as well as carrying supplies like manure and other fertilizers.
- Chopping wood is not just cardiovascular – it requires strength too.
- If a family member is injured, you may end up carrying or supporting them.

To build your strength, you can start out with simple body-weight exercises. Push-ups, crunches, lunges, and squats will increase your strength.

Once you have developed a cardiovascular base, do a training walk at least twice a week. Start off with an extra 10-20 pounds in your pack and work your way up from there until you can walk with a 50-pound backpack.

At-home programs like P-90x and Insanity are also great for strength training. Whatever you choose, keep doing it and keep increasing your resistance.

FLEXIBILITY

Flexibility is the most neglected part of many fitness routines. Flexibility allows you to perform physical activities without becoming injured. The training stretches your muscles and makes them more pliable and less susceptible to injury.

Yoga is a great way to become more flexible. A yoga DVD or website can walk you through some simple stretches and the routine will soon become a pleasant activity that you look forward to—it simply *feels good*! I find that my entire day is off if I don't start out with my 15-minute routine every morning. If you aren't a fan of yoga, basic track and field stretches will net you the same results. If you only stretch for 10 minutes per day, you will notice increased flexibility within two short weeks.

YOU ARE WHAT YOU EAT

Did you know that parts of your body replace themselves?

Your skin every 28 days, your liver every 5 months, and your bones every 10 years. Your body makes these new cells from the food you eat. Therefore, what you eat literally becomes you. If you eat nothing but sugary, processed junk, then you can't expect to perform like an athlete. A fit lifestyle is something that encompasses how you spend your spare time, what you eat and drink, exercise programs, and nutritional awareness. It also includes the things you don't do. Analyze your situation to see if you have some habits that are sabotaging your health and fitness efforts.

Keep these points in mind:

- **Get to a healthy body mass index**. Being in a healthy weight range is incredibly important, especially in the event of an emergency. If you are too heavy, your body undergoes far more stress when asked to take on strenuous physical activity. Imagine hiking up a steep hill with only the clothes on your back. Definitely a challenge, especially if you aren't accustomed to performing that task. Now imagine hiking up that same hill carrying 20 pounds. You will be huffing and puffing at the top of the hill, and that's if you make it up there. Now, think about how your body will feel if you take off the 20 pounds that made your jeans too tight – you can perform the same activity with far less effort.
- **You are what you eat**. Make healthy snacks ahead of time to avoid binge eating. When you are ready for a more dramatic change, get rid of your weaknesses (junk food, sodas, ice cream, chips, etc.) and begin incorporating more healthy meals into your diet.
- **Drink *lots* of water.** We all know that water helps your body and organs function properly, so start drinking more water. It really does a body good.
- **Bring on the protein.** Adding more protein into your diet helps heal your muscle tissue after exercising. Without sufficient protein, you won't recuperate quickly and you will lack energy.
- **Create muscle memory**. Any activity that you perform for a length of time with repetitiveness is a motion that is easier to pick up again later in life. This is muscle memory. If you can predict things that you might need to do in an emergency situation (like chopping wood, for example), begin practicing in order to develop muscle memory. You want your body to be able to fall back on what it knows when an emergency occurs. This "second nature" response is very beneficial in an emergency situation.
- **Take your vitamins.** Vitamins have a beneficial effect on the body. Proper nutrients can help aid in exercise recovery, build the immune system and keep your body's "operating systems" working efficiently.
- **Stop the bad habits.** Make a commitment today to stop consuming anything that is harmful, including alcohol, tobacco products, and harmful drugs and substances. You do not want to be dealing with withdrawal symptoms during an emergency.

What you may find after incorporating physical exercise and stretching is that not only will you begin a physical transformation, your mind and spirit will transform as a result of making healthier choices. Being physically well is realistic and a very important aspect of preparedness. Peter Holy, CEO of 1-2-3 Feel Better.com suggests that, "A physically healthy person is someone who strives to do all that they can to maintain their body at the optimum level of functioning both in times of sickness and good health…Total health reaches far beyond physical wellness, but adequate physical wellness provides a good foundation for a whole and complete life."

PREPS TO BUY:

- Speak with a wellness advisor or physician about what your physical exercise plans are and short/long-term goals.
- See if they can give you any pointers. Buy any exercise equipment needed for your exercise regimen.
- Research the importance of super foods and begin purchasing foods that will enhance your health.
- If you plan on hiking outdoors, consider a good pair of hiking boots.

ACTION ITEMS:

1. Start an exercise routine and make a commitment to do at least 10 minutes a day of physical activities. Gradually build up when your body gets used to the workout.
2. Begin a daily vitamin regimen.
3. Throw away the junk food and plan healthy meals before you go grocery shopping. Stock up on healthy snacks such as fruits, vegetables, seeds and nuts, trail mixes, eggs, yogurt, etc.
4. Always stretch your muscles before doing any type of physical activity.
5. Before starting this or any other fitness plan, consult your physician.

SUPPLEMENTAL INFORMATION AND RESOURCES

Healthy Snacks

Instead of hitting the vending machine at work when the 3 o'clock munchies hit, bring some healthy snacks from home. Some great portable foods are:

- Carrots
- Pepper Strips
- Apples
- Oranges
- Oatmeal
- Homemade granola bars
- Nuts or sunflower seeds (in limited quantities)
- Half sandwich made with whole grain bread and lean meat
- Lean protein meats (chicken, turkey, etc.)
- Hummus and pita chips
- Boiled egg
- Yogurt with fruit and granola
- Popcorn (air popped is best), no butter

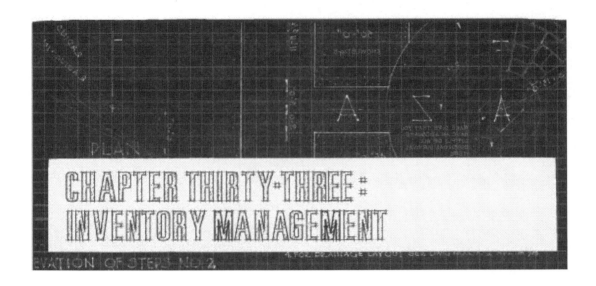

CHAPTER THIRTY-THREE:
INVENTORY MANAGEMENT

From a reader:

I learned the importance of organization when a terrible windstorm hit our city unexpectedly. Not only did the power go out, our kitchen window imploded from the force of the high winds!

Imagine my frustration when I went to hang a piece of plywood over the window and I couldn't find the right head for my screwdriver to fit the long woodscrews that I had for that purpose! We ended up duct-taping a plastic bag over the window and listening to it flap in the wind all night, all for lack of the right drill bit.

Our next dilemma was finding a lighter for the candles we had so carefully stored. Because we aren't smokers, we rarely use lighters or matches. Our lighter had most recently been used in the bathroom to light a scented candle, and had been left there. While searching the kitchen drawers holding a flashlight between my teeth, it never occurred to me to go into the bathroom to search for my lighter. So, because of lack of organization we sat there freezing, in the dark, despite the preps that we had purchased to prevent these issues.

Signed,

I'm Organized Now!

Keeping your preps organized can be very challenging. Most of us do not have a room dedicated to ideal storage specifications. Instead, we tuck our preparedness and food supplies into every free nook and cranny that is available to us. If you're not careful, this can lead to a quick descent into disorganized chaos.

In order to know how much you have and how much more you need, you must be able to account for it. If you are ever in the midst of an emergency, you want your preparedness items and equipment to be accessible and easy to find when you need them the most.

There is no single "right" way to store preparedness supplies. Some store their similar preparedness items in groups (i.e. stored foods, tools, equipment, hardware, and household items) while others store them according to need (baking supplies, short-term food supply, long-term supply, etc.)

Whichever way you choose to organize, ensure that the area chosen is in a room free from natural elements and insects. The best way to keep track of your preps is with a master inventory list. One way that my family has become more organized is by using cardboard filing boxes to organize our short-term food preps. After we label and seal our Mylar bags, we stuff them into labeled file boxes. This method has made for easier access to our short-term food supply. The best part is, when we run out of our short-term food preps in these boxes, we know that it's time to seal more.

Another organizational method we have used is utilizing plastic lidded containers found at dollar stores and super centers. All of my medical supplies are organized for quick access using this method – the medicines, surgical dressings, gauze, Band-Aids, etc. This organization method would be best utilized with smaller items. You can also create emergency response kits[115] using this organizational method as well.

CREATING A MASTER LIST

One aspect of preparedness that most preppers complain about occurrs when they have amassed so many supplies, it is difficult to find them.

Having a master list will help keep things organized and easy to locate.

---

[115] http://readynutrition.com/resources/shtf-survival-first-response-packs-for-medical-emergencies-2_13082011/

Use the following suggestions to get yourself and your preps organized and ready for use at a moment's notice. This will also help calm the clutter down and keep you abreast of how many supplies you have and how much more you need.

- Use Excel or a spreadsheet software program[116] to better organize and categorize your preps.
- List everything! Nothing should be exempt from your inventory list.
- Add the location of where the prep items are stored.
- Alphabetizing the list and including the location of where it is stored can be helpful when you're in a pinch.
- Store your master list in your Emergency Binder.

ORGANIZING THE STORAGE AREA

Spend a couple of days organizing your storage areas and creating your inventories. You can check expiration dates and rotate foods into your kitchen, you can see what you might need, and you can check that your storage methods are working well to keep things fresh and pest-free.

- Take out all your preparedness items from the area where they are being stored.
- Ensure that the area you are choosing to store your food is free of the enemies (natural elements and insects).
- Thoroughly clean the storage area.
- Label each container, bucket, tub or package with its contents, pack date/year and any necessary instructions.
- Assign locations in the storage area to keep items more organized (medical supplies, baking, sanitation, breakfast, canned goods, etc.).
- Grouping items that are used together can be convenient. For example, keep baking needs such as flour, sugar, baking soda, salt, etc. next to one another for easy access.
- Place goods with the longest expiration date in the back and work forward to the closest expiration date. Remember FIFO (First In, First Out).
- Systematically rotate and organize your storage.
- Food storage inventory should be checked every 6 months to make sure that food items are properly rotated and are used within their expiration date.

As you have realized from previous chapters and from your own personal experience, preparedness involves acquiring a lot of gear, tools, and food. Knowing what you have, how much you have and where to find it, is imperative in keeping organized.

---

[116] http://readynutrition.com/resources/if-you-dont-know-what-you-have-you-dont-know-what-you-need_02102012/

PREPS TO BUY:

- Pens
- Labels
- Plastic containers, cardboard filing systems, bins or under bed storage containers
- Shelving units
- Label maker

ACTION ITEMS:

1. Take all of your preparedness items out of the storage area and thoroughly clean the area. Areas that are not clean can invite rodents[117] and other unwanted guests.
2. Organize your preparedness supplies.
3. Develop a master list of your inventory supplies.
4. Store the master list in your emergency binder[118].

---

[117] http://readynutrition.com/resources/rat-proofing-your-food-storage-pantry-in-5-easy-steps_26102011/

[118] http://readynutrition.com/resources/good-manuals-every-family-should-have-one_22102009/

SUPPLEMENTAL INFORMATION AND RESOURCES

Small Space Storage Ideas

If you live in an apartment or another small space, don't despair – you'll be amazed at how much hidden storage is available! Just keep in mind, when storing supplies all over the house, it is even more important to keep your Master List up to date!

There's no rule that says food has to go in the kitchen and storage items have to go into the utility room. Go room by room and look for other nooks and crannies that can be drafted into storage duty!

Bathroom:

Be sure to use bathroom storage only to store items that won't be affected by humidity and temperature fluctuations.

- If your linen closet has that top shelf that is difficult to access, it can be a good location for items you won't use on a regular basis.
- If your linen closet has deep shelves, you can store a layer of preparedness items behind your neatly folded towels.
- Over-the-toilet cabinets are a good place to store small items.
- Under the sink—if you don't have cabinets, use stick-on Velcro and kitchen curtains to make a skirt for the sink.

Hallway

If your hallway is wide enough, it can be an untapped treasure trove of storage space.

- Secure inexpensive bookcases to one wall. Store your prepping library on these shelves and get some attractive boxes for the bottom shelf. Organize small items into the boxes (don't forget to label them).
- Use an armoire to hang extra blankets and tarps.

Bedroom

By nature of having a large object raised off the floor (your bed) – the bedroom has many square feet of storage space!

- Modify your box spring by removing the fabric covering – you can store lightweight boxed goods like Band-aids and feminine hygiene supplies here.
- Get risers for your bed and start using the space under your bed for canned goods and other supplies.
- In the back of your closet, add hooks along the sides and create horizontal rows of bungee cords. Stack canned goods behind the bungee cords – using this method you can go all the way to the ceiling with canned items. This works best with larger cans.
- Place items on the top shelf of your closet.

Living Room

Since this is likely the most public room in the house, take care that your storage here is subtle and attractive.

- Replace your coffee table with a trunk.
- Make a coffee table – use 2 large sturdy identical boxes and fill them with inexpensive items. Place a tablecloth cut to size over the boxes and top the cloth with two attractive serving trays.
- Two 5-gallon food buckets securely stacked are the right height for an end table—cover with a cloth and top with a tray.
- Use the space in your entertainment center for more than DVDs—place small items in attractive containers and intersperse these with the CDs and DVDs.
- Some sofas have storage space built right in.
- Adapt the hallway bookcase idea (above) to the living room.
- Make a window seat. Make the seat deep enough that 5-gallon jugs of water can be stored within—you can store 20-30 gallons of water here, depending on the size of your window.

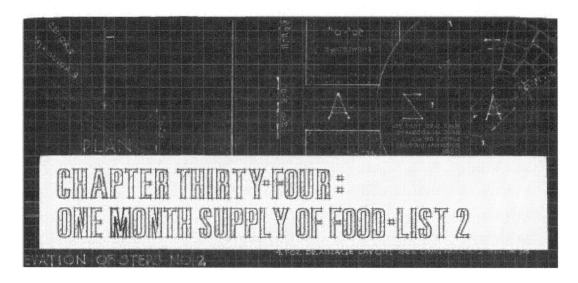

CHAPTER THIRTY-FOUR:
ONE MONTH SUPPLY OF FOOD-LIST 2

The scale of the siege of Leningrad itself boggles the mind; some *three million* residents and soldiers were encircled and entrapped at the beginning of the Nazi incursion into Russia. The two-and-a-half year siege caused the greatest destruction and the deaths that occurred during the Leningrad Blockade exceeded those who died from the atomic bombs at Hiroshima and Nagasaki combined, and constitutes the largest death toll ever known in a modern city.

Supply lines providing a lifeline of food and essential supplies were cut off from the city leaving its inhabitants to fend for themselves. When the food ran out for the people of Leningrad, many died a very slow, agonizing death. Although there was talk of cannibalism, many starved, froze, drowned, were run over by tanks, walked into mine fields, succumbed to a wide range of diseases, were murdered by German soldiers, and sometimes were caught in artillery fire. By the end of the siege, some 632,000 people are thought to have died with nearly 4,000 people from Leningrad starving to death on Christmas Day, 1941.

 Lenina, a survivor of the siege was age 7 at the time it began. She says, 'We were not heroes, but victims. We were children.' She described how her sister, four years older, died from starvation during the siege. Her mother openly declared she'd lost the will to live. 'What about me?' asked Lenina, 'You can go live with the neighbors or an orphanage,' came the devastating reply. Sure enough, her mother died soon afterwards. Lenina owned a cat, Stripey. As hunger took hold and temperatures plummeted to minus 30 degrees and with no wood left for heating, she, along with a neighbor, were left with no choice but the kill and eat the former pet. Well, it was her birthday, Lenina shared with a mischievous grin.

Source[119]

[119] http://www.historyinanhour.com/2012/10/15/900-days-leningrad/

Investing in food is similar to investing in an insurance policy. Food storage, just like insurance plans, allows you to invest a little time and money each month, in order to fall back on a safety net when you need it the most. You might even say food storage is more fruitful, because you can reap the benefits of your food throughout the year, with no disaster required.

My family and I are still living off of dry goods that we stored in 2009. Since that time, I have noticed food prices increase considerably and am thankful for the forethought in investing in my family's well-being. Did we have to sacrifice and forgo certain luxuries? Yes. But that initial investment of food has paid off and it gives me a sense of relief to know that I made a decision that will benefit my family for years to come.

HAVE THE RIGHT TYPE OF FOOD STORED

One of the golden rules of prepping is "It's better to be over prepared than under prepared." Therefore, ensure your family has the right foods stored to maintain a healthy diet in an emergency. Stock up on food with essential nutrients to maintain body functions: proteins and carbohydrates, fats for energy, as well as foods that are not high in salt (the saltier your food is, the more water you will drink).

Those who are thinking of solely investing in canned goods could be surprised at the amount needed and expense of such an investment.

Keep in mind that on average, one person's rations of canned goods for a month is equivalent to:

20 cans of canned meat

34 cans of canned vegetables

26 cans of canned fruit

Now, multiply that by a year. You'd need approximately 960 cans per person for a one-year supply of food – and that doesn't include any grains!

Most of us do not have adequate storage space for that kind of commitment to canned goods, and therefore look to other foods that can help to supply the dietary needs of the family while still providing variety. A food storage calculator can be of help in this process. Take notice of the canned items or pre-packaged foods you typically buy and pick up a few extra the next time you are at the store. Stock the same food items you normally eat. Buying food you don't normally consume is one of rookie mistakes[120] made by new preppers.

---

[120] http://readynutrition.com/resources/8-mistakes-made-by-first-time-preppers_06092013/

ESSENTIAL FOOD PANTRY RULES

To make the most of your emergency food supply, keep these essential food pantry rules in mind before purchasing:

1. **Balanced nutrition is an important factor in survival.** In any disaster situation, you want to avoid malnutrition. Having the appropriate foods stored to prevent this will keep you at your optimum health. Also ensure that you can provide enough calories for the members of your family.
2. **Consider buying multifunctional food items.** Items that can be prepared in several different ways will help your finances, as well as save precious space in the food storage pantry. Items such as oats, pasta, rice, wheat and beans are some great low-cost foods that will serve a variety of uses.
3. **Store high-energy snacks to help boost energy levels.** Eating snacks that are high in complex carbohydrates and protein will provide you with a guaranteed energy boost. Nuts, peanut butter, crackers, granola bars and trail mix can be stored for up to 1 year and will help keep energy levels and spirits high in an emergency scenario.
4. **Bring on the protein!** Protein is an essential ingredient in our daily diets and should not be omitted from a survival diet. Canned meat is a good source of protein and can also help you maintain your energy level. Meats such as tuna, ham, chicken and spam are great additions to the food pantry and are multifunctional. Beans are another great source of protein, and when beans are accompanied by rice, the meal provides a complete protein with all of the amino acids needed to survive. One serving of beans and rice provides 19.9 g, or 40 percent of your daily vitamins.
5. **Don't forget the basics.** Essential staples such as cooking oil, flour, cornmeal, salt, sugar, spices, baking soda, baking powder and vinegar should not be overlooked. If they are present in your kitchen, they should likewise be present in the emergency food supply. These are also multipurpose items for your storage supplies.
6. **Convenience helps in stressful situations.** Many moms know that boxed dinners can be a lifesaver when you are in a time crunch. Having some pre-packaged dinners and meals-to-grab during emergency scenarios will help you begin acclimating yourself to cooking in a grid-down scenario and can provide some comfort at the same time. My family has the "just add water" pancake mixes, cornbread mixes, macaroni and cheese dinners and drink mixes that are a great convenience.
7. **"Variety's the very spice of life that gives it all its pleasure."** Having a well-rounded food supply will cut down on culinary boredom and balance your diet. Stocking up on an assortment of herbs and spices will also enhance your food pantry. Take advantage of your kitchen window to grow fresh herbs and dehydrate them. This will save you money in the long run.
8. **Find comfort in the little things.** Have some comfort food items that provide enjoyment to the family. Popcorn, sweet cereals, hard candy, juice boxes, pickles, applesauce, pudding, or cookies could be a great way to provide a bit of normalcy during an emergency situation.

9. **Have back-ups for your backs ups.** Compressed food bars are lightweight, taste good, and are nutritious. Having food bars as a back-up to your existing food supply can provide you with peace of mind knowing you have an alternative to turn to if you run out of food. Further, these are great additions to your 72-hour bag or bug-out vehicle. MREs are another alternative food choice to turn to if you happen to run out of food in your pantry. Although many have turned their nose up at MRE's (due to the high amounts of preservatives), they will provide you with sufficient calories and nutrition when it counts. *Note: MRE's are designed for short-term food sources only. Over time, you could become nutrient- and vitamin-deficient.* A cost effective way to avoid vitamin deficiency is to make your own MREs[121] and include a multivitamin in with your food.

10. **Rotate and resupply when needed.** Any items bought for the food storage closet should be used, rotated, and resupplied. This is the best way to have the freshest foods available in the event that a disaster occurs. When organizing food reserves, place the item that has the earliest expiration date in the front so that it is used first (FIFO - First in, First out). Do an inventory check every 6 months to make sure that canned goods, preserves and other storage items are within their expiration date.

WHEN YOUR FOOD RUNS OUT

Since we are concentrating on preparing for extended emergencies, we must anticipate and prepare for the scenario that our stored food supplies could dwindle. This could occur from improper food storage calculations, survival garden difficulties, or food depletion over time.

A great resource to learn more about prepping your food pantry for longer-term foods is The Pantry Food Primer, by Daisy Luther. The book places an emphasis on how you can create a healthy food pantry *frugally*. She explains the characteristics of different types of pantries and how to combine them into a layered pantry

---

The Easiest Ways to Begin Preserving Food

1. Dehydrating food is one of the easiest ways to preserve food for long-term storage. Nutritious snacks can be made from dehydrating fruits, vegetables and meat. Dehydrated soup mixes can also be made for on-the-go meals or can be added to bug-out bags or emergency vehicle supplies.

2. Canning is another traditional method to preserve fruits and vegetables. Because the food is canned at the time of the plants' peak nutrient content, they will retain most of their nutritional value, and some foods even gain more nutrients from the canning process. Canned food will keep 12 months (or longer if stored correctly). Start learning these essential skills today in order to be more self-reliant in the event of a long-term emergency situation. The more you practice, the more confident you will feel in your abilities.

---

[121] http://readynutrition.com/resources/homemade-mres_02102012/

system powerhouse that you can rely on. She believes in layering her pantry with fresh foods, adding larger stockpiled foods to the pantry and adding home canned foods for tasty and healthy choices.

A favorite prepper adage is "Two is one, one is none." As preppers, you don't want to solely focus on acquiring one type of food source. This is why we have concentrated on acquiring a short-term food supply and are beginning to build a longer-term food supply. You want to have back-up methods. Learning how to preserve your own food in the case of a long-term, widespread emergency is the ultimate backup plan. To start learning this skill set, I want to redirect you back to the previous chapter on food preservation methods.

Can you imagine the nightmare of living through an extended crisis during which food is not available for purchase? Being prepared can put you way ahead of the game. While many who are unprepared for disasters will be battling to find a way to meet their basic needs, being well-stocked can keep your mind on what matters most: your family's wellbeing.

PREPS TO BUY:

- Dehydrated vegetables and fruit
- High-energy snacks (trail mixes, peanut butter, whole wheat crackers, etc.)
- 2-gallons cooking oil (plant based oils lasts longer)
- Bulk quantities of canned vegetables, fruit, meat and soups
- Monthly dry and packaged goods (pastas, pasta dinners, rice dinners, cereal, dry oats, etc.)
- Bulk quantities of baking goods such as baking powder, baking soda, yeast, salt, vinegar (white and cider vinegars), corn meal
- Tea and coffee – 1 box with 16 bags or 1 (2-ounce) jar instant coffee
- Drink mixes
- Emergency food bars
- MRE's
- Specialty foods for those with special diet concerns
- Pet food

ACTION ITEMS:

1. Use the food calculator at www.ReadyNutrition to estimate how much food you will need.
2. Begin dehydrating different types of fruits, vegetables and meats to gain confidence in this skill.
3. Remember to take into account the calories and nutrients your food storage will provide you.
4. Store the appropriate items to meet any special dietary needs along with your existing food supply.
5. Don't forget to include pet supplies to your emergency food storage. Your furry friends want to eat too!

SUPPLEMENTAL INFORMATION AND RESOURCES

4 Food Types to Avoid Malnutrition

Concentrating on storing foods that have carbohydrates, proteins, fats, vitamins and minerals can assist in maintaining healthy bodies and decrease the likelihood of malnutrition in a long-term emergency. Those who are preparedness-minded may want to take a more in-depth look at the question of *why it is important to store these types of food.*

Carbohydrates – Simply put, carbohydrates provide the body with energy. They also have a symbiotic relationship with protein by protecting the protein stored in the body. The brain optimally uses carbohydrates for energy, but when there is insufficient carbohydrate consumption for several weeks, the body does not metabolize fatty acids completely and as result body protein will also be lost, and the body will generally become weakened.

Preps to buy: white rice, pasta, wheat, oats, dehydrated fruits and vegetables[122], sugars, honey, fruits, roots and tubers (cook these well) and cereals.

Protein - Protein is a part of every cell of the human body. Also, equally as important, proteins provide the body with a special form of nitrogen that one cannot get from carbohydrates or lipids. Proteins also help regulate the pH, or acid-base balance, in the blood, are necessary for the synthesis of many hormones and enzymes, and participate in important cell formation vital for the immune system. In the case of starvation, excessive muscle tissue is wasted and results in diminished health.

Preps to buy: legumes, eggs, nuts, peanut butter, canned meats and fish, oatmeal, grains, wheat, quinoa, MREs, popcorn

Fats - As much as some people attempt to eliminate fats from their regular diets, this food source actually plays a vital role in maintaining healthy skin and hair, insulating body organs against shock, maintaining body temperature, and promoting healthy cell function. They also serve as energy stores for the body. In addition, Vitamins A, D, E, and K are fat-soluble, meaning they can only be digested, absorbed, and transported in conjunction with fats. Fats are also sources of essential fatty acids, an important dietary requirement and also serve as a useful buffer towards a host of diseases. (Source)[123] The USDA suggests that about 30-35% of your daily calorie intake should come from fat.

Preps to buy: whole milk, ensure, peanut butter, oil (preferably plant based oils), nuts and seeds

---

[122] http://readynutrition.com/resources/dehydrate-foods-for-long-term-storage_31032010/

[123] http://www.wellness.com/blogs/sydshahid/1055/why-do-we-need-fats-in-a-balanced-diet/syed-shahid-md

Vitamins and Minerals - Did you know that thirteen vitamins are considered necessary to perform crucial functions in the body? Vitamins and minerals are needed for overall health and provide protection against infection and diseases, help the body grow, help the body's metabolism and assist in the removal of waste products. It is recommended to obtain your vitamin intake through fresh fruits and vegetables with a regular diet. However, when dietary sources are limited, taking vitamin supplements is an excellent alternative. Amounts vary for children, seniors, lactating or pregnant women, smokers, heavy alcohol drinkers, those with chronic diseases or those who consume less than 2,000 calories per day.

Because vitamin deficiencies tend to exacerbate over time, we are typically unaware of being deficient until secondary issues manifest themselves. Eating a balanced diet and taking a multi vitamin is one way to curb this issue and the physiological consequences that go with it. Some physiological consequences of deficiency include: dental problems, inflammation of the mouth and tongue (riboflavin deficiency); diarrhea, dermatitis (niacin deficiency); edema, weakness (thiamin deficiency); tongue soreness, anemia (biotin deficiency); fatigue, tingling in hands (pantothenic acid deficiency); poor growth, inflammation of the tongue (folate deficiency); poor nerve function, macrocytic anemia (vitamin B12 deficiency); and poor wound healing, bleeding gums (vitamin C deficiency).

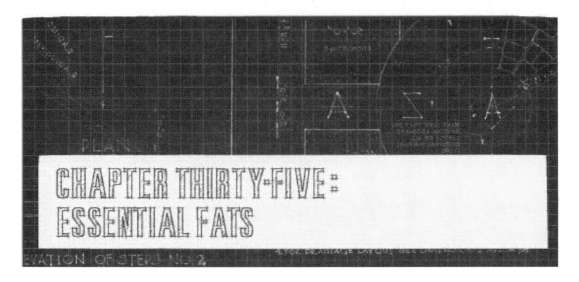

**CHAPTER THIRTY-FIVE:
ESSENTIAL FATS**

Vilhjalmur Stefansson, who spent many years living with the Eskimos and Indians of Northern Canada, reports that wild male ruminants like elk and caribou carry a large slab of back fat, weighing as much as 40 to 50 pounds. The Indians and Eskimo hunted older male animals preferentially because they wanted this back slab fat, as well as the highly saturated fat found around the kidneys. Other groups used blubber from sea mammals like seal and walrus.

"The groups that depend on the blubber animals are the most fortunate in the hunting way of life," wrote Stefansson, "for they never suffer from fat-hunger. This trouble is worst, so far as North America is concerned, among those forest Indians who depend at times on rabbits, the leanest animal in the North, and who develop the extreme fat-hunger known as rabbit-starvation. Rabbit eaters, if they have no fat from another source - beaver, moose, and fish - will develop diarrhea in about a week, with headache, lassitude, a vague discomfort. If there are enough rabbits, the people eat till their stomachs are distended; but no matter how much they eat they feel unsatisfied. Some think a man will die sooner if he eats continually of fat-free meat than if he eats nothing, but this is a belief on which sufficient evidence for a decision has not been gathered in the north. Deaths from rabbit-starvation, or from the eating of other skinny meat, are rare; for everyone understands the principle, and any possible preventive steps are naturally taken."

Source[124]

---

[124] http://www.medbio.info/Horn/PDF%20files/rabbit%20starvation.pdf

These days, most of us live a very blissful reality where strenuous physical activity is not required. Obesity has become a major health factor in our country as a direct result of our sedentary lifestyles. Because of this, the government and multiple health organizations have advocated restricting fats in your diet. As much as many of us strive to eliminate these fats, in a SHTF reality, this nutritional element will actually serve a vital purpose in our survival. Here's why:

1. Fats are an essential component in any diet for proper vitamin absorption. Specifically, vitamins A, D, E, and K are fat-soluble, meaning they can only be digested, absorbed, and transported in conjunction with fats.
2. Fats also plas a vital role in maintaining healthy skin and hair, insulating body organs against shock, maintaining body temperature, and promoting healthy cell function.
3. They also serve as energy stores for the body.
4. Fats are sources of essential fatty acids, which are an important dietary requirement and also serve as a useful buffer towards a host of diseases. (Source)[125]
5. The USDA suggests that about 30-35% of your daily caloric intake should come from fat.
6. Fats are one of the food types you must eat to avoid malnutrition.

SHORT-TERM FAT SOURCES

- **Infant formula** – The oil content in this food source makes it a viable choice for a SHTF fat source. An unopened can of powdered infant formula has a shelf life of 12 months. Once a can of formula has been opened, it should be used within a month and then discarded.
- **Ensure -** This supplement drink has 6 grams of fat, which provides your body with 9 percent of the recommended daily intake. The powdered version of Ensure will last longer than the pre-made drink. Plan on an unopened can of powdered Ensure to last the same as a can of infant formula, roughly 12 months.
- **Oil** – Plant-based oils such as vegetable, olive or coconut oil are best to keep in your emergency supplies, and can last up to a year if stored properly. That said, once opened, the oil could turn within a matter of weeks or months depending on how it was processed and the storage environment.
- **Peanut butter** – Any type of butter made from nuts is a healthy source of fat; if stored properly it can last up to 12 months.
- **Nuts and seeds** – Because of the high oil content in nuts and seeds, their shelf life is usually affected. Nuts and seeds typically last about 12 months.
- **Crisco** – With a shelf life that ranges from 2-8 years, this fat source is the longest lasting. That being said, it is probably the unhealthiest of the choices.
- **Mayonnaise** – Mayonnaise has a relatively short shelf life of 6 months. Therefore, if you plan to stock up on this, ensure that it is frequently rotated in your food supply.
- **Salad dressing** – Salad dressing lasts anywhere from 9-12 months.

---

[125] http://www.wellness.com/blogs/sydshahid/1055/why-do-we-need-fats-in-a-balanced-diet/syed-shahid-md

- **Canned meats -** Some canned meats, such as spam, fish and ham can also provide an adequate source of fat for your survival diet. Due to the high salt content of some of these canned meats, they have a relatively long shelf life of anywhere between 2-5 years.
- **Chocolate –** Although chocolate is considered a high-calorie, high-fat food, it does provide some health benefits as well. Studies have shown that dark chocolate lowers blood pressure and cholesterol levels and also provides more antioxidants than blueberries. Most of the studies done used no more than 100 grams, or about 3.5 ounces, of dark chocolate a day to get the benefits. Chocolate has a shelf life of 12 months; however, if the chocolate is repackaged in Mylar or stored in a plastic container, it could last much longer.

LONG-TERM FAT SOURCES

Storing fats are good for short-term emergencies, however if you are planning for extended or long-term emergencies, you'll need to learn how to get your fat sources by natural means. The following list is of fat sources that one can acquire living in a homesteading environment.

- **Whole milk –** Milk from animals can provide essential fat to our diets, and can also be used for cooking, making cheeses and other dishes.
- **Eggs –** Eggs have 5 grams of fat per egg. Fresh eggs would provide an adequate amount of calories, protein and fat if consumed on a regular basis.
- **Fatty fish –** If you have a water source on your property, consider stocking it with fish. Many homesteaders have found great success in stocking their ponds with: tilapia, channel and blue catfish, hybrid stripers, largemouth bass, trout, bluegill, and freshwater shrimp. Other sources of fatty fish are: salmon, tuna, mackerel, herring, trout, and sardines. (Ensure that you have fishing gear to get those fish with.)
- **Animal fats -** Livestock and game animals can be used as a source of fat. Bone marrow from wild game contains 6.79 grams of fat, which is 10 percent of your daily requirement on a 2,000-calorie diet. Natural fats can also be rendered for other uses or preserved through canning to have a natural source of fat on hand.
- **Nut trees –** Look for the dwarf variety of nut trees. Dwarf trees bear their fruit earlier than the standard varieties, and can produce higher yields in a shorter period of time. They have also been known to be more adaptable. This also goes for dwarf fruit trees.
- **Fruit trees –** Specifically avocado and olive trees provide a substantial amount of healthy fats for the body. Obviously, the following examples are region specific and prefer a Mediterranean-like climate, however check with the USDA zoning map to see if you can plant them in your area. When I lived in the coastal South, I saw many gardeners who grew avocado trees.

In a SHTF reality our diets will be very different from how they are today. Our activity levels will be more physical in order to promote our survival and as a result, our diets should reflect those changes. Continuing to have fat in the diet can help physiologically, as well as psychologically. Ensure that you have incorporated enough fats into your survival supplies.

PREPS TO BUY:

- Infant formula
- Ensure powdered drink
- Shortening such as Crisco
- Lard
- 2-gallons of vegetable based oil
- Mayonnaise/salad dressing
- Canned fish packed in oil
- Waxed cheeses
- Chia seeds and flax seeds
- Nuts and nut butters

ACTION ITEMS:

1. Get smart about survival and research the importance of having certain food sources in your diet.
2. Use the Ready Nutrition Food Storage Calculator to find out how much fat needs to be added to your storage supply.
3. Store your purchased products in a suitable environment where it is not exposed to natural elements. Learn about your food's worst enemies[126].

---

[126] http://readynutrition.com/resources/meet-your-emergency-foods-worst-enemies_06042011/

SUPPLEMENTAL INFORMATION AND RESOURCES

Off-the-Grid Food Preservation Method

Did you know that you can use fat as a preservation method? The popular French entrée confit of goose (confit d'oie) and duck (confit de canard) are usually prepared from the legs of the bird. The meat is salted and seasoned with herbs, and slowly cooked submerged in its own rendered fat. It is then preserved by allowing it to cool and storing it in the fat. Turkey and pork may be treated similarly.

When cooked meat is layered and then covered with hot lard, the air is sealed out by the fat. This is an off-grid way to preserve meat without a refrigerator. Moreover, it utilizes all aspects of the animal.

In a large crock, add layer on layer of the cooked meat and then cover with hot lard. When you are ready to prepare a meal, scrape the lard off each layer and take the amount necessary for a meal. The lard can then be reused in cornbread, pies, baked goods, or in soap.

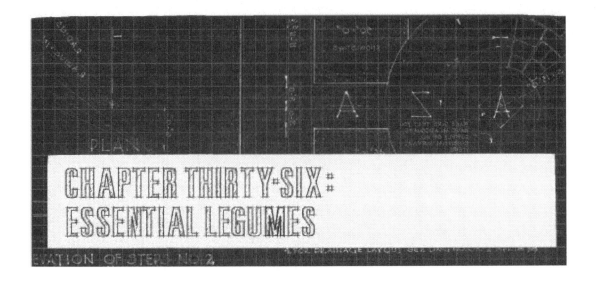

CHAPTER THIRTY-SIX: ESSENTIAL LEGUMES

Ideally, in an extended emergency, many of us would be living in a self-reliant environment where we have access to fresh foods and meats. However, since we are preppers, we make preparations to have back-ups for our back-ups. If, for some reason, our homesteading environment isn't thriving, we will need to be able to fall back on our food storage. Therefore, we want to have a well-rounded pantry in order to meet all of our dietary needs.

In previous chapters, we discussed which essential fats and oils to store in our deep larder. Another layer we need to focus on for our long-term dietary needs is a protein source capable of being stored long-term for SHTF emergencies. Legumes are the most versatile option for storable proteins. Best of all, they are low cost and have the capacity to last a decade if properly stored.

LEGUME NUTRITIONAL BREAKDOWN

In general, it's recommended that 10–35% of your daily calories come from protein. When beans are accompanied with a grain source such as rice or quinoa, the combination forms a complete protein. Having protein in your diet not only provides energy, but also creates a special form of nitrogen that the body cannot get from carbohydrates or lipids. In the case of starvation, the body may actually cannibalize its muscle tissue (called wasting) to acquire the necessary amino acids, or it may borrow the amino acids from the immune system or body functions to meet its protein needs. Beans, peas and lentils are the richest source of vegetable protein, as well as a good source of fiber, calcium, and iron. Aside from using legumes in the usual manner, they can also be ground into an alternative flour source, sprouted[127] for a fresh vegetable source, or made into spreads such as hummus.

[127] http://readynutrition.com/resources/simply-sprouting_16042010/

STORAGE RECOMMENDATIONS

Like most of our preparedness foods, beans should be stored in a manner that protects them from the food enemies: oxygen, moisture, insects and sunlight. Beans in their original, flimsy plastic packaging have a shelf life of 1 year or more. However re-packaging the dry goods in heavy duty Mylar and/or plastic containers can protect and prolong legumes for up to 10 years or longer! Ensure that you have proper storage conditions[128] or else your hard work could be all for nothing. Improperly storing your beans could lead to rancidity of bean oils, color fade, and an overall "off" flavor. To make the most of your legume storage, consider these five tips:

1. When storing larger amounts of food, glass canning jars, plastic storage pails, #10 cans, or Mylar-type bags are best for long-term food storage.
2. If you are using one of the above long-term storage containers, you can keep the beans in their original packaging, or remove the plastic wrapping and pour the contents into a long-term container and properly seal.
3. Oxygen absorbers should be used to remove oxygen from the packages to extend shelf life and minimize off-flavors caused by oxidation.
4. For smaller quantities of storing beans, consider using canning jars. Ensure that the jars are stored in a dark place.
5. Like most stored foods, colder storage temperatures will increase shelf life. 40-75 degrees Fahrenheit is the ideal temperature range for keeping your long-term food storage safe.

Lentils and soybeans have the highest nutrition values in the legume family, so keep this in mind when purchasing for long-term storage. Further, consider the cooking time that legumes require. Larger beans take more time cooking and may require more of your fuel source to cook them. If this is an issue, purchase smaller legumes such as lentils and split peas. They cook faster, thus decreasing your fuel usage. Soaking beans for 6-12 hours can also reduce the cooking time by about one half, and saves vitamins, minerals and proteins that can be lost during hours of cooking.

WHERE TO BUY IN BULK

Those of you planning on putting away bulk quantities of beans can purchase many varieties, including organic beans at www.PrepperPackaging.com. Further, the Latter Day Saints have food storage warehouses that usually carry legumes and an assortment of other food related items. By far, the larger quantity bags will be a better investment compared to purchasing mass amounts of the smaller bags. If you want to purchase these items online, doing a simple search for "buy legumes in bulk" will connect you to many online companies that can take your order.

---

[128] http://readynutrition.com/resources/are-you-packing-5-inexpensive-ways-to-store-your-food_28062012/

PREPS TO BUY:

[In Quantity]

- Lima Beans, Dry
- Soy Beans, Dry
- Split Peas, Dry
- Lentils, Dry
- Dry Soup Mix, Dry
- Chickpeas, Dry
- Black Beans, Dry
- Navy Beans, Dry
- Pinto Beans, Dry

ACTION ITEMS:

1. Get smart about survival and research the importance of having certain food sources in your diet.
2. Use the Ready Nutrition Food Storage Calculator to find out how much protein you need to add to your storage supply.
3. Bear in mind, daily caloric intakes are different with each person, so research how many calories you need to stay at your optimum health.
4. Those with special needs (such as pregnant women) are advised to get more protein sources, so keep this in mind when purchasing.
5. Learn how to package and store your bulk foods for long-term storage.
6. Store your purchased products in a suitable environment where they are not exposed to natural elements.

SUPPLEMENTAL INFORMATION AND RESOURCES

Beans, Beans, the Magical Fruit, the More You Eat….

Lots of people avoid beans because of the unpleasant aftermath of intestinal gas. If you know what causes this problem then you can take steps to lessen the issue. Beans contain a sugar called oligosaccharide. Our bodies do not have the enzyme needed to break this down. When oligosaccharide gets to your lower intestine, it ferments, which creates bloating and gas. The gas cannot be absorbed into the intestines and is rather unpleasantly expelled from the body.

So, what's a bean lover to do?

1.) Soak your beans. Not only does this shorten your cooking time, as mentioned above, but it also leaches out the oligosaccharides. Change your water several times during the soaking and rinse your beans again before you begin cooking them.
2.) Cook beans slowly.
3.) Chew well – this helps to break down the oligosaccharides.
4.) Certain spices work as digestive aids when beans are on the menu. Experiment with recipes that contain fennel, cumin, turmeric, ginger, cloves, coriander, dill, or a dash of lemon juice
5.) Follow up with a mint tea.

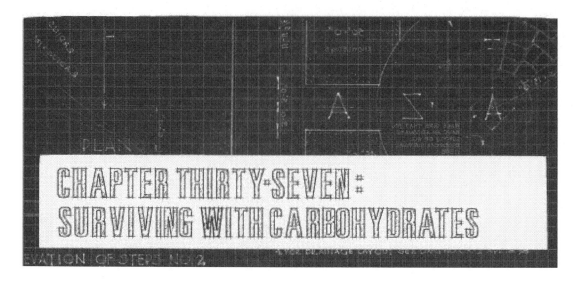

CHAPTER THIRTY-SEVEN : SURVIVING WITH CARBOHYDRATES

Have you ever noticed how many options and varieties of food there are at the grocery store? After all, variety is the very spice of life that gives it all its pleasure. Having a well-rounded food storage pantry will cut down on culinary boredom, as well as balance your diet.

With this in mind, when the veritable "S" hits the fan, you *will* want variety – lots of variety. Diversifying your emergency pantry will ensure you have plenty to choose from. Remember, food has more than one purpose: it comforts us, keeps us well, heals us with nutrition, and provides us with energy to withstand what may come our way. Even if you don't eat many carbs now, in a survival situation, activity levels increase due to the escalated necessity of physical labor (i.e. chopping firewood, planting a survival garden, standing guard or securing a perimeter, hunting, hand washing clothes or dishes, etc.). Harsh weather conditions can also play a role in the amount of carbohydrates we will need to consume: the colder the temperatures are, the more carbohydrates you will need in order to maintain your body temperature.

NUTRITIONAL BREAKDOWN OF CARBOHYDRATES

U.S. guidelines suggest that between 45 and 65 percent of your calories come from carbohydrates. The best choices are complex carbohydrates and come from natural sources that contain a lot of fiber, such as vegetables, fruits, and whole grains.

These types of carbs take longer to break down into glucose and give you the most nutrients along with your calories. As a whole, we grossly underestimate how many carbohydrates we need stored for a long-term emergency.

SPECIAL EQUIPMENT

Because storing grains in their whole form will allow them to stay fresh longer, to make flour, you will need an electric or manual mill to turn your grains into flour. Therefore, start researching and saving up for a quality mill now. These can be a costly, but necessary preparedness investment. Initially, when my family started preparing for a long-term disaster, we purchased a low-cost manual grain mill for around $70. We practiced and used the low-cost grain mill until we had money saved up to purchase our primary mill. For those of you who may be wondering, we invested in a **Country Living Grain Mill**; and although the cost is on the higher end, we feel satisfied with our purchase. Not to mention, now we have two working mills. (Two is one, one is none!)

STORAGE GUIDELINES FOR GRAINS

Many preppers like to choose a multi-barrier system to store their food. This barrier system is for long-term purposes, and will keep natural elements such as sunlight, moisture and air out of the container when sealed.

For the last four years, my family and I have stocked up on long-term food items from a variety of places, including super stores, the LDS food storage warehouse, and preparedness websites such as Ready Nutrition, Emergency Essentials, Five Star Preparedness, and the Ready Store.

From a survival standpoint, if you must forage to find carbohydrates, know in advance which **wild food sources** are available in your area. When food is scarce, chaos and fear begin to set in. However, instead of panicking, step outside and go for a walk. More than likely, food will be right under your nose.

Our goals are simple: to find multi-purpose preparedness items that will help you conserve space, provide versatility and give you the biggest bang for your buck.

Foraging For Food

When food is scarce, consider the following:

- Look for bees (honey)
- Wild apples
- Cattail roots
- Wild potatoes
- Edible weeds
- Wild fruits
- Acorns
- Roots and tubers (cook these well)
- Clover

PREPS TO BUY:

To make the most of your investments, many of the suggested carbohydrates below have a lifespan of 20 years and longer. These items have a 20-year+ shelf life.

[In Quantity]

- Corn (whole kernel lasts longer)
- Pasta
- Wheat – hard red wheat or white wheat
- Rice – white rice
- Oats – steel cut oats, not the instant kind
- Quinoa
- Amaranth

ACTION ITEMS:

1. Get smart about survival and research the importance of having certain food sources in your diet.
2. Research how versatile these foods can be for your food pantry.
3. Use the Ready Nutrition **Food Storage Calculator** to find out how much protein you need to add to your storage supply.
4. Bear in mind, daily caloric intakes are different with each person. Therefore, research how many calories your family needs to stay at optimum health.
5. Keep in mind that pregnant or lactating women are advised to get more daily nutrition and calories.
6. Learn how to package and store your bulk foods for **long-term storage**.
7. Store your purchased products in a suitable environment where they are not exposed to natural elements: temperature fluctuations insects, sunlight and oxygen.

SUPPLEMENTAL INFORMATION AND RESOURCES

5 Most Common Wild Edibles

1. Dandelion – The flower, leaves and root of this plant are edible. This plant has an abundant source of calcium to aid in bone health and also has properties that help disinfecting lungs. Vitamin A is also present in this plant, which acts as a natural antibiotic. The leaves especially are packed full of every vitamin imaginable. The plant can also be made into a tea to alleviate skin irritations such as athlete's foot, scratches and some acne. Collect the root in the late fall to early spring and it makes a great addition to soups or by itself. Dandelion flowers can be eaten raw, sautéed, steamed, fried or used to make wine. Collect dandelion leaves in the spring when they are most tender and sauté them or use in salads or teas.

To Make Dandelion Tea:

Tear six dandelion leaves into a hot cup of water and let it steep 5-10 minutes.

*Any unwanted tea can be used as a natural face wash.

2. Chicory – This plant is rich in vitamin A, B, K, E and C, calcium, copper and zinc and phosphorus. Collecting young plants in March and in November is the best time to harvest. The flowers are stems can be used in salads. The root can be eaten (after being boiled) or used as a coffee substitute, if necessary.

To Make Chicory Coffee:

Scrub the Chicory root, chop it up and toast them at 350 degrees for one hour until dark brown, brittle and fragrant. Grind the root up and mix 1 tsp. of ground roots in one cup of hot water. The taste of chicory coffee is comparable to bitter coffee.

3. Cattails – Cattail shoots provide essential vitamins such as beta-carotene, niacin, thiamine, potassium, phosphorus and vitamin C. Many survival sites view the cattail as one of the most important edible plants to know about. The shoot of a cattail tastes like a combination of cucumber and zucchini.

It is advised to harvest plants after a bout of dry weather, so they are easily accessible. The entire plant (flowers, shoots and pollen) can be harvested, so cut the plant at the base. The best time to harvest and eat these plants is right before spring, when plants are young and just beginning to flower. The older they get, the more fibrous they become. The pollen from cattails provides great energy, nutrition and can also be used as a flour for breads, or breakfast breads such as pancakes and muffins. The pollen does not rise, so it should be mixed with three times as much whole grain flower, or sprinkle it on salads, oatmeal or yogurt.

4. Amaranth – Amaranth, once ignored and thought as a pestering plant, is now getting the notice it deserves. Ancient Aztec civilizations thought this plant had superpowers. This plant is high in fiber, amino acid, essential nutrients, and proteins and comes in a close second (quinoa comes in first) with the lysine content. Whole bread can be made from ground amaranth seed. Substitute 25% of your wheat flour with amaranth flour. According to sources, just 150 grams of the grain is all that is required to supply an adult with 100% of the daily requirement of protein. This plant can be used as a spinach substitute eaten raw or cooked. The leaves are best collected in the spring. Amaranth seeds can also be fermented into beer.

5. Milkweed – This versatile plant has many uses. Not only does it attract butterflies to feed on it and assist you in the garden, but you can also collect the milk, eat the silken fibers from inside the immature pods and use the milkweed fluff as a stuffing for coats or blankets. Milkweed stalks have a fibrous material that can be used as twine for sewing. In more ancient civilizations, Milkweed was eaten as a vegetable. Its shoots are similar to asparagus. Flower buds can be collected in the springtime for a broccoli alternative. Flowers can also be boiled and mashed to create a unique sauce. Additionally, the flower pods can be pickled for winter months. Milkweed provides a multitude of edible parts from late spring until late summer

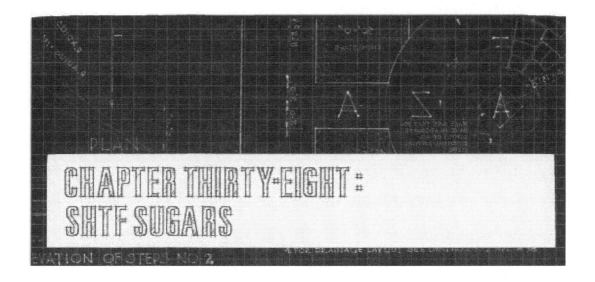

CHAPTER THIRTY-EIGHT:
SHTF SUGARS

I might get a lot of flak for asking this, but before the haters get all up in arms, be honest with yourself: do you really want to sit out TEOTWAWKI without sugar or honey?

I realize there is a long list of diseases attributed to refined sugar in our diet. According to the American College of Sports Medicine a mere 5 to 6 percent of your daily calories should come from sugars. But, have you ever considered that there may be more than one reason for storing these sweet supplies for a long-term emergency? Some uses include:

- Curing/Food Preservation
- Alcohol
- Medicinal Use
- Bartering

MOST POPULAR STORED SUGARS

We are all a bit particular when it comes to our favorite sweeteners. It's a good thing there are so many options! This sweetener list is meant to be a general overview of some of the more popular storage choices. If there is a sweetener that you prefer, by all means purchase some for your preparedness pantry.

Since we are stocking up for long-term preparedness, we want to store sweeteners that have the longest shelf lives. The four most popular long-term sugars to store are:

- **Honey** – This sweetener lasts forever if stored properly. Many honey harvesters say that when honey crystallizes, it can be re-heated and used just like fresh honey. Because of honey's low water content, microorganisms do not like the environment. *Uses include: curing, baking, medicinal, wine (mead).*

- **White Sugar** - Like salt, sugar is also prone to absorbing moisture, but this problem can be eradicated by adding some rice granules into the storage container. Sugar lasts forever if stored properly. *Uses include: sweetener for beverages, baked goods, food preservation, curing agent, making alcohol, gardening, and insecticide.*
- **Maple Syrup** - Maple syrup is another consideration for your food storage. Because of its high sugar level (which is antibacterial), it lasts practically forever. The higher the quality and sugar level, the longer it lasts. *Uses include: baking, medicinal, food preservation, curing agent.*
- **Molasses** - This is actually a by-product of the refining process of sugar cane into table sugar and it actually possesses health-promoting properties. Blackstrap molasses is a very high source of non-heme iron and can be used as a supplement in the event of anemia. Molasses can last up to two years unopened. *Uses include: baking, preservative, food preservation, curing agent, soil amendment, medicinal.*

Sugar Substitution Chart

If your recipe calls for 1 cup of sugar you can replace it with....

- Honey: ¾ cups + ¼ tsp. of baking soda (reduce other liquid ingredients by 2 tbsp.)
- Maple syrup: ¾ cups (reduce other liquid ingredients by 3 tbsp.)
- Molasses: 1 1/3 cups + ½ tsp. of baking soda (reduce other liquid ingredients by 5 tbsp.) – not advised to totally replace sugar with molasses – use a 1:1 ratio

---

OTHER PLANTS THAT MAKE VIABLE SUGAR SOURCES

Although many of the above listed items can last a lifetime, if you are planning for extended or long-term emergencies, it is advised that you educate yourself on some other sugar options. The following list includes some sugar sources[129] that you can grow or raise yourself in a homesteading environment:

- **Sugar beets** - Learning how to extract the sugar from beets can be tricky. During wartime, many people used ordinary red garden beets[130] to make sugar. Please note that getting sugar from beets will require a lot of fuel, so prepare accordingly.
- **Sugar cane** - This is a region-specific plant and one that thrives in tropical-like weather conditions. However, the entire plant can be used. The tops and remaining pulp can be eaten or fed to livestock.

---

[129] http://readynutrition.com/resources/the-sweet-life-sugar-alternatives-for-your-homesteading-needs_12102012/

[130] http://www.sucrose.com/lbeet.html

- **Bees/honey** - There are also many books on beekeeping that can be quite useful. Sometimes it is difficult to keep the bee colony thriving, so find a person in your area that is willing to share his or her experience.
- **Sugar maple trees** - The sap from the sugar maple tree will produce maple syrup. There are many how-to articles and videos on the Internet that can take you step-by-step through the process. Please note, on average you will need 400-500 gallons of sap to make 10 gallons of maple syrup.
- **Stevia** - A fairly easy to grow herb that is good for sweetening drinks, simple syrups and making jams. Within limits, stevia is an acceptable sweetener for diabetics. Here's a trick to keep your stevia producing its sweet leaves: when you see the plant trying to flower, cut the tops off.
- **Sorghum** - Sorghum is a grain cultivated for its sweetness. Amish folk love this grain and use it as a syrup. It is also a popular grain to grow in impoverished regions of the world, and remains a principal source of energy, protein, vitamins and minerals. Grain sorghum has been utilized by the ethanol industry for quite some time because it yields approximately the same amount of ethanol per bushel as corn. *Take note: Some species of sorghum can contain levels of hydrogen cyanide, hordenine and nitrates lethal to grazing animals in the early stages of the plant's growth.*

SUGAR IS A VALUABLE COMMODITY

Have you noticed the price of sugar increasing In some areas, the price of sugar has gone up 22% in the past 12 months, so stocking up on it now would be a good investment for the future.

Hard assets such as sugar, wheat, beans, and food preservation tools are an investment that will have a reliable return, while also securing one's future. Further, these types of investments could make lofty sums in a **bartering situation**.

PREPS TO BUY:

The following is a general list of long-term sugars that can be stored:

[In Quantity]

- Honey
- Sugar
- Brown Sugar
- Molasses
- Corn Syrup
- Jams
- Fruit drink – powdered
- Flavored Gelatin

ACTION ITEMS:

1. Get smart about survival and research the importance of having certain food sources in your diet.
2. Further, research how versatile this food source can be for your food pantry and for your overall survival.
3. Use the Ready Nutrition **Food Storage Calculator** to find out how many sugar items you need to add to your storage supply.
4. Bear in mind, daily caloric intakes are different with each person, so research how many calories you need to stay at your optimum health.
5. Those with special needs (such as pregnant women) are advised to get more nutrition and calories daily, so keep this in mind when purchasing.
6. Learn how to package and store your bulk foods for **long-term storage.**
7. Store your purchased products in a suitable environment where they are not exposed to natural elements.

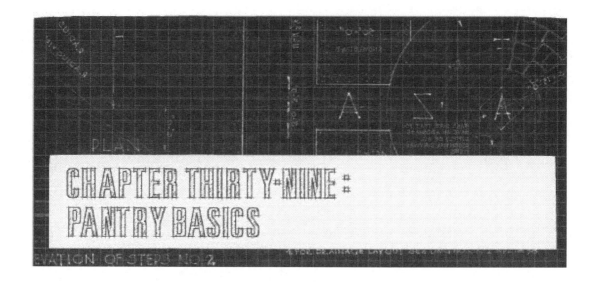

CHAPTER THIRTY-NINE ::
PANTRY BASICS

OUTFIT FOR OREGON

...The amount of provisions should be as follows; to each person except infants:

200 pounds of bread stuff (flour and crackers)
100 pounds of bacon [more like salt pork]
12 pounds of coffee
12 pounds of sugar

Each family should also take the following articles in proportions to the number as follows:

From 1 to 5 pounds tea
From 1/2 to 2 bushels dried fruit
From 10 to 50 pounds rice
From 1/2 to 5 pounds saleratus [yeast]
From 1/2 to 2 bushels beans
From 5 to 50 pounds soap

Cheese, dried pumpkins, onions and a small portion of corn meal may be taken by those who desire them. The latter article, however, does not keep well.

Source[131] - St. Joseph, Missouri Gazette (March 19, 1847) excerpt

---

[131] http://personal.my180.net/thesmiths/oregontrailrecipes.html

When early Americans migrated westward, they had to adapt to a new environment, and their supplies had to be multifunctional. The items we choose should be able to carry us, not only through difficult times, but perhaps through impossible times as well. Having a food supply that not only utilizes the basic kitchen/pantry essentials, but also one that encompasses proper dietary needs will help you thrive in a short or long-term disaster.

When I first began prepping, I had just bought all of the recommended items for a short-term food supply. After carefully stocking the items on our storage shelf, I sat and looked admiringly at my meager supply, imagining all the ways it was going to pull us through a hard time.

Then, a thought crept into my mind—I began to wonder how on earth was I going to use all these supplies? Who uses a pound of yeast? Or two pounds of baking powder? Folks, this was the moment that sealed the deal for me. Because this was when I realized that I didn't have to use two pounds of baking powder for *baking*; I could find another way to use it! And for that matter, I bet that a lot of other items that I had purchased could be used in ways other than their original purposes. That was when I got my hands on every book and website I could find on alternative uses for these items. Inevitably, this is when I went loco for prepping!

OUR PREPS ARE OUR LIFELINE

Our preps are our lifeline and we must know how to make them multitask. Since most of us have limited shelf space, it is only logical to find products that will perform multiple jobs[132] for us. The following is a list of kitchen staples that deserve a space on your emergency food shelves. Keep in mind that in an extended emergency, these items may be very useful in a bartering situation. Print out or save any pertinent information for your preparedness binder.

Baking Soda - This is my favorite item to stock up on because it has so many darn uses!

- Natural antacid
- Dental care
- Electrolyte powder
- Emergency antiseptic
- Natural cleaner and laundry brightener
- Cleans off rust
- Can be used in treating scalding, to prevent blistering and scarring. Cover the scalded area with a liberal layer of sodium bicarbonate and water paste and seek medical assistance
- Can be applied to skin irritations that occur from poison oak, poison ivy and sumac

---

[132] http://readynutrition.com/resources/7-kitchen-essentials-that-deserve-to-be-on-your-preparedness-shelves_15032012/

Please note: Due to the salt content, anyone on a sodium-restricted diet or those with high blood pressure, cardiovascular disease or kidney disease should not take sodium bicarbonate in large quantities as it can elevate blood pressure, aggravate heart disease and lead to edema, or swelling of the legs and feet due to fluid retention.

Baking Powder - Baking soda is actually the primary component in baking powder, so it's no surprise that pretty much anything you can do with baking soda, you can do with baking powder. Some additional uses include, but are not limited to:

- Eliminates odors
- Natural cleaning agent
- Draws out insect stings and jelly fish venom
- Keeps ants away from the house

Salt - Salt is another prepper's favorite kitchen essential to stock up on. It is a multipurpose, low cost prep that will be highly desirable if a long-term disaster were to come around. Salt will be a big bartering item[133]. Stock up on different types of salt: sea salt, table salt, pickling salt, curing salt – they will all have their uses in a long term disaster. Sea salt[134] is not only healthy for your body, but it also provides antiseptic and bactericidal qualities.

- One of the top bartering items
- Eliminates odors
- Natural cleaning agent
- Sea salt has antibacterial and medicinal properties

Yeast - Where would we be without the discovery of yeast? Yeasts are naturally present and live symbiotically on food sources such as grains, vegetables and fruits. It would be prudent to learn how to grow your own baking yeast[135].

Baking Yeast

- Leavening agent
- Currently being studied for a natural cure for cancer

Brewer's Yeast

- Making alcohol
- Nutritional supplement

---

[133] http://readynutrition.com/resources/james-rawles-salt-will-be-the-1-bartering-item_05032010/

[134] http://readynutrition.com/resources/10-health-benefits-of-sea-salt_15092011/

[135] http://readynutrition.com/resources/survival-food-series-3-ways-to-naturally-make-yeast_02032011/

- Assists diabetics in controlling their blood sugar level
- Helps control high cholesterol level
- Is a natural flea control for pets

Vinegar - Vinegar has been around for thousands of years and is so diverse that it would be worthwhile to have a good supply stocked up. The good news is the shelf life is long-term! See a recipe for fresh apple cider vinegar at the end of this chapter.

- Soothes sunburns
- Eliminated bad breath
- Natural facial toner
- Can be used as a fabric softener
- Is a natural hair cleaner/conditioner
- Cleaning product for the home
- Possess medicinal properties

Corn Starch - Did you know that cornstarch offers some health benefits? Crazy, I know. Cornstarch has 488 calories per cup and 117 grams of carbohydrates. I realize this is not an ideal main entree, but if added to dishes it could be a great way of providing additional calories and carbohydrates for extra energy. There are also some additional uses to consider with this product:

- Great for use as a dry shampoo
- Burn treatment
- Treatment for insect bites
- Deodorant
- Gets grease out of fabric
- Cleans windows
- Thickener for soups, sauces and gravies

Powdered Milk - Have you ever wondered how powdered milk is made? Basically, it is made by evaporating milk to dryness. One of the reasons that powdered milk[136] is so popular amongst the preppers and survivalists is it can be stored for long-term use.

Further, due to its low moisture level, it does not need to be refrigerated, thus making it a perfect emergency pantry item! Some uses include:

---

[136] http://readynutrition.com/resources/the-skinny-6-everyday-uses-for-dry-milk_28122012/

- Milk
- Yogurt
- Cheese
- Sour cream
- Whipped topping
- Substitute for milk
- Facial wash

Our ancestors' philosophy of "make do or do without" transferred into many avenues of their life, and they were on to something. They knew the versatility of their supplies and made sure they had enough of them to get by.

We also want to get by. Some of these items may even provide a semblance of what our normal life once was. And how great is it that these items are low-cost, multi-functional, and readily available at practically any grocery store?

PREPS TO BUY:

Start stocking up on these items in quantity and gathering knowledge on your own on other uses for these items.

[In Quantity]

- Baking Powder
- Baking Soda
- Yeast
- Salt
- Vinegar
- Evaporated Milk
- Powdered Milk
- Corn Starch

ACTION ITEMS:

1. Use the Ready Nutrition Food Storage Calculator to find out how many essential baking items you need to add to your storage supply.
2. Bear in mind, daily caloric intakes are different with each person, so research how many calories you need to stay at your optimum health.
3. Those with special needs (such as pregnant women) are advised to get more nutrition and calories daily, so keep this in mind when purchasing.
4. Learn how to package and store your bulk foods for long-term storage.
5. Store your purchased products in a suitable environment where they are not exposed to natural elements.

SUPPLEMENTAL INFORMATION AND RESOURCES

Make Your Own Apple Cider Vinegar

Start your vinegar making as soon as the season's new apple crop is available so you can make several attempts, if necessary. Use your homemade product wherever vinegar is called for... ***except for pickling,*** *which requires a vinegar of proven acidity.*

For 1/2 gallon of cider vinegar you will need:

- 1/2 gallon of spring, rain, or well water

- 2 c. honey

- 12 or more apple peels and cores

- 1/2 package of dry yeast (1 1/2 tsps.)

- 1/2 c. cider vinegar, commercial (for comparison only)

Instructions:

1. Small barrel or plastic gallon jug (used plastic milk jug); cord or lid; sipping straws. *If a plastic milk jug is to be used, wash well and scald with hot water to kill any bacteria.

2. Find a place in the warm kitchen where it can rest on a side, with the narrow opening serving as a bunghole.

3. Cut an opening on the top surface to receive a wide cork or plastic lid (the closing should not be airtight).

4. Boil water, pour it in the jug, and stir in honey, peel, and cores. Cover, set aside.

5. Check mixture daily for bubbling. If none occurs in a week, add the yeast. If mold forms on the surface, skim it off without disturbing the contents.

6. After 1 month, the bubbling will have stopped and souring begun. Now it is up to your taste to tell you when the vinegar is ready to use. To take a sample from the jug, plunge in a sipping straw, close the end with your thumb, and remove the straw half full. Judge the strength by comparing it with the taste of the commercial vinegar.

7. In two months the vinegar may be sour enough to use in cooking and salad dressings. Try to decant a quantity from the bung without shaking up the contents. Replenish the barrel with any fermented matter on hand.

Note: At some point a milky froth may form on or below the surface of the vinegar in the barrel. This is called a "mother," and is a welcome sign of acetic acid bacteria but a possible nuisance. Best remove it, along with the other solid matter in the barrel.

CHAPTER FORTY::
EMERGENCY COMMUNICATION

Parts of coastal Japan have been so badly hit by the recent earthquake and tsunami that communication regarding other possible dangers such as radioactive fallout from damaged nuclear reactors, has only been one-way, coming to residents through portable, battery-operated FM radios.

Without cellular or landline voice or data communications, residents in the most hard-hit locations don't have the ability to reach out for help or contact relatives. It has been difficult or impossible to receive information about aftershocks, further tsunami activity or the potential spread of radioactive particles from damaged nuclear power plants, according to various sources.

Computerworld[137]

---

[137] http://www.computerworld.com/s/article/9214462/Communication_key_to_post_disaster_survival_

Consider for a moment how drastically your life would change without the continuous flow of energy the grid delivers. With the increase of natural and man-made disasters paired with an aging infrastructure, experts from the private and public sector warn that we are just <u>one major catastrophic event</u>[138] away from an incident that could take down the grid, causing a complete meltdown of life in America as we know it today.

MEDIA BLACKOUT

Radio, telephone, and television are critically important before, during, and after a disaster. These communication mediums deliver life-saving information to the community and to emergency responders. However, these methods of contact can become vulnerable, especially following a disaster.

> ### The Chaos of a Media Blackout
>
> If the disaster provides no advance warning, or is widespread and damages vital transportation routes, then the media stations will be unable to provide critical information to the masses. When, and if these generators run out of fuel, there will be a widespread communication blackout.

Adding to the fragility, in the last decade, many of these stations have switched from analog to digital, causing an even larger dependence on an always-available, grid-up scenario. Although radio and television broadcasting stations have enough fuel to run their backup generators for a short time (roughly 3-5 days) after the disaster, the stations will be largely dependent on supplies of back-up fuel in order to continue broadcasting.

The best way to prepare for this serious situation is to equip yourself with the knowledge and the tools for communication. Communication in a grid-down scenario is going to be *vital* in order to listen to events unfolding around you, talk with loved ones, and keep order in your community or surrounding area.

Now is the time to invest in and familiarize yourself with emergency communication devices in order to be proficient with them when the time comes.

FORMS OF EMERGENCY COMMUNICATIONS

The following are suggested emergency communication devices that can help ease the stress of a communication blackout.

---

[138] http://readynutrition.com/resources/when-the-grid-goes-down-you-better-be-ready_28102013/

1. **CB Radio**

CB radio or Citizens' band (CB) radio is a communication device that allows people to talk to each other using a radio frequency. The CB radio user has 40 channels to choose from and uses an 11-meter band or 27 MHz. CB radio was originally intended for use by government divisions such as the military, and in the 1960s, it was mainly used by taxi firms and tradesmen.

Top brands include Cobra 148GTL, Midland 1001Z, Cobra 75 WX ST

2. **Field Telephones**

Field telephones are mobile telephones designed for military use, and have the capability to withstand wartime conditions. They can draw power from their own battery, from a telephone exchange (via a central battery known as CB), or from an external power source. There are some that are sound-powered telephones, and do not require a battery.

For semi-permanent installation, ensure that you buy cable that is rated for underground burial (UB), to conceal and protect all of your lines. Burying your lines will also prevent both intentional and unintentional lines cuts and breaks. Extra field telephone wires could also be purchased to run communication wire to your neighbors and coordinate with them as well. To purchase field telephones, look on eBay, at Army surplus stores, or emergency supply stores.

Top brands are TA-1042 DNVT, TA 838, and TA-312

3. **Transceivers**

A transceiver or transmitter/receiver is a device that combines transmission and reception capability on shared circuitry. In regions where digital coverage is spotty, a transceiver may be equipped for analog to ensure that there will be no loss of signal. Transceivers can handle analog or digital signals, and in some cases, both.

Ham radio transceivers, for example, can broadcast and receive transmissions for over 50 miles, and some can let you talk with people from the other side of the planet. Conversations on a ham radio are not secure or private, so ensure that you do not broadcast any personal information over the airwaves.

Radios range in price and functionality from utilitarian $100 handhelds to do-everything desktop behemoths costing thousands of dollars. Amplifiers and ancillary equipment increase range and functionality as they also add cost. You decide your budget. A small handheld transceiver, called "HT" for short, will commonly allow transmission and reception on VHF and UHF bands. Many ham HT's also receive, but do not transmit HF, aviation bands, marine bands, and commercial AM and FM stations.

The top brands include: MURS (Multi-Use Radio Service), Yaesu VX-3R VHF/UHF, Handheld VHF 2 Meter Amateur Radio Transceiver 5watt, and TYT TH-F5

AMATEUR RADIO

Amateur radio is one communication tool available to us all. My intent here is only to introduce the most basic information about ham radio to the uninitiated. The information presented is *not* intended to provide a comprehensive compendium of technical definitions, formulae, physics, esoterica, ham slang, procedures, equipment choices, or to delineate the astonishing variety of amateur radio disciplines and niches, but *only* to motivate you if you are not yet a 'ham.'

Simple foundational concepts:

Amateur radio always involves some mention of wavelength and frequency, but these concepts aren't easy to visualize. For our purposes here, think of radio waves as ocean waves. The distance from wave peak to wave peak (or trough to trough) is "wavelength." The longer the wavelength, the fewer waves touch the beach per minute (or second). **The longer the wavelength, the lower the frequency; the shorter the wavelength, the higher the frequency—** the first key concept.

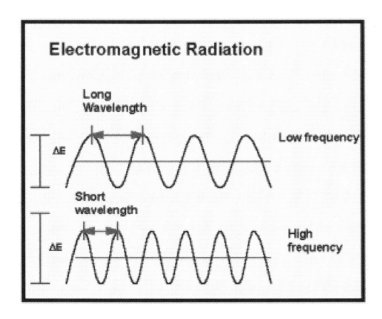

In the radio spectrum, longer wavelengths (lower frequencies) "bounce" better than shorter wavelengths (higher frequencies). These longer wavelengths can be bounced off the ground, off layers of the atmosphere, or even off the moon. The ever-changing activity of the sun (day, night, sunspots) makes an enormous difference in the electrical charges in the ionosphere and so significantly affects how well the longer wavelengths "bounce," "propagate," how far they "go." Shorter wavelengths (higher frequency) do not "bounce" so well and so are limited to line-of-sight propagation. **Since those longer wavelengths can bounce farther than you can see, those longer wavelengths communicate farther than line-of-sight**—the second key concept.

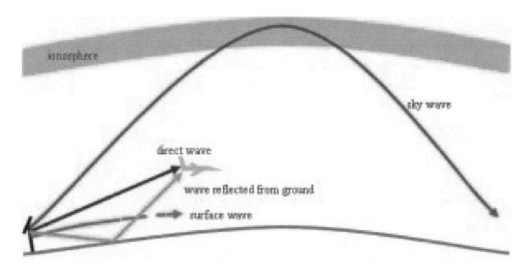

For our purposes here, we refer to the longer "bouncy" wavelengths as high frequency (HF) and the "line-of sight" shorter wavelengths as very high frequency (VHF) and ultra-high frequency (UHF). Radio wavelengths are usually expressed in meters or fractions of meters. Radio frequencies are usually expressed in "per second" or "Hertz" (abbreviated "Hz") or "millions per second" (megahertz, MHz) or even "billions per second" (gigahertz, GHz).

So, the ham radio spectrum looks like this:

HF   3 to 30 MHz
VHF   30 MHz to 300 MHz
UHF   300 MHz to 3,000 MHz (3 GHz).

All this means is that 3.750 MHz in the 80 meter HF band "bounces" better than 144.500 MHz in the 2 meter VHF band. You'll get used to it. These concepts will quickly become second nature for you. Suffice it to say, if you want to communicate over long distances, you will want access to those "bouncy" HF bands.

Why Get Licensed?

Why? To get connected with good people of like mind. To legally operate an amateur radio now, you must be tested, licensed and you must provide an address; a private mailbox or PO Box suffices. Though such government-imposed requirements are repugnant to many, here is why you should start now—to practice important skills that will be very useful later. If you only want to talk to your buddy a few miles away, it is almost as easy to use an amateur radio as a CB radio, but to succeed in regional, transcontinental, or worldwide radio communication requires skills born of practice. If you think you can simply turn on a ham radio and send or receive real time news regionally or globally, you are sorely mistaken.

There are tools today that allow a novice to very easily use an inexpensive handheld radio to talk to other hams around the world, but this capability depends on internet digital linking. When the internet kill switch is used, there will be no more D-STAR (Digital Smart Technologies for Amateur Radio) or IRLP (Internet Radio Linking Project). When the chips are down, you will have only: (1) the short-range line-of-sight capability of VHF and UHF radio and (2) the long-range "bounce" of HF radio. While those short-range line-of-sight VHF/UHF skills are easily acquired, be sure that "DXing," slang for making long-range contacts, requires special HF radios, more skill, more power, better antennas, and practice.

More than local news will be necessary for you to get "the big picture," so I urge you to get your license and equipment now and start practicing. You cannot be an effective sniper with your first round and you cannot be an effective DXer with your first "QSO," slang for "radio contact."

Currently there are three levels of ham licenses being issued by the Federal Communications Commission (FCC): from low to high, Technician, General, and Extra. Each higher level allows more access to bandwidth, more frequencies to use. Morse code is NOT required for any class of ham license. The Technician license exam is very easy. A Technician license gives access to the relatively short-range VHF and UHF bands, but gives none of the HF access necessary for long-range communication. The General license exam is easy, only slightly more difficult than the Technician exam, and a General license allows you to legally enter the long distance world of DXing on HF. A General license is well worth the small increment of effort. The Extra licensing exam is difficult for most, but the Extra license gives access to all the frequencies legally allowed to hams.

Indeed there are many laws currently regulating ham radio usage and I urge you to learn and obey them. Practice, practice, practice... ahem... legally. Let us not review how resistance movements have used clandestine radios against the control grid.

There are two styles of study for the exams. One may simply study to pass the exam or one may study to master the information. You may choose to do both.

Gordon West has a series of books seemingly aimed at passing the exams. The first in the series is Technician Class 2010-2014[139].

---

[139] http://www.amazon.com/Technician-Class-2010-2014-Gordon-West/dp/0945053622

ARRL, the American Radio Relay League, has a series of books and webpages seemingly aimed at mastering the material. The first in the series is Ham Radio License Manual Revised 2nd Edition. In far more detail than I can do here, the ARRL website[140] provides an overview and resources for many aspects and specialty niches of ham radio, niches like "fast scan amateur TV" mentioned below. With little effort on the ARRL website's Find a Club[141] page, you can find a local ham club. Most clubs have training classes and members willing to be your personal ham radio mentor, in ham slang, your "Elmer."

Some Facts, Some Gear

Radio "bands" are named by their wavelength or frequency, so because of the relationship between wavelength (abbreviated by the Greek lower case *lambda*, λ) and frequency (abbreviated by the Greek lower case *nu*, v), the "40 meter band" is the same as the "7 MHz band." As I hinted above, the reciprocal mathematical relationship of wavelength and frequency is quite simple: wavelength (λ) = speed of light (c)/frequency (v).

> ### Radio for Kids
>
> There are even websites dedicated to helping children obtain their licenses. For example:
>
> http://www.nc4fb.org/wordpress/kid-friendly-technician-license-self-study-program/

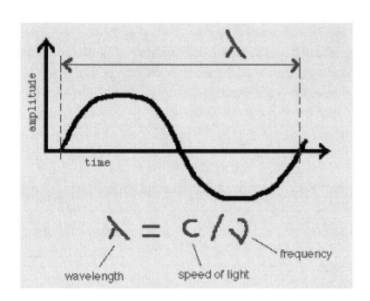

The allocation of frequencies to bureaucratic, military, commercial, and amateur users is agreed through international treaties that are enforced by national agencies. The "band plan"

---

[140] http://www.arrl.org/home

[141] http://www.arrl.org/find-a-club

for US amateurs includes access to band segments from 160 meters (1.8-2.0 MHz) to 33 centimeters (902-928 MHz), covering quite an enormous expanse of the electromagnetic spectrum.

Do not be perplexed or overwhelmed by product specifications as listed in brochures and reviews. The meaning of these specifications will become crystal clear as you study for your exam and use your own radio. Computer software and cables are available that allow you to program and clone the memories and setting of such radios more easily than tapping every memory and setting into the radio using the radios' tiny buttons. RT Systems is among the most respected purveyors of such software. That Yaesu model has broader band access than that ICOM model, but does not have D-STAR or built-in GPS. The ICOM does have both D-STAR and built-in GPS (Global Positioning System), hence easy global access *now* using VHF/UHF (no HF), but, as I mentioned above, those global VHF/UHF capabilities are easily shutdown at the whim of "our" police state. Also, there may be circumstances where you might *not* want to automatically report your GPS location, so you might deactivate or not install such options. The ICOM ID-51A's automatic GPS does allow automatic connection to nearby repeaters and reflectors (see below), a convenience, but you may choose instead to manually enter such information if needed. The line-of-sight range of these tiny 5 watt HT's can be markedly improved, even to 50 miles, by connecting through suitable coaxial cable to a simple, inexpensive, and unobtrusive magnet mount antenna at home or on your vehicle. To help protect against EMP damage, our family keeps our HT radios in Faraday bags.

Vehicle mounted mobile transceivers markedly expand your range and bandwidth. 100-Watt mobile transceivers are common and many add HF capabilities to VHF and UHF. The very newest mobile radios, such as the touchscreen ICOM 7100 reviewed at eham.net, include both HF and D-STAR as well as GPS capabilities *if* you activate it. 1,500-Watt amplifiers are optional and refined tunable antennas are available. Such units give you the best of local and worldwide digital radio now and analog radio when the internet has been killed.

For the dedicated, practiced, and affluent ham with a "ham shack," a 1,500-Watt desktop behemoth (for example, an amplified Kenwood TS-990S) carefully grounded and coupled to a skyful of specialized antennas is the pinnacle of amateur radio capabilities, but is far from portable. There are, of course, competing models such as the ICOM 9100, reviewed at QST, a ham website and magazine, and at eham.net. At about a third of the Kenwood TS-990S's price, expect fewer features and slightly less capability. Your shopping philosophy may differ, but for firearms, optics, and tech gear, I believe, "Buy once, cry once."

Whatever you choose, be sure to consider and purchase backup power sources for your radios—rechargeable batteries, solar chargers, generators, and even your vehicles' batteries.

Ham Radio Outlet is one of the better-known suppliers of new and used equipment, but local and regional "hamfests" usually have swap meets. Experienced hams looking to upgrade their equipment often offer a variety of excellent used equipment at great prices though usually *without warranties*.

CONSIDERATIONS WHEN PURCHASING EMERGENCY COMMS

Some other features to consider when purchasing emergency communications equipment:

- You have more control when you have knobs on the radios rather than buttons.
- Antenna masts that can be telescoped when not in use.
- Vertical yagis antennas stick out, but horizontal types blend in. (They just look like television antennas, to the casual observer.) So consider getting one that pivots for operation in both polarizations. Not only will it give you better OPSEC, but it will give you better versatility.
- With some communication devices, such as the Hamm radio, a license is required to operate.
- The power source it uses to operate.

During emergencies, our dependence on communications becomes all too clear. If the emergency is severe enough, the communication could be limited, if not non-existent for an extended period of time. We have all read enough survival books to know that the "comm down" scenario is a very real threat, and happens more often than not. So, when you are on your own, will you have your communication devices set up to communicate with others, or will you risk being without access to vital information?

Thanks to John Q. Public who assisted in writing a portion of this chapter.

PREPS TO BUY:

- Transceivers such as a Ham Radio and MURS walkie-talkies
- CB radio with SSB capability
- Field telephones with extra communication wire
- Table radio with shortwave bands
- Extra communication gear (i.e., headsets, antennas, etc.)
- Extra batteries
- Solar charger for cell phones

ACTION ITEMS:

1. Read the complete instruction manual for your emergency communication devices.
2. Determine whether you need licensing to operate your emergency communication device.
3. Learn alternative emergency communication sources, such as Morse code.
4. Practice using your emergency communication device regularly to increase your comfort with using it.

SUPPLEMENTAL INFORMATION AND RESOURCES

Morse Code

Amateur or "ham" radios can be operated with voice communications or Morse code. In many cases a message can get through with Morse code when voice messages fail. For emergency signals, Morse code can be sent by way of improvised sources that can be easily "keyed" on and off, making it one of the simplest and most versatile methods of telecommunication. The most common distress signal is SOS: three dots, three dashes and three dots. This distress signal is internationally recognized as a call for help.

A	.-	M	--	Y	-.--	6	-....
B	-...	N	-.	Z	--..	7	--...
C	-.-.	O	---	Ä	.-.-	8	---..
D	-..	P	.--.	Ö	---.	9	----.
E	.	Q	--.-	Ü	..--	.	.-.-.-
F	..-.	R	.-.	Ch	----	,	--..--
G	--.	S	...	0	-----	?	..--..
H	....	T	-	1	.----	!	..--.
I	..	U	..-	2	..---	:	---...
J	.---	V	...-	3	...--	"	.-..-.
K	-.-	W	.--	4	....-	'	.----.
L	.-..	X	-..-	5	.....	=	-...-

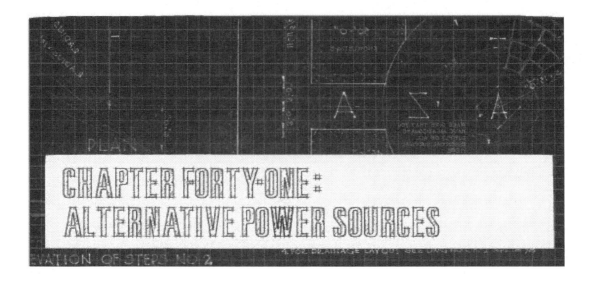

CHAPTER FORTY-ONE: ALTERNATIVE POWER SOURCES

HORRENDOUS and damaging as it was, Hurricane Sandy would be considered only an opening act compared with a powerful "once-in-a-century" solar storm...Although they can come at any time, their likelihood waxes and wanes in 11-year cycles — with the next period of maximum activity being next year [2013] ... A powerful solar (or "geomagnetic") storm has the potential to simultaneously damage multiple transformers ... affecting upwards of a hundred million people in the United States for many months, if not years.

These huge transformers are expensive and difficult to replace, and not many are stockpiled in the United States for an emergency. In the worst case, the impact would be devastating: an outage could cost a few trillion dollars, with full recovery taking years. Not only would parts of the grid be compromised, but telephone networks, undersea cables, satellites and railroads also would be affected.

A 2008 National Academy of Sciences study[142] warned that "because of the interconnectedness of critical infrastructures in modern society," the "collateral effects of a longer-term outage" would likely include "disruption of the transportation, communication, banking and finance systems, and government services; the breakdown of the distribution of potable water owing to pump failure; and the loss of perishable foods and medications because of lack of refrigeration." ... Similarly, a recent Lloyd's of London report cautioned that "a loss of power could lead to a cascade of operational failures that could leave society and the global economy severely disabled" ... So far, however, as an expert scientific panel tasked by the Homeland Security Department recently concluded [pdf[143]], the federal response to this potential crisis has been "poorly organized" and "no one is in charge." We ought to get our act together before a "Solar Sandy" catches us off-guard.

---

[142] http://www.nap.edu/openbook.php?record_id=12507&page=1

[143] http://www.fas.org/irp/agency/dod/jason/spaceweather.pdf

[144] http://www.nytimes.com/2012/11/03/opinion/not-ready-for-a-solar-sandy.html

Those who are moving to retreat properties make it a point to look for land with its own source of fuel in order to accommodate future needs. Whether those sources are an ample wood supply, a natural gas well, or a surface coal seam, these resources will ensure that you can continue to power your home and your equipment.

ALTERNATIVE POWER SOURCES

Those of us who do not have these resources readily available to us on our own land may eventually run out of stored fuel sources[145]. A way to avoid this future issue is to consider investing in devices that collect renewable energy to supply our homes and retreats with a continual supply of power. Consider the following, and keep in mind that all of these items would be ideal for barter situations:

Batteries - Most of our emergency devices require batteries, and having an abundance of them with the capability of being recharged is a good investment in your long-term livelihood. The best batteries on the market right now are NiMH (Nickel-Metal Hydride) that have a low self-discharge (LSD). To prolong the charge of your batteries, store them in a sealed bag in the back of your refrigerator to prevent condensation and extend the life of the battery.

> **Make a battery bank**
>
> Having multiple DC batteries hooked up and working together creates a battery bank and allows you to run more of your household appliances using stored solar energy.

Also, consider purchasing lead-acid deep-cycle (DC) batteries (also called solar batteries). Solar batteries provide energy storage for solar, wind and other renewable energy systems. Different from a car battery, a deep cycle battery is capable of surviving prolonged, repeated and deep discharges, which are typical in renewable energy systems that are "off grid." Deep cycle batteries can be a large expense for a sizeable off-grid system, but with proper care and maintenance, they should last 5-10 years.

Keep in mind that many families who invested in solar panels for their home complained that when the grid went down in their location, they were unable to access any power[146]. Even after the storm or disaster has passed and it is a bright, sunny day (when the PV modules would certainly be generating electricity), they were disappointed that they couldn't access electricity

---

[145] http://readynutrition.com/resources/the-6-most-popular-types-of-fuel-to-store-for-emergencies_10092013/

[146] http://www.nytimes.com/2012/11/20/business/energy-environment/solar-power-as-solution-for-storm-darkened-homes.html?_r=0

for their home. This problem applies to grid-connected PV systems that do *not* include battery banks for back up. This is why battery banks are essential in storing energy for later use.

Solar Energy - Harnessing the sun's magnificent power has become quite the craze lately. And why wouldn't it be? In some states, having photovoltaic panels can make you eligible for a 30 percent federal tax credit!

- **Solar Panels** come in all sizes, ranging from enormous to small enough to fit on the hood of your car for charging small devices. If you are considering purchasing some supplies for solar power, start out with a basic set and then add additional items to the existing set up.

- **Solar Generators** have many advantages: they don't produce dangerous fumes, they run quietly, they are energy efficient and fuel is not required to run them. The best part is these generators can last 25 years or longer! Although the initial expense can be high, there is no additional cost to run the generator, so it's a great investment. And for that matter, who says that a solar generator can only be used during disasters? Running your solar generator regularly will keep your electricity bills down.

- **Mobile Solar Power Systems** would be ideal for bug-out bags. Keep in mind that these systems can easily be stolen, hence the word portable solar power systems. They should be placed in a secure, well-guarded area.

- **Solar Battery Chargers** use trickle charging, and can be somewhat time consuming. To expedite this process, considering investing in two or three chargers to use simultaneously. However, there are solar chargers that can be connected to a photovoltaic panel and can make a huge difference in recharging batteries and providing power to small-scale appliances. Those that live in humid or rainy environments may want to consider a charger that is weather resistant[147]. Lastly, ensure your solar battery charger can charge a variety of battery sizes and has smart capability.

- **Inverters** - An inverter[148] is an electronic device that converts DC power into AC power. Ensure that you find an inverter that can handle your initial needs and anticipated needs. You can get the wattage by looking at the manufactures label on the appliance; if only the amps are there, use the formula (amps x 115 volts= wattage) to convert to watts.

> A solar power system has three components:
>
> Solar panel(s) + Charge controller + Batteries
>
> As the sun's rays hit the solar cells on a photovoltaic (PV) panel, the power is transferred to a silicon semiconductor.
>
> The power is then changed into (DC) direct current electricity and passed through connecting wires to enter a storage battery.

---

[147] http://www.wayfair.com/SOLAR-Battery-Charger-For-Marine-Trickle-1002-IGT1046.html?refid=GPA49-IGT1046&gclid=CJjNjYCSj68CFQFgTAodfG63yA

[148] http://readynutrition.com/resources/prepping-to-survive-the-nautical-series-pt-5-shtf-inverters_05032012/

NATURAL POWER SOURCES

The power from wind and water has been used for centuries and can easily be adapted to fit most self-reliant lifestyles.

- <u>**Wind** energy</u>[149] can be harnessed by mounting <u>wind turbines</u>[150] in high locations such as a rooftop. (Having a professional mount the turbine would be beneficial.) Many preppers do not recommend wind turbines because of their high maintenance and the risks associated with tower climbing. However, if you happen to live in an area that is prone to high winds and has lots of cloud coverage it could be a suitable option.
- **Water (hydro)** energy has a lot of power - anyone who has seen Niagara Falls knows what I'm talking about! Steep parcels of land with large creeks running through them can be ideal spots for water turbines. A water turbine or hydro generator has the capacity to produce 10 amperes around the clock and matches the usable power generated by over 40 amps of solar modules. The power system itself is the same as solar, except that only diversion-type charge controls can be used with hydro.

Batteries of all types and sizes will be a high commodity item during an emergency. In an extended or longer-term emergency, batteries would also be a valuable bartering item. If the subject of peak oil isn't enough, consider the fragility of the grid. As it stands, our country cannot exist without the electrical grid, and sometime in the not-so-distant future our lives could change drastically by a single event or disaster. While there is no way to predict when or if this will happen, we would be wise to prepare for the possibility.

---

[149] http://readynutrition.com/resources/prepping-to-survive-the-nautical-series-pt-4-wind-turbines_27022012/

[150] http://www.hydrogenappliances.com/Hornet1000.html

PREPS TO BUY:

- Rechargeable batteries in assorted sizes – in quantity
- DC Batteries – in quantity
- Solar Battery Chargers
- Solar Photovoltaic Panel (5 watts or more)
- Generator (Solar powered, diesel ran generators are preferable. Also, keep in mind that a typical size for a home backup generator is 4,500 watts continuous and 5,500 watts peak.)
- Inverter
- Seasoned Firewood
- Extra parts for any alternative energy equipment and generators
- Extra fuel sources you regularly use (propane, gasoline, diesel, etc.)
- Fuel stabilizers if using gasoline (such as Sta-bil), or diesel fuel supplements to prevent gelling and a diesel antibacterial additive to prevent both growth and gelling

ACTION ITEMS:

1. Make a spreadsheet of the total wattage the household uses.
2. Purchase your alternative power supply devices and keep in mind if they are compatible to your needs.
3. Purchase spare parts for your equipment.
4. Ensure that your equipment is kept in a secure location and is unable to be stolen if in use. Hardened bolt-cutter-resistant security chains and a padlock can do wonders!
5. When using any alternative power supply, monitor your supply to ensure that the power is not about to run out.

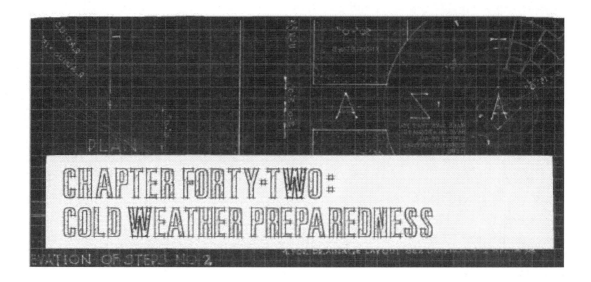

CHAPTER FORTY-TWO: COLD WEATHER PREPAREDNESS

When is the worst time to have your furnace give up the ghost? Why, the day before Christmas, of course. The worst Christmas in memory at our house took place during a terrible cold snap and snowstorm. Not only were we snowed in, but our furnace sputtered to a halt at the same time. None of the heating repair companies were working and phones weren't answered.

The first day wasn't too bad – we were moderately comfortable with just an extra sweater over our clothes. We went about our business and I made sure to cook dinner in the oven to add a little bit of warmth to the house. As it grew dark out it began to get colder so we all bundled into one bed under the covers.

Christmas morning dawned COLD. The kids opened their presents while caped under blankets. We hung blankets in the doorways and congregated in the kitchen as the turkey cooked. We plugged in the tiny electric space heater that we had to take the chill off the bathroom on cold mornings. By evening, the thermometer read 50 degrees in the warmest room of the house. That night, we pulled out the sleeping bags, dragged a mattress into the dining area, and slept in the chilly kitchen, warmed only by the little heater.

The following day, the temperature was down to 37 in the kitchen, the warmest room of the house. We wore hats and gloves and huddled miserably under blankets. The children were lethargic and cranky. Finally, we reached the heating company, who dispatched a repairperson immediately. He very kindly brought in a large electric heater to warm our kitchen while he worked on the furnace. Several hours later I gratefully wrote out a large check as our furnace came to life.

A Reader

We've already discussed in depth the nightmare we would experience during a prolonged or long-term power disruption. Let's take it a step further: what would happen if this event occurred in the dead of winter? This is a serious threat for those who see frigid temperatures during the winter. In this case, it will be up to you to keep yourself and your family warm until the grid comes back up or until spring arrives.

Our society has become so certain that the grid is permanent that many homes built over the past 50-60 years have been designed without the vital elements of a fireplace or a wood stove for heat. In the newer homes, most of the fireplaces are present for aesthetics rather than practicality. For this reason, we must prepare accordingly in order to stay warm.

> **Layer Your Preparedness Efforts!**
>
> Every preparedness layer makes a difference in the case of surviving the winter in a grid-down situation. We can make the most of a dire situation by insulating the body and insulating the home.

HOW COLD AFFECTS US

Hypothermia

When hypothermia occurs, the body functions begin to slow as the temperature drops. Aside from the cold that is felt and the shivering that may occur, mental function is most affected initially. A particular danger of hypothermia is that it develops gradually, and since it affects thinking and reasoning, it may go unnoticed.

Other symptoms include initial hunger and nausea that will give way to apathy as the core body temperature drops. This is followed by confusion, lethargy, slurred speech, loss of consciousness, and coma. Often the affected person will lie down, fall asleep, and die. In some cases, the patient will paradoxically remove their clothes just before this occurs.

There is a direct relationship in the decrease of brain function and the decrease in body temperature (the colder the body, the less the brain function). Brain function stops at a core temperature of 68 F (20 C). The heart is subject to abnormal electrical rhythms as hypothermia progresses and could cause cardiac arrest. (Source[151])

Keep in mind that you can develop hypothermia with temperatures above freezing. The fastest way to become hypothermic is a combination of cold temperatures with wind and rain. In this case, your body loses heat *25 times faster* than it would by just being out in the cold.

Older individuals and small children are at the greatest risk of hypothermia. Diabetics and those who suffer from low thyroid levels are also at higher risk. However, anyone who is subjected to the elements long enough will surely be affected.

---

[151] http://www.onhealth.com/hypothermia/page3.htm

Frostbite

Exposure to the cold for long periods[152] can lead to frostbite. The damage done to the tissues occurs from the formation of ice crystals within cells, thus rupturing the cells and leading to cell death. When the cold causes your core temperature to drop, your body will kick into survival mode by cutting off circulation to the outer extremities first. The fingers, toes, nose, ears, and lips are the first parts of the body to show signs of frostbite.

The signs and symptoms of frostbite depend on the extent and depth of tissue injury. Learn about the signs of frostbite and how to treat it in the supplemental information at end of the chapter.

GETTING PREPARED

Let's begin discussing some solutions and practical ways to prevent frostbite.

1. Having some space heaters on hand will be a Godsend when temperatures start dropping rapidly. Propane heaters, such as the Little Buddy heater, can provide a room with ample heat and are considered safe for indoor use in most states. There are several propane heaters on the market that do not require electricity.
2. Kerosene/Oil heaters are also beneficial to have during cold months. These heaters burn a wick for heat, fuelled by the addition of heating oil.
3. An antique "Perfection[153]" oil heater can be a charming addition to your decor that can be called into service during a grid-down situation.

INSULATING THE BODY

- A large majority of body heat is lost at the back of the neck and at the top of the head, so make sure that you use the layering principle[154] with your clothing. Ensure you have a warm hat to wear and to make sure your chest and neck are covered with a scarf. Lightweight gloves will also help you maintain your warmth. Wear heavy socks and shoes to protect your feet from cold floors.
- Hand warmers and foot warmers are a great way to increase your core body temperature quickly. Here is an easy project to make your own pocket warmers[155] to prevent scalding to the skin.

---

[152] http://readynutrition.com/resources/cold-exposure-emergencies-and-how-to-avoid-it_04022012/

[153] http://www.milesstair.com/Perfection_History.htm

[154] http://readynutrition.com/resources/are-you-ready-series-emergency-clothing-part-3_27112009/

[155] http://readynutrition.com/resources/fight-the-coldhomemade-pocket-warmers_25012011/

- Use heavy sleeping bags. Zipping into a sleeping bag will conserve your body's warmth more than simply getting under the covers.
- Bivvy sacks are ideal for adding an extra layer to your sleeping bags for added warmth.
- Crumbling up newspapers and putting them in your clothing will provide some much needed insulation and extra warmth as well.
- Pitch a tent. This works especially well when you have children because it adds an element of fun to an otherwise stressful situation. Inside a tent, you can combine your body heat to stay much warmer.

INSULATING THE HOME

- Light some candles. Burning candles can add some warmth to a small area. And if you want to make the most of heat emitted from a candle, try making a space heater from a candle[156]. This handy device collects, retains, concentrates, and radiates dry space heat from a candle.
- Seal off a room or a smaller area to heat by using a folded quilt to better insulate the room. You can also hang heavy quilts in the doorways of rooms with a heat source to block them off from the rest of the house. Ensure that you seal any drafts coming from windows in the room as well.
- To prevent heat from escaping from the fireplace when it's not in use, purchase a fireplace plug. It is an inflatable pillow that seals the fireplace damper, eliminating drafts, odors, and noise. The pillow is removed whenever the fireplace is used, then reinserted after.
- Insulate your windows. Rubber weather sealant and/or window insulation film can also keep drafts at a minimum. You can also use a plastic shower curtain or bubble wrap[157] and duct tape, topped by a heavy quilt to keep the wind from whistling through your windows. This has the added benefit of keeping the windows dark if you are concerned about OPSEC. Another option is to purchase a draft door dodger or make your own. Layers of curtains made of heavy fabrics can also keep a room more insulated.
- Here's a way to convert your windows into passive solar heater[158]. This passive solar heater[159] is very simple and can be made with items already in your house.
-
-
-
- Heat some rocks. If you have a place outdoors for a cooking fire, you can add large rocks to the fire. Rocks retain heat for a very long time. When you are ready to go to bed,

---

[156] http://www.heatstick.com/_Process.htm

[157] http://builditsolar.com/Projects/Conservation/bubblewrap.htm'

[158] http://www.instructables.com/id/Solar-Heater/

[159] http://www.instructables.com/id/How-to-Build-a-Soda-Can-Heater/

move the rocks into a cast iron Dutch oven. VERY CAREFULLY take this into the room that you are heating. The stones will emit heat for several hours. This is an excellent way to passively heat your room when you're sleeping. With this method, you don't have to be concerned about the potential of a fire or carbon monoxide poisoning during the night.

BE SAFE

In your search for warmth make certain that you also maintain safety. Keep fire extinguishers handy and invest in a battery operated carbon monoxide detector. Keep children and pets away from items that could burn them or that could tip over, causing a fire. Be sure to store all flammable materials (such as propane and kerosene) according to manufacturer's instructions.

Did you know that snow is an excellent insulator (provided you don't touch it)? For those of you who may find yourself outdoors and exposed to the cold elements, knowing how to make an emergency winter shelter[160] out of snow could save your life.

---

[160] http://www.survivalmagazine.org/survival-forum/showthread.php/6330-Winter-Shelter-Quinzhee-Tutorial

PREPS TO BUY:

- Space heater (preferably propane or non-electric)
- Door draft stopper or windows and doors
- Sleeping bag
- Bivvy sac
- Wool socks
- Thermal underwear
- Hand and foot warmers
- Rubber weather sealant
- Caulk
- Window insulation film
- Bubble wrap or an old shower curtain set aside
- Duct tape
- Fireplace plug

ACTION ITEMS:

Winterize your home before bad weather is expected:

1. Check your furnace and replace filters monthly.
2. Inspect the fireplace and get it ready for use. Ensure your firewood is properly seasoned, and stored away from the home.
3. Insulate your exterior pipes.
4. Inspect exterior of home and seal any crevice cracks and exposed entry points around pipes.
5. Caulk and weather-strip doors and windows.
6. Add insulation to your walls and attic, if necessary.
7. Consider purchasing insulated doors and storm windows to further protect your home from the cold. This will also help lower your heating bill.
8. Replace cracked glass in windows. If it is necessary to replace the entire window, be sure to prime and paint exposed wood.
9. If your home has a basement, consider protecting its window wells by covering them with plastic shields.
10. Inspect roof, gutters & downspouts and clean out any debris.

SUPPLEMENTAL INFORMATION AND RESOURCES

Recognizing Frostbite

A victim is often unaware of frostbite until someone else points it out because the frozen tissues are numb.

At the first signs of redness or pain in any skin area, get out of the cold or protect any exposed skin—frostbite may be beginning. Individuals with superficial frostbite may experience the following signs and symptoms to the affected area:

- Pain
- Burning
- Tingling
- Numbness
- Pale colored skin
- Clear-colored skin blisters may develop
- Firm-feeling skin with soft underlying tissue which can move over bony ridges
- As the degree of injury progresses (1st to 3rd) to involve deeper tissue structures, the signs and symptoms of deep frostbite can develop, which may include the following:
    - Complete loss of sensation,
    - Pale, yellowish, bluish, gray, or mottled skin color,
    - Formation of blood-filled skin blisters, and
    - Firm-feeling skin and underlying tissue, with the affected area feeling hard and solid.

With advanced frostbite injuries, the affected area can subsequently appear blackened and gangrene can develop, placing the affected individual at high-risk for infection.

What to Do:

If you detect symptoms of frostbite, seek medical care. Because frostbite and hypothermia both result from exposure, first determine whether the victim also shows signs of hypothermia, as described previously. Hypothermia is a more serious medical condition and requires emergency medical assistance.

1. If (1) there is frostbite but no sign of hypothermia and (2) immediate medical care is not available, proceed as follows:

2. Get into a warm room as soon as possible.

3. Unless absolutely necessary, do not walk on frostbitten feet or toes—this increases the damage.

4. Immerse the affected area in warm—not hot—water (the temperature should be comfortable to the touch for unaffected parts of the body).

5. Or, warm the affected area using body heat. For example, the heat of an armpit can be used to warm frostbitten fingers.

6. Do not rub the frostbitten area with snow or massage it at all. This can cause more damage.

7. Don't use a heating pad, heat lamp, or the heat of a stove, fireplace, or radiator for warming. Affected areas are numb and can be easily burned.

These procedures are not substitutes for proper medical care. Hypothermia is a medical emergency and frostbite should be evaluated by a health care provider. It is a good idea to take a first aid and emergency resuscitation (CPR) course to prepare for cold-weather health problems. Knowing what to do is an important part of protecting your health and the health of others.

Source: CDC

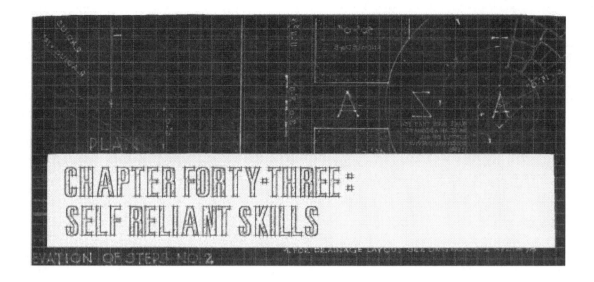

CHAPTER FORTY-THREE: SELF RELIANT SKILLS

Evidence suggests that up to 150,000 people die each year in circumstances where first aid could have helped. It is a subject Ray Mears is passionate about. He says: 'Just knowing the basics can save a life.' He was filming Ray Mears Bushcraft for the BBC, exploring the dramatic landscape of Wyoming, USA.

Ray, the director, the cameraman and the pilot were flying over a ridge to capture a shot of man riding a horse. But, heading downwind, the pilot had insufficient power to maintain height. 'About a minute before the collision, I remember thinking, "We're very low – this isn't right," ' says Ray. 'And then everything turned upside down.' The helicopter hit the ground. 'I went into the brace position and just hoped for the best,' recalls Ray. 'I remember hearing the deafening sound of metal crunching, then everything went eerily silent. 'I clambered out of a small opening thinking I was the only survivor, but I soon heard the cameraman shout, "I'm alive but my legs are broken" from inside the helicopter.'

Amazingly, Ray had suffered only severe bruising so he ran to his colleague's aid. 'His leg was so broken it formed a right-angle out to the side,' says Ray. Using a penknife, he cut the safety harness that was keeping the cameraman in the helicopter and, thanks to the adrenaline pumping around his body, he lifted the 6ft 2in man to safety. 'He felt light as a feather – that strange moment has always stuck with me' adds Ray. 'First aid can just be about being there for someone, which can prevent them going into shock,' he says. 'I slowly moved the leg into a straighter position and made a makeshift splint out of gaffer tape and a camping mat.' Once everyone was away from the helicopter, Ray and the director noted down a list of the injuries. 'I wanted to make sure that when I rang the emergency services, I wouldn't forget anything in a panic,' says Ray. 'I wanted paramedics to be prepared because we came down in the middle of nowhere. I know most people aren't going to be in a helicopter crash but the same rules apply in everyday situations.'

Source[161]

---

[161] http://www.dailymail.co.uk/health/article-2180270/Ray-Mears-helicopter-crash-Survival-expert-reveals-learn-lifesavers.html#ixzz2IpA17njQ

I have often emphasized how important it is to understand that preparedness isn't about how many items you have stored away – it's really about learning the skills necessary to survive. Ultimately, we want to be self-reliant and able to maintain a healthy lifestyle. In order to adapt and transition more fluidly into self-reliant living, our efforts must lie in our learned skills, abilities and knowledge.

I realize the time constraints of our daily schedules can put a dent in our availability; but it is vital that you find the time to learn. When making the decision on what skills you should learn, think: sustainability.

ESSENTIAL SKILLS NECESSARRY FOR SURVIVAL

This is a basic list of skills you should learn in order to survive in a longer-term disaster.

1. **Outdoor Survival Courses**

   Most preppers and survivalists are planning to "re-connect" with nature. Learning the necessary outdoor skills will provide a person with fundamental knowledge on how to better survive. The Boy Scouts offer adult classes as well as some community colleges. Get creative and search around the internet. There are some survival courses offered online (some are free courses) that allow people to learn from the comfort of their home. There are also wilderness courses offered at a variety of facilities such as local colleges, the YMCA, community parks and recreation facilities, etc.

   Additionally, finding books and e-books on survival skills is another way to gather information on this topic. Better yet – practice going out into nature and living in rugged conditions to get an idea of the supplies required and how to better maintain your basic needs.

2. **Medical**

   In a survival situation, medical training is going to be vital. Due to the increased use of saws, axes and knives, there will be more medical emergencies involving deep lacerated cuts. Knowing how to properly clean wounds, stitch wounds, as well as knowing how to treat infected wounds will be extremely important.

   Additionally, there will be an increase in burns from being in closer contact to fires. Burns can get infected very quickly, and knowing how to decipher the degree of the burn and how to treat it will be a concern amongst survivalists and preppers.

   Online courses are offered for basic CPR/First Aid; however, those courses will not give a person the fundamental hands-on training they need. Finding a local Emergency Medical Technician (EMT) class that is offered for paramedics and first responders to accidents will better equip a person to handle emergency medical situations.

3. **Hunting Skills**

As many are planning to hunt wild game for a food source, they will need skills on how to gut the carcass, skin the fur, and properly cut the meat. The "hunter-in-training" will also have to have a proficient knowledge on the different types of hunting tools used to prepare animal carcasses (and these tools come in different sizes based on the animal).

The National Hunting Association is a portal that can take a person to their local area hunting association in order to get more information for their specific area. Also, this website offers hunting guides for all of the states within the USA.

4. **Disaster Training**

Disaster training is typically offered by FEMA, the American Red Cross and other disaster organizations. A person who is equipped with knowledge on how to plan for a disaster, how to properly prepare for a disaster, and how to mentally handle the aftereffects of a disaster will be able to better adapt to the situation more quickly compared to those that are not. The American Red Cross offers extensive courses in disaster safety and training as well as basic First Aid/CPR courses. There are also online courses offered through FEMA.

5. **Gardening Skills**

In a long-term survival situation, seeds will mean the difference between life and death. The only problem is, many have lost the necessary skill of gardening because there is a grocery store on every corner of the streets these days. It's time to get your hands dirty and get back in touch with nature. Learning necessary gardening skills such as companion plants, crop rotations, beneficial insects, natural ways to replenish soil, and knowledge on proper gardening tools will be beneficial.

Another relevant knowledge source is understanding the medicinal value of plants and herbs. It is amazing how many uses there are for plants besides spicing up our cooked entrees. Knowledge of natural medicines is another necessity in a survival situation, especially if a family member has a pre-existing condition.

6. **Firearm Certification and Training**

There are dozens of firearms courses offered through the National Rifle Association. The more you practice, the better your aim gets. This is one survival skill in which a person should be as proficient as possible. Also, practicing gun safety and educating others about gun safety, especially around children, is essential when a firearm is involved.

7. **Canning and Food Preservation**

Knowing how to can and preserve foods to eat during the long winter months is vital. Just think of all the delicious shelf-stable goods a person can store up for when their food supply dwindles in the winter. The canning jars can be a bit of an investment. However, canning jars can often be found on www.craigslist.com, at garage sales and even at second hand stores. Canning jars and lids would also make an excellent bartering item.

8. **Amateur Radio Classes**

Having a radio is encouraged by many disaster relief organizations. Having knowledge on how to operate a ham radio will provide a person with an emergency communication source during a time when most communication is down. The National Association of Amateur Radio provides information based on a person's location and course information on their website.

9. **Sewing Classes**

Typically, if there is a fabric store, there are sewing classes and sewing events offered there. Everyone has heard of how their great grandmothers would sew quilts out of material from damaged or worn clothing, but not many of us have this skill anymore. Sewing classes will not only teach a necessary skill, but it will also get the survival mindset in place: make something new out of what you have available. This skill will also steady your hand if you have to give stitches in an emergency.

10. **Candle/Soap-making**

Soap and candle making are a lost art form in my opinion. Having a background knowledge of these skills would also be a great bartering skill. Search the Internet and community publications to find these classes.

I'd like to conclude by offering a few pieces of advice on learning new skills – practice any chance you get and give yourself time to learn. Like any new thing you try to do, there is a learning curve involved. Finding others in your area that can help guide you through these new skills can be such a blessing, and can open the door to some new mentors.

PREPS TO BUY:

- Written books on skills you want to learn
- Tools or accessories needed to learn these skills
- Extra printer paper to print out any information you find online
- Binders for organizing your information

ACTION ITEMS:

1. Start looking online for any online courses you can take.
2. Make a goal to start learning a new skill set.
3. Purchase written resources for your survival library.
4. Equip yourself with essential knowledge.
5. Get and stay current in any certifications.
6. Continue to educate yourself on skills.

SUPPLEMENTAL INFORMATION AND RESOURCES

Required Reading Lists:

Medical Skills

The Doom and Bloom Survival Medical Handbook

When There Is No Doctor

When There Is No Dentist

Disaster Preparedness

Handbook to Practical Disaster Preparedness for the Family

Disaster Preparedness for EMP Attacks and Solar Storms

Contact: A Tactical Manual for Post-Collapse Survival

Gardening Skills

The Vegetable Gardener's Bible

The Fruit Gardener's Bible

All-New Square Foot Gardening

Lasagna Gardening

Medicinal Plants

Medicinal Plants of North America: A Field Guide

Identifying and Harvesting Edible and Medicinal Plants in Wild (and Not So Wild) Places

Canning and Food Preservation

The Prepper's Cookbook: 300 Recipes to Turn Your Emergency Food into Nutritious, Delicious, Life-Saving Meals

Ball Blue Book Guide to Preserving

Canning and Preserving Your Own Harvest

A Guide to Canning, Freezing, Curing & Smoking Meat, Fish & Game Preserving Food without Freezing or Canning

Build Your Own Underground Root Cellar

The Pantry Primer

Sewing

Singer's Complete Guide to Sewing, Revised and Expanded

Sewing 101: A Beginner's Guide to Sewing

Outdoor/Survival

SAS Survival Guide

SAS Urban Survival Handbook

Wilderness Survival Handbook: Primitive Skills for Short-Term Survival and Long-Term Comfort
How to Survive the End of the World as We Know It

Homesteading

Encyclopedia of Country Living

The Urban Homestead

The Backyard Homestead

The Backyard Homestead Guide to Raising Farm Animals

One Acre Homestead

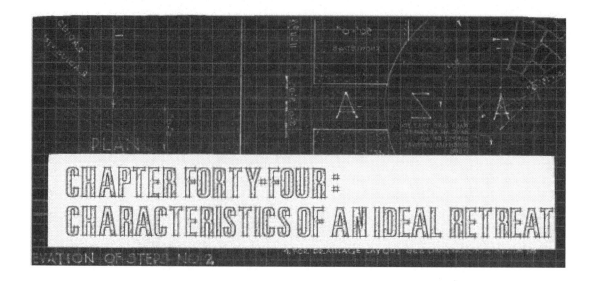

CHAPTER FORTY-FOUR: CHARACTERISTICS OF AN IDEAL RETREAT

By now, you are keenly aware of the different disasters that could affect your way of life. Some of these disasters have the capacity to cause widespread destruction, panic and suffering. Given the pandemonium that would ensue in the more populated areas of our country, some people are ready to take the necessary steps to be more self-reliant. Preparing your home to be a survival retreat allows you to stock more supplies and be more prepared for bug-in situations and longer-term emergencies.

Although many would like to trade in their suburban and urban dwellings to move to more rural settings and start their survival retreats, their jobs keep them from doing so. Let's face it, most jobs are in or around city limits. As much as we would like to leave the city for some wide-open spaces, our jobs will not allow us to. However, some have more flexibility in where they work or can opt to work from home. People in those situations will have more control over where they can relocate.

POPULATION DENSITY IS A MAJOR FACTOR

An important aspect to look into is whether any major cities are in your desired retreat area. Ideally, you want to choose an area that has low population density. If a major disaster occurs, living in a more isolated area (especially far away from major highways) will help to protect your retreat from transient mobs leaving the cities. You don't want to be on the lines of drift from major cities, as towns along these roads will be hit hard by hordes of people, some of whom might not be friendly. See the map below to view the major cities of the United States.

Deciding exactly where to relocate is not an exact science. You can gauge the potential threat and plan accordingly, but you can never be completely certain what will happen and where the safest place will be. However, knowing that you have researched and prepared the best retreat possible puts you at a far greater advantage than many others. In his book <u>Strategic Relocation</u>[162], Joel Skousen analyzes different areas of the United States and offer excellent advice on choosing the best location for your family and resources. Skousen believes the largest threat is population density. Because every crisis that threatens, even a local crisis, can turn exponential because of the close proximity to people who cannot help themselves.

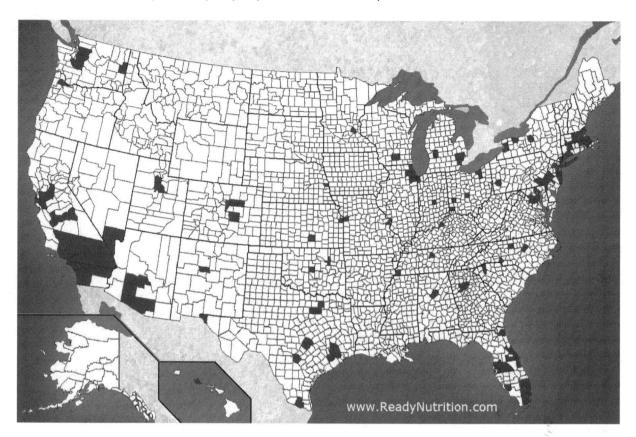

U.S. Most Populated Counties

LAND CHARACTERISTICS

Location and land characteristics are crucial factors when a person is considering purchasing land for a survival retreat. Experts agree on the fact that the area we should choose for a retreat property needs to be a semi-isolated location with a steady water supply and a fair amount of timber for heat in a woodstove/fireplace. If we find ourselves in a grid-down scenario, we want to be able to support our basic needs. These will be the top priorities in the beginning.

While walking the property, note what resources and obstacles your site has before you make a plan. Keep in mind that you want to find a property that can be sustainable. Ask yourself questions such as:

---

[162] http://www.joelskousen.com/strategic.html

- What's there that you can use? Trees, bamboo, stones, sand, soil, clay, etc.?
- Is there plenty of wood or coal for fire?
- Is there a natural water supply?
- Do you know how to work with the available materials? Can you learn to?
- Can the retreat property be seen from the road?
- Is there a major highway nearby?
- Can you protect your land, if attacked?

Keeping these questions in mind will help you determine whether the property is appropriate for surviving long-term disasters.

CLIMATE

Climate is another consideration. Many people believe that living in the warm climates of the south would be ideal for retreats. Bear in mind that most southern states are susceptible to damage brought on by hurricanes, tropical storms, tornadoes, and flooding. As you can see from the map below, most of our states are exposed to one or more climatic issues. Keep this in mind when determining where you want to set up your retreat.

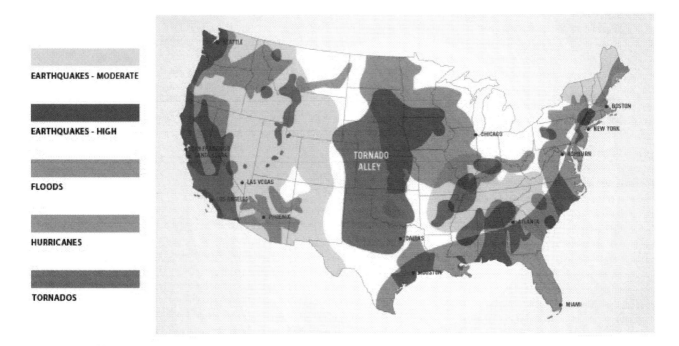

Map provided by Redcross.org and Noaa.gov

IDEAL RETREAT CHARACTERISTICS

- A long growing season
- Property backs up to a state or national park
- Low population density
- Distance from major cities and suburban developments
- Sufficient year-round precipitation and surface water
- Rich topsoil
- Sunny area for solar panels
- No major earthquake, hurricane, or tornado risks
- No flooding risk
- No tidal-wave risk (at least two hundred feet above sea level)
- Minimal forest-fire risk
- Away from interstate freeways and other channelized areas
- Employment opportunities in the area if you are not self-employed
- Diverse economy and agriculture
- Low taxes
- Non-intrusive scale of government
- Favorable zoning and inexpensive building permits
- Minimal gun laws
- A lifestyle geared toward self-sufficiency
- Plentiful local sources of wood or coal
- No restrictions on keeping livestock
- Defensible terrain
- Not near a prison or large mental institution
- Inexpensive insurance rates (home, auto, health)
- Upwind and away from major nuclear power plants[163]

Consider searching within an active farming area. This is beneficial because the barter systems are already in place, not to mention an abundance of livestock and produce.

When thinking about where you'd prefer to buy your retreat and/or retirement home, look at all the factors and whether the piece of land can sustain you and your family's needs. Use this mapping tool[164] to:

- Locate any underground aquifers in the area
- Identify any environmental or climatic issues in the area
- Map the vegetation growth in the area

---

[163] http://money.cnn.com/news/specials/nuclear_power_plants_locations/index.html

[164] http://nationalatlas.gov/mapmaker

PREPS TO BUY:

- Topographic and geographic maps of the area
- Farmer's Almanac to find out growing season

ACTION ITEMS:

1. Research! Compare counties[165] that you are interested in moving to.
2. Look into the local governments and what local laws are in place.
3. Research www.city-data.com to see what the statistics are for the location you are considering.
4. Find out the condition of the soil.
5. Determine if there is a barter system.
6. Learn more about the principles of a retreat.

---

[165] http://www.relocationessentials.com/aff/www/tools/salary/col.aspx

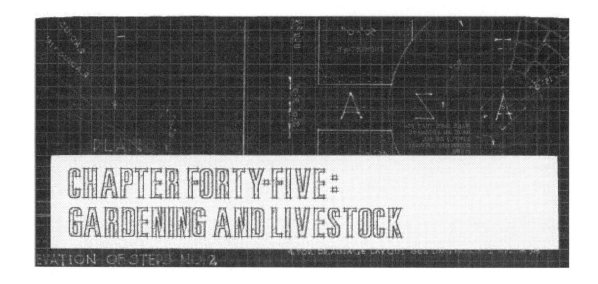

CHAPTER FORTY-FIVE: GARDENING AND LIVESTOCK

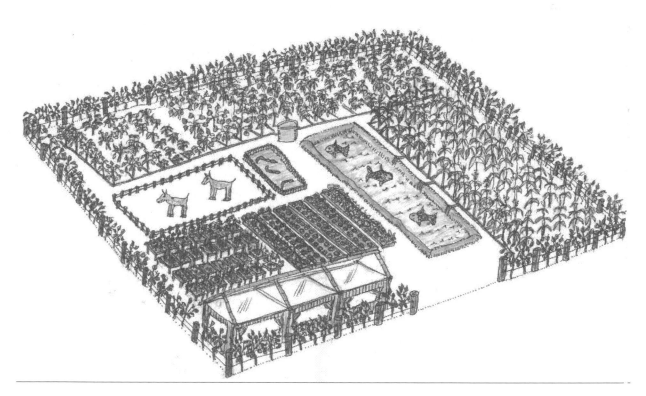

Image Source: Peggy Bradley, Institute of Simplified Hydroponics[166]

Our survival homesteads will be our safe havens to protect us and help us thrive. Living through a long-term emergency will require our attention on many matters. Therefore, we want our land to work for us in the most productive and efficient manner possible.

---

[166] http://www.carbon.org/

The image above is a good example of a micro farm. It shows a great method of making the most use out of the land you have. You want to plan on creating a relationship between your livestock and your gardens for the most efficient, healthy and cost-effective homestead. This is particularly important in a post-disaster world. The more food you can produce for yourself, the better your chances of survival in a long-term situation.

MICRO LIVESTOCK

Especially on a smaller homestead, micro livestock can be a vital element. Smaller animals, such as chickens, goats, ducks and rabbits, are a great addition because they require less space, less care and less food, but can still provide your family with meat, dairy and eggs.

Other breeds to consider are:

- Cattle – Zebu Cattle, Miniature Herefords, Mini Holstein, Red Panda Cow, White Dexter, Lowline, Miniature Longhorns, Miniature Galloways, Jerseys, Ayrshires
- Birds -Turkeys, chickens, ducks, pigeons, quail and guinea fowl
- Goats – Terai, Nigerian dwarf, West African dwarf, Pygmy, Nubian
- Pigs - American Guinea hog, West African dwarf, Chinese dwarf, Criollo
- Rabbits – Cinnamons, Californias, American Chinchillas, Creme D'Argents, Blanc D'Hotot, New Zealand, Palomino, Rex, Sables, Satins, Silver fox
- Guinea Pigs – Long haired, Short hairs, all different color variations
- Miniature Deer – mouse deer, musk deer, blue duiker antelope

Micro livestock can also make helpful farmhands: you can press them into duty and use them to help clear areas of weeds, roots or cover crops, all while fertilizing the land at the same time.

COMPOSTING

Manure from the livestock can be utilized as a rich fertilizer for your gardens. Blood meal and bone meal can both be used to amend the soil, and can also be added to the compost pile.

My favorite type of gardening is sheet mulching, or composting in place. This allows the compost to slowly decompose and be present for the plants that have been planted on top.

There are many benefits to using compost as a soil conditioner. The end result of composting is a nutrient rich soil that will hold water, allows for air flow, controls erosion, and creates a home for the bacteria that protects plants against disease, captures airborne nitrogen, and lures soil-enriching earthworms. In addition to the benefits to the soil, composting cuts down on greenhouse gases as well as naturally discards certain organic materials that would otherwise be thrown into a trashcan. Generally speaking the decomposition process involves both:

Aerobic – oxygen decomposes and stabilizes the composting materials.

> Anaerobic – lack of oxygen – composition breaks down by the actions of living organisms.

"In both of these processes, bacteria, fungi, molds, protozoa, actinomycetes, and other saprophytic organisms feed upon decaying organic materials initially, while in the later stages of decomposition mites, millipedes, centipedes, spring tails, beetles and earthworms further breakdown and enrich the composting materials. The organisms will vary in the pile due to temperature conditions, but the goal in composting is to create the most favorable environment possible for the desired organisms." (Source – Aggie Horticulture Department)

Brown – Carbon Rich Materials

- Livestock manure (horse, cow, sheep, chicken)
- Lawn clippings and dried leaves, pine needles
- Sawdust
- Shredded newspaper
- Straw
- Wood chips and small twigs

Green – Nitrogen Rich Material

- Crop residue
- Culled vegetables
- Kitchen scraps – peels, cores, leftover cooked vegetables (as long as there is no salt or butter on them), and produce past its prime
- Grass clippings (free of pesticide)
- Cuttings from plants, dead headed flowers, pulled weeds
- Coffee grounds and filters, tea leaves, tea bags
- Eggshells

The best compost combines 2 to 3 parts "brown," or carbon-rich materials, with 1 part "green," or nitrogen-rich materials. Cover the first layer with 6 inches of "brown" material and then 3 inches of "green" material. Alternate between the "brown" and "green" layers. Aerate the compost pile every week or two by using a pitchfork to turn it, or by shaking the compost bin.

If all goes well, the compost should be finished in one to four months. Experts have said to let the compost pile sit for two weeks before using. Most gardeners keep two piles, one started about 4-6 months after the first. This way, they can use the compost from the first pile as the other is decomposing.

CONDITIONING SOIL

According to the Soil Science Society of America, "Soil is not dirt. It is a complex mix of ingredients: minerals, air, water, and organic matter – countless organisms and the decaying remains of once living things. Soil is made of life. Soil makes life. And soil is life. We want to keep and protect soil."

Grow Your Soil

Utilizing the way the forest creates soil could be the secret to growing healthy plants. Of course, this is not a new concept. In fact, forest farming[167] has been around for hundreds of years, and has recently become a new way to grow high value crops such as wheat in a natural thriving environment. This is also a great way to grow crops discreetly if you don't want others to know they are present.

The basic premise is the better condition of the soil, the healthier and more productive the plant will be. In order for plants to grow to their optimum capacity, they need nine different nutrients present in the soil. While most of these elements and nutrients are naturally found in soil, sometimes they can become depleted and need to be added to keep the soil healthy.

These are some of the nutrients found in soil. Some of these natural additions can also improve the soil:

- Carbon – found in air and water
- Hydrogen – found in air and water
- Oxygen – found in air and water
- Nitrogen – blood meal, fish emulsion, manure
- Phosphorus – bone meal, rock phosphate, superphosphate
- Potassium – greensand, mutriate or sulfate of potash, seaweed, wood ashes
- Calcium – gypsum, limestone, oyster shells, slag

7 Facts You Didn't Know About Soil

1. Soil is living.
2. There are more than 70,000 types of soil in the United States.
3. One tablespoon of soil has more organisms in it than people on Earth.
4. The very best China dishes are made from soil.
5. It takes more than 500 years to form one inch of topsoil.
6. Nearly all antibiotics used to fight our infections are obtained from fungus found in soil.
7. In one gram of soil, there are over 5,000 different types of bacteria.

http://www.Soils.org

---

[167] http://www.unl.edu/nac/forestfarming.htm

- Magnesium – dolomite, magnesium sulfate (Epsom salt)
- Sulfur – sulfur, superphosphate

No-Till Gardening

No-till gardening, sheet composting, or lasagna gardening is a gardening method that builds the soil on top of already existing soil. More notably, it does not disturb the existing soil, but only enhances it by adding layers. Essentially, before plants are planted into the ground, a miniature compost pile is layered beneath to decay over time and supply the plants with needed nutrients once the root systems grow. This is a very efficient method (because it works with the natural decomposition process already in nature) to gardening, builds the soil to create a welcoming environment for friendly insects such as earthworms, as well as creates a living soil that will benefit your plants or vegetables.

No-till gardening works with nature instead of against it. This type of gardening enriches the soil composition that earthworms and beneficial insects prefer, thus creating a healthy habitat as a result. Finding items that are around your home now to use as sheet mulch is an efficient way to de-clutter and put something (otherwise) laying around, to use.

Think of materials that are normally put in the compost areas. Items such as:

- Newspaper
- Manure
- Hay
- Vegetable/Fruit peels
- Coffee grounds
- Yard waste – grass clippings, leaves, pine needles, plant cuttings, etc.

The author of A Guide to Creating a No-Till Garden[168] provides an in depth recipe for creating this type of garden.

Here are more specific recommendations of layers you might add after the newspaper.

1. First, lay down four to six inches of grass clippings and leaves. If possible, shred the material to help prevent matting.
2. Next, broadcast or dust the leaves and clippings with a light layer of soil amendments such as lime, greensand, and rock dust. You might also layer comfrey and dandelion leaves here, as they are both bio accumulators that concentrate nutrients from the soil in their leaves, and will release these nutrients back into the soil as they decompose. Because both dandelion and comfrey sprout easily from small sections of root, however, be sure to use only their leaves.

---

[168] http://readynutrition.com/resources/a-guide-to-creating-a-no-till-garden_26092010/

3. Finally, add a layer of animal bedding and top it with straw. Enjoy the winter as your new garden bed fertilizes and builds itself.
4. In the spring, you should be able to plant starts directly into the mulch after brushing aside the straw. To sow seeds, you may have to add a thin layer of compost in order to achieve the best consistency for germination.

Folk wisdom has it that a poor gardener grows weeds, a good gardener grows vegetables, and a very good gardener grows soil. Viable soil is the key to a successful harvest. Ensuring the soil is healthy is a wise investment of time on your part, and surely an investment where you will indeed reap what you sow. Allowing the natural decomposition process to take place allows nature to do the work and prevents you from breaking your back. This method also allows you to make better use of your time/energy yield, helps recycle trash, creates a healthy earthworm environment, and supplies plants with essential vitamins and minerals when they need it.

BackyardGardener.com is an excellent website[169] with recipes to make different types of soil.

SEEDS

The most vital element for your garden is, of course, a selection of reliable heritage seeds. Stay away from anything GMO (Genetically Modified). Not only are there serious health concerns related to the consumption of genetically modified crops, but the seeds have been sterilized, so you won't be able to save seeds for following years[170] from these plants. When choosing your seeds, look for the most nutritional value in the least amount of garden space.

These are the top 25 seeds to consider for your survival gardening needs. The seeds chosen were based upon their yield quantities, *ease in growing, nutritional content and for the season they are planted in.

1. **Asparagus -** Although this plant variety takes a few years to get started, it will come back each year, thus keeping you continuously supplied with a harvest.
2. **Barley -** Can be planted in the spring and winter and has the best results when planted early in the season. This grain has loads of health benefits and a variety of purposes such as feeding livestock, grinding the grains for flour, as well as making beer. Barley is high in dietary fiber and manganese.
3. ***Beans -** Beans should be planted in the early summer. One of the easiest vegetables to grow, beans have different varieties such as pole beans and bush beans, kidney beans, etc. Pole beans have a harvest that begins and ends earlier than bush beans. In comparison, pole beans give a high yield production. A stake is needed for the pole

---

[169] http://www.backyardgardener.com/soil.html

[170] http://readynutrition.com/resources/seed-collecting_12102009/

beans. Staggering your plantings will give continuous yields. Beans are very high in fiber, calcium, Vitamins A, C and K.

4. **Broccoli** - Plant seeds in mid to late summer to be ready for the fall harvest. One of the easiest vegetables to grow. This plant has a tendency to give yields past its first harvest and can take light frost with no problem. Broccoli is a good source of protein, vitamins A and K.

5. **Carrot** - Carrots prefer cooler weather and should be grown in the fall, winter and early spring. One of the easiest vegetables to grow. High in beta-carotene and vitamin A.

6. **Cauliflower** - This vegetable is a cool season vegetable. It harvests over a short period of time and cuts out a high head yield. High in dietary fiber, vitamin C and K.

7. **Corn** – This is a warm weather crop and should be planted after last frost. Has a good amount of proteins, calcium and iron. The plant will produce two ears per stalk.

8. **Cucumber** - This is a warm weather crop. This is one of the easiest vegetables to grow. There are large varieties and smaller varieties for pickling. Continuous picking increases the plant's production. Cucumbers are good sources of vitamins A, C, K and potassium.

9. **Eggplant** – Eggplants are warm weather plants and should be planted after last frost. This nightshade vegetable is high in fiber, antioxidants, and a good source of vitamins B1 and B6. This is a very versatile vegetable to cook with.

10. **Lettuce** – Plant two weeks before last frost, as well as in the fall 6-8 weeks before the first frost date. One of the easiest vegetables to grow and one of the earliest crops to harvest. There are many different varieties that offer different nutritional content. This plant grows quickly and harvest can be extended by taking a few leaves at a time. Lettuce is packed with essential vitamins such as A, B6, C, and K as well as protein, iron and calcium.

11. **Kale -** This green is considered a superfood due to its high vitamin content and is very easy to grow.

12. **Melon** - Plant 4 weeks after the last frost as these fruits are intolerant to cold weather. Cantaloupes and Melon varieties need lots of space to grow. Getting the dwarf size of these fruits can save space. One melon plant will produce two melons. Good source of fiber, B6 and folate.

13. **Okra** - Plant 2 weeks after last frost. This vegetable has a variety of uses such as in soups, pickled or canned. High in vitamin A, K and folate, and calcium.

14. **Onion/Garlic** - One of the easiest vegetables to grow. Plant onion in mid to late October. Onions can be pulled earlier and used for green onions. A good source of dietary fiber, Vitamin B6, Vitamin C, folate and potassium.

15. **Peanuts** – This is a hot season plant and should be planted in April until early June. Peanuts are a good source for healthy fats, vitamin E, protein and antioxidants.

16. **Peas** – This is a winter loving plant that is resistant to frost. One of the easiest vegetables to grow. There are many varieties of the pea plant, such as shelling, snap pea, snow pea and sugar pod peas. Most varieties are fast growing. This is a good source of protein, fiber and has a good source of 8 different vitamins including vitamin A, B6, and K.

17. ***Peppers** - Grow after the last frost. There are many varieties of peppers ranging from hot to mild. Sweet peppers are one of the easiest vegetables to grow. The more peppers are harvested, the more the plant will produce. Peppers are high in vitamin A and C.
18. **Potatoes** - Plant 4-6 weeks before last frost. 1 plant yields 5-6 young potatoes. Potatoes are high in fiber, vitamin B6, Potassium and vitamin C.
19. **Pumpkin** - Start pumpkin seeds in the late spring. Pumpkins require lots of room for the vines to grow. Pumpkins are packed with vitamins such as thiamine, niacin, vitamin B6, folate, iron, vitamin A, C and E.
20. ***Radish** – Can be started 4-6 weeks before last frost. Many have had success growing radishes in the fall as well. One of the easiest vegetables to grow. They are very tolerant of weather conditions. Radishes are high in vitamin B6, dietary fiber, vitamin C and iron.
21. **Spinach**- Spinach grows best in cool weather; however, there are some varieties that like warm weather. Many call this a superfood based upon its large array of vitamins such as vitamin A, C, iron, thiamine, thiamine and folic acid.
22. ***Squash** – There are both summer squash and winter squash varieties. One of the easiest vegetables to grow and most are prolific producers. Picking squash regularly encourages a higher yield. A good source of vitamin A, B6, C, K, and dietary fiber.
23. ***Tomato**- Plant tomatoes in the late spring and again in the late summer. One of the easiest vegetables to grow. Tomatoes are a good source of vitamin A, C, K, E, Potassium, thiamine and Niacin.
24. **Turnips/Rutabagas** – Seeds should be sown in late May or early summer. Turnips are fairly disease free and easily cared for. The greens as well as the root can be eaten. Turnips are high in B6, vitamin C, Iron and Calcium.
25. **Wheat**- Winter wheat can be planted from late September to mid-October. This is the preferred variety due to the nutritional content as well as the protection it gives the soil in the wintertime compared to spring wheat. Spring wheat is planted in early spring. This is one of the most commonly used food crops in the world. Wheat is high in copper, zinc, iron and potassium. Planting a 10×10 plot will yield between 10-25 loaves of bread.

Further consider planting some perennial vegetables that come back year after year. This will make less work for you in the long run. Some examples are berries, asparagus, Jerusalem artichokes, horseradish, garlic, perennial onions, and both culinary and medicinal herbs.

When planning your garden, it's important to remember to plant seeds for any pet birds or poultry. Be sure to stock up on seeds that will provide food for them as well. Poultry are fond of millet, sunflower seeds, certain types of corn and grains, sorghum and of course, left over garden clippings. If they are allowed to free-range they will eat grass, weeds, and wild seeds, as well as worms and insects. Growing your own fodder system composed of your chickens' favorite grains and seeds is a great way to practice those self-sustaining skills as well as provide a natural food choice for your flock. Further, larger animals like goats are grazers, and rabbits thoroughly enjoy the scraps from your fodder system as well as any garden scraps you have left over.

Seeds are the key to long-term survival, so it is vital that you choose carefully. Once you collect your seeds, ensure that they are stored properly and protected from the elements.

Seeds are living things and should always be treated that way. Seeds are dormant until they are introduced to natural elements such as oxygen, moisture, sunlight and warmth that create a growth reaction. Keeping these elements away from the seeds will prolong their longevity. Since seeds are alive, they can be stressed out and damaged when subjected to extreme temperature shifts.

If seeds are stored at optimum conditions, they can last for hundreds, maybe thousands of years.   **Source – USDA**

Over time, seeds do succumb to the aging process and begin to lose their vigor. Typically, larger seeds such as beans and corn have superior longevity compared to smaller seeds. Finding resources such as a Seed Longevity Chart[171] will help determine which seeds can be stored longer than others.

Seeds should be stored in an airtight container where the natural elements cannot get to them. Many people use their refrigerators, freezers and basements as a storage facility for seeds. Keeping seeds at room temperature will cause the embryo to consume its stored sugars within the seed casing and will either get too weak to germinate or die altogether. There is no right or wrong method; it mainly depends on how the person plans to use the seeds and for how long they will be stored. Seed packets typically have a "use by" date. Once the seed packet is opened, the seeds should be used that season.

- **Freezing**: Freezing seeds will put the embryo into suspended animation, reducing its need to consume the sugars that are encased in the seed. This increases storage life immensely. If the seeds are frozen, they should sit at room temperature for a few days before they are planted. This is the preferred method of seed storage by leading farmers and agriculturalists.
- **Refrigerating**: Storing seeds in the refrigerator is another method of prolonging the lifespans. Some put the seeds in a Ziploc bag than then place it in a brown bag so that light cannot penetrate through to the seeds. Another method is to use a smaller Ziploc bag, add the seeds and close them up. Get a larger Ziploc bag and place a moisture absorbing material such as dry milk or dry rice to the main large Ziploc bag and then add the smaller bags containing the seeds. Use large bubble mailer to store the large Ziploc bag into and place it in the upper back of the refrigerator and use rubber bands to keep the bubble mailer sealed.
- **Vacuum Sealing**: Many believe that vacuum sealing the seeds is the best course for long-term seed storage. However, some believe this method would harm the seeds due

[171] http://www.hillgardens.com/seed_longevity.htm

to the absence of the oxygen the seeds need to stay alive. Vacuum sealing does extend the life of the seeds by keeping out the natural elements such as excessive moisture and oxygen. If a person lives in a climate where there is high humidity, then this method would be the preferable one. Storing the seeds in a Mylar bag or in a dark container where sunlight and moisture cannot get to it is ideal.

- **Paper Envelopes**: Storing seeds in paper envelopes and then storing them in waterproof containers with gasketed lids or in mason jars is another preferred storage method. One can add desiccant (a substance that removes moisture from the air) to ensure the seeds are not exposed to moisture. Aluminum coated plastic bags in lieu of the paper envelope can also be used. The seeds should be stored away from sunlight in a cool, dark area such as a refrigerator or dark room.

For long-term sustainability, learn to understand the natural cycles of your small farm. The waste products from both plants and animals can be used to nourish the soil, which in turn helps the garden flourish, which in its own turn, feeds the animals. Understanding this symbiotic relationship can allow you to work smarter, not harder. Finding ways to use what most would consider waste is the ultimate form of recycling. Embrace the old ways of farming to enhance your long-term sustainability.

To conclude, I want to emphasize how important it is to practice your gardening skills before you need to rely on them. Learning from master gardeners, gardening groups or from those with more experience can help the learning curve we all seem to experience when starting something new.

Marjory Wildcraft has created a DVD series: Grow Your Own Groceries[172]. In the series, she shares all that she knows about gardening, companion planting, water catchment systems, as well as some handy tips she has learned along the way. This would be a great way for you to learn from the convenience of your own home.

---

[172] http://growyourowngroceries.com/

PREPS TO BUY:

- Books or DVDs on homesteading, gardening, permaculture and animal husbandry
- Heirloom or non-GMO seeds
- Garden tools
- Containers for long-term storage of seeds

ACTION ITEMS:

1. Research the available resources in your area. Are there plants growing wild that would be good grazing foods for your animals? Is there an abundance of organic material for compost?
2. Learn about composting and how to reuse plant waste.
3. Consider taking a vegetable gardening course at a local nursery, community center or gardening club.

SUPPLEMENTAL INFORMATION AND RESOURCES

The 12 Easiest Plants to Grow

Consider starting out with the following components for your homestead. They are not only easy to grow, but will also provide lots of nutrition for your family.

1. Nut/Fruit Trees

2. Squash/Zucchini

3. Berries – Blackberries, strawberries, raspberries, etc.

4. Grapes

5. Peas/Beans

6. Kale

7. Broccoli

8. Peppers

9. Tomatoes

10. Cucumbers

11. Lettuce

12. Pumpkin

Make Your Own Fodder System

What's great about growing fodder is you don't need any soil, any fertilizer or any chemicals. You are frugally creating sprouted vegetation that has an immense amount of nutrients for your livestock to enjoy.

Goats, rabbits and chickens especially love this green treat. Favorite seeds that could be used for your livestock's treats are: wheat, barley, oats, clover, dandelion, alfalfa, corn, beans and lentils. You want to avoid feeding your chickens dry beans as they contain toxins, however when they are sprouted or cooked, the toxins are removed.

Here's what you need:

- Black seedling trays with plastic domes, or disposable aluminum pans
- Seeds you plan to sprout
- Water
- Sunny window
- Spray bottle

Instructions:

1. Gather the seeds you want to sprout and soak them in water overnight.
2. In the morning, drain the seeds and cover with a plastic cover. Place them in the sprouting trays in a sunny location.
3. Water up to 3 times a day – never allowing the seeds to dry out.
4. By day 7, the roots of the seeds will have intertwined and you will be able to peal the fodder out of the pan.
5. Repeat as often as needed.

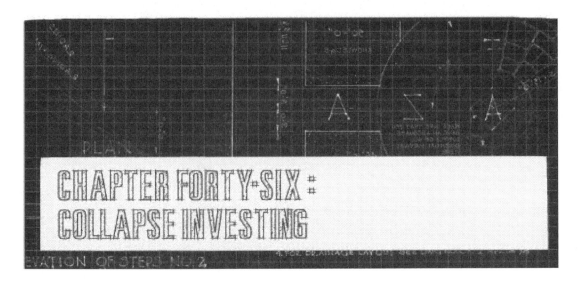

CHAPTER FORTY-SIX: COLLAPSE INVESTING

Experiencing horrible things that can happen in a war – death of parents and friends, hunger and malnutrition, endless freezing cold, fear, sniper attacks.

1. Stockpiling helps. But you never know how long trouble will last, so locate near renewable food sources.
2. Living near a well with a manual pump is like being in Eden.
3. After a while, even gold can lose its luster. But there is no luxury in war quite like toilet paper. Its surplus value is greater than gold's.
4. If you had to go without one utility, lose electricity – it's the easiest to do without (unless you're in a very nice climate with no need for heat.)
5. Canned foods are awesome, especially if their contents are tasty without heating. One of the best things to stockpile is canned gravy – it makes a lot of the dry unappetizing things you find to eat in war somewhat edible. Only needs enough heat to "warm", not to cook. It's cheap too, especially if you buy it in bulk.
6. Bring some books – escapist ones like romance or mysteries become more valuable as the war continues. Sure, it's great to have a lot of survival guides, but you'll figure most of that out on your own anyway – trust me, you'll have a lot of time on your hands.
7. The feeling that you're human can fade pretty fast. I can't tell you how many people I knew who would have traded a much needed meal for just a little bit of toothpaste, rouge, soap or cologne. Not much point in fighting if you have to lose your humanity. These things are morale-builders like nothing else.
8. Slow burning candles and matches, matches, matches.

Advice from a Sarajevo War Survivor

We could spend a significant portion of our time outlining the various reasons why the world's economic, financial and political systems sit on the brink of an unprecedented paradigm shift that promises to change the landscape of the entire system.

I could try to convince you that it's a good idea to prepare for what's coming, but the fact that you are reading this means that you're already in action planning and execution mode. If you've been following the suggestions in this program from the beginning, then you've spent valuable time and resources establishing an emergency and disaster response plan that would probably make FEMA jealous.

You've probably done your research and spent months or years gathering as much information as you can about the many possibilities that could significantly impact your life and the lives of your family members and close friends, and you've actively involved yourself in making sure that you're as insulated as possible from whatever may befall us.

As important as it is to know how to preserve your wealth during times of uncertainty and understand the fundamental economic problems and fraud facing the system; it is also equally as important to ensure you're ready for anything that gets thrown your way – not just an economic crisis.

The strategy that we employ is well rounded and considers as many variables as possible.

- Natural Disasters such as hurricanes, earthquakes, flood, solar flare
- Man-made calamities like currency hyperinflation, cyber-attack, EMP detonation, nuclear fallout or global conflict
- Personal emergencies like a job loss, injury or over-extension of credit

With this idea in mind, when we look at the concept of investing and wealth preservation for uncertain times, we want to employ a strategy that will provide as much coverage as possible so that if we are hit out of the blue with something totally unexpected, we'll at least have the basic necessities to survive.

While I'll stop short of advising you to sell all of the stocks and bonds in your 401(k) account and invest all of your proceeds into 'preps', a little diversification could mean the difference between surviving a disaster, or succumbing to it.

Keep your 401(k), IRA or other investment accounts, but consider expanding your horizons with a new 401(Prep) strategy as well.

THE CURRENCY OF KINGS

> *Gold is the currency of kings, Silver the currency of noblemen, and Debt the currency of slaves.*

While disregarded by mainstream economists as a relic of civilizations past, gold still remains a highly sought-after asset by central banks around the world, including those of China, India, Venezuela, Iran and a host of other countries losing faith in the petro-dollar reserve currency system. We've seen it rise to record breaking nominal highs in the last ten years for a reason. Those in the know – including investors who understand that gold always rises during periods of uncertainty and crisis – have been acquiring gold and its cousin silver for over a decade and have seen its value increase multi-fold.

We need look only at recent history to see what happens when economies and currencies of nations collapse. When the monetary systems of the Weimar Republic, Argentina, and Zimbabwe collapsed, their currencies literally became worthless overnight. During Germany's hyperinflation people were burning wheelbarrows of paper money just to stay warm. When Zimbabwe's currency hyper inflated over a period of about 10 years, a loaf of bread went from one $1 to $1 trillion dollars; today there are people panning for granules of gold in Zimbabwe's rivers so that they can purchase bread to eat for a day.

While nothing is guaranteed, history has proven one thing about gold and silver. There is and always will be a buyer for these precious metals. And if there is a central bank or large investor buying, that demand will always trickle down into the rest of the economy – even if it is operating as a black market.

If you want to expand your portfolio to include precious metals, here are some considerations:

- A single ounce of gold stores more value than silver. If you need portability for a large amount of wealth, gold coins and bars will be your primary precious metals investment. Currently an ounce of gold is about $1550. With less than a pound of coins in your purse or backpack you can conveniently move $25,000 in value.
- What gold offers in portability it lacks in divisibility. This is where silver comes in. You may not be able to move $25,000 of silver conveniently (weighing around 50 pounds!), but because of its lower value per ounce, silver is an excellent mechanism of exchange for things like food, gas, clean water, or tools if the dollar hyper-inflates or crashes. You can purchase silver in bars (100 oz., 10 oz.) or coins (1 ounce, or U.S. government issued pre-1965 halves, quarters and dimes). With the smaller denomination coins like US quarters you will have portability for a small amount of cash (40 quarters is about $150 dollars' worth) and you'll have coinage that should allow you the ability to purchase just about any item someone is willing to sell.
- When buying gold or silver, buy from reputable sources like your local coin shop or an online dealer like Apmex or Kitco.

- The only exception we can make to the above rule is for the purchase of pre-1965 U.S. government minted 90% silver coinage. While we would avoid purchasing any other coins on auction sites like eBay, there are often some great deals to be found on half dollars, quarters and dimes containing 90% silver (pre-1965 coins only!). You can also purchase Kennedy half-dollars dated 1965-1969 containing 40% silver content. Since these coins are government issued and in such small denominations, the possibility that they are counterfeit decreases significantly.
- Silver allows you to make modest, weekly investments of anywhere from $5 to $50 dollars and still build a store of wealth.
- To get the current price of silver and gold, as well as the specific prices for dated U.S. coins, check out the calculators at coinflation.com.
- If you are investing a large sum of money into precious metals, gather details about the types of coins you are buying, especially if you're buying gold. Acquire a coin caliper[173] and/or testing kit to ensure you're getting what is being advertised.

While you may be able to easily utilize gold and silver as a mechanism of exchange at the onset of a crisis, you may be faced with a period of time when no one will be interested in your PM's. Selco of SHTF School[174] points out that gold is not the silver bullet that provides complete insulation from TEOTWAWKI. When all hell breaks loose, as it did in the Balkans in the 1990's, and a war is being fought right outside of your front window, gold and silver may not get you very far, as people are more concerned with the immediate need of getting out of harm's way than they are with anything else.

With that in mind, and for those who (correctly) argue that we can't eat our gold, let's continue diversifying our 401(prep) account.

COMMODITY INVESTING WITH ZERO COUNTER-PARTY RISK

> In this type of environment where nobody can get a safe return on their money within the United States that beats the official rate of inflation, buying canned foods and such is actually a better investment than a Treasury bill. What I would look to do is have a backup supply of at least several months of the basic commodities you need to live with – canned food, toilet paper, as well as barter items...
> -John Williams, Economist, Shadowstats.com

One thing analysts and financial pundits agree on is that, in general, commodities will continue to rise. As central banks continue to inflate their money and hundreds of millions of people in once under-developed nations join the ranks of the global working class, the demand for food

---

[173] http://www.safepub.com/categories/tools-coins-trade-equipment/p/electronic-coin-caliper

[174] http://shtfschool.com/trading/on-buying-gold-silver-for-survival-preparedness/

once reserved for the middle class in America and Europe will rise in countries like China and India. The end result is a higher cost for corn, rice, wheat, meat and other staples.

Thus, as the experts suggest, investing in commodities may be an excellent way to grow, or at the very least preserve, your money. Where I disagree with the experts is how to invest in such assets. While you can purchase Exchange Traded Funds or contracts that follow specific commodities, the inherent problem with these investments is that, even though you have a paper receipt that says you own a particular commodity, if it's not in your possession you are subject to counter-party risk. What I mean by this is that if the investment firm (or the numerous associated firms) has a problem and goes out of business, your paper receipt may become worthless. A recent example of this was the MF Global scandal, where the investment firm headed by a trusted former governor of New Jersey actually took the deposits and commodity investments of their depositors and transferred those assets to other investment banks days before completely collapsing. Their clients, who had receipts to prove ownership, were left with nothing.

If you're investing into commodities because you expect prices to rise dramatically, then you must also assume that those dramatic price rises will result from either a currency crisis, or shortages caused by exceedingly high demand or adverse weather conditions (think Great Depression dust bowl). That being said, the only sound method of investing in these assets is for you to take physical delivery – just like you would with gold.

For food, your best bet would be to look at the 11 Emergency Foods That Last a Lifetime[175]. Dry goods like rice, wheat, beans, salt, honey, and dry milk will provide you with an investment that will grow in value as prices rise, and also offer you peace of mind in case paper markets crash because you'll be in direct possession of your food. How much food should you add to your 401prep investment portfolio? It depends on the size of your family and your time horizon. Think about what could cause a massive price rise in food prices and you'll realize that whatever the crisis is, it could be long-term. The Ready Nutrition food storage calculator[176] can help you to determine how much inventory you may need and allows you to break your purchases into weekly shopping trips so you don't have to invest thousands of dollars up front.

In addition to food, there are a variety of other commodities that you won't want to live without if the system comes crashing down around us – so consider adding these to your preps as well:

- Toilet paper, various toiletries, hygiene products
- Cooking oils
- Off-grid lamps and fuel

---

[175] http://readynutrition.com/resources/11-emergency-food-items-that-can-last-a-lifetime_20082013/

[176] http://readynutrition.com/resources/category/preparedness/calculators/

- Over the counter medicine like ointments, aspirin, anti-diarrheal, anti-constipation meds, alcohol, hydrogen peroxide
- Hand sanitizer (you'll want lots of this because clear water may be hard to come by and disease will be rampant)
- Lighters (highly recommended barter item from the Balkan collapse)
- Ammunition
- Teas, coffee, cigarettes, drinking alcohol
- Off-grid survival tools like hand saws, hand drills, etc. (this may also include low-power requirement tools that you can charge with solar power or other alt energy)
- Antibiotics (here's one survival item that will be worth more than gold in a post-collapse world!)
- Read the Emergency Items: What Will Disappear First[177] for more ideas

Investing in these assets was a sound practice in January of 2010[178] when I first recommended it (you'd be up over 25% now!) and it's a good strategy today, because as you well know things aren't looking any better on the economic and monetary front.

When investing in commodities you'll want to ensure that you are able to physically store your assets so that they are available when you need them post. Be sure to properly store all foods for the long-term.

LAND AND REAL ESTATE

Agricultural commodities are the place to be in for investors. It will be farmers not bankers driving Ferraris.
-Jim Rogers, Contrarian Investor

You may be surprised to see real estate listed here as a 401(prep) related asset, especially considering that the average price collapse in housing since the crash has been about 30%, with some areas of the country seeing in excess of 50% shaved off of bubble-top prices.

With real estate prices still dropping, it's certainly not a bad idea to wait for further price reductions before jumping into a new home, especially if you are planning on paying cash. One thing to consider however, is that if you aren't paying cash for a home and are looking to take on a mortgage then you are in one of the best interest environments we'll experience perhaps in our lifetimes. Money is cheap, and if you happen across the right property, taking advantage of those low interest loans may be the right thing to do. As the dollar continues its decline and confidence in our ability to repay our debt is lost, you will likely see interest rates rise

---

[177] http://readynutrition.com/resources/emergency-items-what-will-disappear-first_11112009/

[178] http://www.shtfplan.com/commodities/buy-commodities-at-todays-lower-prices-consumer-at-tomorrows-higher-prices_01162010

significantly. During the inflation crisis of the late 70's and early 80's some mortgage rates were running as high as 18%, so getting in now may not be a bad idea, especially if you are not planning on flipping your house any time soon and you have an investment time horizon in excess of a decade.

But what is the right property?

Being prepper-minded, I immediately dismiss the possibility of buying a home in an urban or suburban setting. The fact is that these kinds of homes are, in my eyes, liabilities. They have absolutely no productive capacity whatsoever, thus I have hard time looking at them as assets. Moreover, if we're planning on the S hitting the fan, we want to be in a low population area, something that our typical cookie cutter neighborhoods in big cities simply can't provide.

When we talk about real estate and land investments during times of crisis we want to focus on a property that will give us the ability to produce something – anything of value. In the event you lose your current income flow, or if the system falls apart, you'll want to be on a piece of property that allows you to produce some of the commodities we discussed above – either for personal use or to run as a business if employment becomes difficult or impossible to acquire.

Thus, when looking at land, look for land that will provide you and your family with productive capacity. If you can do this, you'll have turned your home and land into an asset instead of the typical liability held by most Americans.

You'll also be much closer to achieving self-reliance by being as off the grid as is possible, so you are no longer dependent on services provided by the government or large business conglomerates.

Here are some thoughts on real estate investing based in part on <u>Ten Things That Make a Survival Homestead</u>[179]:

- Does your land have the space and soil to allow you to grow a vegetable, herb or fruit garden? Even limited space can be used to product a huge amount of food, so you can be flexible on land size if your financial situation requires it.
- Are you able to produce your own energy – perhaps install solar panels, mini-wind turbines or some type of hydropower if you have a stream or river? Whether the world collapses around us or not, energy self-reliance is a long-term benefit that will reduce or eliminate your utility bills, something that will insulate you from not only a collapse of our power grid, but keep the energy flowing to your home if you experience a personal financial catastrophe that makes it difficult to pay your bills.
- Do you have enough land to raise livestock? The bottom line is that people will always need food, and if you can provide that food you'll always have customers willing to buy it or trade for it. Space is an important consideration for livestock, but there are ways to

---

[179] http://readynutrition.com/resources/ten-things-tha-make-a-survival-homestead_20012010/

raise poultry, goats and even micro Dexter cows without a huge pasture. Look into _raising livestock[180] for some ideas (it's something you can even do in suburbia if your HOA allows it!).

- You need a water source. This is self-explanatory. You can't grow food or keep animals if you don't have water. Either make sure you have a well, river, or stream with easy access so you can collect or divert water to irrigate your garden.
- Another water solution that provides multiple benefits is a pond. Not only will it provide water, but you can expand your offerings by raising fish to boot!
- Can you defend your property? In addition to the commodities listed above, other physical assets to look at acquiring are property and self- defense supplies like barbed wire fencing to protect your inner perimeter, flood lights or another alarm system for the external perimeter, empty sand bags that you can quickly fill if needed.

Owning land is a dream held by most individuals. But, few people understand the difference between their homes being a liability vs. an asset. If you're going to be buying (or even renting) land I strongly suggest you look into how you can make your home work for you, instead of the other way around.

GET SOME SKILLS!

> *I don't even have any good skills. You know, like nunchuck skills, bow hunting skills, computer hacking skills...*
> -Napoleon Dynamite

I have a friend who is a specialist in piping design and engineering. In his spare time he builds high quality copper water/alcohol distillation units. Sitting around testing his first unit, my friend and I began discussing the various applications for such an apparatus and how knowledge of manufacturing such units would be an essential skill in a post-collapse world. With his distillation units one can not only purify their water over an open fire, but can also produce drinking alcohol, antiseptics and fuel grade ethanol to run a generator. His project initially started as a hobby, and has since turned into a fledgling side business. If the system collapses, and my friend loses his job in the engineering sector, he will always have his skills of manufacturing to fall back on. In addition to producing distillation units, he is a lifetime prepper, so he is well versed in the manufacture of anything from traps and snares for animals, to making his own ammunition.

The point of this story is that every one of us, even though some of us may sit at a computer all day or work a retail counter, has something we know how to do. Get better at it and consider how you may be able to apply these skills in a post-collapse world.

Also note that if you are skilled at something – machining, sewing, food preservation or some other skills – stock up on the necessary supplies to run your business now, because they won't

---

[180] http://readynutrition.com/resources/category/homestead/micro-livestock/

be available. My friend who manufactures distillation units is heavily invested in copper piping and related materials. While copper may not be a practical investment for you because of your skill set, perhaps yarn or canning jars are.

Every one of us is unique, and we each have different life experiences, skills and backgrounds. This is great news for post-collapse survivors, because you can be assured that American innovation will always return with a vengeance. Necessity will be the mother of invention in a post-collapse world, and while knitting sweaters for the Holidays may be a hobby for you now, it could be the skill that sets you apart and keeps your family fed if traditional commerce breaks down.

The following list is based in part on The Barter Value of Skills[181] and will give you some ideas on ways you will be able to exchange your time and energy for yield (money, trade, etc.) in a post-collapse world:

- First Aid or Critical Aid (Whether you are an EMT or just have basic first aid training, your skills will be in high demand during a serious crisis)
- Midwifery/delivering babies because there won't be any hospitals
- Animal Husbandry – Those who haven't developed animal rearing skills will call on you to help them with their animals or ranching. If you have a large enough post-collapse survival property, you may even be able to lease space on your property for others.
- Blacksmithing, Carpentry, Construction, Machining, and any host of other skills that will be required for jobs that we take for granted today because of home improvement mega stores.
- Mechanics – Whether it's for small engines like generators or understanding the inner workings of alternative energy, there will always be a need for skilled mechanics. After a collapse it will be difficult if not impossible to buy new items like we do in our current consumptive paradigm. Learning to fix what's already out there will be a fantastic way to make a living.
- Food preservation, sewing/mending, soap and candle making, production of alternative medicines (with herbs from your garden) will all be skills that are in demand.
- Also see Top Post-Collapse Barter Items And Trade Skills[182] for more ideas

PLANNING FOR THE UNKNOWN WITH 401 (PREP) INVESTING

If there is one thing we can say about our current economic, financial, social and political climate, it's that we have entered an era in human history of total unpredictability. While we can theorize about what may or may not happen, we need to understand that we are operating on limited information. As Secretary of Defense Donald Rumsfeld once said[183]:

---

[181] http://readynutrition.com/resources/the-barter-value-of-skills_23042012/

[182] http://www.shtfplan.com/emergency-preparedness/top-post-collapse-barter-items-and-trade-skills_06102011

[183] http://www.youtube.com/watch?v=GiPe1OiKQuk

There are known knowns – there are things we know we know.

We also know there are known unknowns – that is to say we know there are some things we do not know.

But there are also unknown unknowns – the ones we don't know we don't know.

As humorous as Rumsfeld's comments were to the press in the room, there is quite a bit of insight to be gleaned from them.

The key takeaway is that we really don't know what we know or don't know, so plan for the worst. Furthermore, ensure that your preparedness plans are flexible enough to be applied to situations that we haven't even contemplated as even being possible.

Special thanks to Mac Slavo for contributing to this section of the Prepper's Blueprint. For more insight on collapse investing, as well as a host of other preparedness related subjects, visit his website, www.SHTFPlan.com.

PREPS TO BUY:

Using the tips and suggestions provided, look into preserving your wealth. Keep in mind that you do not want to go into debt! Set aside money each month and make small investments to accumulate over time.

- Precious metals (gold, silver, copper)
- Hard commodities (sugar, flour, beans, etc.)
- Toilet paper, various toiletries, hygiene products
- Cooking oils
- Off-grid lamps and fuel
- Over the counter medicine like ointments, aspirin, anti-diarrheal, anti-constipation meds, alcohol, hydrogen peroxide
- Hand sanitizer (you'll want lots of this because clear water may be hard to come by and disease will be rampant)
- Lighters (highly recommended barter item from the Balkan collapse)
- Ammunition
- Teas, coffee, cigarettes, drinking alcohol
- Off-grid survival tools like hand saws, hand drills, etc. (this may also include low-power requirement tools that you can charge with solar power or other alt energy)
- Antibiotics (Here's one survival item that will be worth more than gold in a post-collapse world!)

ACTION ITEMS:

1. Research how other countries used alternative currencies in post-SHTF emergencies. Some great online resources are Ferfal's Surviving in Argentina[184], Selco's SHTF School[185].
2. Familiarize yourself with alternative currencies that could be deemed valuable during a post-SHTF scenario.
3. Familiarize and become proficient in skill sets that would be seen as profitable during an extended emergency.

---

[184] http://ferfal.blogspot.com/2009/12/post-shtf-currency.html

[185] http://shtfschool.com/trading/on-buying-gold-silver-for-survival-preparedness/

SUPPLEMENTAL INFORMATION AND RESOURCES

Emergency Items That Disappear First

1. Generators (Good ones cost dearly. Gas storage, risky. Noisy...target of thieves; maintenance etc.)
2. Water
3. Water filters and purifiers
4. Portable toilets
5. Seasoned firewood. Wood takes about 6 – 12 months to become dried, for home use.
6. Lamp oil, wicks, and lamps (First choice: Buy CLEAR oil. If scarce, stockpile ANY!)
7. Coleman fuel (Impossible to stockpile too much)
8. Guns, ammunition, pepper spray, knives, clubs, bats or slingshots
9. Hand-can openers, hand egg beaters, whisks
10. Honey, syrups, white and brown sugar
11. Rice – beans – wheat
12. Vegetable oil (for cooking) Without it food burns/must be boiled etc.,)
13. Charcoal, lighter fluid (will become scarce suddenly)
14. Water Containers of any size. Small: HARD CLEAR PLASTIC ONLY – note – food grade if for drinking.
15. Propane Cylinders (Urgent: definite shortages will occur)
16. Survival Guide book
17. Mantles: Aladdin, Coleman, etc. (without this item, longer-term lighting is difficult.)
18. Baby supplies: diapers, formula, ointments, aspirin, etc.
19. Washboards, mop bucket with wringer (for laundry)
20. Cook stoves (propane, Coleman and kerosene)
21. Vitamins
22. Propane cylinder handle-holder (urgent: Small canister use is dangerous without this item)
23. Feminine hygiene, hair care, skin products
24. Thermal underwear (tops and bottoms)
25. Bow saws, axes and hatchets, wedges (also, honing oil)
26. Aluminum foil regular and heavy duty (great for cooking and bartering item)
27. Gasoline containers (plastic and metal)
28. Garbage bags (impossible to have too many)
29. Toilet paper, Kleenex, paper towels
30. Milk – powdered, condensed (shake liquid every 3 to 4 months)
31. Garden seeds (Non-Hybrid) (A MUST)
32. Clothes pins, line, hangers (A MUST)
33. Coleman's pump repair kit
34. Tuna fish (in oil)

35. Fire extinguishers (or large box of baking soda in every room)
36. First aid kits
37. Batteries (all sizes...buy furthest-out for expiration dates)
38. Garlic, spices, vinegar, baking supplies
39. Dog food
40. Flour, yeast, salt
41. Matches ("Strike Anywhere" preferred) Boxed, wooden matches will go first
42. Writing paper, pads, pencils, solar calculators
43. Insulated ice chests (good for keeping items from freezing in wintertime.)
44. Work boots, belts, blue jeans, durable shirts
45. Flashlights, light sticks, torches, "No. 76 Dietz" lanterns
46. Journals, diaries, scrapbooks (jot down ideas, feelings, experience; historic times)
47. Plastic garbage cans (great for storage, water, transporting – if with wheels)
48. Men's Hygiene: shampoo, toothbrush, paste, mouthwash, floss, nail clippers, etc.
49. Cast iron cookware (sturdy, efficient)
50. Fishing supplies, tools
51. Mosquito coils, repellent, sprays, creams
52. Duct tape
53. Tarps, stakes, twine, nails, rope, spikes
54. Candles
55. Laundry detergent (liquid)
56. Backpacks, duffel bags
57. Garden tools, supplies
58. Scissors, fabrics, sewing supplies
59. Canned goods: fruits, veggies, soups, stews, etc.
60. Bleach (plain, not scented: 4 to 6% sodium hypochlorite)
61. Canning supplies
62. Knives, sharpening tools: files, stones, steel
63. Bicycles and parts: tires, tubes, pumps, chains, etc.
64. Sleeping bags, blankets, pillows, mats
65. Carbon monoxide alarm (battery powered)
66. Board games, cards, dice
67. d-con Rat poison, MOUSE PRUFE II, roach killer
68. Mousetraps, ant traps, cockroach magnets
69. Paper plates/cups/utensils (stock up, folks)
70. Baby wipes, oils, waterless, antibacterial soap (saves a lot of water)
71. Rain gear, rubberized boots, etc.
72. Shaving supplies (razors, creams, talc, after shave)
73. Hand pumps & siphons (for water and for fuels)
74. Soy sauce, vinegar, bullions, gravy, soup base
75. Reading glasses

76. Chocolate, cocoa, tang, punch (water enhancers)
77. "Survival-in-a-Can"
78. Woolen clothing, scarves, ear-muffs, mittens
79. Boy Scout handbook, and/or Leaders catalog
80. Roll-on window insulation kit (MANCO)
81. Graham crackers, saltines, pretzels, trail mix, jerky
82. Popcorn, peanut butter, nuts
83. Socks, underwear, t-shirts, etc. (extras)
84. Lumber (all types)
85. Wagons, carts (for transport to and from)
86. Cots, inflatable mattresses
87. Gloves for work, warming, gardening, etc.
88. Lantern hangers
89. Screen patches, glue,
90. Hardware - nails, screws, nuts and bolts
91. Teas
92. Coffee
93. Cigarettes
94. Wine, liquors (for bribes, medicinal, etc.)
95. Paraffin wax
96. Glue, nails, nuts, bolts, screws, etc.
97. Chewing gum, candies
98. Atomizers (for cooling, bathing)
99. Hats, cotton neckerchiefs, seasonal clothing needs
100. Livestock – goats, chickens, etc.

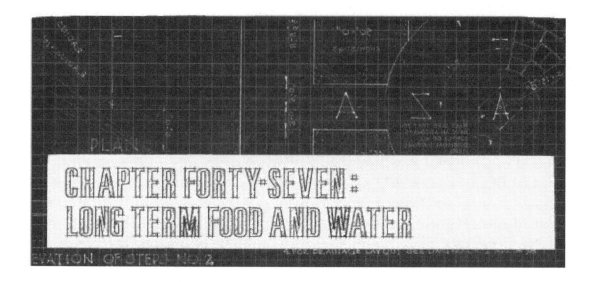

CHAPTER FORTY-SEVEN: LONG TERM FOOD AND WATER

From *The General Historie of Virginia, New England & the Summer Isles*

By John Smith - published in 1624

...within six moneths after Captaine Smiths departure, there remained not past sixtie men, women and children, most miserable and poore creatures; and those were preserved for the most part, by roots, herbes, acornes, walnuts, berries, now and then a little fish: they that had startch in these extremities, made no small use of it; yea, even the very skinnes of our horses.

Nay, so great was our famine, that a Salvage we slew, and buried, the **poorer** sort tooke him up againe and eat him, and so did divers one another boyled and stewed with roots and herbs:

And one amongst the rest did kill his wife, powdered her, and had eaten part of her before it was knowne, for which hee was executed, as hee well deserved; now whether shee was better roasted, boyled or carbonado'd, I know not, but of such a dish as powdered wife I never heard of.

This was that time, which still to this day we called the starving time; it were too vile to say, and scarce to be beleeved, what we endured: but the occasion was our owne, for want of providence, industrie and government, and not the barrennesse and defect of the Countrie, as is generally supposed...

HISTORY SPEAKS FOR ITSELF

When the settlers came from England to Jamestown, they had left with what they felt were an abundance of supplies. However it wasn't long before their supplies ran out. During the first winter, called The Starving Time, only 60 of the original 214 settlers survived. Their needs had exceeded their expectations and many perished from starvation.

Throughout history, we have read and studied about times of famine, widespread natural disasters, and unforeseen circumstances. We simply cannot ignore they exist. In the Old Testament of the Bible, Joseph had prophetic dreams. He convinced the Pharaoh to allow him to store away food from the 7 years of good harvest to survive the 7 years of famine that were to come. Joseph told his family, "God sent me ahead of you to preserve for you a remnant on earth and to save your lives by a great deliverance." Genesis 45:7.

Archaeologists keep discovering caches of food that some archaic soul had stored away. For example, in Arkansas, a village of the Woodland Indians[186] dating back to 600-900 AD was discovered the settlement was a small farming village. Scientists found caches of nuts and seeds that had been lightly roasted, then buried in covered pits. The crops became larger as the Indians learned new methods for storing their harvests.

The Great Depression was another disaster that caused widespread economic downturn and famine. This disaster alone strikes sadness into the eyes of the survivors. In history books it was suggested that a disaster such as this could never occur again. Yet, here we are standing the cusp of a new Great Depression.

Let's assume for a moment that a devastating disaster occurred and you have realized that the life you formerly knew has ended. You are now in a fight for survival. Luckily, unlike many of those around you, you have provisions in place and have planned accordingly for a long-term emergency. But, the longstanding disaster is now threatening to exceed your food supply. What do you eat after your food supply is depleted or, if it is ruined by insects[187] or rodents[188]?

To be truly prepared, we must plan for the unexpected by finding food and supplies that can withstand the test of time. It is my hope that by now your preparedness supplies are diverse and large enough to cover both short-term and long-term emergencies. Eventually, it's possible that you will discover that life has changed to such an extent that there is no way for you to

---

[186]
http://arkarcheology.uark.edu/indiansofarkansas/printerfriendly.html?pageName=Woodland%20Period%20Cultures

[187] http://readynutrition.com/resources/meet-your-emergency-foods-worst-enemies_06042011/

[188] http://readynutrition.com/resources/rat-proofing-your-food-storage-pantry-in-5-easy-steps_26102011/

replenish your supplies other than harvesting them yourself, through farming, hunting and water catchment and filtration.

LONG-TERM FOOD SOURCES

Listed below are some examples of long-term supply sources. If you are planning for emergencies such as EMPs, nuclear attacks, economic collapse, grid-down scenarios, apocalyptic epidemics, etc., then I would strongly encourage you to invest in the following prep items.

Lifetime Foods – Foods that can last for up to 10 years or longer will be a solid investment for your future, as well as your best bet at surviving a long-term disaster. Foods such as wheat, sugar, salt, white rice and corn are items that can last a lifetime.

In chapter 22, we went into detail about the 11 forever foods that should be stored for long term storage. Keep the many uses in mind when investing in these foods.

    1. Honey - Uses: curing, baking, medicinal, wine (mead)

    2. Salt - Uses: curing, preservative, cooking, cleaning, medicinal, tanning hides

    3. Sugar - Uses: sweetener for beverages, breads, cakes, preservative, curing, gardening, insecticide (equal parts of sugar and baking powder will kill cockroaches).

    4. Wheat - Uses: baking, making alcohol, livestock feed, leavening agent

    5. Dried corn - Uses: soups, cornmeal, livestock feed, hominy and grits, heating source (do a search for corn burning fireplaces).

    6. Baking soda - Uses: teeth cleaner, household cleaner, dish cleaner, laundry detergent booster, leavening agent for baked goods, tarnish remover

    7. Instant coffee, tea, and cocoa - Uses: beverages, flavor additions to baked goods

    8. Non-carbonated soft drinks - Uses: beverages, flavor additions to baked goods

    9. White rice - Uses: breakfast meal, addition to soups, side dishes, alternative to wheat flour[189]

    10. Bouillon products - Uses: flavoring dishes

---

[189] http://readynutrition.com/resources/prepping-with-wheat-allergies_07112009/

11. Powdered milk – in nitrogen packed cans - Uses: beverage, dessert, ingredient for certain breads, addition to soup and baked goods.

Ensure that these foods are stored properly and away from your food's worst enemies.

Freeze-Dried Food – Freeze-dried food can last for 20 years. There are a variety of freeze-dried ingredients and cuisines to choose from for breakfast, lunch and dinner. The best part of investing in this long-term food source is that different cans of freeze-dried ingredients can be mixed together to create new entrees. The best way to get your money's worth is to purchase the #10 cans. Further, purchasing by the case will save you even more on your investment. Due to the preservation measures, they can be pricey, but when you work out the math per serving, it is quite reasonable. Many preppers have stocked up on this as their initial food source for a disaster. Because of the long expiration date, I prefer to use up my existing food supply and keep the freeze-dried foods on standby in the event that I run out of my other foodstuffs. Please keep in mind that due to the sodium used for preservation in the freeze-dried foods, it tends to back up the intestines. Therefore, if you choose to stock up on these essential long-term foods, I would advise for you to also stock up on stool softeners.

Seeds – As indicated in previous chapters, non-GMO or heirloom quality seeds are the best types of seeds to store and grow during long-term emergencies as these seeds produce seeds you can save for future harvests. However, some believe that having a few packets of GMO seeds stashed away would be beneficial during times of long-term crises as they have been formulated to survive droughts, have larger yields and be disease resistant. Having dependable seeds and dependable fertilizers and soil amendments in times of a crisis is another example of having back-up for your backups. Further, if stored properly these seeds can last much longer than their expected expiration dates. Consider growing vegetables that have high yields and high amounts of nutrition and vitamins, as well as finding varieties that possess medicinal[190] pro perties.

Water Catchment Systems - Those who do not have access to their own water sources run the risk of being completely dependent on municipal water supplies. Having knowledge about how to harvest water through means of rainwater catchment systems[191] is a great place to begin this path towards self-reliance. Some suggested low-cost options are: collapsible water containers or 5-gallon buckets, rain harvesting containers or barrels, rainwater downspouts routed to water tanks by PVC pipes. If outside water catchment systems are being used, learn more about which catchment system[192] is best for your home.

---

[190] http://readynutrition.com/resources/survival-food-series-medicinal-plants-for-the-survival-garden_04012010/

[191] http://readynutrition.com/resources/using-water-harvesting-as-an-emergency-water-source_28082011/

[192] http://www.harvesth2o.com/rainwaterstorage.shtml

Water Filtration Units – In an extended emergency, possessing the knowledge of how to properly clean water will be essential in keeping sanitation related illnesses at bay. Water filtration systems with extra filters and parts, water purification tablets, chlorine granules, and bleach are essential in having clean drinking water. There will be a high risk of water-borne viruses, so electrolyte or re-hydration powders and anti-diarrhea medications will also be valuable to stock.

For many of us, our core motivation is to provide for our families and keep them safe. But, according to societal mores we should only provide safety up to a certain extent. It is a taboo to think in terms of worst-case scenarios. But sometimes, we must break through societal codes to do what is best for our family. In the case of preparedness, thinking in worst-case scenarios may help you to better prepare. Unexpected events *will* happen during SHTF scenarios, and it will be up to you to be ready for them.

PREPS TO BUY:

[In Quantity]

- Foods for long-term storage such as wheat, rice, sugar, salt, honey, and corn.
- Freeze-dried foods
- Stool softeners
- Seeds, both GMO and Non-GMO
- Fertilizers (enough for 3 seasons)
- Water catchment system items
- Anti-diarrhea medicines
- Re-hydration powders or drinks
- Filtration units such as the Berkey Water Filter

ACTION ITEMS:

1. Ensure that you have enough food supplies to last for a long-term emergency. Refer to the Ready Nutrition Food Calculator to make sure.
2. Research ways that you can conserve water or harvest water on your property.
3. Look for natural water sources, and underground reservoirs to turn to for an emergency water supply.
4. Practice necessary skills that will help you thrive during long-term emergencies: gardening, food preservation, and water harvesting.

SUPPLEMENTAL INFORMATION AND RESOURCES

DIY Rain Water Catchment Systems

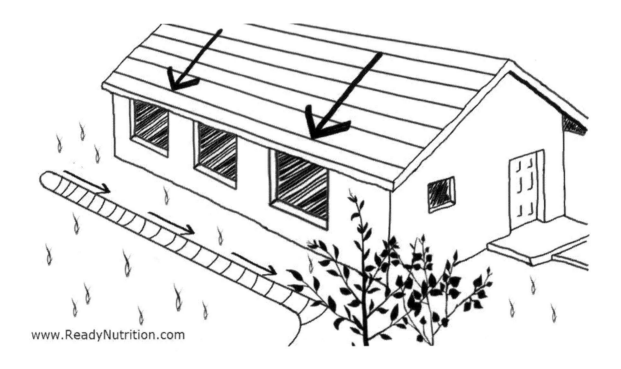

www.ReadyNutrition.com

In this illustration, rainwater is harvested from the rooftop and directed into a furrow that flows to a holding area where water percolates into the soil, watering the plants.

www.ReadyNutrition.com

Barrels collect rainwater from the gutters of the house. A hose is connected to the barrels, which waters nearby landscape plants.

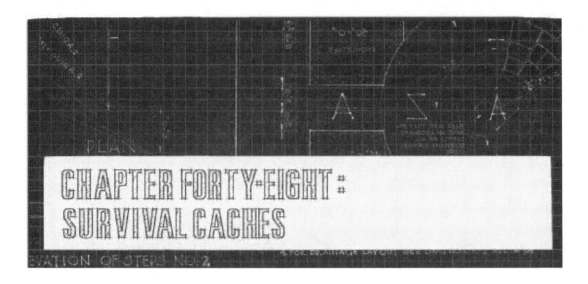

CHAPTER FORTY-EIGHT: SURVIVAL CACHES

For decades it waited in secret inside the masonry foundations of the Brooklyn Bridge, in a damp, dirty and darkened vault near the East River shoreline of Lower Manhattan: a stockpile of provisions that would allow for basic survival if New York City were devastated by a nuclear attack.

City workers were conducting a regular structural inspection of the bridge last Wednesday when they came across the Cold War-era hoard of water drums, medical supplies, paper blankets, drugs and calorie-packed crackers -- an estimated 351,000 of them, sealed in dozens of watertight metal canisters and, it seems, still edible … Transportation Commissioner Iris Weinshall said, "We find stuff all the time, but what's sort of eerie about this is that this is a bridge that thousands of people go over each day," she said. "They walk over it, cars go over it, and this stuff was just sitting there."

The most numerous items are the boxes of Civil Defense All-Purpose Survival Crackers… Nearby were several dozen boxes with sealed bottles of Dextran, made by Wyeth Laboratories in Philadelphia. More mysterious were about 50 metal drums, made by U.S. Steel in Camden, N.J. According to the label, each was intended to hold 17.5 gallons and to be converted, if necessary, for "reuse as a commode."

Source[193]

---

[193] http://www.sfgate.com/news/article/Cold-War-survival-cache-found-under-Brooklyn-2500998.php#ixzz2J1y96xZx

Archaic food caches have been found all over the world. The fact that our ancestors planned for the unexpected gives us a clear picture into their unpredictable lifestyle. Foods such as nuts and dry goods, as well as foraging tools were put away for a time when they needed them the most (source[194]). Today, we face the same uncertainties in life, and preparing for this sudden upheaval is the best way we can secure our odds at survival.

SURVIVAL CACHES ARE THE ULTIMATE BACK-UP PLAN

If you are going for your survival cache, that means Plan A and Plan B went awry. In this case, you may be left to survive with only the contents in your cache. You must plan out those contents accordingly.

Given the seriousness of this preparedness issue, many preppers see the value in having multiple caches spread out geographically to fall back on in order to lessen the risk of losing everything. Ideally, you want some of your caches to be away from your retreat.

Survival Caches

Survival caches can be buried or hidden in secure areas around the property to ensure you have extra survival items to fall back on. Keep in mind that before you hide a cache, you need to have chosen a good location preferably within the parameters of your evacuation route or retreat. You also want to keep in mind that the best evacuation route would be one that does not require use of highways or frequently used roads.

CACHE LOCATION

Choosing a cache location is equally as important as what to stow in it. You want to find a location where your cache contents are protected from water and natural elements. Many preppers have considered hollowed out trees, under outdoor sheds or barns and even behind large shrubberies. If at all possible, find a cache location along your bug-out route. To go a step further, you could plant edible native plants and roots along the way to use as an emergency source of food.

A GPS would be ideal as you can program the location of the cache as a waypoint in the navigation system. Ensure that you keep track of where you hide your survival cache by marking it in some way (spray paint, rocks, etc.) to provide concealment. Further, it should go without saying, but remember to keep the location of your cache quiet. The more people who know about your survival cache, the more vulnerable the cache is to being found and used by someone else.

---

[194] http://research.amnh.org/anthropology/research/naa/hidden_cave

PREPARING A CACHE

Many preppers have chosen to hide or bury their caches in different locations and in an assortment of containers ranging from <u>enclosed PVC pipes</u>[195], waterproof ammunition containers, 50-gallon drums and even small water bottles.

The items you store in the cache and your cache location are going to dictate a lot of what you need to consider for protection. Different locations will have different cache preparation needs. Water damage is the largest concern with caches. There are steps you can take to waterproof your container, but choosing an area that isn't prone to high humidity levels or high amounts of moisture will be your best bet.

Many preppers suggest that before the supplies are placed into the cache and buried, you want to ensure your container will be protected from natural elements. Water and temperature fluctuations can damage your cache container over time. When this happens, the contents of the cache can be damaged. Therefore, take precautions and individually seal your items in Ziploc bags or vacuum-sealed bags for added measure.

> ## Water-Proofing Your Cache
>
> If you are using a PVC pipe as a cache, you will want to take steps to waterproof the container.
>
> To waterproof the edges of a PVC pipe use an extra bead of silicone sealant as a fail-safe.

Other considerations:

1. Keep your storage space in mind. The best storage space for survival supplies will be in a cool, dry location that features elevated shelving and is sealed against rodents.
2. Disaster caches should stock enough water to last a set number of people for several days. Normally, a person needs 2-liters of water per day. If your cache is for an isolated cabin with a reliable water source, a distiller or carbon filtration system and boiler are more important than a large supply of bottled water.
3. Select and purchase a wide variety of canned goods. Most vegetables, many fruits, and all meats are best stored in canned form, and the typical canned food product has a shelf life measured in years. Note: don't forget to include a can opener, or purchase canned goods that are of the "pop top" variety.
4. Supplement the canned goods with a multi-vitamin.
5. Stock coffee and tea. Or, if you have small children, consider storing some packages of Kool-Aid or powdered drink mixes. These treats will boost morale, and they have a long shelf life.
6. Stock cooking oil and extra cooking fuel. These are critical for cooking in the long haul.

---

[195] http://democratherald.com/news/opinion/blogs/over-my-dead-body/how-to-build-a-cache/article_872af492-5f43-11e1-bcc4-001871e3ce6c.html

7. Store dried grains, such as flour, rice and corn or corn meal. Beans are also a good idea. These items will last almost as long as the canned goods.

8. Consider growing mushrooms. If you have a cool, dark space (such as the cellar of an old cabin) you can set up a mushroom farm and let it take care of itself for months at a time. This is the only food that can be put into a survival cache that will partially replenish itself.

9. If room allows, add necessary clothing items for more rugged terrain. A good pair of waterproof hiking boots could save your life.

10. If you plan to be near water sources, have a fishing kit.

11. In a SHTF world, you will need to plan for ways to defend yourself. Store a handgun or rifle and as much ammunition as think you can carry. For added measure, I would also suggest disassembling the weapon and storing lubricant away. Store the weapons in a Ziploc bag and add lots of desiccant to absorb any additional moisture while in the cache.

12. Topographic maps of the terrain would also be a good choice if you are bugging out on foot.

WHAT GOES INTO A CACHE?

What items would you stash away? Would they be day-to-day essentials like canned goods and freeze-dried foods, or would you stash hunting gear so that you could hunt for wild game?

Depending on the size of the container, you could also include other necessary supplies that will benefit your basic survival needs. For example, if you were burying a 50-gallon drum or a large waterproof ammunition container, you could bury a fully packed bug-out bag.

Choose the best survival cache container to fits your needs. Remember, you may need to solely rely on the contents in this container one day so be thorough when stocking it and keep track of where you hide it.

HIDING A CACHE

You will want to hide your cache near your bug in location, along your evacuation route or towards a secondary bug-out location. In an article written on the subject at www.SHTFPlan.com, there are three principles you need to learn: disguise, distraction, and concealment.

What Items To Place in a Cache

- First aid kit
- MRE's or canned goods
- Small fire starting kit (matches or lighters)
- Knife
- Water filter
- Duct tape
- Handgun or rifle
- Ammo
- Fishing supplies
- Spare clothes, wool socks and hiking boots
- Emergency shelter
- Rain and cold weather gear
- Maps

Disguise your cache so that it hides in plain view. You can hide supplies such as canned food, tools, and weapons in a bin labeled "chicken feed," for example. Just place the stuff in the bottom of the bin and cover it with chicken feed.

An effective form of distraction is the use of decoys and "false positives." A decoy is what you want someone to find instead of your cache, so after you've hidden the cache you want for yourself, you can place another one that's more easily found. That way the thief or whoever will make off with whatever you're willing to sacrifice, safeguarding what really matters. For example, bury your cache two or three feet in the ground, then tuck the decoy under some roots and partially cover it with leaves.

A "false positive" is pure distraction — a failure for the thief. Your cache can most likely be found with a metal detector. If you bury guns and ammo, bury them under a junk pile or collapsed barn. All the scrap metal will make a metal detector useless, and a digging operation becomes a random search.

You can also scatter scrap metal like buried plugs of rebar and junk iron. This is controversial — it might signal the alert scavenger that he's close to scoring. He might give up as night falls, or a storm approaches, but if he's determined he'll watch the area, and you'll have to be very careful about your recovery methods. See the discussion of Recovery, below.

Another way to generate a false positive is simply to prepare an empty cache. Consider a scavenger on the hunt. You have two caches, one full, the other empty. By deliberate search he finds your empty cache. His likely response is to figure the stash has already been depleted, and move on. But even if he assumes he's been fooled, he might well abandon the search in frustration and seek easier targets. If he stumbles across your real cache, well, you should have done a better job of setting the decoy, but you'll then have to rely on redundancy (see below).

Concealment is that which impedes visual acquisition of your cache. Burial is the paradigm of concealment. Camouflage is a type of concealment in which your cache is made to blend in visually with its surroundings. If you paint a PVC tube brown and gray and hang it in a tree, it will be visually difficult to distinguish from the tree trunk, unless you know right where to look. Or imagine trying to spot a white PVC tube in a field of snow, even with binoculars. You could frankly set a gray case in the open on a rocky mountain slope and expect to find it undisturbed many years later.

PREPS TO BUY:

- PVC
- Silicone sealant
- 50-gallon drum, or waterproof container
- First aid kit
- MRE's, freeze-dried food, canned goods
- Small fire starting kit (matches/lighters)
- Knife
- Duct tape
- Handgun
- Ammo
- Fishing kit with collapsible fishing rod
- Spare clothes, wool socks and hiking boots
- Emergency shelter – tent or tarp
- Rain and cold weather gear
- Hand-crank radio
- Flashlight and extra batteries

ACTION ITEMS:

1. Have multiple evacuation routes planned in the instance that Plan A and Plan B do not work.
2. Make list of what items you want to have in your survival cache.
3. Find a good location, along the planned evacuation routes and bury or hide your survival cache.
4. Practice getting to the survival cache using different modes of transportation to see how long it will take to get there.
5. Create multiple caches if necessary.

SUPPLEMENTAL INFORMATION AND RESOURCES

HOW TO BUILD A CACHE

1) How it's built: two ways because I have several different caches. First is out of PVC pipe with threaded ends, sealed using screw on caps; threads sealed with plumber's tape and then duct-taped on outside. Second, using locking hard cases such as those from Storm Harding. Contents determine size of box or length of tube.

2) How it's stored: dependent on location. Buried in one case, stored in two others in the basements of people I trust. If I don't claim the cache within X-number of days of certain pre-set events, they get to use it.

3) How close to home? Buried one is relatively close, along the path of bug-out travel. Others are within driving distance of about a half-tank of gas of my bug-out vehicle(s). I have three different bug-out paths and there is a cache along each one.

4) Finding it: The two stored at friend's houses are easy. The buried one is in a preselected location far away from any utilities but easily found by landmarks. Just in case, I do have the longitude and latitude written down.

5) What's in it: each one contains a complete set of what I deem necessary to serve basic needs of shelter, food, water, first-aid and self-defense. This can get complicated to explain but I'll do the best I can without writing a book. "Shelter" (to me) can be as simple as a military-surplus poncho, some paracord and a few aluminum tent stakes. Or it can be a tent, or a large tarp w/ tent poles. Dependent on the size and location of the cache, I've tried to guesstimate my needs along that travel route and included shelter accordingly.

Food and water: Since it's ludicrous to store water, I have a water filtration system and a "water bottle" in each cache. Water bottle is in quotes because in one case it's a hydration bladder, and in the other two its collapsible 5-gallon jugs w/ taps. Each filtration system should clean 1,000 gallons of water each. The food I have stored is an assortment of MREs and other dehydrated food, some having a shelf life as much as 25 yrs. I have enough in each cache to feed my family three meals per day for three days.

Each cache also has a prepackaged basic first-aid kit that includes basic trauma care items (tourniquet, pressure bandages, chest seal, pneumothorax needle, etc.). The only thing we really can't treat are dental issues (obviously there's no field surgery stuff or vision "repair" items).

For self-defense I will simply say that there is one folding and one fixed knife in each cache. There is also one firearm with 250 rounds for that firearm.

There is plenty of other "stuff" that could be included but in addition to the caches I have a layered and redundant preparedness plan enacted at my home. My vehicle bug-out stuff stays packed; my bug-out bag stays packed; my vest stays prepared; my gun belt and weapons stay ready.

I'd like to extend my cache "reach" further, but realistically speaking, they are placed to support initial travel away from the population density of the eastern seaboard along preplanned evacuation/bug-out routes. They would support me getting far enough to relax, recoup and recover, to plan further travel and assess needs.

Source - Frank at NewAmericanTruth.com

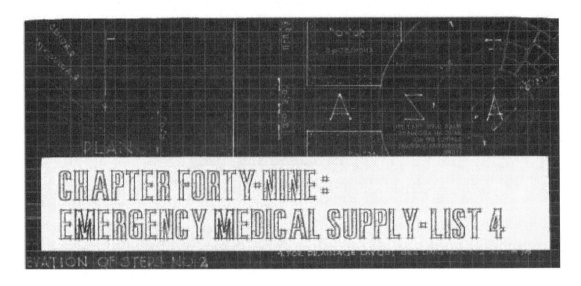

CHAPTER FORTY-NINE:
EMERGENCY MEDICAL SUPPLY-LIST 4

BY JOE ALTON, M.D. AKA DR. BONES AND AMY ALTON, A.R.N.P., AKA NURSE AMY

As a retired physician and nurse team whose entire focus is figuring out strategies for survival situations, we are often asked what medical issues are the most likely to be encountered in times of trouble. The answer depends somewhat on what event you expect to throw society into disarray. Knowing what situations to prepare for and making provision for it will make you a more effective medical resource and might save lives.

ARE YOU EXPECTING?

Economic Collapse? If some event causes us to collapse financially, it stands to reason that food from farm areas will cease to be delivered to supermarkets (who's paying the truckers?). As such, you'll be dealing with malnutrition among your people. Besides food storage, you should be stockpiling multivitamins (either commercial or natural) to prevent deficiencies that cause disease, such as Scurvy (lack of vitamin C), Beriberi (lack of vitamin B1) or Rickets (lack of vitamin D in children).

Civil Unrest? Many collapse events will be fraught with episodes of civil unrest, so you should be well acquainted with how to deal with traumatic injuries such as fractures and hemorrhagic wounds. Supplies here will be lots and lots of gauze bandages (keep old sheets, they can be used to improvise), antiseptic solutions such as Betadine, and some method of closing wounds (butterfly closures, Steri-strips, surgical or super glue, staples, and/or sutures) when appropriate.

You can expect that many wounds will be contaminated with dirt and debris, and therefore bacteria or other microorganisms. It is essential to know when to close a wound and when to leave it open; this is much more important to understand than how to throw a stitch or place a staple. The young Georgia woman in the news who had a laceration from a zip line injury had her wound closed with 22 staples. Doctors unwittingly sequestered bacteria deep in the injury that caused a serious infection called "necrotizing fasciitis", costing her a leg and threatening her life.

Pandemics? If your area is invaded by a superflu, you will need plenty of extra masks (both N95 and standard) and gloves (nitrile is less allergenic than latex). You will have to know how to plan out a sick room protocol that will isolate the ill members of your group and you might consider antivirals like Tamiflu.

Tamiflu is helpful in decreasing sick time if taken early, and may actually have a preventive effect. Be sure to ask your doctor for a prescription for each member of your family each flu season.

Radiation events? Meltdowns, dirty bombs, nuclear apocalypse, EMPs, Coronal Mass Ejections, whew! If this is something you're concerned about, learn how to make a shelter in your home that will block radiation effects.

Learn about "halving-thicknesses", the thickness of a material that will decrease your exposure by half. These multiply as you add additional thicknesses of a substance (1/2 x ½ x ½ x ½ = 1/16 total exposure, for example). Here are the halving-thicknesses of various materials:

- Lead: 0.4 inches or 1 centimeter
- Steel: 1.0 inch or 2.5 centimeters
- Concrete: 2.4 inches or 6 centimeters
- Soil (packed): 3.6 inches or 9 centimeters
- Water: 7.2 inches or 18 centimeters
- Wood: 11.0 inches or 30 centimeters

Also, consider the accumulation of Potassium Iodide (KIO4) tablets. These will help prevent certain thyroid cancers, which can be a long-term complication of radiation exposure.

MEDICAL ISSUES

You may ask, "How can I know what medical issues I'll have to deal with if the you-know-what hasn't hit the fan yet?" Well, many physicians have found themselves in this circumstance and learned the hard way.

Responders to the Haitian Earthquake, Peace Corps caregivers and Doctors Without Borders are just some of the medical personnel that have compiled this information for us.

In no particular order, here is a top ten list from one physician that spent 15 months as the sole medical resource in a remote and austere location:

- Minor Musculoskeletal injuries (sprains and strains)
- Minor trauma (cuts, scrapes)
- Minor infections (cellulitis, "pinkeye", urinary infections)
- Allergic reactions (some severe)
- Respiratory infections (pneumonia, bronchitis, influenza, common colds)
- Diarrheal disease (minor and major)
- Dental issues (toothache, loose crowns and lost fillings)
- Major traumatic injury (fractures, occasional knife and/or gunshot wounds)
- Burn injuries (all degrees)
- Pregnancy (!) and Birth Control

You may have thought of the top nine, but have you given some thought to number 10, pregnancy and birth control? Pregnancy is a natural process and usually ends with a healthy mother and baby, but not so long ago the announcement that someone was pregnant was met with concern as well as joy.

Complications such as miscarriage, bleeding, and infection are easily dealt with in most cases today, but were a common cause of maternal deaths in the past. If modern medical care is unavailable, you may find yourself thrown back to that era. Consider birth control strategies such as the Rhythm Method and learn the basics of how to deliver a baby.

You'll benefit from storing as many medical supplies as you can. How much is too much? You can NEVER have too many medical items in your preps; any "extras" you are willing to let go of will be extraordinarily valuable barter items in a collapse situation.

Accumulate stockpiles of antibiotics as well; these will deal with many of the listed issues above if they are used judiciously. My research shows that some aquarium antibiotics may be identical in dosage, action, appearance and even numbering as those stocked in human pharmacies, and may be purchased in quantity without a medical license from a number of online sources.

All of the above topics are discussed in detail for free on our website at www.doomandbloom.net and more so in our recent #1 Amazon Bestseller (Survival Skills Category) "The Doom and Bloom™ Survival Medicine Handbook"[196]. It's not your everyday first aid book, as its main assumption is that there are no longer hospitals, clinics or doctors, and that YOU are the end of the line when it comes to the medical well-being of your loved ones in times of trouble. You can find it at www.doomandbloom.net, or at http://www.createspace.com/3697264, and Amazon.

---

[196] http://www.amazon.com/Doom-Bloom-Survival-Medicine-Handbook/dp/0615563236/ref=sr_1_fkmr0_1?ie=UTF8&qid=1340330606&sr=8-1-fkmr0&keywords=%C2%93The+Doom+and+Bloom%C2%99+Survival+Medicine+Handbook%C2%94

Please, as you learn how to treat medical problems in hard times, you are learning a skill, not a trade. The practice of medicine or dentistry without a license is illegal and punishable by law. If modern medical care IS available, seek it out.

Dr. Bones and Nurse Amy

Copyright Doom and Bloom, LLC 2012

Dr. Bones and Nurse Amy are a husband and wife team have shared with the preparedness community their experience and knowledge on how to utilize traditional medicine, alternative remedies, and medicinal/survival gardening in emergency situations. Their website, www.DoomandBloom.net and their medical manual, The Doom and Bloom Survival Medicine Handbook, contains a wealth of information that gives the layman the practical answers and strategies we have been searching for to equip ourselves with medical information and develop skills that could be needed when we least expect.

Special thanks to Dr. Bones and Nurse Amy for contributing their time and effort on this portion of The Prepper's Blueprint.

PREPS TO BUY:

An assortment of the following:

- Multi-vitamins
- Gauze bandages
- Antiseptic solutions such as Betadine
- Butterfly closures, Steri-strips, surgical or super glue, staples, and/or sutures
- Extra masks (both N95 and standard)
- Gloves for treating medical wounds
- Antiviral medicines such as Tamiflu
- Potassium iodide (KIO4) tablets
- Benadryl or allergy medicines
- Contraception
- Anti-nausea medicine
- Electrolyte drinks or rehydration powders
- Braces for sprains
- Moleskins for foot relief
- Stethoscope
- Gloves
- Duct tape
- Potassium iodide capsules
- Snake bite kit
- Anti-diarrhea medication (for adults and children)
- Antibiotics
- Stool softeners
- Petroleum jelly or other lubricant
- CPR mask
- Colloidal silver

ACTION ITEMS:

1. Make a list of the medical emergencies you could foresee occurring during an emergency and research (in depth) the preventative measures, treatment and care.
2. Take an advanced first aid or medical course. Many of the preparedness/survival expos going on offer these sorts of classes. Also doing a simple Google search of "survival courses" will provide you with a long list of region specific courses being offered.
3. Do inventory and keep an organized list of medical items you have on hand.
4. Continue to invest in medical emergency manuals and books in order to familiarize yourself with up-to-date medical information.
5. Be proactive and create first response packs for wounds[197] in order to expedite the emergency care process.
6. If childbirth during a sudden emergency is a possibility, research and learn the correct procedure in how to assist in the birth as well as ways to keep the baby and mom healthy.

---

[197] http://readynutrition.com/resources/shtf-survival-first-response-packs-for-medical-emergencies-2_13082011/

CHAPTER FIFTY: ESSENTIAL TOOLS—LIST 4

Like many Americans, Mach Arom ['89], caught the news of the December 2004 Asian tsunami on television and watched the death tolls rise in horror. By some twist of fate, this Thai American who grew up with a foot in each country and typically spends the holidays with family in Thailand, was at home in New York when disaster struck 11 Pacific countries and took the lives of more than 160,000 people. "I called my parents to make sure they were in Bangkok, watched television, and tried to get information from the web. The videos were horrifying. I was simply stunned," he recalls.

As the shock began to wear off, Arom saw past the immediate outpouring of international aid and began to form a plan. "It was similar to how I felt about being in New York for 9/11," says Arom. "Both tragedies were in my backyard, in different geographic ways. The scale was huge, [and I knew] something this big would fall off the radar of the mainstream media relatively quickly because it happened so far around the world." While many relief organizations were collecting donations to send overseas, Arom and his brother Dan wanted to get dollars into the right hands and deliver manpower for smaller-scale projects with immediate impact for local Thai. They formed the Phuket Project, a non-profit volunteer organization to support local communities on Phuket — a tropical island roughly the size of Singapore, some 500 miles south of Bangkok — and in other southern provinces...Projects ranged from relatively simple — the first was to construct a bathroom with four plywood walls — to rebuilding homes and schools, as well as building boats, playgrounds, and holding one-day art therapy workshops for Thai children in conjunction with The Art Reach Foundation. One of the most dramatic: a partnership with the Bangkok Phuket Hospital to rebuild the Kamala Pre-School. Source[198]

198

http://www.conncoll.edu/camelweb/index.cfm?fuseaction=publications&circuit=cconline&function=view&id=4473053&uid=20

Throughout the course of this program, we have touched upon the basic tools you should have to be ready for emergencies, discussed top survival tools, and emphasized the importance of tools to build, repair, and maintain our homes and gardens in the face of damage or breakdown.

Some of you may ask why such rudimentary tools are placed at such high importance during emergencies. Well, quite simply, you cannot place a timeline on how long emergencies last and these tools will be a lifeline for you in a reality where electricity and fuel may not be as available as it is today. Tools will help you build, repair, and fortify your homes or property.

DIVERSIFY YOUR TOOLS

It is important to have a diversified collection of tools, because, after all, you never know when you will need them and for how long you will dependent on them.

For example, my husband purchased a socket set one day at the hardware store. In all honesty, I thought it to be useless. To my disbelief I realized how wrong I was and how many uses there are for the socket set. If you are changing wheels or fastening washers and nuts, then you will be using a socket wrench. With that said, I stood corrected.

PREPS TO BUY:

Take the following items into consideration, but do not limit yourselves to what is on the list. Remember that these lists should serve as suggestions and it is up to you to create a personalized preparedness supply that you and your family can rely on.

- Welding torch and fuel
- Clamps
- Sledge hammer
- Crowbar
- Files
- Bolt cutters
- Crowbar
- Machete
- Ratchet set
- Chainsaw (gas or electric)
- Circle drawing compass
- Tin snips
- Chisels (Cold chisel and wood chisel)
- Wire stripper
- Side cutter pliers
- Wood plane
- Stapler with assorted size staples
- Stud finder
- Fish netting
- Duct tape
- String/twine
- Rebar tie wire
- Measuring tape or ruler
- An assortment of nails, bolts, nuts, washers and screws

ACTION ITEMS:

1. Rather than purchasing two of the same tools, consider investing in spare parts for the tools such as extra blades, sharpening tools, and lubricants such as WD-40 or Vaseline.
2. Ensure the tools you purchase are of good quality.
3. Be mindful of your dependence on the grid and find ways to offset it.
4. Purchase resources that may help you learn skills like building structures, masonry, installing wells or creating shelters that may be needed in a long-term disaster. (For example, an outdoor solar shower would do wonders for morale during a long-term emergency.)

SUPPLEMENTAL INFORMATION AND RESOURCES

In 35 seconds, a devastating earthquake changed the lives forever for Haitians. Their city was destroyed and thousands were displaced. Habitat for Humanity has worked with the displaced Haitians and are taking steps to provide them with permanent housing. They are constructing "core houses," that is, homes that can be expanded on in the future.

Core houses are small, but well-constructedwell constructed and durable, permanent structures that provide adequate living space and sanitation facilities for the average Haitian family of five.

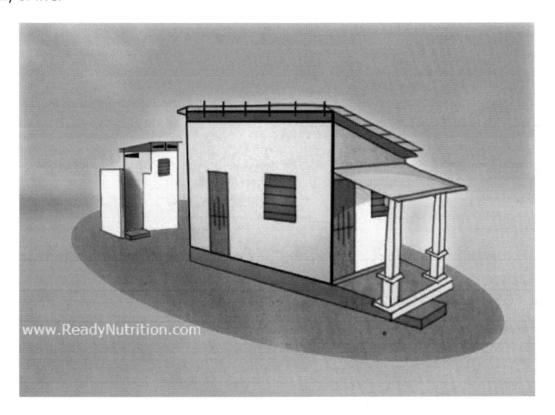

The house, which involves flooring and a roof with a single room, a door and windows, provides provision for water and sanitation and complies with international humanitarian standards.

Core houses are designed with the expectation that the homeowner partner will add on to the structure—expanding its square footage—when circumstances permit.

- **Earthquake-resistant design**
  Core houses are designed with earthquake-resistant features that work as a whole system to resist damage in the event of another earthquake. These structural features include:
- **Walls with embedded steel bars.**
  All cells surrounding doors and windows will contain embedded steel bars. Additionally,

each wall will have a horizontal steel bar for every two layers of blocks. The steel bars will absorb the shear stress of an earthquake.

A portion of the walls will be constructed with concrete blocks. Other materials used may include pre-fabricated micro concrete panels, interlocking blocks and compressed earth block.

- **Reinforced concrete footings, columns and a bond (ring) beam which tie the concrete block walls together.**

  The bond beam absorbs and resists the horizontal forces of an earthquake—transmitting these forces to the columns, footings and eventually to the ground. Additionally, the columns are designed to resist and absorb bending movements.

- **Properly supported, light roof structure.**

  Core house design uses a light roof structure and roof cover, in addition to a proper structural system.

Source – Habitat for Humanity[199]

---

[199] http://www.habitat.org/disaster/active_programs/Core_houses.aspx#P0_0

CHAPTER FIFTY-ONE: NUCLEAR DISASTER PREPAREDNESS

Natalia Manzurova, was a 35-year-old engineer at a nuclear plant in Ozersk, Russia. In April 1986, she and 13 other scientists were told to report to the wrecked, burning plant in the northern Ukraine...also known as the Chernobyl disaster.

"It was like a war zone where a neutron bomb had gone off. All the houses and buildings were intact with all the furniture, but there wasn't a single person left. Just deep silence everywhere. There are really no words to describe it... First, we measured radiation levels and got vegetation samples to see how high the contamination was. Then bulldozers dug holes in the ground and we buried everything -- houses, animals, everything. There were some wild animals that were still alive, and we had to kill them and put them in the holes... The people had only a few hours to leave, and they weren't allowed to take their dogs or cats with them. The radiation stays in animals' fur and they can't be cleaned, so they had to be abandoned. All the animals left behind in the houses were like dried-out mummies. ...All sorts of things happened. One colleague stepped into a rainwater pool and the soles of his feet burned off inside his boots.

I started to feel as if I had the flu. I would get a high temperature and start to shiver. What happens during first contact with radiation is that your good flora is depleted and the bad flora starts to flourish. I suddenly wanted to sleep all the time and eat a lot. It was the organism getting all the energy out... They found it [the tumor] during a routine medical inspection after I had worked there several years. It turned out to be benign. I don't know when it started to develop. I had an operation to remove half the thyroid gland. The tumor grew back, and last year I had the other half removed. I live on (thyroid) hormones now...

Source[200]

---

[200] http://www.aolnews.com/2011/03/22/chernobyl-cleanup-survivors-message-for-japan-run-away-as-qui/

Some believe that the subject of nuclear disaster preparedness is all hype and sensationalism. Since the dawn of nuclear weapons, we have always been wary of a trigger-happy world leader hastily pushing a nuke detonator.

According to history, though, the two worst nuclear events that occurred were accidental. Chernobyl, (being the first event) had a fire and explosion that released large quantities of radioactive contamination into the atmosphere, and spread over much of the Western USSR and Europe. The second largest nuclear event is the infamous Fukushima Daiichi nuclear disaster that occurred in 2011.

NUCLEAR DISASTERS

Each day we are exposed to nuclear radiation, some naturally and some through un-natural means. Those of us who live close to nuclear power plants are exposed more than others. Those that live near nuclear power plants should be especially concerned with nuclear disaster preparedness; especially the area is prone to natural disasters (hurricanes, earthquakes and tornadoes) that could damage the nuclear facilities.

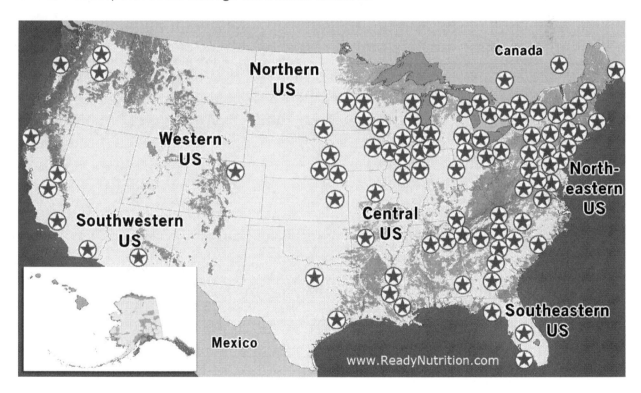

Nuclear Power Plants in the United States

If radiation leaks occur, they will affect all of us, not just those in the immediate vicinity. If you think that the Fukushima emergency is over and done with, think again. We are still dealing with the aftereffects of this one.

For instance, the Fukushima nuclear disaster has already affected our food supplies[201], water sources, and even our health has become affected from the radiation dispersed into the water and atmosphere.

Radiation tests conducted since the nuclear disaster in Japan have detected radioactive iodine and cesium in milk, beef, and vegetables produced in California (Source[202]).

PREPARING, PREVENTING AND PROTECTING OURSELVES FOR A NUCLEAR EVENT

Although the idea of preparing for an EMP or nuclear disaster is not something we want to think about, there are multiple ways to prepare, prevent and protect ourselves from the effects of radiation.

1. One of the easiest ways to minimize the effects of radiation is to know where our food comes from. This can help us to limit our exposure to radioactive foods and water sources. Keep in mind that foods, especially seafood from the West coast will be the most affected by radiation.
2. An electroscope that gauges how much radiation you are receiving daily can be a useful tool. A Kearny Fallout Meter[203] can give daily readings of radiation levels in your area.
3. Thoroughly wash your produce. Despite arguments to the contrary, you *can* wash radioactive particles off of produce. (See below)
4. Adopting an anti-radiation diet can provide natural alternatives to assist the body in ridding itself of radioactive toxins.

> Foods such as kelp, rosemary, spirulina, miso soup and niacin all assist the body in fighting radiation damage. Other foods that may help in combating radiation sickness are foods that naturally detoxify the body. Foods that are high in potassium such as apples, oranges, pineapples and pomegranates are foods that are also good cancer fighters.
>
> Foods that are high in antioxidants will also assist your body in ridding itself of radioactive particles. Foods such as green and black teas (make sure that your tea is not from Japan), garlic, cumin, nettles, dandelions, ginseng, lentils, collards and mustard greens are also suggested.

---

[201] http://daisyluther.blogspot.com/2012/04/pardon-me-your-food-is-glowing.html

[202] http://www.foxnews.com/health/2011/06/29/radiation-in-our-food/#ixzz22hjYk1yl

[203] http://readynutrition.com/resources/a-step-by-step-guide-for-how-to-make-a-kearny-fallout-meter_08082012/

5. Any food or water stored in sealed containers that have any fallout dust is safe to consume as long as the fallout dust is brushed or rinsed off the outside of the container. Take caution not to allow the fallout dust to get inside the container.

6. You need access to pure drinking water. Water that comes from an underground source, such as a spring or a covered well, is likely to be safe. Water can also be filtered to remove radioactive particles. The most effective way to remove the particles from water is a double process. First, water should go through a reverse osmosis filter, and then, a deionization resin filter. This double process removes 95% or more of radioactive particles.

7. If levels of radiation are high, this double-filtered water should be used for drinking, cooking, bathing and washing dishes. This purified water would also be the water you would use to wash your produce.

8. Drinking apple cider vinegar can also assist in flushing toxins and radiation from the body. Look for a natural unfiltered, unpasteurized apple cider vinegar that contains the "mother", like Braggs, for best results. Baking soda and water is another option as it also flushes radiation and cleans the stomach lining. You can also put baking soda in dish soap, body soap, and laundry detergent. The radiation will bind to the baking soda, which neutralizes it.

9. Did you know that the Spiderwort plant is Nature's Geiger counter? This plant naturally has very dark purple flowers and when they are exposed to radiation or near an area where radiation is high, the flowers turn pink. Planting these in your yard will be a great way to know if you are taking in excess radiation.

> **What's Your Annual Radiation Amount?**
>
> Knowing in advance how much radiation you are exposed to through natural and un-natural means can help you calculate your annual radiation dose. To find this out, go to:
>
> http://www.epa.gov/radiation/understand/calculate.html

During or following a nuclear disaster, radioactive ionic particles attach themselves to dust floating in the air. Therefore, these particles can be ingested, inhaled, or absorbed through the skin.

WHAT TO DO DURING A NUCLEAR DISASTER

If you are told to evacuate or bug in due to a nuclear disaster, keep the following points in mind:

1. If you are driving, keep the car windows and vents closed, and use recirculating air.
2. Due to the fear of panic and gridlock that will ensue from mass evacuations, most governments will delay mandatory evacuations until the last minute. This will only cause mass confusion and chaos at gas stations, grocery stores and on the streets. The best way to prevent this is to stay ahead of the crowd and prepare ahead of time.

3. If told to stay indoors, turn off the air conditioner and other air intakes and go to a basement. Seal basement windows and entrances to prevent fallout from getting inside. If you go outside, you will need to remove your outer clothing before coming inside the shelter.

4. Likewise, creating a sealed area near the entrance of the shelter will prevent fallout dust from entering. Seal the entryway with blankets, bubble wrap or plastic sheeting to prevent the dust from coming in. Have water and baby shampoo near the entrance to wash and thoroughly rinse any exposed skin and hair. Exposure to fallout radiation does not make you radioactive, but you need to assure that you don't bring any inside. Some experts suggest having a rain poncho to take on and off when you go outside.

5. To go a step further, covering the windows with wood, and then sandbags followed by masonry bricks will create a multi-layered protection against you and radioactive particles.

6. If you find yourself outdoors when a nuclear blast occurs, duck and cover for 2 minutes. You will first see a blinding light followed by tornado force winds. When all danger is gone, seek shelter immediately. Remove your clothing at the door and place in a sealed plastic bag. You can remove 80% of the particles by removing your clothing. Showering immediately following exposure is another way to remove the remaining particles.

7. If you have signs of radiation on skin, soak in a tub of equal parts baking soda, apple cider vinegar and Epsom salt. Skin brushing can be very beneficial, because the skin is a primary avenue for detoxification – scrub along with the lungs, kidneys, liver, and colon. An unused vegetable brush would be very helpful with this process.

8. Getting caught out in the rain can also cause you to have more exposure to radioactive particles. If you do have to go out in the rain, completely cover yourself. Experts are suggesting that if your clothes get wet to take them off and seal them in a plastic bag, immediately shower and change clothing. (The detox bath solution and skin brushing would be good here. If radioactive materials get on your skin, burns and blistering can occur. *Note: If you are exposed to radioactive particles, you will also need to get your urine tested for traces of cesium at your local medical center.*)

9. When fallout is first anticipated, but has not yet arrived, anyone not already sheltered should begin using their N95 particulate respirator masks and hooded rain ponchos. Everyone should begin taking Potassium Iodide (KI) or Potassium Iodate (KIO3) tablets for thyroid protection against cancer causing radioactive iodine, a major product of nuclear weapons explosions. If no tablets are available, you can topically (on the skin) apply an iodine solution, such as a tincture of iodine or Betadine, for a similar protective effect. (WARNING: Iodine solutions are NEVER to be ingested or swallowed.) Absorption through the skin is not as reliable a dosing method as using the tablets, but tests show that it will still be very effective for most. Do not use if allergic to iodine. If at all possible, inquire of your doctor NOW if there is any reason why anybody in your household should not use KI or KIO3 tablets, or iodine solutions on their skin, in the event of a future nuclear emergency.

> - For adults, paint 8 ml of a 2 percent tincture of Iodine on the abdomen or forearm each day, ideally at least 2 hours prior to possible exposure.
> - For children 3 to 18, but under 150 pounds, only half that amount painted on daily, or 4 ml. For children under 3 but older than a month, half again, or 2 ml.
> - For newborns to 1 month old, half it again, or just 1 ml. (One measuring teaspoon is about 5 ml, if you don't have a medicine dropper graduated in ml.) If your iodine is stronger than 2%, reduce the dosage accordingly.

10. When you know that the time to take protective action is approaching, turn off all the utilities into the house, check that everything is sealed up and locked down, and head for the shelter. You should also have near your shelter fire extinguishers and additional tools, building supplies, sheet plastic, staple guns, etc. for sealing any holes from damage. Your basement should already be very well sealed against fallout drifting inside. Now, you'll need to seal around the last door you use to enter with duct tape all around the edges, especially if it's a direct to the outside door.
11. Do not use the telephone unless absolutely necessary. Staying on the phone will congest phone lines making it impossible for others in your area to make or receive calls.

Source[204]

If you are told to evacuate or shelter in place due to nuclear attack or nuclear leak disaster, don't panic. This type of disaster *is* survivable.

---

[204] http://www.ki4u.com/guide.htm

Symptoms of Radiation Sickness Include:

- Bloody stool
- Bruising
- Confusion
- Dehydration
- Diarrhea
- Fainting
- Fatigue
- Fever
- Hair loss
- Mouth ulcers
- Nausea and vomiting
- Open sores on the skin
- Skin burns (redness, blistering)
- Sloughing of skin
- Vomiting blood
- Weakness
- Inflammation of exposed areas (redness, tenderness, swelling, bleeding)
- Bleeding from the nose, mouth, gums, and rectum
- Ulcers in the esophagus, stomach or intestines

PREPS TO BUY:

- Long-term supply of food and water
- Medical supplies
- Sanitation supplies
- Emergency communications (at least a hand-crank or short-wave radio)

In Quantity:

- Apple cider vinegar
- Baking soda
- Epsom salt
- Ingestible bentonite clay
- Duct tape
- Activated carbon
- Soap, sponges and/or bristled brush (vegetable scrubbing brush)

For each group or family member:

- Geiger counter
- Kearny fallout meter
- Potassium Iodate (KIO3) tablets for all family or group members
- Nuke suit
- N95 particulate respirator masks
- Hooded rain ponchos for all family or group members
- Home air filter
- Gas masks with extra filters
- Filtered ventilation system, powered with manually-powered back up
- A nuclear shelter that has an entrance designed to reduce fallout exposure.

ACTION ITEMS:

1. Do an inventory on your food, water, and preparedness supply to see where you are in terms of short and long-term preparedness. At this point, you should have a multi-level stock of preparedness foods to last long-term (up to 12 months).
2. Consider purchasing more freeze-dried goods (They last for 25 years, so it's a great investment in your long-term preparedness).
3. Find out if you are near a nuclear power plant and use the annual radiation calculator to see what your levels are.
4. Start practicing those survival and homesteading skills!

SUPPLEMENTAL INFORMATION AND RESOURCES

Removing Radiation with Calcium Bentonite Clay

Calcium Bentonite clay is a natural substance that actually *absorbs* radiation. According to the website, <u>About Clay</u>, "Calcium Bentonite Clay has a uniquely strong negative ionic charge. When activated with water it works like a strong magnet, adsorbing and absorbing anything with a positive ionic charge (i.e., toxins, pesticides, radiation). The clay captures these substances and removes them as it is eliminated or washed off."

To wash produce with Bentonite Clay:

Mix 1 part Calcium Bentonite Clay to 8 parts of purified water in a large non-metallic bowl. Toss your produce in this clay water, making certain the produce is completely covered, and let it sit for 10 minutes. Rinse well with more purified water.

For additional protection, peel thin-skinned fruits like peaches and apples after washing them.

(Republished with permission from <u>Daisy Luther</u>[205])

---

[205] <u>http://www.theorganicprepper.ca/</u>

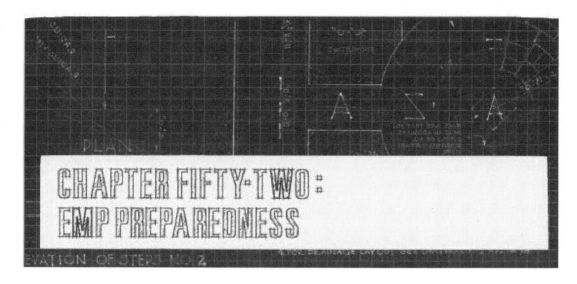

CHAPTER FIFTY-TWO::
EMP PREPAREDNESS

When you think about the possibility of an EMP, do you think it's nothing more than the plot of a Hollywood movie or television series?

If you look back in time to around 1859, there occurred a solar flare so intense that the explosion itself was visible to the human eye. Even more disconcerting, telegraph systems worldwide went haywire. Spark discharges shocked operators and set the telegraph paper on fire. Even when telegraphers disconnected the batteries powering the lines, aurora-induced electric currents in the wires still allowed messages to be transmitted. This ferocious geomagnetic storm was dubbed the Carrington Event.

Fast-forward to 2013, where scientists are anticipating a rather abnormally active sun activity and believe it is not too far out of possibility that a solar flare could take out parts of the grid.

So you decide: are these types of disasters merely sensationalism?

ELECTRO-MAGNETIC PULSE

EMP's are a force to reckon with. An Electro-Magnetic Pulse[206] can be the result of natural events (solar flares) or a man-made attack (a nuclear bomb that has been detonated over a given area). Either type of EMP event would take out the electrical transformers, as well as any unprotected devices (anything electrical – cell phones, computers, cars, electrical appliances, etc.).

In other words, we would be thrown back to the pre-electricity days of the 1800's, without the benefit of homes that were built to run without electricity.

If an enemy planned to attack our country by means of an EMP, all they would need to irreparably cripple us is a small-scale, five to ten kiloton weapon detonated 200 miles above Nebraska, or a few weapons detonated 50 miles or so above the eastern, western and central United States.

The lasting effects would be nothing short of disastrous – literally the end of the world as we know it.

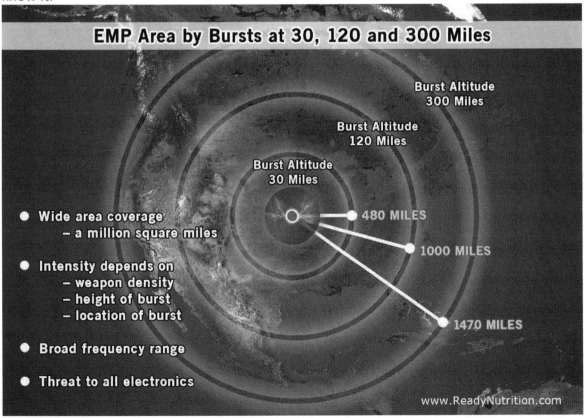

With an EMP disaster, not only would we be without electrical power until transformers could be replaced, a prospect that could take many years, but all unprotected and unhardened

---

[206] http://readynutrition.com/resources/emp-an-event-that-could-cripple-our-way-of-life_05052012/

electrical devices would be left useless and would eventually need to be replaced due to the circuits and boards being fried beyond repair.

You can take steps to protect important electronics by purchasing or constructing an enclosure made of conductive material that blocks both static and non-static electrical fields. This is also called a Faraday cage.

Some preppers question the necessity of a Faraday cage. They wonder, why protect items that must be plugged in if the entire electrical grid is down?

- First of all, if the grid does come back up at some point, a person with devices that have been protected will be in the vast minority of people to possess a working unit. If a device has not been protected, even with the return of electrical power at the flick of a switch, the item cannot be repaired and used in the future.
- Secondly, if you have planned other sources of power (such as solar or wind power) then the items that you have protected can be used with those power sources. If this is the case, also be certain to protect the proper inverters or solar chargers to be used with the stored devices.

Everything about our current way of life would be affected by an event that takes down the power grid.

1. Food manufacturing and transit would completely cease.

2. A vast majority of people would no longer be able to heat or cool their homes.

3. We would not be able to access money in banks.

4. All types of manufacturing would completely cease.

5. We would lose access to vital medication and medical assistance.

6. Our personal security could be threatened.

Over the course of this program, I have often emphasized the importance of being "ahead of the pack" in terms of preparedness. The faster you can react to the disaster in front of you, the more quickly you can be prepared. Once an EMP outage occurs, your paper money will be worthless within a matter of days. Don't hesitate to spend it!

Last minute purchases could include:

- Ammunition and weapons
- Climate appropriate clothing
- Practical shoes/boots
- Long-term storage food
- Seeds and gardening tools
- Bottled water and gravity fed water filtration systems
- Fuel such as propane and kerosene
- Medications, both prescription and over the counter
- Solar devices
- Candles, solar yard lights and other alternative light sources
- Gold or silver
- Batteries in multiple sizes

I have also stressed that although having supplies are important, especially during a short term event, your skill level and knowledge will be what helps you adapt more fluidly to a longer term event such as an EMP.

Taking this a step further, in an EMP survival situation, you would be taking those skills and applying them to an off-grid environment. For example, if you have non-working electrical appliances from the EMP detonation, you will be canning and preserving your food off the grid. Have you practiced that technique?

One of the first things we should do following a disaster (assuming the danger has passed and everyone is safe) is to begin to see how everyday items can be used as tools for off-grid living. A simple credit card or a busted cell phone can go a long way in surviving an emergency. We can easily find items around our home to promote our security and wellbeing.

8 Ways to Use Items to Adapt and Survive

1. **Gravity fed water filter** - Water is key to survival and your number one priority when all hell breaks loose. When you drink unpurified water, it can cause severe illnesses, even death. If you haven't invested in a water filtration system, then you need to learn how to purify water for consumption.
2. **Rope** – Rope or paracord can serve <u>multiple purposes</u>[207] in off-grid living. One of my favorite uses is to line dry clothing.
3. **Busted motors** – Essentially any motor with a copper wire can be converted into an energy producer. You could easily convert your <u>washing machine into a windmill</u>[208] to make power. This is an essential skill to have for surviving a long-term emergency.

---

[207] <u>http://readynutrition.com/resources/paracord-the-most-versatile-item-in-your-bug-out-bag_07062012/</u>

[208] <u>http://readynutrition.com/resources/video-convert-a-washing-machine-motor-to-create-free-</u>

4. **Stationary bikes** - Did you ever think that stationary bikes could help to promote your self-sustainability? Attaching your wheat grinder to your stationary bike by a pulley will help you put the pedal to the metal and grind grains more efficiently. Here are few additional ways to produce energy using a bicycle[209].

5. **Passive solar heater** - We tend to think of solar heating as an expensive option, but with a few 2×4's and a stash of soda cans spray painted black you can create a passive solar heater. This could be a life-saving item if you find yourself living in a grid down environment in a cold climate.

6. **Cellular phones** – As mentioned previously, cell phones have many uses in a survival situation. If your phone is still intact, you can download survival programs now (some are even free) to learn and practice in your free time. However, if your phone is busted during a disaster there are core parts that can be utilized towards your survival. Some of these parts are the speaker, LCD screen, metal divider, wire, circuit board and battery. You can easily make a survival reflective mirror, magnets in the speaker systems can be used as navigational devices, circuit boards can be made into spears, and almost any battery can be short-circuited to generate either a spark or a hot enough wire to ignite flammable tinder.

7. **Credit Cards** - These are great for a good deal more than use as currency. Scraping out a sting with the edge of a plastic card is preferable to fingernails or tweezers, both of which can pump the last bit of venom from the sting into the skin. Cut into strips, credit cards are excellent splints for broken fingers, and the gaps between the strips allow for swelling. Position either side of the finger and tape into place.

   Used whole they can help inflate a deflated lung caused by a sucking chest wound. Put over the hole and tape on three sides only, the card acts as a flutter valve, preventing air from entering the wound but allowing air outside of the lung but inside the chest cavity to escape as the lung inflates. Source[210]

8. **Biomass briquettes** – Your trash could save your life. Biomass briquettes[211] are a green fuel source and are comprised of compressed organic compounds such as corn husks, coconut shells, grass clippings, dried leaves, saw dust, cardboard or paper. Biomass fuel sources are equivalent to that of common fuel sources and can be inside or in outside settings.

---

energy_24022014/

[209] http://readynutrition.com/resources/3-uses-a-stationary-bike-has-when-the-grid-goes-down_28022014/

[210] http://undergroundmedic.com/

[211] http://readynutrition.com/resources/bio-mass-briquettes-an-alternative-fuel-source-made-from-paper_19012014/

The threat of an EMP, regardless of the source, is very real, and we must prepare ahead of time in order to survive the aftermath. Having all of your items prepared and in place before the disaster will keep your family or group safe and ready to bunker in more quickly.

PREPS TO BUY:

- Off-grid cooking methods along with the appropriate fuel
- Emergency lighting sources
- Heat sources
- Emergency communications (at least a hand-crank or short-wave radio)
- Alternative power sources
- Manual tools
- Manual kitchen items like grinders
- Supplies for off-grid laundry, like a wringer bucket and a scrubbing board

ACTION ITEMS:

1. Decide which electronics are the most vital and protect them with a Faraday Cage.
2. Ensure that you are comfortable with using your alternative power sources.
3. Do an inventory to be sure you have plenty of spare parts for alternative power systems and manual tools.

SUPPLEMENTAL INFORMATION AND RESOURCES

How to Make a Simple Faraday Cage

Many websites have complex instructions on how to build a Faraday cage. There are also expensive Faraday bags and boxes that can be purchased. They are "guaranteed" to protect your items from an EMP strike, but collecting on that guarantee could be rather difficult, given the circumstances that would cause the necessity for that protection.

There are many less complicated ways that you can improvise an EMP-proof container of your own for a far less expensive price tag. Although these homemade Faraday cages are perhaps not as stylish and elegant as the retail units, they should be just as effective. The following items can be pressed into device protection duty:

- An aluminum garbage can with a lid
- A metal filing cabinet
- A metal tool box
- A gutted microwave oven
- Tin canisters or ammo cans

Insulate items by lining the container in a non-conductive material, like cardboard. You can also make cardboard sleeves for your devices. It is vital that none of your electronics directly contact the metal of the container. It is important to add that your makeshift Faraday cages should be grounded in order to disperse the energy.

What to Put in a Faraday Cage

What should you store in your Faraday cage? Anything that you don't want to live without post-EMP and anything that you can charge in an alternate manner is a good candidate for residence within the container.

Some items that you might want to prioritize for a place inside the cage are:

- Radios (shortwave or windup)
- DVD players
- Extra hard drives
- USB drives
- Batteries
- Flashlights
- Laptop and charger
- Solar device chargers
- iPods
- Walkie talkies
- Invertors and charge controllers for solar power system
- Small pieces of medical equipment

CHAPTER FIFTY-THREE:
BARTERING AND COMMUNITY

Buyers and sellers gather in a sweltering, previously abandoned building in the Greek city of Volos, some 200 miles north of Athens. There's a bit of everything available here — books, eggs, clothes, kids' toys, and even an old fax machine.

But there isn't a euro in sight. On the eve of a vote which may determine whether Greece stays in the euro zone, these Greeks have moved beyond the euro, at least here. This market is the brainchild of a network of people who have chucked the euro in favor of the TEM — the Greek shorthand for "Alternative Local Currency."

"In the network, people can trade their goods and services. They don't need money for that. They just need time and the desire to do it," said Christos Papaioannou, one of the network's founders. It's kind of like bartering on steroids, he added.

"We can see it as exchanging favors, if I do a service for you, then you owe me a favour, and I can use that favour to get some service from someone else. So, we don't have to exchange directly, I can get it from some third person."

...More than 1,000 people have joined or are waiting to join in this city of 150,000. Katarina, who joined a month and half ago, is selling homemade liqueurs, jams and sweets. For her, the network isn't just about creating an alternative social structure. It's about survival. She uses her credits to buy staples — vegetables, fruits and eggs — from others in the network.

Source[212]

---

[212] http://www.theworld.org/2012/06/greek-town-adopting-system-of-bartering-on-steroids/

One of my favorite chapters in <u>Patriots</u>[213] was when the main characters were invited to a community market where they bartered with other like-minded individuals for supplies. Personally speaking, that chapter expressed hope – hope that our civilization would not crumble, hope that a community would flourish and that business exchanges would still carry on. Ultimately, it was the beginning of a community coming together again.

If a long-term emergency causes an end to our existing monetary system and an end to the exchange of fiat currency that our world currently operates on, people will resort back to bartering for skills and services in order to make transactions.

Living in a bartering environment means one must possess certain goods or skills that others find value in. As <u>Brandon Smith</u>[214] writes on the subject:

> "If you wish to survive after the destruction of the mainstream system that has babied us for so long, you must be able to either make a necessary product, repair a necessary product, or teach a necessary skill. A limited few have the capital required to stockpile enough barter goods or gold and silver to live indefinitely. The American Tradesman must return in full force, not only for the sake of self-preservation, but also for the sake of our heritage at large."

So what items or services would be ideal or deemed valuable for bartering in a long-term emergency?

Ideally, for bartering in a short-term emergency, you want to consider the basic survival items that may quickly disappear. Keep in mind the list of 100 items most likely to disappear and focus your efforts on investing in these.

GOODS

Barter items can be purchased at the dollar store, the flea market or at liquidation houses. Some categories for barter could be: basic survival items, comfort items, tools, currencies, etc.

Many who are investing in bartering items purchase the smaller quantities of certain items. For example, if someone wanted to stock up on soda for a bartering situation, they would stock up on the cans and not the liter versions of the product. This helps you sell more products.

Yard sales, estate sales, and thrift stores are also great places to purchase "trash to treasure" finds. Items that you can acquire inexpensively may one day be more valuable than gold.

What kind of items will be worth their weight in gold? Here are a few additional suggestions:

---

[213] http://www.amazon.com/Patriots-Surviving-James-Wesley-Rawles/dp/156975599X/ref=sr_1_1?ie=UTF8&qid=1345835212&sr=8-1&keywords=patriots

[214] http://alt-market.com/articles/146-top-post-collapse-barter-items-and-trade-skills

- Matches and lighters
- Seeds
- Canning jars, lids and rings
- First aid items
- Tools
- Water Filtration Supplies
- Sewing supplies
- Vitamins
- Salt
- Feminine Hygiene Supplies
- Vitamins
- Fishing Supplies
- Fuel (gasoline, propane, kerosene, etc.)
- Sweeteners such as honey, sugar and syrup
- Coffee/Tea
- Carbonated beverages
- Liquor
- Cigarettes/tobacco
- Small packages of food (baggies of beans/rice, etc.)
- Livestock
- Cooking oil
- Firewood
- Farm supplies (pesticides, fertilizer, etc.)
- Weapons, Ammo*
- Batteries
- Warm clothing
- Hats/Gloves (think about those little dollar store stretchy items)
- Soap/shampoo
- Hand sanitizer
- Dental care items (toothbrushes/toothpaste/floss)

Barter items can be purchased at the dollar store, the flea market or at liquidation houses. Don't forget yard sales – even though you already possess a meat grinder, someone who has ammo that you need might not have one. Items that you can acquire and store inexpensively may one day be more valuable than gold.

Don't forget about the items that you can produce yourself. This goes hand-in-hand with the barter of skills. Stock up on the supplies you need to create the following items for a long-term flow of "income."

- Fresh produce
- Ammunition (see *caution above)
- Home canned items
- Preserved meats (jerky, ham, etc.)

- Warm knitted or crocheted items (mittens, hats, scarves)
- Yarn spun from animal fibers
- Homemade candy
- Homemade soap
- Homemade candles
- Wooden or clay bowls and plates
- Herbal remedies

Use this list to get your creative juices flowing. What items do you possess the ability to make? Which of these items will be particularly useful if the grid goes down or if the economy crumbles?

SKILLS

Physical items are not the only currency of barter. Certain skills will be in very high demand.

If the grid goes down or the economy collapses in a long-term way, gone are the days of making your living doing IT work or ringing through purchases at the grocery store. You will need to become not only self-sufficient, but a provider of goods or services.

Consider what abilities and knowledge you possess that can be shared with others. And don't stop there: consider acquiring new skills that could be used as a bartering exchange during a long-term emergency. There is no limit to the skills that could be used in a barter situation.

Some examples would be:

- First Aid for traumatic injuries
- Sutures
- Midwifery/delivering babies
- Dental care
- Herbal remedies
- Animal Husbandry
- Veterinary Skills
- Teaching children
- Teaching skills to adults like knitting, gardening, machine repair, etc.
- Mechanic's skills: the ability to fix solar generators, small machines, automobiles, etc.
- Other repair skills: the ability to repair tools, woodstoves, plumbing, etc.
- Gardening/Farming
- Construction
- Gunsmithing/Weapon repair
- Security services
- Food Preservation
- Sewing/Mending
- Making soap and candles

- Blacksmithing

PRECIOUS METALS

Precious metals are the only form of currency that has stood the test of time. Keep in mind, that if you plan to use precious metals for barter, it may be difficult to make small trades.

To circumvent this issue, invest in a supply of pre-1965 US silver coins:

- These will be useful as cash, due to their known bullion content, and low, easy-to-use value, when the paper money crashes in purchasing power. A dime is now worth about $3 and may be worth $30 or more after the crash.

- Silver is less likely to be confiscated by the government (not worth the political and physical effort). FDR did it for gold in 1933.

While you may be able to easily utilize gold and silver as a mechanism of exchange at the onset of a crisis to buy much needed supplies during a currency meltdown and use it to exchange for land or equipment during a recovery period, you may be faced with a period of time when no one will be interested in your PM's. Selco of SHTF School[215] points out that gold is not the magic bullet that provides complete insulation from TEOTWAWKI. When all hell breaks loose, as it did in the Balkans in the 1990's, and a war is being fought right outside of your front window, gold and silver may not get you very far, as people are more concerned with the immediate necessity of getting out of harm's way than they are with anything else.

WHERE TO PURCHASE PRECIOUS METALS

If you plan on purchasing larger quantities or diverse investments of precious metals, there are many different ways to acquire gold and silver. Here are a few of the safest:

• Purchase the pieces from mints or exchanges
• Purchase old pieces of jewelry or coins from yard sales, estate sales, thrift stores and Craigslist
• Purchase from reputable sellers on eBay

Mints and exchanges offer a sure thing. These businesses are built on trust and integrity. If you are investing a large sum of money into precious metals, gather details about the types of coins you are buying, especially if you're buying gold. Acquire a coin caliper[216] and/or testing kit to ensure you're getting what is being advertised.

---

[215] http://shtfschool.com/trading/on-buying-gold-silver-for-survival-preparedness/

[216] http://www.safepub.com/categories/tools-coins-trade-equipment/p/electronic-coin-caliper

When you purchase from everyday people or take a gamble on buying something at the thrift store, you need to be able to identify and test the metals yourself.

1. Look for markings. Jewelry made from precious metals in the US began to be required to be marked for metal content in 1906. On silver pieces you are looking for the numbers "925" – this indicates that the piece is Sterling Silver or 92.5% silver. If the piece you are considering is gold, you are looking for 10K, 14K, 18K, etc. 24K is 100% gold, and is very soft, so the other numbers are indicative of the gold content that has been mixed with a harder metal to make it less pliable.

2. Inspect the piece carefully. Is it rough near the edges? Is it discolored in places? Is the finish chipping or flaking? These are all indicators that the piece may only be plated with silver or gold. These items require further testing. (Note: Sterling Silver will "oxidize" and tarnish – don't be put off by black discoloration. This should wipe off with a soft cloth.)

3. If the piece has been marked, then you will want to test it further. Carry with you a strong magnet. Precious metals are NOT magnetic, nor are the other metals that are used in jewelry to harden them. If the piece of jewelry or coin reacts to the magnet it is not gold or silver.

4. Test it with ceramic. You can purchase a small piece of unglazed ceramic tile at your local hardware store. If you have a piece of questionable gold, run the piece across the ceramic tile. If it leaves a blackish mark, it is not genuine gold.

Once you have performed these quick tests, you may want to go further. There are two more definitive tests – the "Archimedes Test" and the acid test.

Archimedes Test

Break out your physics hat and perform a density test to determine the content of the metal you have on hand. For this you will require a vial marked in millimeters in which you can submerge the item in question.

Do not fill the vial to the top, since you will be displacing water with the jewelry item. Note exactly the amount of water in your container. Weigh your item on a digital jewelry scale, marking down your result in grams. This is the "mass" of your item.

Place your piece in the vial and note the new water level.

Calculate the difference between the two numbers in millimeters. This is the "volume displacement" of the item.

Use the following formula to calculate density:

Density = mass/volume displacement

Here is a sample calculation:

Your gold item weighs 38 g and it displaces 2 milliliters of water. Using the formula of [mass (38 g)]/ [volume displacement (2 ml)], your result would be 19 g/ml, which is very close to the density of pure 24K gold.

Remember that different gold and silver purities will have a different g/ml ratio:

o 14K – 12.9 to 14.6 g/mL
o 18K yellow – 15.2 to 15.9 g/mL
o 18K white – 14.7 to 16.9 g/mL
o 22K – 17.7 to 17.8 g/mL
o 999 Silver – 10.49 g/mL
o 925 Silver – 10.2 to 10.3 g/mL

> ## A Word to the Wise
>
> *Caution: Exercise great discretion when bartering with weapons and ammunition. It is entirely possible that those items could be used against you to take your supplies. These are items to be bartered only with someone you trust implicitly or as an absolute last resort.*

Nitric Acid Test

This is the most definitive way to test the metal in question. This test is where the saying "passing the acid test" originated.

WARNING: Nitric Acid is highly corrosive. Wear safety eyewear and protective gloves when working with this product. Protect all surfaces that could come into contact with the acid.

To perform an acid test, you will require Nitric Acid, a non-reactive dropper, and a stainless steel container in which to perform the test.

Place your item in the stainless steel container. Using the dropper, apply a very tiny drop of acid on a non-exposed part of the item in question. (Remember: If the item is not gold or silver, the acid may permanently mar the finish.)

If you suspect that the item is merely plated, you can make a small scratch in a hidden place in which to test the item.

The acid will turn different colors in reaction to different metal contents:

Cream: 90 to 100% silver
Gray: 77-90% silver
Green: less than 75% precious metal content
No reaction: Gold

Test kits containing the chemicals and instructions can be purchased through Amazon for less than $10.

Finally, when purchasing gold or silver, always trust your instincts. You may not always have access to your testing kit when an opportunity arises. If an item looks suspicious or the price seems too good to be true, it probably is.

KNOWN DANGERS

Given the nature of disasters, those who are unprepared or ill equipped to live in this new reality will do whatever is necessary to take care of their needs – and that includes taking what you own.

When you are traveling to bartering grounds or community markets, be aware of frequented raid routes. These areas could become a nesting ground for thieves. Travel in a group and be weary of roads that lead to community markets, as they can easily be areas where desperate individuals will steal from you. Further, always have another person with you to "have your back" in case the meeting turns for the worse. Pay close attention to those you are bartering with. Always have your guard up and trust your gut. If you don't feel comfortable around this person or group, stay away.

To conclude, if studying preparedness has taught me one thing, it's that we can't go it alone. Psychologically speaking, we are social creatures and naturally prone to gravitate toward others. Bartering will not only serve as a way of trading goods and services, but will also serve as a way to grow closer, to bring the community together.

PREPS TO BUY:

- Matches and lighters
- Seeds
- Canning jars, lids and rings
- First aid items
- Tools
- Water filtration supplies
- Sewing supplies
- Vitamins
- Salt
- Feminine hygiene supplies
- Condoms, birth control
- Vitamins
- Fishing supplies
- Fuel (e.g., gasoline, propane, kerosene, etc.)
- Sweeteners such as honey, sugar and syrup
- Coffee/tea
- Carbonated beverages
- Liquor
- Cigarettes/tobacco
- Small packages of food (e.g., bags of beans/rice, etc.)
- Livestock
- Cooking oil
- Firewood
- Farm supplies (e.g., pesticides, fertilizer, etc.)
- Weapons, ammo*
- Batteries
- Warm clothing
- Hats/gloves/mittens (think about these the next time you are at the dollar store)
- Soap/shampoo
- Hand sanitizer
- Dental care items (e.g., toothbrushes/toothpaste/floss)

ACTION ITEMS:

1. Refer to the Top 100 Items to Disappear First. This is a great guide to provide ideas of what you can use for bartering and research which items will be most valuable in an emergency.
2. Make a point to research, take a class or practice one set of skills per month.
3. Stock up on necessary items for bartering.

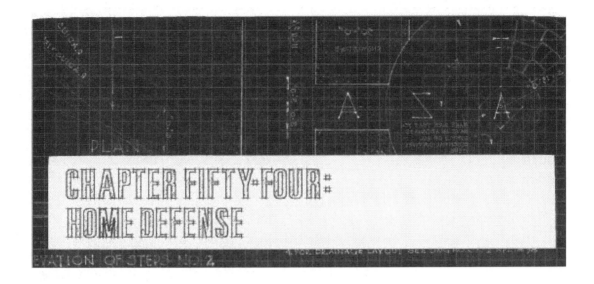

CHAPTER FIFTY-FOUR:
HOME DEFENSE

In the aftermath of Hurricane Isaac, the widespread lack of electricity seemed to embolden opportunistic criminals.

In one incident, a masked gunman walked into Hi-Ho Lounge at 2239 St. Claude Ave. about 10:35 p.m. Saturday and ordered all the bar's patrons onto the floor, according to police reports. The robber threw a bag to the bartender, demanding money from the cash register.

In a separate incident, five juveniles armed with a gun carjacked a 22-year-old woman as she sat in her car...

All told, police arrested 41 people for looting. Most of them targeted convenience stores, stealing food, alcohol and cigarettes...

A 37-year-old woman and two 17-year-olds were booked on counts of looting and contributing to delinquency of a juvenile after being caught rummaging through a store's food shelves with a 13-year-old boy. When caught inside Selena and Serena Sweet Shop at 8135 Oleander Street, the woman "apologized and stated they were hungry," according to a police report.

Source[217]

IF YOU CAN'T PROTECT IT, YOU DON'T OWN IT

[217] http://www.nola.com/crime/index.ssf/2012/09/new_orleans_police_report_wide.html

The unprepared have a certain mentality about you and your preps. Theft is a reality and a concern you should not take lightly. The fact of the matter is that crime only seems to escalate in the aftermath of a disaster - something we have seen many times, and as recently as Superstorm Sandy.

Throughout this preparedness program, we have discussed how important it is for security measures to be in place especially during and after a widespread disaster. In an earlier chapter on the subject of external security measures, I wrote that "a 'bug-in' scenario may be our only choice after a disaster strikes and we must prepare not only for our basic needs, but also for our safety. Since the grid may be down following a disaster, each household should prepare for crime."

I realize there are some who believe a gun does not belong in the home; that is your God-given choice. If we are talking about protecting ourselves in a short-or long-term disaster, then we have to assume that local emergency responders will not be as readily available and crime could be a threat to our property and personal safety. If that is the case, then a firearm should be as much a part of your preparedness plan as having the coveted beans and Band-Aids.

I don't know about you, but if someone kicks in my door, I know they aren't looking for a cup of sugar. Their motivation is purely to take something that you have or cause harm to you or a family member, and you must assume the worst. Trying to communicate with him or her will not do the trick if they are inside your home. A rifle pointed directly at the intruder's chest, however, would make a very clear statement.

I would like to emphasize that a gun should never be in the home of someone who does not understand gun safety protocols. This is an accident waiting to happen.

Ten Commandments of Gun Safety

1. Always keep the muzzle pointed in a safe direction.

2. Treat every firearm as if it were loaded.

3. Always keep the action open except when actually hunting or preparing to shoot. Always wear approved shooting safety glasses and hearing protection.

4. Be sure the barrel and action are clear of obstructions and that the ammunition is appropriate for the firearm.

5. Always be sure of your target and beyond prior to firing.

6. Avoid all horseplay with a firearm and never point at anything you don't want to shoot.

7. Never climb a fence, tree, or jump a ditch with a loaded firearm.

---

8. Never shoot at a flat hard surface or water.

9. Firearms and ammunition should be stored and locked separately.

10. Do not use alcohol and/or drugs at any time while handling a loaded firearm.

If you plan on keeping a gun in the home, it is my recommendation that every family member, including children, learn the gun safety and handling rules. Every time you pick up a firearm, you must assume that it is loaded. Go one step further and check the magazine and chamber to make sure a bullet is not lodged.

FIREARMS FOR CHILDREN AND FIRST TIME USERS

So what's the best all-around gun for the entire family? In my humble opinion, the .22 rifle or .22 pistols are the best choices for first time gun owners or for teaching children how to shoot. A great selling point of this caliber is it has little to no recoil, and can be used in a multitude of situations, including home protection and used in hunting small game (and even large game from a certain distance).

An added benefit is the ammunition is reasonably priced, which means that a .22 can be an excellent practice rifle to learn basic rifle shooting skills at a fraction of the cost of other rifles.

FIREARMS FOR HOME PROTECTION

My #1 choice for overall home protection is the shotgun. Either a 12-gauge or the slightly smaller 20-gauge would be excellent choice. In the article, "An Introduction to SHTF Home Defense, Guns and Safety", at www.SHTF Plan.com, the author agrees with these sentiments and goes on to suggest that the best all-around shot gun to purchase is a 12-gauge.

"During my concealed weapons permit course, the instructor said something to the effect of "for a home defense shotgun, you can pick any gauge you want...as long as it is 12-gauge." First, 12-gauge shotguns offer a generous spread (i.e., you don't have to be that accurate) and stopping power (depending on the type of ammunition of course). Second, 12-gauge shells are BY FAR the most common and the easiest to find (compared to .410, 20-gauge, etc.) and often the least expensive. As far as what bullets to use, the author explains that 2 ¾ shells are the most common, and most shotguns can use them.

For a SHTF scenario, as opposed to home defense, 00 ('double ought') buckshot, which is essentially 7-9 pellets (for a 2 ¾ shell) similar in size to a 9 mm bullet, is probably the way to go, as it offers some spread and SERIOUS stopping power, and decent range (maybe 50 yards or so). If you want more penetration (but no spread), you may want to consider a rifled slug. ...BUT for home defense, 00 buck and slugs MAY not be the best choice. One of the concerns with firing at an intruder in your house is what happens to the bullet/pellet if you miss the bad guy, or it goes through the bad guy? Some ballistics tests have indicated that various types of buckshot can easily pass through several layers of sheetrock because of the relatively high momentum of the projectiles.

Therefore, some experts recommend a lighter load if the shotgun is intended only as an "under the bed" weapon. One commonly recommended load is No. 4 birdshot, which has a higher number of smaller pellets compared to 00 buck. While still offering 'decent' stopping power, it will spread a bit more than buckshot and really cut down the possibility of injuring someone in the next room, or possibly even the next house.

Another thing to keep in mind is that you can load your shotgun with alternating rounds (e.g., #4 bird, slug, 00 buck, #4 bird, etc.), just be sure to have the series memorized. Two of the most popular, reliable and cost effective shotguns available are the classic Remington 870 and the Mossberg 500. Both are pump shotguns that have been tried and tested in real life situations with excellent results.

PISTOLS FOR HOME DEFENSE

Pistols are another popular choice for home defense weapons. Some of the most popular pistols to purchase are .9 mm, .40 cal., and .45 cal. (which means that the ammunition is also widely available).

In a situation where ammunition has become scarce, having one of these three calibers, especially 9mm and .40 caliber may allow you to use it as a medium of exchange to trade for other goods. Likewise, it will be much easier to find than other 'specialty' ammunition.

Before you purchase a weapon for home defense, you want to take into consideration:

- The price of the firearm, magazine and ammunition
- How much recoil it will have
- Whether or not there is a safety mechanism on the firearm
- What type of firearm offers up the highest capacity for magazines
- And of course, which firearm offers the most stopping power

9 mm firearms recoil the least, so it's generally the easiest of the three to keep on target after pulling the trigger, and usually offers higher capacity magazines compared to the others. The 9 mm is usually the least expensive of the three. A con to this type of firearm is it does have the least stopping power.

.40 caliber firearms offer (in a defensive round) more stopping power than 9 mm, but usually 'snaps' (or recoils) more than BOTH 9 mm AND .45. Many law enforcement personnel have switched from 9mm semi-automatic handguns to the .40 caliber in recent years because of the increased stopping power.

.45 caliber firearms offer the most stopping power, but you'll generally have to sacrifice a few rounds of magazine capacity and a bit of penetration (which might be a good thing depending on the situation). Comparably speaking, between the three calibers discussed, there usually isn't that much of a price difference between them, although the .45 is the most expensive.

Handguns come in numerous price points ranging from $300 to $1000, so there is certainly a good, reliable weapon out there for anyone who needs to acquire one. The Beretta 92FS 9mm is a favorite in our family and has been used by officers in the United States military since the early 1980's. Glocks in 9mm or .40 caliber are proven in the field as well. The 1911 model .45 caliber is an excellent choice for those looking for more serious stopping power and has been standard issue (M-45) for the Force Recon element of the United States Marine Corp. since 1985.

ASSAULT RIFLES AND LONG RANGE WEAPONS

When discussing home defense preparedness we can't ignore the possibility of a total breakdown of law enforcement capability in our immediate local region. In an event such as this we may be faced with multiple attackers attempting to overtake our homes and land. While shotguns or handguns are both excellent close proximity defense weapons, they will not fare well at longer distances. If you have a property with acreage that needs to be defended, you'll want to seriously consider acquiring an assault rifle.

It would be quite difficult to neutralize a target at 100 – 200 yards with a handgun or shotgun, but for an assault rifle it becomes much more feasible.

Like handguns, there are numerous choices available. Here are a couple of excellent options we have found for our own personal defense.

AR-15 - One of the more popular "zombie weapons" out there is the AR-15, made by multiple manufacturers and based on the military version of the M-16. This rifle is chambered in 5.56mm x 45mm round, which is essentially a .223 caliber (there are some special circumstances here, so do your research on ammunition for this rifle if you choose to go with this model). The recoil on an AR-15 is negligible compared to other assault rifles of higher caliber, so it's easier to control. It is highly customizable, allowing operators to add force multipliers that include after-market equipment like scopes, magnification, night vision, flash lights, suppression, etc. Because of its popularity, the AR-15 is fairly inexpensive with base models starting in the $800 range. It's also widespread in the United States, so parts are readily available. So, too, is the ammunition (for now).

Most families will want to have the same weapons platform – (a his and hers model) so that they can share ammunition, after-market equipment and parts. If one gun breaks, you can always use it for parts for your other weapon. Buying two AR-15's would run at least $1600 for basic models, so cost may be an issue for some.

SKS - One alternative option for an excellent "SHTF weapon" is the SKS. Somewhat similar to an AK-47, the SKS is chambered in a standard round of 7.62mm x 39mm. It is not as easily customizable as the AR-15, but as a perimeter defense assault rifle can be just as effective in the right hands. At a starting price point of around $350 it is an excellent choice for those on a budget. There are numerous manufacturers of this weapon, all foreign and originating from Russia, China and Yugoslavia. Certain models of this rifle have been banned in some states (making it all the more desirable!), but they are readily available for purchase online or at local gun shows.

For some, home defense also means being able to protect your property at long range. While assault rifles are effective for a couple of hundred yards, a long-range hunting weapon may be a better option for anything exceeding 200 yards.

.308 - As with AR's and handguns, you have lots of options. And like AR's and handguns, consider looking into a weapon that utilizes popular ammunition. The .308 is one such caliber and is effective up to roughly 800 yards (though most of us would have a hard time hitting a target at that range). In addition to being able to provide long-range, highly accurate firepower and support, a .308 is an excellent hunting rifle. If society has broken down, there's a strong likelihood that food will become scarce, so you'll want to have a weapon with which you can hunt effectively.

Depending on your personal preference, you can consider looking at a traditional bolt-action single shot 308, or going with an assault rifle model like the Armalite AR-10 (used for guard duty by some military personnel because they can stop oncoming vehicles) or the FN AR semi-automatic 308. A bolt-action model can be had for $300 – $600 for basic models, and in excess of $1000 for the semi-automatic rifles mentioned.

MAGAZINES

In addition to the magazines that come standard with your firearm – usually two – you'll want to consider having some in reserve. You can never have too many reserve mags, but stockpiling these can become expensive, so consider having at least three primary magazines and one in reserve.

You can purchase "factory" mags that are manufactured by the same company that made your firearm, or you can purchase after-market magazines manufactured by a number of different companies. The factory magazines are almost always more expensive, and for good reason. They will almost always perform better than those manufactured by other manufacturers. If you have to purchase non-factory magazines, I strongly recommend that you read multiple reviews from others who have tried them. You are depending on your magazine to work to specifications 100% of the time. Failure can mean death, so it's in your interest to spend the extra money on the best magazines you can acquire.

Different states have different laws regarding "high-capacity" magazines. In some states like California, magazines cannot hold more than ten (10) rounds, while other states, like Texas, have no restrictions. Unfortunately, in many states right now, restrictive new gun control laws are being passed.   In recent years federal legislation for high-capacity magazine restrictions has been introduced, which means at some time in the future owning a 17 round magazine may be illegal in any part of the country. This, of course, poses a problem in a situation where the rule of law breaks down and you are forced to defend yourself against multiple targets.

One solution for those living in states where high-capacity magazines are illegal is to only keep parts on hand. Though I am not advocating that you break or circumvent laws in your state, having parts or a parts kit, as opposed to assembled magazines, may be one way to still be prepared for a scenario where you could be threatened by multiple attackers and a higher volume of firepower is required. If you are ever presented with the worst case, you could re-assemble those parts.

Certain states, like California, also have laws that require "fixed magazines" in rifles that cannot be removed with a simple push of the magazine release. They require a special, external tool (like a screw driver) to remove the magazine. This, of course, poses a serious problem when dealing with an external threat. Though you'd never want to circumvent these laws, in a situation where lawlessness reigns, having parts on hand to make necessary modifications may be beneficial.

Note: Research pertinent laws in your state, as firearm restrictions do vary. The better you understand the laws, the better equipped you will be to make quick decisions when under great stress.

AMMUNITION

Over-penetration in a home defense situation IS a concern, especially with Full Metal Jacket (FMJ) ammunition. A 'nightstand' pistol, in any of the above calibers, with a defensive round, such as some sort of hollow point, is STRONGLY recommended, as it increases stopping power significantly and reduces the odds of injuring an innocent party.

Purchase a 'defense' type (e.g., hollow point) bullet (as opposed to 'ball' or full metal jacket) in any of these three rounds provides plenty of stopping power.

How much is enough? In all honesty, you can never have too much ammunition[218]. In a long-term emergency, you will want to have ammunition not only for protecting your home, but for hunting purposes as well. Before we get to a specific number, you need to take into account that you will also need a few thousand rounds in reserve for target practice. At one target practice, a person can easily blow through a few hundred rounds. Having a minimum of 500-1,000 rounds for each of your guns is a good starting point. If you can, purchasing ammunition in bulk will be more economical, but purchasing a box of ammunition every chance you get is all right too. Just stick to what is within your budget!

For something like a .22 which can be used for hunting, personal protection and target practice, you can stock even more, especially since ammunition is so cheap. Additionally, take into consideration that the purchase of bulk ammunition for popular calibers could supply you with a HUGE bartering item.

PRACTICE MAKES YOU A PERFECT SHOT

Being consistently accurate when shooting is a skill that takes frequent practice. Your ability will depreciate over time if the skill goes unused. Therefore, visit the shooting range[219] regularly

---

[218] http://ammo.ar15.com/ammo/project/hist_fmj.html

[219] http://find.mapmuse.com/interest/shooting-ranges

and take an assortment of firearm training classes to maintain or improve your skill level. Courses such as a handgun class to teach you the right stance, grip, and how to position your body to absorb the recoil would be a great starting point for beginners.

One more point regarding practice: if you come under attack for any reason, you will be under a great amount of stress. It is vital to feel comfortable with the firearm in your hand. When you practice regularly, you become familiar with the gun and subsequently develop muscle memory. If the time comes when you need to use a firearm for defensive purposes, you will be confident in your abilities and in your firearm.

One other recommendation for those serious about improving their skills is to attend simulations. Paintball and Airsoft battles add some realism to your training, as you will be firing at live targets (and trying to evade getting shot as well!). It will give you the ability to hone your skills in environments that will be similar to the real thing.

Simulated battles like this will also allow you and your team to learn to work together in high stress, fast-paced environments. What's more, you can purchase your own equipment and work together in learning how to defend your own property by setting up simulated scenarios.

Make Your Own

If you have enough land and live where shooting is acceptable, you can build your own range. Having a gun range at home is convenient and promotes regular shooting practice to refine your skill. Remember, the more you shoot, the better your hand/eye coordination becomes. Your trigger pulls improve and the overall process of shooting becomes more natural.

Here are some ideas to help you build your own range:

- Use or build a picnic table for a bench
- Fill a couple of sandbags for a rest
- Build a target stand out of 2x4s
- Use cardboard or paper plates for targets

If you'd like a bit more serious shooting range, companies like Caldwell Shooting Supplies and Shooter's Ridge manufacturer everything you need.

BODY ARMOR

Here is the reality of it: if you are shooting downrange or shooting to protect your home, there is a very strong possibility that someone will be shooting back at you. This is especially true should the world as we know it fall apart and you alone are left to protect your family, your home and your supplies.

One of the absolute best investments you can make to reduce your chance of serious injury or death is body armor. This includes a helmet, a vest to protect your chest, neck protector, groin protector, and even side guards to protect your ribs and vital organs.

As is the case with firearms, there are numerous options for body armor. My advice is that you go with the absolute best protection you can afford.

Here is a brief breakdown of the different levels of body armor:

Type I (.22 LR; .380 ACP)
This type of armor protects against .22 long rifle lead round nose (LR LRN) bullets. Type I body armor is light. This is the minimum level of protection. *(Note: In my opinion, this is not going to cut it.)*

Type II-A (9mm; .40 S&W)
This armor protects against 9mm full metal jacketed round nose (FMJ RN) bullets and .40 S&W caliber full metal jacketed (FMJ) bullets. Type II-A body armor is well suited for full-time use by police departments, particularly those seeking protection for their officers from lower velocity 9mm and 40 S&W ammunition. *(Note: It'll stop a lower caliber handgun, but that's it.)*

Type II (9mm; .357 Magnum)
This is the next step up from Type II-A and is worn full time by police officers seeking protection against higher velocity .357 Magnum and 9mm ammunition. *(Note: It's good for lower velocity handguns, but that's about it.)*

Type III-A (High Velocity 9mm; .44 Magnum)
This armor protects against 9mm full metal jacketed round nose (FJM RN) bullets and .44 Magnum jacketed hollow point (JHP) bullets. It also provides protection against most handgun threats, as well as the Type I, II-A, and II threats. Type III-A body armor provides the highest level of protection currently available from concealable body armor and is generally suitable for routine wear in many situations. *(Note: For the prepper planning on worst-case scenarios my opinion is that this is the absolute minimum in body armor protection.)*

Type III (Rifles)
This armor protects against 7.62mm full metal jacketed (FMJ) bullets (U.S. military designation M80), with nominal masses of 9.6 g (148 gr), impacting at a minimum velocity of 838 m/s (2750 ft/s) or less. It also provides protection against Type I through III-A threats. Type III body armor

is clearly intended only for tactical situations when the threat warrants such protection, such as barricade confrontations involving sporting rifles. *(Note: If you are in a situation where you are firing an assault rifle at the enemy, they are probably doing the same. You'll want at least this level of protection for those situations.)*

Type IV (Armor Piercing Rifle)

This armor protects against .30 caliber armor piercing (AP) bullets (U.S. military designation M2 AP). It also provides at least single-hit protection against the Type I through III threats. Type IV body armor provides the highest level of protection currently available. Because this armor is intended to resist "armor piercing" bullets, it often uses ceramic materials. Such materials are brittle in nature and may provide only single-shot protection, since the ceramic tends to break up when struck. As with Type III armor, Type IV armor is clearly intended only for tactical situations when the threat warrants such protection. *(Note: If you are digging in, this is the body armor you would want. It is expensive. It is also going to be heavier than other types of protection. Combined with other gear you may be carrying when mobile, the added weight with this body armor may require serious physical conditioning. But, it will stop high power armor piercing rounds – something other protection levels simply can't do.)*

Source[220]

CONCLUSION

The fact that we have the luxury of discussing this issue means that the proverbial you-know-what has not hit fan. In reality, if we were in the midst of a true SHTF scenario, you wouldn't care what firearm you had – just as long as you had something to keep the bad guys at bay. We are lucky that we still have time to research, practice and fine tune this pertinent skill. It seems that every day the news brings a new attack on the freedom to protect ourselves, so use this time wisely.

I leave you with this advice; do not be solely dependent on a firearm for protection. As much as I value my firearm, I know that it can be taken out of my hands and used against me. Learning other forms of personal protection such as hand-to-hand combat, Krav Maga, martial arts and other forms of self-defense for last resort measures will only make you more capable of protecting yourself, your loved ones and your preps.

---

[220] http://www.shtfplan.com/emergency-preparedness/body-armor-because-if-youre-shooting-down-range-you-can-bet-someones-shooting-back-at-you_04252012

Related Information:

National Rifle Association[221]

Gun Laws State by State[222]

Portions of this article have been inspired by <u>*An Introduction to SHTF Home Defense, Guns and Safety*</u> *written by Rick Blaine*

---

[221] http://home.nra.org/#/nraorg/gallery/3

[222] http://www.nraila.org/gun-laws/state-laws.aspx

PREPS TO BUY:

Guns and ammunition are some of the most expensive items you will be adding to your preparedness supplies, so it's understandable if you can't purchase all of these items in one week. Prioritize what's important and keep your needs in mind when buying items for self-defense. You may need to stretch out these purchases over a longer amount of time. Be sure to do your research on state regulations and considerations for which type of firearm to purchase.

- Firearm for home defense
- Ammunition (500-1,000 rounds per firearm)
- Extra magazines
- Spare parts or kits
- Gun cleaning kits
- Ammunition storage case (waterproof)
- Protective gear (i.e., helmet, a vest to protect your chest, neck protector, groin protector, and even side guards)
- Gun enhancement equipment (i.e., scopes, magnification, night vision, flash lights, suppression)

ACTION ITEMS:

1. Check the pertinent laws in your state, as firearm restrictions do vary.
2. You may want to consider going to a gun range that rents firearms to test which equipment is best for you and your needs.
3. Take a handgun course to familiarize with proper stances and grips to gain better accuracy.
4. Consider taking a hand-to-hand self-defense class.
5. Minimize the threat of a home break-in or home invasion by adding layers of security[223] to prevent your home from being a possible target.
6. Designate a safe room in the home and discuss proper protocols with all family members.

---

[223] http://readynutrition.com/resources/home-invasion-preventitive-security-layers-to-protect-the-home_30062010/

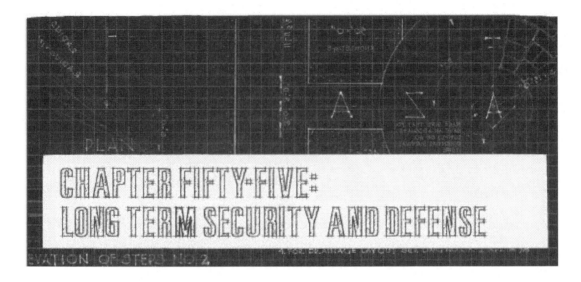

We cannot predict now exactly what conditions will look like after a collapse and as such I urge you not to make too many assumptions based on your particular idea of what such a post-SHTF situation will look like. The purpose of this chapter will be to give you the general principles and techniques of defending a location, which you can tailor and apply as necessary and appropriate. It is best to adopt a mindset of flexibility and gather mental and physical knowledge and 'tools' in order to be able to develop your response and put some of these measures in place as you find them necessary and appropriate. For this chapter, I will assume a broad post-SHTF situation of societal collapse with a general absence of law and order.

LONG-TERM SECURITY AND DEFENSE OF YOUR RETREAT LOCATION

What is the threat? As a prepper hunkered down at your home with food stores, the most likely threat will be from looters and marauders. These could take many forms, from a simple beggar, starving neighbors, mobs, tricks and deceptions, to a tactically organized group with weapons and equipment. The worst case is some sort of organized paramilitary style force with heavy equipment, bent on forced redistribution. Therefore, remain flexible and have an emergency rally point and extraction route should you be overmatched. Know when you have no alternative but to bug out. You can make this decision if you have the information before the threat arrives and conduct the bug out in good order. Alternatively, you may be forced to make the decision as the attack progresses and have to 'break contact' and withdraw under enemy fire; this is one of the most difficult tactical maneuvers. Work on your leadership, decision making and decision points so that your response under the pressure of both time and enemy is optimal. Tied in with this is the need for clear rules of engagement and for the use of force appropriate to the threat.

This chapter is mainly concerned with defense of a single location and as such will not go into techniques such as mobile and area defense, which could be useful for a larger community.

Remember, the best form of defense is to avoid the fight. But that may not be possible and you have to always plan and prepare for that fight. You can better avoid confrontation by adopting a lower profile at your location, attempting to conceal your supplies and capabilities. The opposite of this is to have a high profile and try to use threat of force as a deterrent. Remember that a good rifleman could sit out at long range and simply shoot your defenders in their sentry positions.

In my opinion, the best approach for a small survivor group is to adopt a lower profile while maintaining the capability to defeat threats as they are encountered. The following are some principles of defense that you should consider and apply to your location and plan:

- All Round Defense, in order to anticipate a threat from any direction.
- Depth, in order to prevent penetration of your defended position.
- Mutually Supporting Sectors of Fire, in order to increase the strength and flexibility of a defense.
- Concealment and Deception, in order to deny the adversary the advantages of understanding.
- Maintenance of a Reserve.
- Offensive Action (where appropriate), in order to seize or regain the initiative.
- Administration, to include:

  o *Appropriate numbers of trained personnel.*
  o *Appropriate weapons, ammunition and equipment.*
  o *A watch system for early warning.*

Most modern family homes do not lend themselves to defense. The structure is vulnerable to high velocity rounds which can pass through multiple frame, wood and plasterboard walls. Simple mechanical breaches are possible with tools and even vehicles used as rams. These homes are also very vulnerable to fire. If you try and defend your house from the windows, then you will not be protected by the walls framing those windows and the room can be filled full of high velocity rounds by an attacking group.

There is a real danger of being suppressed by superior firepower. If you stay back from the windows as you should, then you limit your fields of fire and unless there are enough of you defending, the enemy will be able to take advantage of blind spots to close with and then breach the house. You need a basement or other ballistic-protected safe room for your noncombatant personnel (kids etc.) to shelter in; otherwise they will not be protected from the violence and from the high velocity rounds ripping through the walls.

KEYS FOR GOOD PREPPER DEFENSE

Trained Personnel

One of the key things for a prepper defense of a location is to have an appropriate number of trained personnel with appropriate firearms, ammunition and equipment. You will also have to take measures to harden the building to slow down attempts to breach.

Hardening your Retreat

You need to consider whether or not you want your property to look derelict; this could be a good or bad tactic in the circumstances.

1. **Boarding up or shuttering ground floor windows.** It would be worthwhile to consider boarding up or shuttering at least the ground floor windows and think about putting up door bars or even board up some of the doors. This will also help with light discipline. External boards can make the place look derelict, but looking derelict could also encourage approach by potential squatters. You could put up the boards internally, or something similar, in order to maintain a low profile and slow any breaches. There are a lot of pros and cons each way. When boarding up doors, ensure that you have at least two independent exits that can be used both for routine tasks but also for egress if you have to escape. Boarding up your windows and doors does not make them ballistically hardened.

2. **Sandbags.** You could have sandbags ready to go, and you will need to consider a big pile of dirt to fill them from. Consider the benefits of simple mass of soil in protecting you from high velocity rounds, and for the construction of fighting positions. Sandbags need to be at least two deep to protect against high velocity rounds. If you try stacking enough of these on a modern upper floor, or even a ground level floor with a basement beneath, then the weight of a constructed fighting position may cause a collapse. You could stack sandbags externally around designated window fighting positions on the ground floor, but you will need a lot of them. Other alternatives would include filling a chest of drawers with soil to create firing positions, or maybe even material such as steel plates that will weigh less but will provide ballistic protection.

   From the principles of defense it is clear that we need to establish a plan that provides early warning, all round defense and mutually supporting sectors of fire.

3. **Create depth.** This is best utilized outside the building rather than with fallback positions inside the house. We can create depth using external fighting positions to keep attackers away from the house, which will also aid mutual support.

A key method in the defense of a house is to have a second or more positions outside of the main building that can provide fire support, supporting each other by keeping the enemy away from the house. This position(s) could also be another house or cooperating neighbor if it works out that way.

This creates a 'cross-fire,' so you must enforce fire discipline and allocate sectors of fire to ensure you do not cause 'friendly fire.'

4. **A very important concept is that of 'standoff.'** This can be created with a combination of fighting positions in depth and cleared fields of fire with obstacles. If you have an obstacle, such as wire, it must be covered by fire to be effective. Utilize standoff distances to keep enemy away from the property, combined with obstacles to slow vehicle and dismounted approach. Wire is good for dismounted personnel and also vehicles if it is correctly laid concertina wire.

   Obstacles such as steel cabling, concrete bollards or planter boxes and felled trees will work well against vehicles. This will also have the effect of reducing the risk of attackers getting close enough to set the place on fire, which they are likely to try if they can't get in to get your stuff.

   If we expand this concept we can see how a mutually supporting neighborhood with checkpoints/roadblocks and observation/fighting positions will provide a great advantage. Standoff is also important in terms of engaging the enemy with accurate effective fire at the longest range that is physically and legally possible. If you are competent and have the equipment for long-range effective suppressive fire, this can have the effect of keeping the enemy at arm's length, thereby reducing the accuracy and hence effectiveness of their fire. This will also prevent them from successfully suppressing you and subsequently maneuvering onto your position to breach or burn your property.

   In addition, consider the presence, placement and potential hard protection of any flammable sources on your property or close to your buildings, such as propane tanks and fuel supplies. Ensure the enemy cannot repeatedly fire upon them to cause a fire or explosion.

5. **Long-range defensive fire.** The ability to generate accurate, effective long-range defensive fire depends on skill, equipment, positioning of fighting positions, your policy for the use of force and also the way the terrain affects weapon killing areas and ranges. To engage at long range you have to reasonably fear that the enemy presents a threat of lethal force against your defended location. However, if you are in a closer urban or wooded environment you may find some of your fields of fire are limited and you will have to plan and position accordingly.

6. **Administration is a key factor.** While you are maintaining your defense you need to look after the welfare of the team, equipment and the site itself. Administration is what preppers usually concentrate on. This is your "beans, bullets and Band-Aids." This is an area where those that are non-combatants can really pull their weight and make a difference. You must maintain a watch system which will be tied in to 'stand to' positions and maybe some form of 'Quick Reaction Force' or reserve, depending on the resources and numbers available to you.

   Your watch system can be augmented by other early warning sensors such as dogs and mechanical or electronic systems. Day to day you will need to keep the machine running and this will be the biggest challenge as time goes on. Complacency kills!

   Depending on the extent of your preparations, stores and the resources within your property, this will have a knock-on effect to your ability to remain covert and the requirement to send out foraging patrols. People will also start to get cabin fever, particularly kids, and you will need to consider how to entertain them. Consider that while mundane tasks are being completed, there is always someone on watch. People who are not on watch need to have weapons and ammunition carrying equipment close or on their person while doing other things.

   Consider carrying long rifles slung as well as handguns everywhere you go on the property, with at least a light bit of web gear with some additional magazines in pouches. Rifles should never be out of your arms reach if there is any kind of threat of attack. You should put rifle racks or hooks/nails on walls in key rooms, out of reach of kids, so that rifles can be grabbed quickly if the alarm is sounded.

7. **Protecting personnel and noncombatants in group.** Regarding your noncombatants or protected personnel; what you do with them depends on who they are. The younger kids will need to be protected in the safest location you have. Others will be useful to do tasks such as re-load magazines, distribute water and act as firefighting crews. Note that you need to have fire extinguishers, buckets of water and /or sand available at hand during a defense to put out any fires.

   The more tasks you give people during a crisis, the more the activity will take their minds off the stress of the situation and the team will be strengthened. Ammunition replenishment, water distribution, casualty collection point, first aid, watching the rear and looking after the younger kids are all examples of tasks that can be allocated to make people a useful part of the team when personnel resources are tight.

DETECT, OBSERVE AND ENGAGE YOUR ENEMY

Firearms

Firearms and equipment has been covered under the home defense chapter of this program. For this kind of defensive situation you will be well served by the ability to detect, observe and accurately engage enemy at the longest range possible by day and night. This is easily said, but would take throwing money at it to get all the equipment you need to best do it.

In terms of firearms, I would recommend:

- Tactical type, high-capacity magazine rifles for the main work, backed up by handguns and pump action 12-gauge shotguns.
- The shotguns are good for close work and if the enemy gets in to the building, last ditch stuff.
- Long range hunting type rifles are good for observation (scope) and longer distance engagement.

Other Equipment

- Binoculars, Night Vision and Thermal Imaging. You would be best served with good optics for your weapons and also observation devices such as binoculars. Think about night vision and even thermal imaging if you can afford it. You will also have to consider that even if you can afford a night vision device, it will only work for whoever has it— how will the rest engage? What type and configuration of these night vision devices will be used, on weapons as sights or not? Without night sights you can fire at muzzle flash or use whatever illumination is available, white light or whatever. A good option is to have parachute illumination flares.
- Loose, barking dogs on your property are perhaps the best low-budget early warning system; however, consider that they may give away your position if you are trying to be totally covert.
- Decide on your priorities and strategy and tie that in with what money you have to spend on equipment. You can get expensive systems such as ground sensors, lights and alarms, but these cost money and you have to consider their use in a long-term grid-down situation. I would prefer to spend money on optics and night observation devices, which will last without grid power (but will require batteries) and can also be taken with you if you have to move locations.

Here are some basic suggestions for equipment to augment such a defense:

- Appropriate tactical firearms and ammunition
- Web gear and magazines
- Ear and eye protection
- Body armor and helmets, NIJ Level III or Level IV
- Barbed wire, coiled (concertina) and for low wire entanglements
- Sandbags or other ballistic protection options
- Night vision devices
- Binoculars plus optical rifle sights
- Black out curtain and pre-cut plywood for windows
- Parachute illumination flares
- Trip-flares
- Trauma medical kit incl. CAT tourniquets
- Range cards
- Two way radios and/or field telephones
- Multiple fire-extinguishers and/or buckets of water

Defense Training for Group

If you have put a group together for such a defense, they need to be trained not only on tactical shooting and basic small unit tactics and movement, but also briefed and rehearsed on the defensive plan, including fighting positions and sectors of fire. Consider that depending on your circumstances and the terrain, you may be benefited by running periodic clearance patrols around the property to mitigate against surprise attack. To do this your team needs to be able to patrol and move tactically, as well as respond to any enemy contact. You will preferably have a medic with a trauma bag.

You do not ever want to run out of ammunition, so make sure you have as much as you can reasonably purchase. Like tactics, ammunition quantities are a subjective argument with many solutions.

Training Your Group

Train your team to engage positively identified enemy, or suppress known enemy positions. A rapid rate of fire is 30 rounds per minute; a deliberate rate is 10 rounds per minute.

I recommend a personal load of six to eight thirty-round magazines on the person, with at least as many full magazines for resupply. And once you have used that, you need another resupply! In a real life contact you will likely use less ammunition than you may during training, so you must concentrate on effective, accurate fire rather than simple quantity.

Some other key points for training your group are:

1. Practice and rehearse the command and fire control procedures at your location, including the communication of enemy locations and actions.

2. Use range cards to tie in sectors for mutual support and to prevent 'friendly fire.'
3. Run 'stand to' drills like a fire drill by both day and night, and be able to call out which direction the enemy threat comes from.
4. Be aware of diversions and demonstrations intended to distract you from the main direction of attack.
5. Always cover all sectors, even with just one observer looking to the flanks and rear in a manpower crisis.
6. Keep unnecessary noise and shouting down, allowing orders and target indications to be passed around the position.
7. Every team member is a sensor and a 'link man' to pass on information.

BE MINDFUL

Having said all that, you are not going to open fire on just anyone coming to your location. Any actions that you take should be justifiable as self-defense. Do be mindful of tricks and the potential for snipers. However, don't give up on morality and charity and don't illegally open fire on anyone that comes near your defended location.

You need to agree on rules of engagement for your sentries and you should apply escalation of force protocols to meet a threat with the proportionate and appropriate force necessary to stop that threat. Have the ability to warn anyone approaching, whether you have permanent warning signs or something like a bullhorn that you use as part of your escalation procedures as you begin to identify threats. Remember that escalation of force is a continuum and you can bypass the early stages and go directly to lethal force if taken by surprise and faced with a lethal threat that must be stopped.

Max Velocity:

Special thanks to Max Velocity of <u>MaxVelocityTactical.blogspot.com</u> who was kind enough to dedicate his time and professional insights to our preparedness community. He has an extensive military background, having served in both the British and the U.S. armies and also as a high threat security contractor. He has served on six military operational deployments, including to Afghanistan immediately post-9/11, and additionally he spent five years serving as a security contractor in both Iraq and Afghanistan.

During his career in the British Army he served with British SOF (The Parachute Regiment), to include a role training and selecting recruits for the Regiment. More recently, he has served in a Combat Medic and Civil Affairs role in the US Army Reserves.

He is the author of two books: <u>Contact! A Tactical Manual for Post Collapse Survival</u> and <u>Rapid Fire! Tactics for High Threat, Protection and Combat Operations</u>. With his vast military background and real world experience, Max provides the kind of information that every prepper needs to learn, understand and integrate into their long-term security and home defense plans.

My sincere thanks to Max Velocity for contributing this portion of The Prepper's Blueprint.

PREPS TO BUY:

- Appropriate tactical firearms & ammunition
- Web gear and magazines
- Ear and eye protection
- Body armor and helmets, NIJ Level III or Level IV
- Barbed wire, coiled (concertina) and for low wire entanglements
- Sandbags or other ballistic protection options
- Night vision devices
- Binoculars plus optical rifle sights
- Black out curtain and pre-cut plywood for windows
- Parachute illumination flares
- Trip-flares
- Trauma medical kit incl. CAT tourniquets
- Range cards
- Two way radios and/or field telephones

ACTION ITEMS:

1. Create a defensive plan including fighting positions and sectors of fire and ensure that all group members know the plan and rehearse the plan regularly.
2. Agree on rules of engagement.
3. Train each group member on tactical shooting and basic small unit tactics and movement.
4. Practice and rehearse the command and fire control procedures at your location, including the communication of enemy locations and actions.

Conclusion

Throughout this preparedness program, we have invested in, researched, and practiced ways to get our families prepared for the unexpected. This investment of time, energy and supplies is not yet complete. You are at pivotal point in your preparedness journey: either you feel comfortable with the preps and skills you have attained and feel they can carry you through an extended emergency, or you have begun to see that it is necessary to take your preparedness journey to the next level.

Some of us find that we are never finished preparing, researching or learning new skills to help carry us through a given emergency. This need to learn and develop more is what I want to discuss in this chapter - because it won't require you to go and invest your money into preps. This next step is about a change you will make to your existing mindset. You are now at a point of shifting from *preparing* for a preparedness lifestyle[224] into *living* a preparedness lifestyle.

TAKING THINGS TO THE NEXT LEVEL

My need to take preparedness to the next level has changed my entire outlook on life. It simplified my life[225], because I no longer am concerned with what the latest fad is or what the newest series on television is. In fact, for the better part of 3 years I severed my ties to television and didn't watch it. Each of us will make our own choices as to what is best for our families, but my choice has been to concentrate on my preparedness path and work on going forward with it – and I must say that it has been a wonderful blessing. I'm much more immersed in caring for my chickens, finding ways to get my garden to grow, appreciating my surroundings, and making sure that my family is cared for.

There are challenges to shifting to a preparedness lifestyle, but I continue to stay positive and view mistakes that I make as learning experiences. Sometimes things work out, and sometimes they don't, but at least I am working towards my goal of being 100% self-reliant. I am fortunate that I still have the time to make these mistakes and learn from them. After all, there may be a time in the not-so-distant future that mistakes can be costly.

---

[224] http://readynutrition.com/resources/8-prepper-principles-for-a-prepared-mind_04062012/

[225] http://readynutrition.com/resources/simply-simplifying_06102010/

NEVER GIVE UP!

Throughout your preparedness journey, no doubt many of you have become frustrated because you can't seem to wrap your head around a certain skill, or you can't seem to prepare enough because of the rising food prices, or you are growing more and more concerned that a large-scale disaster is around the corner and you won't be ready in time. Don't get discouraged! We have a wonderful community that is there to encourage us through these bumps in the road; I am here for you as well. The bottom line is this: we can only prepare so far, then we have to trust our skillsets and leave the rest to God.

In closing, I wish each and every one of you the very best of luck in your preparedness endeavors. I hope that if the day ever comes where you have to use the ideas and information in the program that you will be well equipped and be mentally and spiritually prepared to handle what may come your way.

I want to leave you with a quote. "Remember, that even though we are preparing for rainy days, it's important to enjoy the sunshine we have." Waiting for the bomb to drop is no way to live. In my experience, I have learned the importance of living in the now. We must make time, no matter how small, to enjoy the love and the gifts that are surrounding us right now. After all, these are the moments that we are going to look back on and remember.

Best of luck to you all,

    Tess Pennington

Acknowledgements

Thank you to the community at Ready Nutrition for your patience in allowing me to create this guide. Your kind words and encouragement mean the world to me. If it wasn't for you all, this book may not have happened.

Special thanks to my friend and usual partner in crime, Daisy Luther. Your friendship and assistance on this preparedness program were a Godsend. Thank you for your input, knowledge and always encouraging me along the way.

To my kooky, goofy, wonderfully big-hearted brother and friend, Peter. Thank you for all of your help with the illustrations you created for the book. As usual, everything you touch becomes more beautiful.

To my family, thank you for your patience in allowing me to write this book, your support and for being so incredibly wonderful. I love you all.

Index